Social Change in America

Christopher Clark

SOCIAL CHANGE IN AMERICA

From the Revolution

Through the Civil War

Chicago
IVAN R. DEE

www.ivanrdee.com

The paperback edition of this book carries the ISBN 1-56663-754-6.

Library of Congress Cataloging-in-Publication Data:
Clark, Christopher, 1953–
   Social change in America : from the Revolution through the Civil War / Christopher Clark.
      p. cm.
   Includes bibliographical references and index.
   ISBN-13: 978-1-56663-686-5 (cloth : alk. paper)
   ISBN-10: 1-56663-686-8 (cloth : alk. paper)
      1. United States—Social conditions—To 1865. 2. Social change—United States—History. I. Title.
   HN57.C548 2006
   303.40973'09034—dc22

                                                     2005031811

To my students

Contents

Households, Labor, and Society

T HIS BOOK offers a brief interpretation of the processes of social change in America between the eve of the Revolution and the aftermath of the Civil War. Since the emergence of the "new social history" in the 1960s there has been a massive outpouring of scholarship on American society in this period, and especially on the roles played by men and women at all levels of social status and wealth in the momentous developments that took place. Social historians have explored the complexities of class, race, and gender; suggested how these shaped patterns of opportunity and inequality; and traced connections with political and cultural change and with American economic development. Because these subjects involve studying human interactions in specific contexts, much social history has been conducted at the local level, using particular places, instances, or regions to illustrate broader historical tendencies. Any attempt at an overall account of social change is therefore inevitably partial and wide open to challenge. This book is no exception.

The period in question encompasses the creation of the United States as an independent nation, its occupation and settlement of an increasing portion of the North American continent, and—in the Civil War—its cataclysmic division into two hostile regions. The nation's expansion involved two trends: the rapid growth of rural societies based on family labor, slavery, and wage labor; and an intensification of economic activity that fostered the growth of commerce, towns, and manufacturing, witnessed the application of new technologies to transport and communications, and initiated mass immigration from overseas. The account that follows, which necessarily is highly selective, traces the interaction of these processes of expansion and intensification and their implications for American society.

The changes I examine were rooted in the social relationships between individuals and groups that emerged in different regions of North America during the colonial period. In turn, the changes that occurred between the Revolution and the Civil War reshaped social relationships and the interactions they entailed. In particular I suggest six themes that are essential for understanding these processes:

—Families and households, and the social relationships they encompassed, were central to American economic activity throughout this period, though with some diminution of their importance from the mid-nineteenth century on.

—The various forms by which work and labor were organized and extracted were crucial to national growth.

—New social structures emerged from the interactions of households, labor, and property.

—Social elites of differing character benefited most from exercising power and accumulating wealth, but also at critical times faced challenges from non-elite groups. Throughout America, though to different degrees, social elites achieved influence through wealth, power, or command of others' deference. At times, such as in the onset of the Revolution, or before and after the Civil War, elite groups played a vital role in shaping events. But they were often confronted, as they were in the Revolution and more subtly during the nineteenth century, by popular claims to share access to political power, land, or other resources. The relationships between elites and other groups influenced both social structures and the dynamics of social change.

—Regional differences were essential characteristics of society and social change. Regional differences in social structures worked, on one hand, to channel change along consistent paths during the period but also, on the other hand, helped create new social patterns as they interacted with one another. Elites in different regions were rooted in varied and distinct relationships to land, commerce, and other economic activity.

—There was also a consistent yet dynamic tension in America between the conditions that pressed for territorial expansion, or "extensive" growth, and those promoting development, or "intensive" growth in already settled regions of the continent.

Social change in America's first century of independence emerged in the interactions of these six characteristics.

The thrust of what follows is chronological. Social change occurred in a process of interactions and consequences that can only be understood in sequence. Chapter One lays out the principal regional divisions of the late colonial period, and subsequent chapters illustrate how those divisions worked into new patterns of change in the two generations that followed. Competing views of patterns of expansion set up some of the most vital political and social tensions that early Americans confronted. As Chapter Two suggests, the American Revolution itself sharpened these tensions by providing new commercial and territorial opportunities. Different regional patterns of relationship between elites and non-elite households, between elites and labor, and between elites and economic activity were critical to the United States' evolution into the mid-nineteenth century. Chapters Three, Four, and Five trace those interactions in stages from the 1790s to the 1840s. Tensions between expansion and development also helped tear the United States apart. Different regional conceptions of labor, property, and society were brought, as Chapters Six and Seven indicate, into the fatal conflict of civil war, and then into the imperfect resolution provided by Reconstruction.

The discussion that follows touches on many themes avidly debated by historians. Social history is, as I have noted, most often a study of localities and regions, and I offer a perspective that places regional social differences at the heart of an argument about national developments. These differences were not variations or exceptions to general trends; rather, their interactions were the essence of social change in eighteenth- and nineteenth-century America. Similarly, I suggest that the inequalities of status between individuals within households played almost as significant a role in driving social change as conflicts and tensions arising from inequalities between social groups.

From these perspectives, the American Revolution appears less of a radical transformation than a partial modification of colonial era social assumptions and practices. The constraints established in colonial societies survived to provide powerful impetus to patterns of expansion and development in the nineteenth century. These changes, in turn, reshaped views about personal dependence and independence, and produced an evolving debate about the meanings of freedom and unfreedom. The growing tensions between slave and nonslave societies in America were not those between a "traditional" or backward-looking social system and a "progressive" or modernizing one, but between two models of social structure, each with its own logic and dynamism. The slave society's dynamism was enough, indeed, to cause its leaders to gamble it away in a reckless bid for self-determination. The Civil War resulted in the destruction of slavery but entailed costs and imposed conditions that have continued to reverberate in American history ever since. Although the abolition of slavery was nineteenth-century America's sharpest and most important break with its past development, other changes, more subtle and incomplete, marked the relationships between men and women, work and property, power and subordination.

C. C.

Storrs, Connecticut
January 2006

Acknowledgments

I AM INDEBTED to Ivan Dee for suggesting this project and for awaiting its fruition with great patience. I am grateful for the invaluable support I received from a Small Personal Research Grant of the British Academy, a Leverhulme Research Fellowship from the Leverhulme Trust, a Residential Fellowship at the University of Connecticut Humanities Institute, and a Research Leave Award from the UK Arts and Humanities Research Board. I also wish to thank the University of York and the University of Warwick for grants of research leave, and the Master and Fellows of St. Catherine's College, Oxford, for their hospitality during my tenure as a Visiting Fellow.

Professor John Braeman read the draft manuscript in full and made many helpful suggestions. Numerous other individuals have contributed ideas or practical assistance, for which I am very grateful: Joyce Appleby, John Ashworth, David W. Blight, Richard D. Brown, Bruce Collins, Robert Cook, Martin Crawford, William Dusinberre, Richard Follett, Robert A. Gross, Nancy Hewitt, Daniel Walker Howe, Catherine Kelly, Gary Kornblith, Carol Lasser, Timothy Lockley, Stephanie McCurry, Jonathan Prude, Daniel Vickers, Altina Waller, and Peter Way. Colleagues and students at York, at Warwick, and at the University of Connecticut have been a constant inspiration, and I thank them.

As always, I owe much to Carol MacColl and Don Michak for their warm friendship and hospitality, and to Margaret Lamb for everything.

Social Change in America

CHAPTER 1

Households and Regions at the End of the Colonial Period

THE CENTRAL social institution in eighteenth-century America was the family household. Households were the primary, and almost universal, agents of social and economic organization, and it was under their auspices that most productive activity took place. Of course, households differed greatly from one another. Above all, there were wide variations in the property and income they controlled, from destitution to great riches. Most colonial Americans saw society as a hierarchy of social standing and authority in which individual households held positions according to their wealth, family connections, and other determinants of status. At the same time, though, most commentators also saw households as models of the wider society, because they conceived households themselves as miniature hierarchies, whose (usually male) heads had control of property and resources, and had legally and culturally recognized authority over other family and household members. Individual households contained within them many of the divisions and gradations of wealth, gender, age, color, and legal status that characterized the society at large. Foremost among these distinctions were those between people who were "independent" and legally free, and those who held one or another form of "dependent" status and were thus to a greater or lesser degree unfree. Freedom conferred civic and political rights, often including the right to vote and participate in public affairs, and the right to sue and to testify in court. In the British American colonies on the eve of the American Revolution, four of every five people did not have these rights because they held a status legally defined as dependent.[1]

Of these the largest number were women and children, who were excluded from most civic rights and activities. Married women in particular were also substantially excluded from exercising rights over property. Legally and practically, they and their children were dependents of their husbands and fathers. Under most circumstances married women were deemed to be *femmes covertes*, that is, legally covered by their husbands, and with no separate legal standing. Although marriage was regarded as a reciprocal arrangement between husband and wife, women when they married customarily vowed to obey their husbands, and any man who did not entirely neglect his own responsibilities could seek to compel obedience from his spouse. One recent historian has referred to the "structural social conditions that cast marriage as a prison for many women." Children too were legally as well as morally subject to their parents' authority. "Honor thy father and thy mother" was a biblical commandment with practical meaning.[2]

Although in many places rural household heads were freeholders—outright owners of their land and other property—access to land and resources was not equally distributed. In certain regions significant numbers of household heads were tenants or squatters, themselves in subordinate positions or with uncertain control over the means of earning their livelihoods. Within households especially, servants, apprentices, and slaves as well as women and children held subordinate positions, with varying degrees of restriction on their freedom but all with obligations to their masters. Even among the adult population (people aged twenty-one or over), more than half were legally dependents. "Freedom" and the privileges of legal and economic independence were enjoyed by no more than one in five colonial Americans.

Labor

FREEDOM CONVEYED not just family authority, civic rights, and legal standing but power over others' labor. All who were not independent or legally free were to some extent subject to having their labor directed by those who were. With property ownership largely in male hands, the historian Jeanne Boydston has noted, there was "a widespread dissociation of wives and wives' work from the symbols of economic value." Even in the poorest families, husbands and fathers could command the labor of their wives and children, and custom, law, and religion backed them up. In the New England colonies, which alone made legal provision for divorce, several eighteenth-century divorce petitions claimed that wives had refused to perform household tasks, such as cooking and washing, that custom required of them. By contrast, cases in which women secured divorce for their husbands' cruelty or desertion were rare or nonexistent. Divorce was usually regarded as a male prerogative and was indeed mostly initiated by husbands who were dissatisfied with their wives' conduct. Given their lack of economic means or other sources of independence, divorce was an avenue few women could seek to pursue anyway.[3]

The notion that households were miniature versions of society at large was more than just an intellectual conceit. Society was in fact built up of households with various patterns of dependency within or between them. Household authority provided either the basis or the model for a range of means by which labor could be compelled from others. In a labor-scarce economy, only great incentives or strong compulsion could secure the assistance of others, and with land and other resources readily to hand, compulsion was often the more effective method. Of all the possible means one could imagine for commanding labor, early Americans at one time or another employed a considerable number. In addition to the patterns of authority within marriages and families, these included indentured servitude of various kinds; apprenticeship; the binding out of children or the poor to other families; various forms of tenancy, sharecropping, and contract labor; debt liens and imprisonment for debt with the object of compelling work to pay off obligations; and systems of vagrancy laws, settlement laws, and workhouses intended to curtail the "idle" or itinerant poor.

Many of these methods functioned on a household basis. Merchants' clerks became members of their employers' households. Indentured servants and apprentices belonged to their masters' families and were bound by contract to labor for them for a specified term or until they reached adulthood. Afloat too, seamen were legally obliged to obey the commands of ships' masters and officers until they reached port and were paid off, or were granted "liberty"—a run ashore temporarily beyond shipboard authority. Adults could also be bound to service in others' households. Like young servants or slaves they became temporarily the legal property of their masters, subject to being bought or sold and to the master's authority and discipline. In many localities householders could bid to the authorities for contracts to house and employ the poor. If someone else injured a servant or apprentice, or seduced and impregnated a female servant, it was the legal right of the master, not of the individual concerned, to sue for damages. The law held that, as the owner of the injured party, it was the master, not the servant, who suffered loss in consequence.

Often enough, dependents had little effective power to enforce obligations masters might have to them. Apprentices, for instance, were supposed to be taught their masters' trades, but this did not always happen. John Fitch of Connecticut, apprenticed to a clockmaker in 1762, found that his master simply wanted his labor rather than to teach him the craft, and even though he kept an account so as to insist on being trained, Fitch found he "learned little of clockwork." Managing to switch to another master, Timothy Cheney, he found things no better: he learned little, was fed poor food, and found Cheney "a proud imperious hasty man," to whom "I dreaded saying much . . . till after I was of age." In most situations, masters and household heads had legal authority to compel performance or enforce discipline, and to inflict punishment or exact penalties for noncompliance. They could whip bound servants for disobedience or poor work, and a common form of punishment was to extend the term of service. John Fitch stood up to his second master only once he had come of age; when Cheney threatened to hit him, Fitch replied, "Mr. Cheney do not strike me now for I am no longer your apprentice." Later he wrote that this was "the first time [I] recollected that I was a subject on an equal footing with him." Although in some jurisdictions, such as Massachusetts, husbands were legally prohibited from using corporal punishment on their wives, the very small number of prosecutions for violating this rule suggests that it was not generally enforced. Numerous memoirs of children or apprentices noted the rough justice exercised by fathers, elder brothers, or masters who held household authority, and scholars of what is today called domestic violence are only beginning to explore a largely hidden history of marital and family punishment. Among the tasks of this scholarship will be to clarify the roots of spousal and child abuse in the legally sanctioned areas of patriarchal household authority.[4]

Such authority underscored the personal and hierarchical character of relationships between "independent" masters (or superiors) and their "dependent" inferiors. Coerced labor was ubiquitous, existing in a spectrum of forms that were not sharply distinguishable from one another. But the most complete and coercive form of dependency was slavery, which had grown up in conjunction with indentured servitude in the seventeenth century and applied exclusively to nonwhite people, most of them of African origin. Slavery was legal in all the American colonies, though historians distinguish between regions where slavery existed but was not common ("societies with slaves") and those where slavery was a key element in the social and economic fabric ("slave societies"). By 1774 about 20 percent of the thirteen colonies' population was wholly or partly of African descent, and of these people no fewer than 96 percent were held as chattel slaves, that is as the outright property of others. Although unique in that they were permanently the property of their masters, in certain respects slaves were different only in degree from other groups of dependents in early American society. In its most common form, chattel slavery was simply a type of household servitude without a limit of term. Most slaves lived singly or in small numbers with their owners and worked as farm laborers or domestic servants. But larger units of slaves, including the plantations common in the South that held slaves in groups of from twenty or so up into the hundreds in exceptional cases, could also be seen as magnified households. Many a nineteenth-century plantation owner liked to talk of his "slave family." In one sense, slavery was merely at one end of a spectrum of dependent relationships that were characteristic of household production. In 1808 a Massachusetts court noted that until slavery had been abolished in that state twenty-five years earlier, "the condition of a slave resembled the connection of a wife with her husband, and of infant children with their father. He is obliged to maintain them, and they cannot be separated from him."[5]

Yet slaves' situation was indeed extreme. Slaves were denied most of the legal privileges obtainable by free people, and unlike some other dependents—such as free male children who could expect to grow up to become independent adults—often had little hope of shedding their status. Slaves' marriages and households had no legal standing. Slaves were unprotected by laws governing fornication or bastardy. The heads of slave households had none of the legal recognition or powers granted to free husbands and fathers. Rather, all slaves were formally subject to the authority of their masters and owners. To those who could afford to buy and maintain them, slaves' labor was essential to raising and processing crops and livestock, clearing and improving land, and undertaking the many other tasks that successful farming and household production demanded. Among free individuals, therefore, the ability to own and control slaves was itself often a badge of social standing. The very existence of slavery was an important hallmark of societies rooted in concepts of hierarchy and dependency.

Structures of Compulsion

THE CIRCUMSTANCES that supported coerced and dependent labor in North America were not simply cultural and ideological. From their inception, colonial societies in North America had been shaped by one condition above all: the small size of the settler population in comparison with the land area potentially available to it. Land was not literally empty wilderness, or *terra nullia*, as its original European claimants and many later commentators portrayed it. It was occupied by Native American groups whose removal by disease, warfare, or displacement had been a constant theme, and most of whose remaining members either withdrew beyond settlement zones or took up marginal, often practically invisible, roles in white societies. Throughout early American history the growth of settler populations and of their legal, military, and practical means of acquiring territory served not only to preserve but also to extend the land area potentially available to them. In spite of population growth, territorial expansion sustained a high ratio of land to labor well into the nineteenth century, exercising a crucial influence on the conduct of social and economic life. Above all, it sustained the conditions that supported forms of compelled or coerced labor.

Households and Regions

Having ready access to land has usually been associated with freedom. In North America, as in some other parts of the world where colonial settlement and extensive expansion was occurring, cheap land and the ability of households to settle on and develop it did indeed provide opportunities for greater prosperity, family independence, and social mobility than were often available in the more crowded regions of Europe. Yet access to cheap, plentiful land was at least as strongly connected with unfreedom. Holding land had little purpose unless there was labor to do something with it. As John Adams would write in an essay of 1790, "the great question will forever remain, *who shall work?*" Scholars have long noted that the relative scarcity of labor where there is a high land-to-labor ratio tends to prompt the use of mechanisms for controlling labor and obliging people to work the land. For those with the freedom and the resources to get hold of it, abundant land was an emblem of escape from the restraints of older, more crowded societies. But for many of those who had to work on it, the availability of land was often a source of oppression. Hector St. John de Crèvecoeur noted this when he wrote about the conditions of American farming in the 1780s. Land was available for new settlement both in the North and in the South. Southerners "who have capital and can purchase Negroes," wrote Crèvecoeur, could use slave labor to work the land for them. Northern farming, though often based on abundant and good land, was "not so advantageous as a European might at first imagine." In the North labor was scarce, and consequently farms were "fit only for people capable of working [themselves]." "I am but the first slave on my farm," claimed one man Crèvecoeur wrote about, and in most independent farm households his wife, children, and any servants will have been the others. The range of devices obliging people to work reflected the stringent needs for labor in a land-abundant environment.[6]

Although land and resources were available for use, and although forms of compelled labor grew up in response to the risks of indiscipline and disorder that this availability posed, some of these forms also reflected different aspects of the social inequality and marginality of many people in early American society. While slaves were involuntary subjects of servitude, many others in subordinate positions had been placed there for more or less discretionary reasons. Even in prosperous areas there were large numbers of people for whom the margins between independence and poverty were very slim. Young men and women, either at their own behest or at that of their parents or guardians, often entered into dependent forms of labor, as servants or apprentices, to secure protection for themselves and to provide a start toward marriage or personal independence. In Maryland in the 1770s, for example, 35 percent of all children aged five to fourteen were at service in households not headed by a relative. Even among the children of the free population about 15 percent of boys and 11 percent of girls were in this position. For people without means of their own, the effort to obtain employment or income, property or skill entailed making specific personal arrangements and often involved submitting to the discipline of unfree labor. Even amidst abundance, employers wanted a hold over the labor they could obtain, and dependent individuals were often obliged to accept their authority.[7]

The actual mixture of patterns of free and unfree labor varied considerably from region to region, however. Although they had certain things in common, the colonial societies founded in North America in the seventeenth and early eighteenth centuries developed under a range of circumstances. Cultural origins, systems of crop production, and, above all, social structures evolved differently in different places. Even though independent households were the most common social institutions throughout the American colonies, the circumstances in which they functioned varied widely from region to region.

The Middle Colonies, or Mid-Atlantic region, from New York to Pennsylvania, was already by the late colonial period displaying some pluralist features that now appear as characteristics of the modern United States. It was religiously diverse and home to a variety of ethnic groups. Although these groups had religious, cultural, and political differences among them, the differences were not themselves systematically the basis of social or economic inequalities. Wage labor was beginning to take on importance. Indeed, the most widespread basis of social distinction in the Mid-Atlantic region was that of class derived from patterns of wealth and occupation. But if the Mid-Atlantic appeared to hold the key to a future pluralistic America, the regions to the north and south of it were to have more influence on major political events and would indeed sustain that influence across the period from the Revolution to the Civil War. The South, with its many subregional variations, would become particularly associated with its dominant labor system, chattel slavery. There the preeminent form of social distinction appeared to be that of race. Rural New England, meanwhile, combined a degree of cultural homogeneity with relative egalitarianism that put gender and age ahead of class and race as the bases of social distinction. But this regional variety, together with the many further variations in pattern that existed within the major regions, poses a problem for historians. Only when they came to act together and declare their national independence in the mid-1770s did the thirteen colonies that formed the United States appear to be anything like a cohesive whole. How did this political cohesiveness arise in the first place among such disparate societies, and why was it these colonies and not others elsewhere that found common cause together? In examining the regional diversity of the British American colonies of the mid-eighteenth century, we must also draw attention to some similarities of social structure that enabled them to emerge as distinctive among the dozens of European colonies and settlements in the Americas.

The Middle Colonies

THE LATE-EIGHTEENTH-CENTURY populations of New York, New Jersey, and Pennsylvania were ethnically among the most diverse in North America. Before the Revolution, though settlers of English descent were the largest group in most parts of the region, they formed only 45 percent of New York's population, 40 percent of New Jersey's, and 30 percent of Pennsylvania's. Descendants of early Dutch colonists in New York and parts of New Jersey, and substantial numbers of German migrants and their families in Pennsylvania, together almost equaled the region's "English" population, while immigrants from Ireland, especially Protestants often identified in America as "Scots Irish," also grew in number during the century, forming more than one-fifth of Pennsylvania's population. Whether they were traversing the countryside or observing life in the streets of Philadelphia or New York, visitors to the region often noted its people's varied origins.

Ethnic diversity also meant religious diversity. Pennsylvania's Quaker origins especially pointed it away from attempts to secure religious conformity, and there was no attempt there to establish an official state church. But pluralism and weak connections between churches and governments also marked other parts of the region. Fear that the creation of King's (later Columbia) College in New York in the 1760s was a stealthy attempt to make Anglicanism the colony's established religion formed part of the background to New Yorkers' protests against British rule in the prologue to the Revolution. Across the Middle Colonies, cultural and religious diversity often necessitated forming political alliances across ethnic and denominational lines.

Like everywhere else in early America, the Mid-Atlantic was primarily a farming region. Yet circumstances and social structures in parts of the region pointed toward more widespread developments in the American economy. Fertile soils and favorable climatic conditions encouraged the many thousands of European settlers who had flocked to take up land in the region between the settlement of Pennsylvania in the 1680s and the eve of the Revolution. For its access to land and relative prosperity, eighteenth-century rural Pennsylvania secured a reputation as "the best poor man's country in the world." As in many other places, mid-Atlantic farming was primarily conducted by families; the labor of household members, and a division of labor between men, women, and children, governed farming life.[8]

Still, landownership patterns helped determine the character and prosperity of farming. In some parts of New York and New Jersey, many farmers were outright owners (freeholders) of their land, but in both those states and in Pennsylvania much land was not owned on a freehold basis. The Penn family, colonial proprietors of Pennsylvania, had retained formal title to the land they leased to settlers and farmers, requiring payment of an annual fee known as a quitrent from the occupiers. In practice, the Penns' policy had been to encourage settlement and the creation of farms, rather than to profit highly from rents, so Pennsylvania quitrents remained very low, farmers were not subjected to other obligations, and most controlled their land effectively as if they owned the freehold. In parts of New Jersey and New York, however, large proprietors did seek to gain income from their ownership and control of land. New Jersey had relatively high rates of tenant farming and a history of conflict between tenants and landlords that would help divide the population's loyalties during the Revolution. Large parts of the Hudson River Valley north of New York City also remained in the hands of powerful landed families, such as the Philipses, the Livingstons, and the Van Rensselaers, some of whom were descended from Dutch *patroons* who had been granted manorial estates there in the seventeenth century. Farmers on these manorial lands were subject to rents, to fees and restrictions on purchasing or selling land, and to other obligations derived from the feudal system in Europe. The Hudson Valley had consequently been settled less rapidly than Pennsylvania in the eighteenth century. A struggle over the eastward extent of New York's jurisdiction before the Revolution also led to an assertion of independence by New England settlers of the area that later became Vermont; they were determined not to become subject to the control of landlords under New York law. In the post-Revolutionary period, the desire to attract and retain tenants led landlords to relax their conduct of the manorial system, but as population then rose and labor scarcity eased, landlords' renewed diligence at enforcing their prerogatives was to breed further conflict in the Hudson Valley in the nineteenth century. Unlike Pennsylvania, therefore, parts of New York and New Jersey supported a landed elite, a provincial gentry whose wealth and influence was rooted in the ownership of landed estates.

However it was owned, most land in the Middle Colonies was divided into moderately sized rather than large farms. Eighteenth-century prosperity, especially in Pennsylvania, derived from the region's emergence as a supplier of wheat, a staple agricultural export that was increasingly in demand from Europe as populations there grew. Income from wheat cultivation provided for purchases of cloth and other manufactured goods, and also funded agricultural diversification, such as the development of dairying in parts of Pennsylvania during the second half of the eighteenth century. Such household production relied heavily on the work of farm women and daughters. The French visitor Jacques-Pierre Brissot de Warville was surprised when he encountered an unmarried farmer near Philadelphia in 1788, and noted the disadvantages this involved. The man could not keep poultry, pigeons, make cheese, have any spinning done or collect goose feathers—all tasks, Brissot remarked, which could be carried on well only by farm women.[9]

Patterns of social organization and equality sometimes varied by ethnicity. There is evidence that some groups made use of forms of unfree labor to give their members access to the chance of prosperity. Some

"English" farmers in Pennsylvania, for example, used rented land to grow wheat that they could sell for export as a step toward farm ownership. Large numbers of colonial-era German migrants to Pennsylvania arrived in family groups, about one-third of them as "redemptioners," indentured servants who were sold to employers on arrival and who owed labor for a period of years to repay (or "redeem") the charge for their transatlantic passage. Over time, different patterns emerged among English and German-descended farmers in the wheat regions. In German-settled districts, such as Lancaster County, Pennsylvania, farmers kept control over family members to secure labor for plowing and harvest. English farmers in other parts of the region tended to seek people they could employ on their land as their commercial output increased. Often they leased small amounts of land and cottages to landless tenant-laborers known as "inmates," who worked partly for themselves and partly for the main farm. By 1783 the number of inmates in Chester County, Pennsylvania, had reached more than one-fifth of the population.[10]

At points across New Jersey, Pennsylvania, and adjacent Maryland, ironworking and smelting had also grown up in the late colonial period, in places where iron deposits were accessible in pine barrens or mountainsides. Ironworks, many of them quite large organizations by eighteenth-century standards, were operated by a combination of free and unfree labor, usually around a company-run store to furnish supplies, and often in conjunction with farm leasehold arrangements. Men would be employed for wages or on shares to cut trees and saw lumber for fuel, and to undertake the heavy, continuous work of maintaining a smelter while it was in operation. Iron provided another of the region's staple exports: in the late colonial period, the Mid-Atlantic region was supplying about one-seventh of the world's rapidly growing demand for iron. After the American Revolution ironmakers would also find increasing home markets for their output.[11]

Wheat and iron generated prosperity but were produced in ways that meant this wealth was not equally distributed. Increasing numbers of the Mid-Atlantic's workforce were men and women without land or property, who were obliged to take leases as inmates or to find work for wages. In Chester County, Pennsylvania, for example, there were fifty-six landless laborers for every hundred propertied householders in 1756, and the proportion was rising. A significant percentage of the population were white apprentices, servants, cottagers, or wage earners, in a pattern that was more comparable with parts of Europe than with other North American regions. Yet the expansion of the region, the prosperity of the economy, and the character of its products helped give it several distinctive features.

Prosperity attracted migrants. The colonial Mid-Atlantic region was in some senses a prototype for the large-scale immigration from Europe that the United States would experience from the mid-nineteenth century on. Pennsylvania in particular became a magnet for European settlers, many of whom arrived either as single young men or—like many of the German redemptioners—as families to undertake unfree labor. But both wheat cultivation and ironworking made highly seasonal and uneven demands for labor. This seasonality and the ready availability of European labor meant that owning slaves—though it was legal in colonial Pennsylvania—was relatively unattractive to rural employers. Only about 2.5 percent of the pre-Revolutionary population of Pennsylvania was of African descent, of whom some were free but most were slave laborers in Philadelphia. Indeed, with the exception of some pockets of slave labor in the New Jersey and Hudson Valley countryside, most slaves in the Middle Colonies were urban, working as domestic servants, laborers, or skilled craft workers in the region's growing towns and cities. For the most part, this region could be counted a "society with slaves" rather than a "slave society."

Towns came to have particular significance for the Mid-Atlantic economy. Grain exports, commercial development, markets for agricultural goods, and craft production all stimulated the growth of port towns, both the region's larger cities and small centers with access to seaways, such as Burlington, New Jersey. Philadelphia emerged in the colonial period as North America's largest town, a position it would retain until after 1800. New York, which would overhaul Philadelphia then, had grown more slowly in the colonial period. Both cities provided homes for an expanding commercial class of merchants and shipowners whose prosperity from Atlantic commerce and their trading connections with the region's hinterlands gave them increasing sources of wealth and influence. Philadelphia's overseas merchants rose in number from 230 in 1756 to 320 by 1774, and their ranks continued to grow thereafter. They and their counterparts in New York and smaller ports formed urban elites not primarily rooted in the land or the direct employment of labor to cultivate it.[12]

Towns were the main locations for slavery in the region. Slaves formed about one-tenth of the New York City population in 1770, for example. But the seasonality of rural work made urban areas targets for internal migration as laborers moved to and from towns in search of different kinds of employment, and their position as centers of Atlantic commerce also made these towns important destinations for immigrants from Europe. First Philadelphia and then New York became homes to important pools of legally free labor, especially of young single men. One consequence was that slavery declined in significance. In Philadelphia the proportion of formally unfree laborers in the workforce fell markedly in the late colonial period; whereas in 1750 almost 40 percent of Philadelphia workers were servants or slaves, by 1783 the proportion was little more than 6 percent of the city's growing workforce. With immigrant labor available, wages in the city and nearby farming areas like Chester County were low compared with those in other regions. Fewer and fewer employers sought to take on the costs and obligations of having indentured servants or slaves when casual wage labor could be found inexpensively. By 1775 the proportion of untaxed persons (mostly laborers without property) in Philadelphia had grown to about 10.5 percent of the city's taxable population, a proportion almost double that twenty years earlier. In light of the pace of population growth and the underrepresentation of the poor in official records, these figures imply a rapid expansion of Philadelphia's free laboring poor during the last years of the colonial period.[13]

Urban growth and seasonal fluctuations in the demand for labor in wheat farming also produced significant flows of migration back and forth between town and country, and made labor available for a wider range of urban and rural activities. Farm households' demand for cloth, for example, was met in Pennsylvania both by imports from Europe and by weaving undertaken by male workers, some itinerant, some working in urban workshops. Their presence would later influence patterns of industrialization in Philadelphia and its hinterland. Together the combination of wheat farming, rural demand, immigration, and urban growth led to a reliance on forms of free labor and to social divisions based on class that elsewhere would emerge only in the nineteenth century.[14]

Many Souths

SOUTHWARD FROM Pennsylvania, stretching down the seaboard to Georgia and westward into the Appalachian Mountains, was the region that would remain until the Civil War marked by its continued reliance on slavery, and which was also the base for nineteenth-century expansion west as far as Texas and the Missouri Valley. Although two-fifths of its population in 1770 was enslaved, and though slavery would eventually come to denote this region's unity as "the South," in the late eighteenth century the states from Delaware to Georgia were noteworthy more for their disparities than for their uniformity. Indeed, as long as it remained legal, even if in decline, in the Mid-Atlantic region and parts of New England, slavery alone did not distinguish the South from those areas. Just as significant in the eighteenth century were the South's patterns of landownership and social structure, and its economic functions. Slavery and staple-crop production were important factors in them, but these characteristics varied considerably across the South.

To begin with, it is important to note that independent household or "yeoman" farming was as telling a characteristic of the Southern colonies as it was elsewhere. On the eve of the Revolution about half, for example, of Virginia's population consisted of small landowners and their families, and another 10 or 20 percent were tenant farmers. Slaveholders made up only a minority of landowners and would continue to do so. The white yeoman farmers who lived in plantation districts or in the piedmont or upland areas across the South engaged in patterns of cultivation that reflected their primary reliance on their own family labor, similar to that in other early American regions. In the upper South, many of them undertook tobacco cultivation, which was as amenable to production on small farms as on plantations. In the lower South, white farmers engaged in mixed crop production, often together with hunting and other activities that made use of unoccupied or uncultivated land that formed a common open range. In the piedmont and uplands, such farmers usually constituted a large majority of landholders; the proportions of cultivators owning even a small number of slaves fell away with distance from the coasts. Only 22 percent of Lunenburg County, Virginia, householders owned slaves in 1750, and only 2 percent owned more than five. In Tazewell County, organized in 1799 in upland southwestern Virginia, there were four times as many adult white men in 1801 as there were adult slave men, and no slaveholder in the county owned more than seven slaves. Tensions between yeoman farmers and slaveholders would emerge in various contexts over the next sixty or more years, though only in upland regions where slavery remained virtually nonexistent would outright opposition to planters' policies become politically significant.[15]

The Chesapeake Bay area of Virginia, parts of Maryland, and adjacent Delaware included some of British America's oldest settlements and had emerged as its first "slave society." Early engaged in staple-crop production for export, especially of tobacco, the Chesapeake had come to rely on slave labor during the late seventeenth century, when sources of white indentured servants had dried up and planters became keen to keep the poor who were growing in number around them divided by race and status. By the late colonial period the spread of tobacco cultivation supported small farms, with and without slave labor, across the region, but in the longer-settled districts in particular, considerable numbers of larger farms and plantations relied substantially on slaves to produce crops. Across the tidewater and piedmont regions of Virginia about seven in ten slaveholders owned eleven or more slaves each, a proportion that in frontier counties fell to 57 percent.[16]

The modest-sized properties of the Chesapeake's yeoman farmers were interspersed with the larger estates of planters, whose land was either worked by slaves or divided up and rented out to tenants. About 10 percent of white men in Virginia were members of the gentry, but they owned half the land and almost half the personal property in the colony. Such inequalities persisted. In Appoquinimink Hundred, south of Wilmington, Delaware, in 1797, only 45 percent of taxpayers owned land, 43 percent were tenants, and 12 percent were landless. In Prince George's County, Maryland, too, a majority of the population owned no land; many whites and some free blacks were tenant farmers on short leases, with high rents. In contrast to Pennsylvania, where some farmers used rented land to help them work toward greater prosperity, tenancy in the Chesapeake was primarily associated with poverty. In Delaware tenancy rates would rise between the late eighteenth and mid-nineteenth centuries. The uneven division of land and the existence of slavery and tenancy denoted a rural economy in which wealth and income inequality was marked, and in which owning wealth denoted social power. When Joseph Doddridge traveled from frontier western Pennsylvania to a school in Maryland in 1777, he noted these inequalities and the "arbitrary power of one man over another" that they implied.[17]

The existence of slavery meant that divisions by race and status were more significant in the Chesapeake than the ethnic diversity characteristic of the Mid-Atlantic colonies. In the 1760s about 45 percent of the population of Maryland and 35 percent of that of Virginia were of English descent. African-American slaves accounted for another 40 percent or so in each case. The balance included immigrants and their descendants, most of whom had origins in other parts of the British Isles, such as Ulster and the Scottish Highlands, and had made their way southwestward into the valley of Virginia after arriving or initially settling in Pennsylvania. But social and political life in Maryland and Virginia had historically been dominated by a slaveholding gentry sustained by tobacco cultivation, by the wealth this had generated, by the political power that had derived from control of local church vestries and county courts, and from election to the assemblies. Here was a social elite closely tied to the land that it owned and to the control of the slave labor it employed to work it. Urban settlements in the Chesapeake region were rare, small, and widely scattered. The region remained overwhelmingly rural, with a complex mix of large and small, slave-worked farms, a white majority of yeomen, tenants, and landless laborers, and a distinct gentry class.

This pattern's emergence during the colonial period had helped create a slave population that more than sustained itself. Although Virginia had imported about a hundred thousand slaves during the colonial period, by 1800 it had a slave population roughly three times that many. The observation that the American slave population could expand by natural increase would underpin many calculations about the future of slavery and its political implications during the Revolution. Slaves in the Chesapeake had always lived under a variety of conditions. Many were the only slaves their holders owned, and others lived grouped in small numbers; but a substantial minority lived in large groups on plantations housing twenty or more slaves. In Richmond County, Virginia, in 1783, 54 percent of slaveholders owned only one to five slaves each; but 41 percent of slaves lived in units of between sixteen and fifty slaves each. This pattern of slaveownership distributed across plantations and smaller farms remained a characteristic of the upper South into the nineteenth century.

Further south, however, in the Carolina-Georgia Lowcountry, a different pattern of slave society had emerged. This was organized first around cattle raising on large tracts of land, then became concentrated on raising staple crops such as indigo (which was exported to make dyes) and rice, both of which were grown on coastal plantations. In coastal parts of South Carolina in particular, concentrations of slaves were larger than in the Chesapeake and had come to represent an absolute majority of the population. As in the Chesapeake, plantation owners in the Southern Lowcountry came to form a distinct regional elite. Even though indigo production would decline during the Revolution because British subsidies for growing it ceased, the extension of tidal rice planting on the Carolina and Georgia coasts and Sea Islands in the 1780s, and the introduction of long-staple Sea Island cotton cultivation, ensured the survival and consolidation of the area's plantation system and its planter elite. Partly because of the character of their crops; partly because the slaves' skills, derived from the African experience of rice-growing, were essential to success; partly because the climate led many whites to avoid the plantation zone in the hot, disease-ridden summer months, Lowcountry elites divided their time between their plantations and town residences they maintained in Charleston and, increasingly, Savannah. Charleston, the only important port town between Baltimore and New Orleans, was North America's fourth largest urban center in the 1770s. Because of the residential patterns of the planter elite, Lowcountry society had a more distinctively urban dimension than that of the Chesapeake, but the wealth of most prominent Charleston and Savannah families was nevertheless derived from the plantation land and slave labor they owned and controlled.

Plantations in the lower South were generally larger than those in the Chesapeake and housed larger slave workforces. Interspersed even among the biggest plantations, however, were substantial numbers of smaller farms owned by white yeoman farmers or small slaveholders.

Compared with the Chesapeake, monitoring of slaves' work was more commonly left to overseers or to enslaved supervisors (called "drivers") than assumed directly by slaveholders themselves. Indeed, during the colonial period there had evolved a set of practices for slave work that were largely distinct from the direct oversight or gang labor that predominated on farms and plantations in the upper South. This "task" system identified work to be completed by slaves, often in small groups or in isolation, and left them with a relatively wide degree of autonomy. Here, even more than in the Chesapeake grain areas, slaves relied on their own activities, fishing or tending gardens, to provide much of their sustenance and goods for informal local trading. Yet this autonomy was only relative, and it involved harsh constraints. Life in the rice swamps and coastal regions was tough. Slaves were exposed to disease and debilitation. Adult and child mortality rates among slaves were higher than in the Chesapeake, so that the rate of natural increase of the slave population, though still positive, was comparatively slender. As planters or their overseers sought to maintain control over their labor forces, punishments dealt out for slack work, absences, or attempted escape were often severe.

Two New Englands

IF RACIALLY based slavery marked the most crucial social distinctions in the South while incipient class differences were emerging in the Middle Colonies, many parts of New England could lay claim to relative equality. New England's rural economy was based on household-run farms, whose heads were usually freeholders of the land they worked and who conducted mixed-crop agriculture to supply household, local, or intraregional markets. Yet the image of a society of households relatively undifferentiated by marks of status or great disparities of wealth should be qualified in two important ways. First, disparities of power and authority across age and gender within households, though they were no greater than those elsewhere, played a more decided role in explaining the particularities of New England society: to a greater extent, these were the divisions that mattered here. Second, there was also a significant geographical division within New England itself. Especially in

southern New England, coastal towns and their adjacent districts functioned differently from the rural interior. It is valid to speak of New
England as in some respects a "dual economy," a region in which distinct
patterns of society and economic activity existed alongside one another
and require separate examination. In each case, however, the social influence and power associated with landholding was much more muted
than in the plantation South or the Hudson Valley.[18]

By comparison with either the South or the Mid-Atlantic, eighteenth-
century New England appeared socially and ethnically homogeneous. In
1760, for example, about 85 percent of the Massachusetts population was
of English descent. When Timothy Dwight, president of Yale College and
one of New England's most traveled observers, visited New York City in
the 1790s, he was struck by the variety of peoples and cultures he encountered on its streets. Rural towns also displayed quite high levels of
what anthropologists call residential kin propinquity: many people related
to one another by blood or marriage lived in close proximity. As one contemporary observer put it, people in New England settlements were "all
in some degree related to each other." Charles Gleason, who taught winter school at Dana, Massachusetts, in 1799, recorded the names of his
fifty-four "scholars." They shared seventeen family names between them,
and twenty-nine of them shared only five names.[19]

Surpluses from farming districts reached urban markets and were
shipped by merchants there to supply the plantation districts of the West
Indies, but New England did not have significant staple export crops like
the wheat of the Mid-Atlantic region or the tobacco and rice of the
South. Farm families conducted a variety of tasks, based on a distinct but
fairly flexible gender division of labor. Property ownership was not
equally distributed, but landowning was widespread and tenancy less
common than in other regions. In Revolutionary Era Connecticut, for
instance, only about 5 percent of households owned no landed property.
Although most young adults were propertyless, there was a realistic expectation in rural regions that they would acquire it, and the distribution
of landownership was usually correlated with age.[20]

Farm households calculated on doing much of their work with family labor. Nevertheless wealth and age distinctions, and different stages in
families' life cycles, created disparities that required outside help. This
was often supplied by exchanging labor between households (known as

"'changing works") or by hiring servants and farmhands locally for domestic and outdoor tasks. Young families with small children might have neighbors or relatives to help them out. As children grew up and were capable of contributing their own labor, they would take on a larger share of the household's work, or might work by the day for neighboring farmers or be hired to live out and work for another household. Prosperous farmers might hold one or a handful of slaves as servants and farmhands; the future general Benjamin Lincoln of Massachusetts acquired a man called Cato, the first of several slaves he would own, in 1772. But except for small parts of Rhode Island and southern Connecticut where a handful of wealthy farm families owned groups of slaves to work in gangs, rural slavery remained rare in New England and in many areas was virtually nonexistent. Even the prosperous, fertile town of Hadley, in western Massachusetts, in 1774 counted only four slaves among its total population of more than nine hundred. In southern New England as a whole, slaves accounted for about 3.5 percent of the population, and in Massachusetts only 1.8 percent. But conditions for slaves, though they varied according to circumstances, were not notably more benign than they were in the South. Like slaves throughout the colonies, those in New England faced poverty and arbitrary treatment, dependence on their owners' will, and the burdens of racial prejudice.[21]

Hiring of labor for wages in rural New England was often intermittent; only wealthier households relied permanently on the waged labor of others and, compared with southeastern Pennsylvania, relatively few laborers could rely on being hired for particular jobs. The region's household-based economy created few opportunities for outsiders. In the late eighteenth century, for example, the wages paid in the New England countryside were significantly higher than those paid in Pennsylvania, but the two labor markets remained separate. The lower Pennsylvania wages were attributable to the higher rates of immigration into that region. Rural New England in this period was not attractive to migrants, either from abroad or from within North America, because few households hired labor continuously, and much hiring that did occur was from among neighbors who were already settled in the region. Very few British or Irish migrants set out for America with New England as their intended destination; in the years immediately before the Revolution, fewer than one in a hundred emigrants did so.[22]

From the mid-eighteenth century on there were growing numbers of itinerant laborers and men and women of the "wandering poor," who moved from place to place throughout the colonies in search of employment. They often found short shrift in the New England countryside. Town officials, wary of the risk that they might have to provide poor relief for those who became destitute, issued formal "warnings-out" to prevent wanderers from obtaining legal residence, and sometimes they literally removed them from town. Demand for labor was uncertain, intermittent, and based on having local connections.

Many farm households with means also undertook craft production in addition to agricultural tasks, a tendency that would grow during the Revolution when demand for home-produced manufactures increased. In Concord, Massachusetts, about 15 percent of household heads were craftsmen in 1771, a proportion that more than doubled over the next three decades. At Northampton, Massachusetts, at the beginning of the Revolution an estimated one-third of households had nonfarm incomes. The French traveler Brissot de Warville noted in the 1780s that many New England farmers were also small manufacturers, a fact he applauded, "for it detaches fewer from the great object of agriculture." Men might acquire skill at shoemaking, harness making, or any one of a variety of woodworking trades. Women also conducted trades as needlewomen, tailors, or gownmakers, or as midwives with skills in nursing and the use of herbs and other medicaments. A considerable number of rural households were engaged to some degree in textile production, and this activity would also grow during the Revolution. Many women or their daughters spun wool, or flax for linen yarn, and many households owned spinning wheels or flax wheels for this purpose. A smaller number took in yarn to weave into cloth. Across the interior of Connecticut, Massachusetts, and New Hampshire, between 60 and 90 percent of households owned spinning wheels in the 1770s, and in Hampshire County, Massachusetts, about one-third owned a loom. In New England, unlike Pennsylvania, weaving had become a woman's craft during the eighteenth century, reflecting the central role of family labor in the region's economy.[23]

Many rural New Englanders subscribed to notions of deference and social order based on length of residence, position in the clergy, and, above all, age. Where fathers ruled and controlled access to the land their sons would one day inherit, deference to age was proclaimed as a prominent social virtue. Inequalities of wealth and income meant, in fertile farming regions such as the Connecticut Valley, that local and regional elites could establish some preeminence among their neighbors. In Hampshire County, Massachusetts, these families were known as the "River Gods" for their control of political and judicial offices, and their prominence in the clergy and the provincial militia. But these inequalities were modest by comparison with those of the Chesapeake or Southern Lowcountry, and they were not characteristic of many parts of New England. In most areas, among the freeholders who were the majority of farmers, a rough equality prevailed, reflected in the disposition of town offices and in traditions such as the election of militia company officers. As some Revolutionary War officers from other regions would come to complain, New England soldiers, especially those from rural districts, seemed incorrigibly attached to egalitarian notions.

These rural patterns offered a contrast to the societies that grew up in and around the port towns scattered along New England's coasts. Boston, the largest of these towns, with a population of about fifteen thousand at the end of the colonial period, was a significant commercial and governmental center—capital of Massachusetts and home to between three hundred and four hundred merchants, many of whom engaged in Atlantic trade. A host of smaller ports, too, including Salem and Newburyport in Massachusetts, Newport and Providence in Rhode Island, and New London and Middletown in Connecticut, similarly based their activities on shipping, fishing, or other maritime trades. The port towns were as much oriented to the commercial world of the Atlantic as they were to the rural society in their immediate hinterland. Unequal and class-based social structures had grown up there since early in the process of colonial settlement. In Boston by the period 1765–1775, more than 90 percent of wealth listed in estate inventories was held by only 40 percent of estates, and significant numbers of the urban poor had no property at all. Even so, household production was significant. Across Essex County, Massachusetts, in the 1770s, almost three in five households had spinning wheels, and one in five had a loom.[24]

The pools of available labor in the port towns were poorly integrated with those of the rural interior, largely because each was still strongly connected to household and family networks that tended not to overlap.

Crews hired locally by merchants in Salem, Marblehead, Nantucket, and other ports plied their fishing craft as far as the cod banks off Newfoundland. They were often ill paid and in debt for the supplies with which they had been outfitted. Coastal and oceanic trading vessels sailed with crews employed for wages and exposed to dangers, disease, and harsh living conditions and discipline. Skilled and unskilled labor in the docks, ropewalks, and chandleries of the port districts was subject to fluctuation from the seasons and the ebb and flow of trade. Maritime communities like Marblehead or the waterfront districts of the larger ports were areas of relative poverty and economic instability. In particular, the port towns were home to considerable numbers of households headed by women, whose marginality in a society where men usually controlled property was exacerbated by the accidents of maritime life. Across the colonies as a whole, fewer than one in ten households had female heads, but in port towns such as Boston or Newport the proportion could be more than double that. Widowhood and abandonment, as husbands were drowned, died from disease, or simply never returned from the sea, struck great numbers of port town households, creating further pockets of poverty in an unequal society. Small ports, like Salem, Newburyport, and New London, had higher proportions of their workforce directly employed in maritime occupations than large towns like Boston; accordingly, their incidence of impoverished families was relatively greater.[25]

On the New England coast, as in the Mid-Atlantic region, influential elite groups were more strongly connected with commerce and shipping than they were with the land. The principal leaders in New England port towns were the merchants and shipowners whose wealth could contrast strikingly to the poverty that was often to be found around them. While most of the rural interior made little use of slave labor, slaves were not uncommon in the ports, and New England merchants were active in conducting the international trade in slaves from Africa to plantation regions in the Americas. Some prominent merchants would remain loyal to Britain during the Revolution and either withdraw into obscurity or go into exile in England. But a notable proportion of New England merchants would support the patriot cause, and the opportunities that some gained from military supply, privateering, and other commercial activities would help reshape and consolidate a substantial, prosperous commercial class in the Revolution's aftermath.

Nevertheless, despite the sharper social distinctions and wealth differentials of the port towns and maritime activities, the contrasts between the conduct of rural and coastal economies were not absolute. Businesses in the maritime trades were usually conducted on a household basis, just as farming was. Families and kin connections remained central to these enterprises and to the recruitment of labor for them. Late-eighteenth-century fishing crews from New England ports were overwhelmingly recruited from maritime areas. Although the composition of crews in commercial vessels at sea embodied a social hierarchy in which status and authority were sharply differentiated and power vested at the top of the structure, this did not wholly reflect the character of maritime New England society in general. Officers and ship captains from towns such as Salem had usually served as seamen and risen through the ranks. The families that had placed them, as boys or young men, as hands in their own or other merchants' ships regarded seagoing much as rural households regarded farming or artisan skill—it was a craft that had to be learned from the bottom up. On land, in the artisan crafts that grew up in rural village centers or in the port towns to service the maritime trades or to process trade goods, household-based patterns prevailed.[26]

Regional Variety and Social Divisions

S O S O C I A L structures, cultural patterns, and productive activities varied from region to region across the colonies. Different labor systems, different patterns of connection between towns, countryside, and wider markets, and the different character of elites all contributed to regional distinctiveness. This is why it is important to ask how such disparate colonies might ever act cohesively.

Their differences in society and resources, coupled with the effects of British trading regulations, often meant that individual colonies had stronger trading links with Britain, the West Indies, Africa, or the Mediterranean than they did with other parts of North America. Political culture and practice, too, varied considerably from colony to colony. Each was to some extent a political world of its own, with more important connections to London than to its neighbors. Nine of the thirteen colonies were direct possessions of the British crown and headed by governors appointed from London. Pennsylvania and Maryland were owned by proprietors, the Penn family in one case and the Calvert family (the earls of Baltimore) in the other, while Connecticut and Rhode Island remained comparatively autonomous, choosing their own governors under their original colonial charters. Its form of government could much influence a colony's politics. The Penn family's proprietorship, for example, was a key issue in Pennsylvania throughout the mid-eighteenth century. But because each colony, whatever its formal arrangements, also had its own representative assembly, with members elected by freemen qualified to vote, political life invariably centered on local and provincial issues. Only temporarily, during the Seven Years' War in the 1750s, and again during the Stamp Act crisis of 1765, did delegates from the different colonies gather to consider matters together. Other than in these exceptional instances, each colony conducted public affairs in its own way, with little reference to the others, and regarded itself as a distinct entity.[27]

Like most political entities, individual American colonies were often internally riven by political and social divisions. The religious revivals that began in the 1730s and 1740s, often known as the Great Awakening, challenged the authority of established clergy in Virginia and parts of New England. Rhode Island and New York were constantly subject to political factionalism, in the latter case between groupings headed by the Livingston and DeLancey families who were among the province's wealthiest landowners and merchants. New York, New Jersey, and other regions witnessed repeated conflicts between landlords and tenants. Pennsylvania and the Carolinas faced strong disputes between older-settled regions and provincial government policies and the claims of new backcountry settlers who were pushing out the boundaries of frontier settlement and fomenting friction with Native American groups. The new settlers wanted governmental protection and the right to equal participation. In 1763 western settlers calling themselves the Paxton Boys marched on Philadelphia and threatened the colonial assembly. Armed "Regulators" on the South Carolina frontier sought to exclude Native Americans and to extend the colony's system of local government to their settlements, only at length proving persuasive with a planter elite reluctant to share influence in the provincial assembly. North Carolina's coastal elite was more recalcitrant, resisting the claims of the colony's own backcountry Regulators and inflicting a military defeat on them in 1771 when argument turned to armed insurrection.[28]

What Did the Colonies Have in Common?

HISTORIANS HAVE long debated the kinds of common ties and experience that might have bound the American colonies together despite their differences. From our survey of the regions, we could note that the colonies did have common features, among them the predominance of agriculture, the centrality of households in social and economic activity, and the effects of a high land-to-labor ratio. But these were underlying patterns that only occasionally became explicit features of public discussion. They were not unique to North America, and they had in any case been important facets of colonial societies since the start of European settlement. To these common patterns we need to add an understanding of changes that were taking place in America by the mid-eighteenth century.

Some historians have interpreted American independence in the 1770s as an outgrowth of the growing maturity of the North American colonies, their demographic growth and prosperity, and their acquisition of characteristics—such as town growth and greater population density—that were reminiscent of European societies. Benjamin Franklin famously estimated around 1760 that British America's population was doubling in size every twenty-five years, and that in another century the colonies would have more inhabitants than Britain itself. Reflecting on the growing confidence that came with size and prosperity, Franklin even suggested that in time the British Empire's center would gravitate to North America. But growth and prosperity did not necessarily point to intercolonial unity. Equally likely, they could sharpen regional differences and rivalries among the colonies and deepen the existing connections between the colonies and Britain.[29]

Recently, though, the historian Timothy H. Breen has argued that prosperity did create an important set of common circumstances across the colonies in that colonial people—especially among the wealthy and middling classes—were becoming significant consumers of British goods.

This common experience bound otherwise disparate colonists together. A writer in the *Connecticut Courant* claimed in 1765 that the acquisition of tea, household goods, and other "modern superfluities" that were becoming increasingly important elements both of Atlantic trade and of colonial culture had "jointly and severally conquered more than sword, famine, and pestilence." Perhaps with tongue in cheek, this writer was suggesting that consumption and fashion were more powerful forces than war or disease. Yet of course within a decade sword and pestilence, together with the threat of famine, were hanging over the American colonies as they embarked on their struggle with Britain. While it is undoubtedly true that trade and consumption became crucial elements of the disputes that drove colonial Americans to seek independence, there are grounds for skepticism that it was their common status as consumers that bound colonial patriots together in the Revolution. Above all there were many colonial consumers, both among the wealthy and among poorer sections of society, who would stay loyal to Britain or attempt to remain neutral during the conflict. Consumption of British goods may indeed have become a common experience across the colonies between 1750 and 1774, but it is not clear that this in itself cemented an alliance between otherwise disparate colonial peoples.[30]

Two sets of circumstances did, however, play a crucial role in drawing the different colonies toward a common political struggle. First, the impact of evolving British colonial policies during and after the Seven Years' War provided political issues across the colonies' diverse political systems that advocates of colonial rights were able to paint as common assaults on Americans' liberties. In the specific context of debates over the conduct of British colonial policy, similarities between different colonies' relations with Britain could establish common ground between otherwise disparate societies and political cultures. Second, it is necessary to remember that the thirteen colonies were not the only territories in the British Empire or in the Atlantic colonial world. Their ability to recognize common interests in challenging British rule in the 1770s came about not because of experiences such as consuming British goods, which they shared with other parts of the empire, but because by chance some social characteristics both linked these British colonies together and distinguished them from others.[31]

Why the Thirteen Colonies?

THE THIRTEEN British colonies that broke with Britain in 1776 to create the United States of America did not form a natural or inevitable grouping. Why did these colonies, and not others also, form the nucleus of the new nation?[32]

First, they were what historians term "colonies of settlement." All had received substantial influxes of people who migrated from Europe to occupy and cultivate land. The large majority of their populations were not indigenous peoples, whose societies had largely been destroyed or pushed back beyond the areas of colonial settlement, but voluntary or involuntary immigrants and their descendants. By the eighteenth century, natural increase and immigration had accelerated their growth to levels even beyond what Benjamin Franklin had estimated. With population increase came strong popular interest in extending the bounds of settlement into new areas of the continent. Conflicts between colonial aspirations and the British government's efforts to control this expansion were among the Revolution's root causes. At the end of the Seven Years' War the British government sought to control settlement west of an artificial boundary (the "proclamation line" of 1763) drawn along the length of the Appalachians. This conflicted not only with the interests of prominent colonists who had invested in land speculation schemes west of the mountains but also with the more general colonial aspiration to continue the process of expansion across the land that had now been going on for 150 years.

Second, the largest settler groups across the thirteen colonies had British origins or ancestry. Although free migrants from other European countries had settled in many places, especially in the Middle Colonies and the Southern up-country, and though race-based chattel slavery was legal throughout the colonies and was important from Delaware southward, affinities with Britain were strong. This did not lead to cultural uniformity: different migrations replicated conflicts originating in the British Isles' own social, ethnic, and religious antagonisms more than they instilled a sense of common heritage. But broadly understood concepts of political liberty and "the rights of Englishmen" defined many colonists' attitudes to British policies and ensured the influence of radicals' arguments when these rights were under assault. As the merchant Christopher Gadsden of South Carolina claimed in 1765, "the sons of Britain would have been . . . very thinly scattered on this side of the Atlantic Ocean" had "the natural liberties of British subjects" not applied as fully in the American colonies as in the home country.[33]

This was possible because, third, each colony had established its form of local, representative government, usually with an assembly that became the focus of provincial political power. Each to some extent suffered from the revision of British colonial policies during and after the Seven Years' War, and came to perceive a common interest in joining with the others to resist further impositions. Whereas in Britain only a small minority of the population was qualified by heredity or property holding to participate in politics, among adult white men in the colonies a substantial proportion owned property and hence the qualifications for political participation.

Creole Elites

FOURTH, POLITICAL influence within each colony was exercised by elite groups whose principal connections lay within their own colonies rather than in Britain or elsewhere. Because the North American colonies had been colonies of settlement, the chief groups exercising landed or commercial power were "creole elites," drawn from people who were born in the colonies and who had strong roots there. In the late colonial period, North American contacts with Britain became stronger and more complex. Much Chesapeake trade came to be handled by Scottish-based tobacco merchants and their agents. Links between Philadelphia, New York, and Britain grew with each decade. Yet the majority of elite figures, North and South, remained colonials whose property and interests lay in North America rather than in Europe. The same political boundaries contained the sources of both their wealth and their political power.[34]

Each colony had evolved its own version of a colonial gentry of wealthy and well-connected individuals, linked by ties of kinship and held together by patterns of inheritance. Although these creole elites existed throughout the colonies, and though there were connections among them, there are few grounds for suggesting that they formed a unified grouping. The North American colonies never had a formal, titled aristocracy and lacked the wide disparities in wealth and privilege that characterized much of Europe. But late colonial society did express habits and assumptions of formal behavior and deference that betokened a social order rooted in concepts of birth and hierarchical social status. Although their estates were modest indeed by comparison with those of England's greatest landed families, the colonial gentry of Virginia and Maryland occupied houses, wore clothes, and expected to be accorded day-to-day politeness that marked them off from their less privileged neighbors. Seating arrangements in the Anglican churches of the Chesapeake region and the South reflected a social hierarchy based on rank and race. Some *patroons* or great landlords of the Hudson River Valley held or aspired to similar indications of their status. Leading merchants in the main port towns also enjoyed residences, dress, and other symbols of their exalted rank. Even in the relatively egalitarian countryside of New England and Pennsylvania, more prosperous farmers and merchants, especially if they held legal or political office, were regarded as being "in the first place" and might enjoy two-story houses or other modest indications of their position.[35]

Despite their differences, it was the presence of these elites that, above all, marked the thirteen colonies out as distinct from other New World colonies in the mid-eighteenth century and helps explain why they and not others joined together in rebellion against imperial rule. On one hand, they differed in important respects from most Spanish, Portuguese, and French colonies in the Americas and the Caribbean. On the Spanish American mainland and in the French Canadian interior, settlers from Europe had intermixed with indigenous populations to a much greater extent than in the British colonies, and Native Americans in those areas were regarded as belonging to colonial populations rather than being separate from them. In the Caribbean islands, European settlers were vastly outnumbered by the slaves whom they had brought in to work on the plantations—mainly sugar-growing—that made the region a principal source of European wealth. Only coastal South Carolina and Georgia, with their rice and indigo plantations, had population structures remotely like those of the Caribbean, but with smaller slave majorities in most localities. Spanish, Portuguese, and French territories in the New World had no representative political institutions that could serve, as those in the British colonies did, as loci of autonomous political activity, debate, and opposition.

On the other hand, by comparison with other British territories in the New World, the thirteen colonies also displayed distinctions that help explain why they could act together but why others did not join them in rejecting British authority. Some British West Indian colonies, such as Jamaica, did have their own representative assemblies, for example. But the wealth of these islands, and their plantation systems, made them of much greater interest to British elites in the eighteenth century than the mainland colonies, which were either less lucrative or more marginal to British interests. The British Caribbean did have policy disputes with Britain, but it was also in a variety of ways much more closely tied to Britain than the mainland colonies. Many of its wealthy plantation owners were from British families who sent members to the islands to run their estates for them. Powerful families with West Indies interests formed an influential lobby in the British Parliament, giving them the kind of political influence in London that mainland North American colonists lacked. Although some Jamaican planters sought greater autonomy, they did not see independence from Britain as either practicable or attractive. Their close ties there, the protected markets for their sugar, and the importance to them of British naval and military protection of their trade and against slave insurrections discouraged thoughts of breaking away from the mother country. British Caribbean planter groups were not creole elites to the extent that those on the mainland were.

Britain's Canadian colonies, too, were little more likely than those in the Caribbean to seek independence. None yet had a representative assembly that could have formed the basis for political opposition. Newfoundland, the oldest British possession in the New World, consisted of scattered coastal fishing settlements. Nova Scotia was a relatively new, still sparsely populated center of fishing and farming, whose small capital, Halifax, was a significant British naval and military base. Quebec, captured from France in the Seven Years' War, consisted predominantly of French farmers and had only a small English-speaking merchant community at Montreal. Early in the Revolution, American patriots tried to induce their Canadian cousins to join them, invading Quebec, capturing Montreal, and unsuccessfully laying siege to Quebec City in the hope of provoking an anti-British uprising. But few settlers in the province saw much to gain by rejecting British rule. Quebec's French Catholic majority had just had their legal and religious institutions confirmed by Parliament in the Quebec Act of 1774 and were readier to rely on this indication of Britain's tolerance than to take their chances with the often fiercely Protestant American provinces. Canada's English-speaking minority relied on Britain to secure their own position.

Elites and Social Relations

SO THROUGHOUT the American colonies creole elites and the political institutions over which they held sway marked their distinction from other parts of the New World. Whether they were landed elites, like the planter gentry of the Chesapeake and the Southern Lowcountry, or commercial elites, like the wealthy merchant groups of Boston, New York, and Philadelphia, their principal ties were to the colonies of their birth rather than to Britain or to other parts of the empire. Unlike many Caribbean planters, or merchants in the Spanish American colonies, they tended not to see themselves as only temporary colonial residents, carrying out functions for families or business partners based at home, where they would in due course expect to return. American elites *were* at home. The leadership of the planter elite in Virginia, the support of radical sections of the commercial elites in the North, and the susceptibility of many conservative merchants to popular and radical pressure helped bring about American independence. Only in the thirteen colonies, in other words, had there emerged independent elites with access to their own political institutions, whose economic connections and personal networks were such as to enable the overthrow of British rule to be a feasible or attractive prospect. As much as anything else, it was the existence of elites—who had both social and political influence and a strong interest in and identification with their colonies—that shaped the geography of revolution and the initial boundaries of the new United States.

But it was not elite groups alone who shaped revolution. Revolution grew also from the conflicts and disputes that these colonial creole elites had had with more democratic elements of their own societies. As the Scottish political economist Adam Smith wrote on the eve of Independence, Americans enjoyed "more equality . . . than among the inhabitants of the mother country," and "their manners, . . . and their governments . . . have hitherto been more republican too." The contest between elite rule and democracy would become one of the American Revolution's hallmarks. The colonies' creole elites would often play a significant role, either in pushing the Revolution forward, as in Virginia, or in seeking to control it, while in the Middle Colonies in particular many of their members would find themselves resisting the impetus to rebel. Whatever stance the elites took, the Revolution derived its character not from them alone but from the alliances, conflicts, and friction they generated with other, more popular groups.[36]

CHAPTER 2

Change and Continuity in the American Revolution

S OME WEALTHY colonists might have wished for it, but social circumstances did not support the formal aristocracy and deep gradations of rank that characterized British society. Inequalities of wealth among white males were notable but by European standards comparatively slender. The colonies' political systems and absence of great social distinctions brought members of the gentry and mercantile elites into the orbit of middling and poorer colonists and to some degree subject to their influence.

Members of political elites found themselves of two minds about this situation, and much of the politics of the American Revolution resolved around their ambiguous responses to it. They sought to preserve conceptions of hierarchy and their fitness to exercise leadership. All the same, they either made common cause with farmers, artisans, and laboring folk to exert political pressure, or were obliged to concede popular claims to participate in public affairs. The Revolution entailed a complex rebalancing of elite and popular influences in politics, introducing new elements of democracy and formally recognizing "the people" as the sovereign power in a republic. Although elite power and influence remained highly important, and was to some degree reinstated as the Revolution progressed, in public and political arenas assumptions about social hierarchy were called into question.

In the private and domestic spheres, however, change was much less apparent. Although there were challenges to patriarchal and hierarchical assumptions in the private sphere, and although groundwork was laid during the Revolutionary Era for some later changes in these areas, the Revolution left intact all the elements of household and family authority. Households remained the central form of social and economic organization. Common forms of personal dependency continued. Property rights and marriage law left control of economic resources mostly in male hands. Only in limited respects were slavery and other aspects of personal dependency undermined or altered. The authority of household heads, the dependent status of many laborers, and the coercive power of masters were preserved.

A Popular Challenge

OPPOSITION TO British taxation and administrative measures, to the activities of customs officers, the Proclamation Line of 1763, the Stamp Act and Townshend Duties, quartering acts, the Tea Act, and a range of provincial or subsidiary policies that became controversial chiefly in light of the developing crisis, arose in three main arenas. They acquired revolutionary implications as the three became intertwined. First were the provincial assemblies, usually dominated by members drawn from local elites, which already had a long record of contention with royal or proprietary governors whose actions they disliked. Second was a tradition of popular protest "out of doors," often in the form of ritualized rioting or mob action by people of varying social status, whose purpose was to correct perceived injustice and restore established norms of fairness and good government. Often during the 1760s and early 1770s, local and provincial political elites found themselves faced with popular protests or with popular claims to participate in political deliberations. Both traditions drew upon and fostered the concept that as settlers within the British Empire, American colonists were entitled to the "rights of freeborn Englishmen," including the rights of assembly and of protest they often enacted.

As the perception of a crisis of British rule in the colonies gathered weight in the mid-1760s, these two mechanisms gave rise to a third: the elaboration in political writings, newspapers, popular protests, and petitions to the crown of increasingly sophisticated responses to British actions. American political thought evolved into new theories of the Anglo-colonial relationship and the right to rebel against unjust rule. Left to themselves, elite-dominated assemblies would have been unlikely to reforge the "rights of Englishmen" into a right of revolution; even if this had been thinkable, it would have been too much of a risk to social order. But with pressure from popular action, and with key alliances between elite and non-elite groups, traditional assembly politics became sharpened over time into a tool that could overthrow the authority of an empire.

Opposition to Britain began within the bounds of assumptions about social hierarchy and deference. Assemblies complained and petitioned London with forthright but respectful pleas for the redress of grievances. Street protests and even violent mob actions employed rituals that signified the inversion of the existing political and legal order. Forcing public apologies from officials implicated in unpopular policies, adopting forms of disguise, burning or hanging targets in effigy, or even tarring-and-feathering officials or opponents—all reversed normal assumptions about authority, or subjected targets to ritual humiliation that indicated their abasement before the demands of the people. Rituals of inversion, however, presume the existence of an order to be reversed, and do not usually threaten hierarchy; their object is to restore something that has gone awry rather than to overthrow the system. Yet as resistance became revolution, and petitioning for redress turned into the pursuit of independence, the overthrow of British power did call hierarchical assumptions into question. When protests against Britain mobilized into a throwing-off of British rule and replacement of the old monarchical order with new republican institutions, the question of who should rightly govern in America became a central issue.

Social Divisions and Mobilization for Revolution

ALTHOUGH THE Revolution evolved from disputes over British policies in North America, those disputes were influenced by social divisions within the colonies themselves. Members of the Virginia gentry, who provided the colony's leadership in protests against British policies in the 1760s and spearheaded its support for the Revolution, acted in the context of sharp internal religious divisions and economic uncertainty that arose at the same time. Politics and gentry culture were roiled by political scandal and by the influence of a spreading evangelical revival, which called into question the gentry's claim to authority and led many individuals—including members of the gentry—toward a more egalitarian ideology. Meanwhile the growing ties of tobacco producers with Britain, and their increasing indebtedness to British-based tobacco merchants, helped underscore the political opposition to royal administration in the colony.[1]

In the northern port towns, objections to British commercial policies also developed against the background of social divisions. Crowd actions in Boston, New York, and smaller ports against the Stamp Act of 1765 and the Townshend Duties of 1767 were carried out by merchants, artisans, laborers, and seamen who did not always agree among themselves on the tactics they should pursue. Although disputed British actions were usually the focus for protests, divisions within these unequal urban societies helped shape events. The destruction of Massachusetts Lieutenant Governor Thomas Hutchinson's Boston house in August 1765, or the disputes between British soldiers and local laborers that precipitated the Boston Massacre in 1770, reflected the town's social tensions rather than a coordinated response to British policies. Protests against the Tea Act of 1773 addressed not only broad aspects of political principle but the power that commercial interests might gain over ordinary people. In a poster distributed in Philadelphia, "A Mechanic" noted that the British East India Company, the Tea Act's beneficiary, had "become the most powerful Trading Company in the Universe," with "a designing, depraved, and despotic Ministry to assist and support" it. If it had its way, he asked, would "our Property, and the dear-earned Fruits of our Labour," be "at our own Disposal, or . . . be wantonly wrested from us, by a Set of luxurious, abandoned, and piratical Hirelings?" Boston radicals' destruction of a cargo of tea aboard a ship in Boston harbor in December 1773 defied not just Britain but also the merchants whom the British had granted the privilege of importing it. Like the sacking of Hutchinson's house, this was a serious attack on property as well as on political authority. British officials nevertheless contributed to the conflict by posting troops and enforcing trade regulations more rigorously, helping to turn the northeastern port towns into tinderboxes of discontent. Parliament's punishment of Boston and Massachusetts by the Coercive Acts of spring 1774 set the tinder alight.[2]

To this point the preponderance of colonial protest against British policy, particularly in the North, had been centered in the port towns and commercial centers that were often most directly affected by trade regulations or the activities of customs officials and other crown officers. The port towns alone, however, were not capable of launching a revolution. Rural America would be the key to this. The crisis over British policies and colonial opposition posed no certain threat to Britain's control of the colonies until the disquiet produced by British reactions to urban protests spilled over into the countryside. The Coercive Acts accomplished this by exercising unprecedented interference in Massachusetts county and local government, not least by restricting the activities of the town meetings that embodied participatory politics throughout the province. Only when, in response to British coercive actions, significant numbers of Massachusetts farmers and then Virginia planters were provoked to take political action in their own right did an urban-based protest movement become a popular revolution.

During the second half of 1774 and early 1775 many rural New Englanders prepared for armed confrontation with British troops. In western Massachusetts and elsewhere they took steps to remove or curb the power of local officials loyal to the king. British actions had spread a dispute over urban commerce into a general assault on one colony's institutions. American radicals responded by rallying other colonies to support Massachusetts, convening the First Continental Congress in September 1774, agreeing on measures to boycott British trade, and urging local patriots throughout the thirteen colonies to organize committees to enforce these measures. In some colonies and localities over the next few months, these extralegal committees and provincial congresses began to take over political control from crown-appointed officers and institutions. These committees were ready to act when fighting broke out between Massachusetts "minutemen" militia and British troops in April 1775.

The colonies' decentralized character and the weakness of their government structures helped radicals seize the initiative. In parts of Virginia a broad consensus among the gentry enabled them to direct their local political influence against the colony's royal officials. In parts of New England, popular anger at British policies enabled local radical leaders, drawn from among farmers, merchants, and ministers, to direct opposition against members of the elite who sought to uphold British authority. Elite leadership in Virginia and popular participation in New England produced a substantial political coalition behind the patriot cause as protest turned to war against Britain in the spring of 1775. But in other colonies, even as they sent representatives to participate in the Continental Congress, social and political divisions over the war, based on divisions already in society, tempered or delayed radicals' influence.

Political Allegiance

IN THE Hudson Valley, parts of New Jersey, and many areas of the lower South, earlier social or ethnic divisions and rivalries kept populations divided. In New York City and Philadelphia, mobilization for war came about only as radical merchants and artisans succeeded in displacing moderates or loyalists on the committees that were elected to run the towns. New York remained under conservative control in 1774, though radical handbills urged the city's artisans to follow their Boston brethren and refuse to work for the British forces stationed there. After news arrived of the outbreak of fighting at Lexington and Concord in April 1775, radical committees took over the city and began regulating orderly protest and taking action against suspected British sympathizers. Philadelphia too was divided. As in New York, important groups among Philadelphia's merchant elite were indifferent, hesitant, or opposed to the radical course pursued by New England and Virginia patriots as the protests against British rule deepened from 1774 on. Philadelphia was home to five hundred or more merchants, whose wealth and connections made it one of the most important centers of the Atlantic world, and their influence worked to put a brake on the radicalism of the actions against Britain.[3]

But as a prosperous town with a growing rural hinterland, Philadelphia was a center of production as well as trade. A large number of skilled artisans and laborers inhabited the city. As the crisis with Britain deepened and the Continental Congress met in Philadelphia, printers, journalists, instrument makers, and other skilled craftspeople became important in pressing the radical cause. It was to this Philadelphia environment that Tom Paine had come in 1774, in self-imposed exile from England. There he quickly honed the writing skills that produced his powerful and widely popular argument for independence in *Common Sense*, published early in 1776. As the Continental Congress debated measures to secure redress of American grievances from Britain, and found its efforts at settlement rebuffed, wide differences emerged between Philadelphia's leadership and popular advocates of radicalism. Men like John Dickinson and George Galloway, with support from many among the city's elite, urged moderation in the Congress. Galloway would, in the end, oppose independence and depart for England; Dickinson stayed but withdrew from politics. Radicals, with support from the artisan community, gained seats on the committees that were founded to conduct the city's affairs during the crisis, and ultimately gained control of them, adding their weight to the decision for independence. In both Philadelphia and New York, the pressure for independence had a class dimension. It would be reflected in later debates and contests over the best form of revolutionary government.[4]

Splits within elite groups, and between them and the rest of the population, helped create the patterns of loyalism and neutrality that made the Revolution in many localities a struggle among Americans as much as a struggle against the British. At Annapolis, Maryland, about one-quarter of the wealthiest residents were loyalists, who left the town in 1776 when the war spread. Even in New England and Virginia, where there was greatest consensus in favor of the patriot cause, prominent families and individuals sought exile in Britain or Canada, or were obliged to curb their businesses or commercial activities because of their suspected sympathies with the crown. Several members of the leading colonial families in the Connecticut Valley of Massachusetts were driven from public life, some of them subjected to humiliation and continued suspicion. Suspected Boston loyalists had their property temporarily sequestered. But the majority of established leaders in these regions supported the patriot cause, and so did not find their positions disturbed by popular threats.[5]

In the Mid-Atlantic region, where loyalties were more divided and where military actions crisscrossed the landscape for several years, established leaders found it more difficult to retain their positions. Patriot leaders in New York City lost property in 1776 when they had to flee to escape the British capture of the city, and New York State later confiscated considerable property from loyalists. At Burlington, New Jersey, a modest commercial center that was the state's half-capital, loyalist sympathies remained strong, and the town's Quaker-dominated merchant group found itself harassed by patriot committees and militia for its reluctance to support the war against Britain. Many Philadelphia merchant leaders had opposed the move for independence or been at best lukewarm toward it; Quakers among them, in particular, had held aloof from active service in the war. It was popular radicalism rooted in the artisan and small-trader communities that had driven the city toward independence. Temporary occupation by the British army in 1777–1778 complicated the political position of Philadelphians and exposed many to suspicion of loyalist sympathies. After patriot leaders placed the Quaker merchant Abel James under house arrest, he was ultimately ruined: in 1784 he went bankrupt. The brothers Thomas and Joseph Wharton, also prominent Quaker merchants, were also suspected of Tory sympathies: Thomas died in ruins in 1782, having been arrested and had his Pennsylvania property confiscated, while Joseph ended the Revolution bankrupt and living in genteel poverty.[6]

Throughout the regions where war and support for revolution were most contentious, those suspected of loyalism had their property confiscated or were subject to other sanctions. Large numbers were forced into exile. More than seven thousand from all the colonies, including many of the wealthiest citizens, departed for Britain and later filed claims for compensation from the British government. Some thirty thousand others, many of them of poor or middling status, moved to Nova Scotia or to the new colony of New Brunswick, established in 1783 to receive them. But the Revolution, though it called elite power into question, did not destroy it. Instead the experiences and difficulties of revolution suggested to some members of the elite the need for greater cooperation among themselves if their power, control of wealth, and hold on the social order were not to be disrupted by the forces that independence had unleashed.[7]

Social Conditions and the Conduct of War

URGING AMERICANS early in 1776 to take the final steps toward independence from Britain, Tom Paine assured them in his pamphlet *Common Sense* that "we have it in our power to begin the world over again." With this stirring phrase Paine expressed the optimism that independence could enable Americans to remake their political and social system and strike out in directions unthinkable in the colonial world. By year's end, however, Paine was writing the equally famous phrases of his first *Crisis* paper, lamenting the inconstancy of "the summer soldier and the sunshine patriot" and the difficulties of "the times that try men's souls." The bravado of claiming independence confronted the profound difficulties that securing independence actually entailed.[8]

The social structures and circumstances of thirteen autonomous, widely spaced, and disparate colonies framed the war that advocates of American independence had to conduct against Great Britain, the world's strongest maritime power and one of its greatest military powers. In the end this struggle for independence would succeed, and the new United States would survive and thrive. As it turned out, the colonies' social characteristics created even more difficulties for Britain than they did for the revolutionaries. Yet the obstacles they presented to the success of the cause of independence are also hard to overestimate, as one early patriot setback illustrated.

On December 31, 1775, American militia units commanded by General Richard Montgomery and Colonel Benedict Arnold sought to capture the well-defended city of Quebec on the St. Lawrence River. Hampered by a snowstorm and alert British defenders, the attack failed. Along with numbers of his men, Montgomery was killed and so became an early patriot martyr. Many militiamen were captured. The other survivors made a long, painful retreat in the harsh North American winter to their homes, which were mostly in New England and New York. Montgomery, Arnold, and their comrades had been executing the Continental Congress's plan to draw Britain's Canadian provinces into the rebellion against British rule. Another American force had already captured Montreal. But the failed assault on Quebec meant that the Canadian campaign too was lost. A key reason lay in the circumstances in which the rural militiamen who carried it out, especially the New Englanders among them, had been recruited to serve.[9]

As noted earlier, New England farming was conducted largely by independent farmers who owned their own land and relied substantially on their families' labor to work it. Militia service, long a tradition and obligation, was structured to meet rural needs. It included provisions for short-term enlistments that could avoid removing ablebodied men from the farm labor force for extended periods of time. A factor in Richard Montgomery's decision to attack Quebec in unfavorable weather was the expectation that some of the troops he commanded would depart when their terms of service expired with the turn of the New Year. His fate was, therefore, conditioned by late-colonial New England society and the constraints it imposed on military activities. Such constraints repeatedly hampered the American war effort.

The difficulties of military supply and finance, coupled with the demands of rural society, made army life especially onerous and often austere. As William Hooper, one of North Carolina's signers of the Declaration of Independence, remarked, "A soldier made is a farmer lost." In such an overwhelmingly rural society, this was a serious issue. In late 1775 only a portion of the troops under George Washington's command near Boston agreed to reenlist. In New Jersey in 1777 and again in South Carolina in 1779, militia companies suffered desertions as farmer-soldiers went home to help with spring planting. In Virginia in 1781 military recruiters provoked riots as they tried to fill the ranks during planting time. Poor harvests and harsh winters in the late 1770s made the provision of food supplies and the very operation of the economy dangerously precarious.[10]

Increasing reliance had to be placed on the service of the regular Continental army, in which altogether about half of the 200,000 or so who served during the war were at some point enlisted. Soldiers who undertook long-term service in the Continental army were primarily young, unmarried, transient, or relatively poor, and included significant numbers of African Americans and European immigrants as well as American-born whites. Continental forces became the mainstay of the campaign against Britain. The ability of Washington and other generals to keep them intact in the face of strong British opposition was the single most important guarantee of the new nation's proclaimed independence. A comprehensive defeat of the Continental army might have derailed the Revolution altogether. But success exacted a considerable price in suffering. At winter quarters in places like Valley Forge, Pennsylvania, in 1777 and Morristown, New Jersey, two years later, Continental soldiers faced severe hardships from cold, disease, and shortages of food and clothing. Smallpox, dysentery, and other diseases killed troops and hampered campaigns. About 2,500 soldiers died of disease in the winter of 1777–1778 alone. Between 1777 and 1783 as many as twenty-eight mutinies occurred in Continental units, mostly over shortages of food and other supplies. As in many wars, soldiers contrasted the hardships they faced with the comparative comfort of civilian populations and especially with the opportunities that some seized to prosper from the war. Critics, such as Reverend Israel Evans, lambasted "the langour of the country, and their inattention to the starving situation of the most patient . . . army in the world." Before defecting to the British in 1780, the American general Benedict Arnold condemned the hypocrisy of a civilian population that had allowed its armies "to starve in a land of plenty."[11]

Meanwhile merchants and others in the ports and trading centers achieved new fortunes from military provisioning, privateering, or other commercial activity. Those with access to shipping and commercial expertise were well placed to win government contracts for supplying the armies, or the "letters of marque" that licensed armed vessels to attack and seize enemy ships. The Continental Congress issued almost seventeen hundred such bonds, and Massachusetts alone issued almost a thousand more. Although they faced high risks (Salem, Massachusetts, lost about one-third of its two hundred or so privateering vessels during the war), privateers captured £18 million in British ships and cargoes, and much of the profit went to private individuals. The opportunities of war enabled figures such as James Bowdoin, Jr., of Boston, grandson of a merchant and son of a Massachusetts governor, to reap a significant fortune. The merchant Stephen Higginson of Salem received an estimated $70,000 from privateering.[12]

Slaves and the Revolution

THE UPHEAVALS of revolution and the difficulties of military recruitment also created opportunities, of a quite different character, for many slaves. From all regions there is evidence of slaves' desire for freedom, and now many of them had some chance to seize it. As white colonists had asserted their rights as "freeborn Englishmen" and warned that British tyranny might enslave the colonies, slaves pointed to the connection with their own situation. In Charleston in the 1760s a group of slaves watching a Sons of Liberty demonstration caused consternation when they joined in chants for "freedom." By 1774 some Boston slaves were petitioning for their personal freedom. Virginia experienced an unsuccessful slave uprising, while in Georgia a slave revolt in December 1774 caused the murder of four white people before the slaves concerned were captured and then, as both punishment and warning to others, burned alive.[13]

War's outbreak in 1775 especially provided male slaves of military age with more certain opportunities to achieve freedom. The war efforts of both sides required labor and recruits. If slaves were recruited to military service, as necessity suggested they should be, it seemed axiomatic that they could not later be reenslaved. In November 1775, Lord Dunmore, Virginia's last royal governor, offered freedom to slaves who volunteered for the British army. The British general George Clinton later made a similar offer to slaves in the New York area. Such policies may have harmed the British war effort by driving otherwise neutral whites to support the patriot cause. Enraged by Dunmore's proclamation and the threat of insurrection or escape that it posed, Virginia slaveholders took countermeasures, some of them moving their slaves to inland locations. Landon Carter of Sabine Hall, who owned more than four hundred slaves at the time of his death in 1778, feared that the Revolution would undermine the social order, including slavery.[14]

But slaveholders could not suppress the slaves' desire for freedom. Among those answering Dunmore's proclamation were eight of Carter's slaves, who ran away in 1776 to join the British army. Proximity to British forces persuaded many slaves to escape, and George Washington among others protested this British "rescue" of runaways. Many of the

1,000 or so Virginia slaves recruited by the British after Lord Dunmore's proclamation quickly succumbed to a smallpox epidemic, but thousands of other slaves survived to achieve postwar freedom. Thomas Peters, an Egba-Yoruba born in eastern Nigeria in the late 1730s, captured by slave traders in 1760 and shipped to Louisiana, had probably escaped several times before being sold in 1770 to a Scots immigrant at Wilmington, North Carolina. This man, William Campbell, a member of the local Sons of Liberty, worked Peters as a millwright, and Peters settled down with a young family in the early 1770s. But when the British raided the Cape Fear River in 1776, Peters ran off with other slaves and joined a detachment of Black Pioneers that served at Charleston and Philadelphia before being moved to the main British base at New York. In 1779 a nineteen-year-old slave called Boston King ran off from South Carolina's Tranquil Hall plantation to the British lines near Charleston; he too was later sent to New York. As many as 12,000 South Carolina slaves may have escaped while the war raged in the region. When peace was signed in 1783, the British resettled thousands of black soldiers in eastern Canada. Thomas Peters and Boston King were among 2,775 who were evacuated to Nova Scotia from New York City.

Slaves also sought freedom by joining the patriot ranks. While the Rhode Island soldier Jeremiah Greenman was a prisoner of war, quartered with a Tory landlord on Long Island in 1781, he recorded that the man's slave had run away with a marauding party of New Jersey militia. Greenman's home state had been among the first to recruit soldiers from among its slave population. Fear of insurrection caused much agonizing over the arming of slaves, but the pressure to find soldiers and military labor was such that every state except South Carolina enrolled slaves in its service, with freedom as the prize for those who lived to see out the war.[15]

But the chances of war did not always point to freedom. In 1779 South Carolina tried to solve its recruitment problems by promising one hundred acres of land and ownership of one slave to every white man who served a twenty-one-month enlistment in the army. South Carolina's refusal to recruit slaves had at least one serious military consequence. In 1780 the port of Charleston came under assault from a British force. Key to its defense was a detachment of the Continental army commanded by the Massachusetts-born general Benjamin Lincoln. Outnumbered by the

British, Lincoln urged South Carolina's leaders to arm slaves and reinforce the militia units that were supporting his troops, but they refused.
Lincoln prepared to withdraw his force from Charleston to avoid capture,
but the South Carolinians compelled him to remain, threatening to use
the militia—effectively in alliance with the British—to keep the Conti-
nentals in place. This ensured that when the British captured Charleston,
they also captured Lincoln and his men, dealing a serious blow to the
American cause. Preserving slavery was a priority that South Carolina
planters could not abandon, even in such dire circumstances.

In any case, not every slave who survived military service obtained
the freedom promised him. John Anderson of Virginia served in the patriot forces, yet at war's end he was not granted the manumission he expected. Slaves fighting for the British who fell into American hands were
frequently returned to their owners and punished. When the British
garrison at Yorktown surrendered in 1781, they abandoned many runaway slaves who had worked at the fort or taken refuge there, many of
whom American soldiers found dead or dying of hunger or disease.
Some patriot soldiers earned cash by helping masters recapture the
slaves who survived. For these people, the end of the war spelled consignment to the bondage they had sought to escape.[16]

Regional Patterns of Revolution

AREAS OF strong support for the patriots' cause included large parts
of New England, the Chesapeake, and the sections of the Carolinas that
had previously supported colonial assemblies against Regulator insurgencies. Reflecting its greater degree of ethnic and religious diversity,
as well as some of its pre-Revolutionary conflicts, patterns of political
allegiance in the Mid-Atlantic region were more complex. The longest-
settled parts of Pennsylvania, particularly the rural areas around
Philadelphia, were home to substantial numbers of English-descended
Quakers and German-speaking settlers, who formed a significant bloc
of neutrals in the Revolution. Many Quakers and members of such
German sects as the Mennonites were pacifist by religious conviction,
and with some success resisted attempts to oblige them to undertake
military service during the war. Other German settlers, among them

Lutherans, were more strongly attached to their own communities than to either the American patriots or the British. Southeastern Pennsylvania therefore offered strong support to neither side in the Revolution. In the New York City region and the Hudson River Valley, not only did existing social tensions and allegiances help influence how people took sides during the war, but circumstances often made it hard for them to avoid taking sides and remain neutral. On the Hudson Valley manors it was not uncommon for tenant farmers to take sides with their land-lords' opponents. Tenants of the patriot Livingston family sought help from the British during the war to remove the Livingstons from their land. The Livingstons' great political rivals the DeLanceys, meanwhile, largely abandoned their holdings for exile in Britain, as many of their tenants became enthusiastic patriots. Indifference to either side was common in New Jersey, where farm prosperity, prior conflicts, or loyalist influence curbed support for the patriot cause. But after 1776 New Jersey's location between New York City and Philadelphia brought it into the center of military action. The repeated passage and retreat of British and American forces aggravated local antagonisms and made effective neutrality difficult for many families and individuals to sustain. In this region especially, civilians faced the fear and actuality of robbery and rape by marauding soldiers. A war widow later recalled that "there was so much suffering . . . in our neighborhood . . . that it has always been painful for me to dwell upon."[17]

In frontier areas that abutted territory still controlled by Native American populations, international as well as local antagonisms shaped political outcomes. From northern New England to the Ohio Valley and the mountainous Southern up-country, frontier zones became the site of a double contest—between Britain, its Native American allies, and their patriot opponents, on the one hand, and over local control of land and institutions on the other. For many inhabitants the Revolution provided opportunities to seize control of land, to attack or disperse native groups who lay in the way, and to carry out activities that had more to do with their own purposes than with the political disputes between Britain and the colonies. Because of the significance of the western frontier, and because British strategy included mobilizing Indian allies against its enemies, the two elements of the conflict became entwined. But the impact of frontier war on the outcome of the Revolution was determined more by patterns of local settlement and land acquisition than by the dictates of either imperial or Continental policy.[18]

In central New York State, which had been the territory of the dominant Iroquois "six tribes" before the Revolution, but into which white settlers had been infiltrating for some years, violent conflicts arose between patriot settlers and their militia units and British-supported Iroquois fighters. Attacks and counterattacks in this region in the late 1770s produced massacres and village destruction on both sides and led to the withdrawal of white settlers to relative safety, closer to the Hudson and Mohawk Valleys, until the war ended. Farther west, meanwhile, in the upper Ohio River Valley, white Moravian settlers allied to Delaware Indians and other tribes were subject to violent pressure from patriot forces. A massacre of Moravians at the village of Gnadenhütten in 1782 led to the exile of many survivors and other early settlers to Canada, and helped pave the way for further white incursions into the Ohio country in the 1780s.

In parts of New Jersey, New York, and the western frontier, the struggle took on aspects of a civil war. This was even more notable in the lower South after 1779, when British efforts to defeat the Revolution shifted to that region. Capturing Savannah and Charleston, the British then sought to use an army under Lord Cornwallis to restore Georgia and the Carolinas to royal control, but they also relied heavily on loyalist militias raised among the local population. Almost all the nearly 2,600 combatants on both sides at the battle of King's Mountain in South Carolina in 1780 were Americans. Prewar social divisions, like those between Scots Highlander and Scots-Irish settlers in the piedmont and up-country, and prewar struggles, like those of the Regulator movements in the Carolinas, shaped vicious antagonisms that made military confrontations across the region particularly violent. Loyalist and patriot militia units, drawn from opposite sides of earlier conflicts, battled each other separately as well as in conjunction with British and Continental forces. A British officer wrote in 1779 that two-thirds of settlements he saw in the Georgia Lowcountry had been ruined as loyalists and patriots "both vengefully destroyed the property of each other." One patriot militia officer in South Carolina was reputed to have twenty-five notches in his rifle, one for each Tory or British soldier he claimed to have killed. "Few," wrote the state's first historian David Ramsay after the war, "did not partake of the general distress."[19]

Change and Continuity in the American Revolution

The difficulties of war, the inequalities it entailed, and the tensions between regions and groups helped foster new outlooks in the institutions that had assumed control of the war effort. The Continental Congress brought together leading figures from different colonies and charged them with coordinating a war to be fought together. This did not in itself erase provincial outlooks. Indeed, Congress's struggles with the separate provinces and states over military policy, recruiting soldiers, raising and paying for supplies, and conducting the war as often as not reinforced regional loyalties. But there were some loci of a new, more unified perspective. The Continental army was one. For the first time there was an American military force not tied by command, finance, or recruitment to a particular province or state, as militia units continued to be. Many of the men involved in the Continental army acquired a sense of common experience and identity that set them apart from others and attached them more directly to the new nation. Senior officers, too, found themselves serving outside their home regions. George Washington, a Virginian, first took up command of the Continental army in New England, then spent much of the war in the Mid-Atlantic provinces. Benjamin Lincoln, though he served at first in or near his native New England, was moved to the South in 1778 and ended the war there. Such regional swapping helped forge a "continental perspective" among such figures: as Lincoln wrote to Washington in March 1778, "We are all embarked in the same bottom and shall be saved or lost together." Critical events after the war helped convert this perspective, in the minds of some members of the elite, into a program for the peacetime development of American politics and government.[20]

Beyond creating divisions between patriots and loyalists, however, preexisting political and social tensions also promoted factions or divisions among patriots themselves. The harshness of wartime conditions, the overall weakness of the economy to provide for military needs as well as for the civilian population, and the effects of inequalities all contributed to these fissures. Although the British had great difficulty reconquering the thirteen states, and eventually gave up trying, their military and naval strength imposed severe restrictions on the American economy and the revolutionaries' latitude for action. States and local committees, often with popular backing, sought to levy price controls, wage ceilings, curbs on profits, and other regulations; they also faced the constant challenge of requisitioning troops and supplies to keep military forces in the field. Tensions over these policies, and their conflicts with the interests of farmers and wage earners as well as wealthier merchants and military provisioners, provoked protests and disturbances as the war continued.[21]

Elites and Democracy

THE MILITARY conditions that ultimately spelled success for the Revolution and secured independence for the United States arose from smart maneuvering, the acquisition of European allies, and Britain's incapacity both to secure its other possessions and to surmount American resistance. They did not arise from social or political unity within the former colonies, whose divisions indeed often seemed to hamper the cause. Nevertheless the preexistence of active political life in each colony meant there would be debate and dispute even among the supporters of independence about the future shape their new society and political system should take. Disconnected from their former allegiance to the British crown, with its empire-wide system of social status and hierarchy, members of American elites faced the prospect of securing local and provincial power and influence. But their exposure to popular, democratic pressure also led some of them to explore means of forging elite collaboration across state and regional lines.

The Revolution replaced an older colonial pattern of social hierarchy and deference to existing rulers, such as the king, with a more democratic, egalitarian ethos. But this change did not come about easily. The efforts of colonial creole elites to criticize and resist British policies in the 1760s and 1770s had not only brought about the movement for independence but also unleashed a protracted discussion about the appropriate forms of newly independent state and federal governments. Popular and democratic pressure called hierarchical assumptions into question and pushed new governments in a democratic direction. But in most cases they did not create direct democracies and in many respects only initiated a process of democratization that would continue into the nineteenth century.

Some Revolutionary leaders saw the maintenance of social hierarchy as a key aim of military mobilization. New York's James Duane wrote to the Hudson Valley landlord Robert R. Livingston, urging him to recruit a company of troops from among his Livingston Manor tenants, "to render landed property secure." To preserve order, Duane argued, military leadership should be in the hands of a social elite: "Licentiousness . . . can only be guarded against by placing the command of the troops in the hands of property and rank who . . . will preserve the same authority over the minds of the people which they did in the times of tranquility." As they took command of soldiers from more egalitarian regions, some officers found this authority difficult to maintain. Of Connecticut troops under his command at Fort Ticonderoga in 1775, New York's General Philip Schuyler complained, "It is extremely difficult to introduce a proper subordination among a people where so little distinction is kept up. . . . I really believe [they] will make good soldiers, as soon as I can get the better of this nonchalance of theirs." Schuyler's colleague Richard Montgomery, an English emigrant who had married into the Hudson Valley's Livingston family, found few of his troops satisfactory as he advanced northward in 1775 on his ill-fated invasion of Quebec. His New Yorkers, he claimed, were "the sweepings of the New York streets," while "[t]he New England troops are the worst stuff imaginable. There is such an equality among them, that the officers have no authority." "[I] wish," he mused, "some method could be fallen upon of engaging *gentlemen* to serve; . . . that class of men would greatly reform discipline, and render the troops much more tractable."²²

This elite vision proved difficult to maintain in the throes of revolution. Even though the Continental army would come to be trained according to European methods of discipline, and sustained a clear distinction between its officers and enlisted men, entry to its officer corps in practice became open to talent and was not reserved for "gentlemen." Often the symbols of deference quickly dissolved. Fairfax County, Virginia's gentry-dominated militia began drilling for war in September 1774 with its members dressed in their customary gentlemen's attire, but by February 1775 the same men were drilling in farmers' clothing. Gentry delegates to the Virginia provincial assembly took their seats later that year dressed in coarse hunting shirts and carrying tomahawks; Virginia Tories complained of the "damn'd shirtmen" who opposed them. A member of the prominent Randolph family remarked that "everyone who bore arms esteems himself upon a footing with his neighbors." Unlike before the war, "no doubt each of these men considers himself, in every respect, my equal." Near the end of the decade the Boston shoemaker George Hewes enlisted to serve aboard a Massachusetts warship. But "not liking the manners of the Lieutenant very well, who ordered him one day in the streets to take his hat off to him—which he refused to do for any man," Hewes switched to another vessel, seeking more egalitarian treatment. Farmers and artisans forced their way into public life, negotiating terms with the "gentlemen" to whom they had previously deferred, and shifting the balance of politics in a markedly democratic direction.[23]

Officeholding became more democratically distributed. A study of the Northern states of New Hampshire, New Jersey, and New York found that before the Revolutionary War about 17 percent of assemblymen came from the "moderate" income bracket, and 23 percent were farmers; after the war 62 percent had "moderate" incomes, and 55 percent were farmers. Conversely, the proportions of assemblymen who were wealthy, or who were merchants or lawyers, fell markedly. Similar though less pronounced shifts occurred in Maryland, Virginia, and South Carolina. In Massachusetts the proportion of state representatives classified as "wealthy" or "well-to-do," which had stood at one-half in 1765, fell to 21.5 percent in 1784. Small property holders, members of the "middling classes" of farmers and artisans, had greater chances to influence policy after the Revolutionary War than before it.[24]

Old elites were in some states broken up or disrupted. The destruction of British power in the thirteen colonies led to the emigration of a significant number of the wealthy and to the confiscation of land and other property in states like New York, where political rivalries and animus against loyalists ran strongly. But the disruption of elites was not limited to loyalists. British occupation of New York City and other regions equally put propertied patriots in jeopardy from arrest, destruction, confiscation, or disruption of business. New Yorkers who fled from the British capture of the city in 1776 risked losing their property. Some returned after the war to find their houses burned or looted. On either side of the ideological divide, wartime economic disruption ruined family fortunes or businesses. Under the terms of the Treaty of Paris of 1783, the resumption of trade at the end of the war also meant the resumption of British merchants' efforts to collect their American debts. The year 1784 saw a rash of bankruptcies among commercial families who had suffered heavy financial losses over the previous few years and whose resources were now inadequate to repay old debts that had once more become due. Even in more stable elites, as in Virginia, where the planter gentry had been largely patriot and so not much depleted by loyalism and emigration, and where existing patterns and rituals of political power continued, subtle shifts occurred in the character of hierarchy and deference. Church vestries lost much of the importance they had enjoyed when Virginia was a colony. State laws passed in the 1780s eroded legal provisions derived from England, such as primogeniture (the passage of property to the eldest son) and entail (confining the passage of property to lineal descendants), intended to keep propertied estates intact.

Wartime also created new contenders for elite status. Opportunities in military supply, privateering, or commercial ventures had refreshed the wealth of some families and created new wealth whose holders could fill the gaps left by loyalist exiles or by others ruined during the Revolution. Men such as the wheelwright William Cooper of Burlington, New Jersey, rose to a degree of prominence they could never have anticipated before Independence, achieving a prosperity and obtaining personal connections that helped them take over from others who were displaced. In Massachusetts, where loyalist departures were relatively few, older families muttered at the rise of new wealth and the intrusion of new members into the ranks of the influential. James Bowdoin noted in 1783 that "you will scarcely see any other than new faces." In 1777, Lucy Knox had told her husband, the Continental general Henry Knox, of the reversals of fortune going on in Boston. Anyone, she wrote, "if he understands business might without capital make a fortune—people here without a shilling frequently clear hundreds in a day, such chaps as Eben Oliver are all men of fortune while persons who have ever lived in affluence are in danger of want."[25] Such social mobility had paradoxical effects. Although it did, on one hand, help endorse democratic claims, it also reinforced the social inequalities that continued to underlie elite status. Many members of the patriot leadership, witnessing the chaos and disruption of the war, affirmed a determination to regain elite control of law and government once the war had ended. Horrified by the effects of disorder, especially on property, they sought at both state and national levels to secure forms of government that could curb what they saw as the excesses of democracy.

Independence confirmed the political autonomy of the individual states. Most enacted new constitutions, but these varied widely in the extent to which they protected either elite or democratic interests. Under the Articles of Confederation, continental government remained weak and largely dependent on the will of the states. The upheavals of the Revolution and the financial difficulties that dominated the 1780s both spurred advocates of elite influence to reassert their position and caused advocates of greater democracy to fear that their newly gained influence was under threat. Members of provincial gentry groups such as those in Virginia witnessed with alarm the extent to which loyalists had lost their property and propertied patriots had been exposed to the risks of competition and business failure. Members of the gentry might deplore their loss of standing, but many among them, and among the newly wealthy that the Revolution had thrown up, sought to protect at least their own property.

Struggles for Dominance in the 1780s

THE REVOLUTION provoked deep controversy over the regulation of economic life, particularly of prices. It sparked a series of complex struggles over property and property rights, and ushered in a period of serious social and economic disruption in the 1780s as elite and popular groups clashed over the terms for conducting the new nation's financial affairs. The pre-Revolutionary suspicions of many farmers and frontier settlers were renewed, not allayed, by the political changes of the Revolution. Late-colonial-era conflicts had been directed against colonial governments or elites as much as against Britain itself, and were revived after 1783 in numerous places. The 1780s and 1790s were marked by a series of such confrontations, some of which influenced the ways political leaders shaped their visions of the nation's independent future.

The key issues were economic and took several forms. The Revolution's costs left severe financial problems, both private and public. Wartime disruption to production had spread poverty and personal indebtedness. The coming of peace released a pent-up demand for goods, and 1783–1784 witnessed a significant surge of imports from Britain as Americans replenished stocks depleted during long years of protest and war. These goods would have to be paid for in addition to the unpaid prewar debts that the peace terms between Britain and the United States permitted British creditors to collect. By 1784–1785 the combination of old and new debts imposed substantial private obligations, especially in rural regions still recovering from the disruptions of war. In addition to this arose the severe effects of public financial burdens. The war had left state treasuries empty and their finances in chaos. In an effort to replenish them and repay their debts, states raised taxes by amounts ranging from double to six times their pre-Revolutionary levels. These demands were imposed on a society where inequalities had widened sharply.

The war had been largely financed by the issue of paper money and by the payment of soldiers and others in paper warrants and other instruments entitling them to land or cash in the future. Most holders of these paper instruments, however, needed ready cash or goods to live on, and could not afford to keep them. Meanwhile the crises of wartime and uncertainties about the future of Revolutionary governments severely deflated the current values of this paper, and many holders were obliged to sell it to others for mere fractions of its face value. Wealthier men, often connected with political and financial elites, together with "new men" who had obtained their means from the opportunities of wartime, accumulated significant quantities of these paper promises, which gave them title to significant amounts of land or to the potential repayment of debts owed by the states. In Annapolis, Maryland, from 1781 on, merchants were buying soldiers' pay certificates and land warrants at one-seventh of their face value. In 1783 the Rhode Island merchant Nicholas Brown paid out goods worth £246 in Rhode Island currency for Continental certificates with face values totaling almost fifty times that amount. Of Pennsylvania's $4.8 million in outstanding wartime debt in 1790, more than 96 percent was in certificates held by just 434 individuals, and 40 percent was held by just 28 individuals, most of them merchants, lawyers, or brokers in Philadelphia.[26]

Commercial and public debt, taxation, and the unequal distribution of credit and paper produced social unrest. In some states, popular pressure produced measures designed to alleviate the burdens on individual debtors or farm families. In Connecticut, Georgia, New York, and New Jersey, state governments issued more paper money, risking the continued decline of their states' credit in return for providing immediate relief to hard-pressed citizens. In Rhode Island the legislature made the state's paper legal tender for the payment of debts, obliging creditors to accept it as payment, and sending many of them fleeing from their debtors so as to avoid having to receive it.

Pennsylvania, by contrast, tried to restrain the issue of paper currency, and by value per head of the state's population its circulation declined sharply, from $1.88 in 1786 to 31 cents in 1790. Massachusetts also restricted the amount of paper in circulation and tried to insist that debts and taxes be paid in ready money. In both states commercial elites based in the port towns influenced government to maintain a tight financial regime. In both states there was a price to pay. Merchants' correspondence filled with reports of uncollectible debts and the pleas and excuses of those who owed money. Forced sales of the property of those with unpaid taxes or debts mounted. In Pennsylvania, between 1787 and 1795, the unpopularity of these sheriff's sales provoked a campaign of roadblocking and harassment of officials in hinterland and frontier regions as farmers and others determined to defend their own or their neighbors' homes and possessions. One political effect was the defeat of the ruling party in the state legislature.[27]

Agrarian Revolt

IN MASSACHUSETTS, conflict became more serious still. In Worcester County in 1784 alone, around two thousand lawsuits for debt were brought in the county courts. Petitions and political conventions in the interior of the state in 1785 and 1786 called for a change of policy but did little to move the government from its position. Crowds gathered to close courthouses and prevent debt cases from being heard. In parts of central and western Massachusetts in the winter of 1786 these actions evolved into outright rebellion. Armed men calling themselves "Regulators" gathered to ensure that courts remained closed, or to counter militia groups mobilized to resist them. In January 1787 two

Regulator bands converged on the federal armory at Springfield, Massachusetts, intending to capture its arsenal of weapons. A mistimed rendezvous allowed militia defending the armory to put one of them—led by a former Continental officer, Daniel Shays, from the upland town of Pelham—to flight, inflicting some casualties. As they retreated into the hills, Shays's men were pursued by a state militia force that had been hastily assembled in Boston and marched west under General Benjamin Lincoln. When Lincoln surprised the Regulators in an attack on their encampment at Petersham, Massachusetts, they were scattered. Skirmishes between militia and Regulators continued in parts of rural Massachusetts into the spring of 1787, but the rout of his force marked the effective defeat of the rebellion that came to be remembered by Shays's name. Shays and many others fled the state. Regulators who stayed, having laid down their arms, signed oaths of allegiance to the Commonwealth. Arrested leaders were tried and sentenced to death, though in most cases the sentences were commuted in a show of judicial mercy. The consequences of Shays's Rebellion, however, were symptomatic of broader themes emerging from the Revolutionary period.

On one hand, the rebellion aggravated the anxiety already evident among American elites about the potential disorder of post-Revolutionary government. Benjamin Lincoln, given the task of raising a militia to counter the Shaysites, presented the situation in stark terms to the prosperous men he sought to recruit. Persuading leading Bostonians to finance and support the army, he portrayed the rebellion as an attack on property, urging them to be "loaners of a part of their property if they wished to secure the remainder." As Lincoln marched west an observer noted that he had "a fine body of men, well-officered, the whole of the monied men to support him." The fear instilled by Shays's Rebellion galvanized elites to protect their own interests. But the rebels' defeat did not reduce popular sympathy for their cause. In spring 1787 elections, Massachusetts' incumbent governor and many members of the legislature were voted out of office and replaced with men more sympathetic to the rebels' position. Shays and other leaders never returned to Massachusetts and remained under official condemnation for rebelling, but future Massachusetts governments took care not to repeat the harsh policies that had brought about the crisis. Here at least, elites would henceforth have to curry popular support.[28]

Responses to other agrarian protests in the 1790s also embodied elite fears of disorder. At various places in hinterland or frontier zones, rural people saw themselves oppressed by powerful opposing groups or interests. Retreating Shaysites united with eastern New York protesters in 1791 to put pressure on Hudson Valley landlords and their system of manorial tenancy. This phase of "anti-rent" agitation met defeat at the hands of New York authorities determined to suppress rebellion, but it left a legacy of protest that would culminate in a more successful anti-rent agitation in the 1840s. Farmers in central and western Pennsylvania, for whom distilling grain into liquor was the most effective way of shipping it to distant markets across mountainous terrain and poor roads, joined together in 1794 to resist a new federal excise duty on whiskey. George Washington's administration was so alarmed that it mobilized an army to suppress this "Whiskey Rebellion," but the protesters melted back into the farms and hills, and no large confrontation ensued. Four years later, in a climate of sharp political contention and division over a prospect of war with France, a local Pennsylvania protest against imposition of the federal Direct Tax, which included a levy on houses according to their size, elicited another heavy-handed response in the arrest and conviction for treason of a farmer, John Fries.[29]

Meanwhile, on the Maine frontier of northern New England, repeated conflicts between squatter-settlers on uncleared land and the surveyors and lawyers of large landholders who claimed title to the property signaled the persistent inability of elites to control popular activity outside the bounds of older existing settlements. "We once defended this land at the point of a bayonet," a group of Maine farmers proclaimed, "& if drove to the necessity are now equally united, ready & zealous to defend it again the same way." Only after the election of 1800, when the Jeffersonians brought federal government more into line with the aspirations of settlers, and the extension of party organization and voting rights brought protesters closer to the political system, did such conflicts lose much of their apparent threat to the nation's future integrity. Popular demands to occupy land came to be seen less as a threat to elite control than as an extension of national interest.[30]

The Constitution and "Balance"

INFLATION AND the financial weakness of the Confederation government, coupled with the fear of popular unrest spread by agrarian protest, caused influential figures to convene at Annapolis, Maryland, in 1786 to consider measures to strengthen federal government. They agreed to call a larger convention at Philadelphia the following year to take steps to modify the Articles of Confederation. By the time the convention met in 1787, the explosion and subsequent suppression of Shays's Rebellion in Massachusetts had underscored the elites' sense of alarm. Their deliberations rapidly turned not to modifying the Articles but to scrapping them altogether and replacing them with something they could regard as more robust. The outcome was the United States Constitution.

In drafting the Constitution the 1787 convention achieved an awkward balance between the claims of democracy and those of propertied elites. Popular influence was embodied in the direct election of congressional representatives and by the apportionment of seats in the House of Representatives according to the population of each state. But the indirect election of senators (which until 1913 was conducted by state legislatures) and of the president (by the Electoral College), and the assignment of equal representation in the Senate to states regardless of their population, were intended to check excessive democracy. Provisions guaranteeing the sanctity of contracts and constraints on the government's tax-raising powers also protected the claims of property. Opponents, who argued against the Constitution when it was sent to the states for ratification between 1787 and 1789, primarily worried that it might eclipse state governments or erect too powerful a central administration. But many of these Antifederalists, as they became known, were also anxious about its influence on social equality and the conduct of democracy. At the Massachusetts ratifying convention the farmer Amos Singletary expressed the fear that under the Constitution "lawyers, and men of learning, and moneyed men . . . would swallow up us little folks." When Massachusetts came to vote on ratification, Shaysite regions of the state remained bastions of Antifederalist sentiment. Only an alliance of the state's commercial elite with urban artisans and other coastal supporters ensured the Constitution's ratification there by a narrow margin. In New York's convention the merchant Melancton Smith, who had himself risen from a modest background, argued that government under the Constitution would favor "the few and the great," to the exclusion of "those of the middling class of life." Many contemporaries saw the revolutionary settlement as a struggle between what the radical Massachusetts writer William Manning would later call "the Many" and "the Few," between "those that labour for a living and those that get one without."[31]

The doctrine of political balance, which was incorporated into the Constitution from a number of previous state constitutions, helped prevent the seizure of governmental power by any one group or interest. Supporters also argued that it could protect the weak against the strong: "In all the governments," such as the Articles of Confederation, "which were considered as beacons to republican patriots and lawgivers," wrote James Madison to Thomas Jefferson in 1788, "the rights of persons were subjected to those of property. The poor were sacrificed to the rich." The Constitution, he claimed, would serve them better. But in many instances the concept of balanced government was seen as a safeguard for property rights and of those who held property. Even though they opposed each other while in office, Thomas Jefferson and John Adams could agree in their later correspondence that democracy should not be allowed to lead to social leveling or chaos.[32]

As the federal constitution was being debated in the late 1780s a campaign was under way in Pennsylvania to alter the state's own radical constitution, which had been adopted in the democratic excitement of 1776. With a single legislative house, a president rather than a governor, and a weak executive, this original constitution had made Pennsylvania's one of the most democratic of all state governments. Wealthy and conservative Pennsylvanians had opposed it from the outset. By the late 1780s a coalition of Philadelphia merchants and artisans succeeded in obtaining a constitutional convention to revise it, and did so in 1790, over opposition from a constitutionalist party rooted mainly in the countryside and western part of the state. Pennsylvania's new constitution more closely matched the pattern of balances against democracy already present in the federal Constitution and those of other states.

Hierarchy Challenged

THE DOCTRINE of balance mirrored the Revolution's two distinct effects in society at large. On one hand, though largely carried out by adult white men and contested by proponents of elite rule, the Revolution's proclamations of equality nonetheless refocused cultural and political attitudes, destroying many aspects of colonial social deference and elevating participation in labor as a basis for social standing. On the other hand, the Revolution did not entirely destroy concepts of social hierarchy. To the extent that it did so, this tended to be confined to the public realm, and even there the process was ambiguous. In the private sphere it left them almost untouched.

Campaigns to ratify the Constitution provided opportunities for public demonstrations of a new social order. Federalist newspapers published tracts, rhymes, and even cartoons urging the advantages of the new form of federal union, stressing its democratic aspects. Verses such as those from "The Raising: A New Song for Federal Mechanics," published in 1788, portrayed the federal government as a building that would be erected by the people and fashioned out of its skills and hardy materials. Independence Day celebrations held in the main port towns that year became Federalist parades providing a visual display of a social and political system composed of working people. The "Grand Federal Procession" that took place in Philadelphia reportedly involved five thousand marchers and seventeen thousand onlookers—numbers that, if correct, totaled more than half the city's entire population. The procession consisted of members of Philadelphia's trades and other institutions, marching in some fifty divisions. They included cabinetmakers, dressed in similar aprons and hats, farmers, shoemakers, staymakers, ship carpenters, coopers, upholsterers, and brewers. Their position in the line of march was determined not by rank or social precedence but chiefly by drawing lots, which symbolized equality and the exercise of God's will. With marchers attired in the "dress and character" of their trades or professions, the emphasis was on citizens as workers and on the inclusive character of the political system. Richard Willing, a prosperous assemblyman from nearby Delaware County, marched "in a farmer's dress." One onlooker wrote that "every tradesman's boy . . . seemed to consider himself as a principal in the business. . . . Rank for a while forgot all its claims." Boston's procession, unlike those of most other towns, was organized by the tradesmen themselves.[33]

The Revolution had unseated some members of elites from power and had brought assumptions of hierarchy and social deference into question. It weakened elite rule, securing the entry of modest and middling men into politics in unprecedented numbers. Some elite families, such as the wealthy Livingstons of New York's Hudson Valley, withdrew from politics and concentrated on private concerns during the Revolution, even though they supported independence. To the extent that it broadened the concept of citizenship to embrace most white men with means, the Revolution also established a robust rhetoric of social and political equality.[34]

Yet the conservative reaction to the Revolution's most democratic impulses, though it did not restore colonial-style concepts of political hierarchy, also ensured that the idea of equality faced many challenges in the post-Revolutionary period. The ideal of elite rule was not displaced; instead it enjoyed a long afterlife. Especially in Virginia and New England, elite figures retained a major influence, because their broad support for revolution had preserved them from the upheavals faced by their colleagues in the Mid-Atlantic states or the deep South. Benjamin Lincoln became something of a figurehead for the farmers and professional men who formed the backbone of New England federalism, men from middling and prosperous families who adhered to the notion that rule was best exercised by "the best men," an elite based on birth, education, and ability.

There were several further qualifications to the claim that the Revolution was "democratic." Many groups, especially women and nonwhites, remained excluded from politics and the benefits of citizenship. Inequalities of social status and legal position remained, even among the white men who were the Revolution's chief beneficiaries. Furthermore, the idea of the legitimacy of elite rule or influence remained potent. Most advocates of the new United States' republican forms of government rejected the hereditary principle by which birth conferred social and political status, but the influence of such aristocratic concepts remained strong. Post-Revolutionary political groupings such as the

McKean/Dallas faction in Pennsylvania and the Clinton/Livingston faction in New York State clung to the notion that control of government should properly lie in the hands of "great" families. Others, including Thomas Jefferson, advocated the political influence of what they called a "natural aristocracy"—those whose background, education, talents, and accomplishments lifted them above the commonality of men and fitted them for the responsibilities of governing. The contest between these notions and more democratic ideas would continue to shape American politics. Political success tended to go to those elite groups who were most astute at accommodating the outlook and demands of yeoman farmers, artisans, and others with more democratic claims to inclusion in public affairs.[35]

Hierarchy Sustained: Slavery

THE REVOLUTION'S ambiguities were clearly reflected in its effects on slavery. War had helped some slaves gain their freedom. Legal and ideological changes also broadened the chances for liberty. Aside from slaves who secured their freedom through military service, thousands of others benefited from a Revolutionary egalitarian impetus that looked likely to weaken or destroy slavery in the latter decades of the eighteenth century. Since before the war Quaker slaveholders in Pennsylvania had been enjoined to free their human property. Under the influence of evangelical revivals and Revolutionary idealism, considerable numbers of slaveholders in Virginia and other Southern states took steps to free slaves, either by manumitting them (granting freedom) on the spot or by making provisions in their wills for eventual freedom. Largely as a consequence, the United States' free black population for a short period grew faster than its slave population: between 1774 and 1790 it rose from about 4 percent to 8 percent of the total. In Virginia, for instance, private manumission had been prohibited under a statute of 1748, but in 1782 the state passed a law permitting manumission on certain conditions. The free black population grew from about two thousand in 1782 to thirteen thousand in 1790 and twenty thousand by 1800.[36]

In the North's "societies with slaves," the relatively small numbers of slaves in the population, coupled with their military service, led to steps that eroded slavery after the Revolution. In Massachusetts in 1783, followed by New Hampshire the following year, courts found slavery inconsistent with constitutional declarations of equality. Although it took time for individual slaves to achieve their freedom, the institution of slavery was effectively abolished in these states from this point. The new republic of Vermont also prohibited slavery in its constitution while the U.S. Congress's 1787 Ordinance setting out governmental arrangements for the North West Territory across the Appalachians and north of the Ohio River permanently banned slavery from that region as well, though this prohibition was sometimes ignored.[37]

Other Northern states whose populations included substantial numbers especially of urban slaves took more hesitant steps toward abolition. Between 1784 and 1804 each state between Pennsylvania and Rhode Island enacted gradual emancipation laws, freeing individuals born after a certain date when they reached adulthood or a certain age. Military service, manumission, and purchases of freedom during the Revolution had already eroded slavery there; in Connecticut, for example, the number of slaves fell from 5,101 in 1774 to 2,648 in 1790. Gradual emancipation drove the number of slaves down further. From 50,000 in 1775, the total Northern slave population fell to 27,000 by 1810. Yet under gradual emancipation slavery took a long time to disappear entirely. New York freed all its remaining slaves in 1827, but as late as the 1840s New Jersey and Connecticut still had small numbers of slaves who had by law not yet qualified for freedom.[38]

Despite these steps toward emancipation in the North, the Revolution also secured conditions that would, in time and in conjunction with other circumstances, reinforce the slave societies of the South. Manumission benefited only a small portion of Southern slaves. Even in Maryland, where it was comparatively common, free persons made up only 16 percent of the black population in 1800. Virginia's 13,000 free blacks of 1790 were vastly outnumbered by its 300,000 remaining slaves, and by 1800 only 5 percent of Virginia's black population was free. Laws and constitutions in the South took none of the steps toward emancipation attempted in the North but instead tended to strengthen the slave system. Under the Articles of Confederation individual states remained sovereign, and under the Constitution the principle of state sovereignty remained largely unchallenged. Political compromises ensured that slavery was protected wherever it retained the white population's support. The Constitution precluded any ban on the importation of slaves in international trade before 1808 and, in its "Three-Fifths" clause, enhanced the political weight of the Southern states by counting each slave as three-fifths of a free person when population was calculated for the purpose of apportioning congressional representation. Article IV, Section 2 provided for the return of all persons "held to service or labor in one state" who had escaped into another, which led to the federal Fugitive Slave Act of 1793 and its successor of 1850. The Constitution's upholding of property rights deflected legal interference with slave ownership where states permitted it, and its provision for free trade among the states guaranteed the continuation of an internal slave trade. In the South, economic interests, property rights, cultural assumptions, and ideologies all helped strengthen slavery's position.

Yet while constitutional arrangements, reflecting the political influence of slaveholders, permitted slavery's continuation, they did not mandate this outcome. It was the strength of the institution and the reliance of slaveholding groups upon it that ensured few steps were taken to dismantle it. South Carolina's John Rutledge remarked in Congress in 1797 that "most of the [South's] property consisted of slaves, and . . . the rest was of no value without them." As various recent studies of the Founding Fathers have shown, even those who—like George Washington and Benjamin Franklin—expressed objections to slavery found it difficult to disentangle themselves from it. Many slaveholders, like Thomas Jefferson, had so much invested in their slaves or were so mired in debt that they could not divest themselves of their human property even if they had wished to. For the great majority of them, the sacrifice involved was too great, and their need for bound labor in a labor-scarce economy was too strong for emancipation to become common. Instead the persistence of slavery reinforced the power and influence of slaveholding elites. In his annual message in 1798, Governor Charles Pinckney urged the South Carolina Assembly to strengthen the state's slave code, to give "all the security and protection in our power to this species of property . . . the instruments of our cultivation, and of the first importance to our wealth and commercial consequence." As James Madison had ruminated in an unpublished comment six years earlier, "In proportion as slavery prevails in a state, the Government, however democratic in name, must be aristocratic in fact." Constitutional compromises over slavery helped seal the fate of the system for two generations to come and ensured that, contrary to the hopes of many slaves and of a handful of advocates of abolition, for most African Americans the Revolution would not secure freedom.[39]

The continuation of slavery was also attributable in part to the willingness of Northerners to perpetuate slavery where it was strong and to avoid meddling with what they saw as the property rights of their Southern counterparts. In the debates over the Constitution, Northern political leaders secured the support of Southerners for their own plans in return for their acceptance of the right to continue slavery. Some were influenced by a widespread late-eighteenth-century belief that slavery was an outmoded or doomed system, which the natural law of progress would soon bring to an end. Many Northerners were also aware that their commercial systems, since the colonial period, had benefited from involvement in the transatlantic slave trade. Even if relatively few Northern merchants and shippers had been directly involved in the traffic in slaves, many more—together with many farmers—had traded goods to the Caribbean or the South to supply those regions' plantation-based economies. This business of supplying slave regions would only grow in the late eighteenth and early nineteenth centuries.

Hierarchy Sustained: Families and Households

STILL, ANOTHER key reason for the perpetuation of slavery was that in the late eighteenth century it continued to appear consistent with general hierarchical concepts of labor and social relationships. Particular groups in the Revolutionary crisis—especially white men who were traders, artisans, and farmers—had succeeded in lodging their claims to freedom and equality, and had helped reshape the political system to reflect these claims. Conservative voices, however, thwarted the efforts of the more radical among these groups to press their ideology further, to achieve more general emancipation and egalitarianism. The political mechanisms erected by the constitutional system, in individual states as well as at the federal level, reflected the influence of elite groups who sought to temper the more radical influence of democracy with checks and balances tied to wealth, position, or privilege. The Revolution did much less to alter hierarchical assumptions in domestic life, which increasingly came to be seen as a "private" realm separate from the male-dominated "public" sphere of politics.

Some women sought changes in private or family law and practice that built upon the egalitarian implications of revolutionary politics. Lucy Knox wrote to her husband General Henry Knox in 1777 to discuss his future life at home after the war, suggesting that "I hope you will not consider yourself as commander in chief of your own house, but be convinced that there is such a thing as equal command." In New England, where laws permitting divorce already existed, there is some evidence that women made more use of them after the Revolution than they had in the colonial period. When Abigail Strong of Connecticut petitioned for divorce in 1788, she suggested that since "even Kings may forfeit or discharge the allegiance of their subjects," husbands might also, by their behavior, forfeit the loyalty and obedience expected of their wives. The possibility of divorce was indeed extended from New England to other states. But this did not markedly change the character or stability of marriages. Although New York, for instance, enacted a divorce statute in 1787, in practice it was rarely used.[40]

Indeed, little happened to undermine hierarchical assumptions in the private realm of households. Masters continued to enjoy the same authority over apprentices, servants, or slaves that they had had in the colonial period. Household heads, master craftsmen, ships' masters, military officers, and slaveholders could still inflict corporal punishment on their dependents and subordinates. Married men still owned or controlled their wives' property. State statutes and common law continued to embody the obligations and duties that women were held to owe to men, and children to parents. John Adams wrote to his son John Quincy Adams in 1799 that stable government depended on family authority, including "a marked subordination of mother and children to the father." The full freedoms of citizenship in the post-Revolutionary period were available only to men; married women continued to be held in "marriage bonds." Even radical artisans, farmers, and merchants still operated in a household system in which women, servants, apprentices, and children, as well as slaves, were regarded as unfree dependents, constrained by law from acting with the freedom of independent men. In 1807, Massachusetts courts considered the case of a woman who had refused her husband's demand that they move from their son-in-law's house, where they were living, and set up house separately. The state superior court declined, in this instance, to compel the wife to comply, but only on the limited grounds that she was free to live in the household of another relative if she chose. But the court made clear that had she been her son-in-law's employee, rather than his guest, her husband could have required her to move because that would have curtailed his own right of access to her and her labor.[41]

The freedoms secured by the Revolution were mainly those of proprietors, those able to place at the service of national independence the personal independence rooted in property ownership. As John Adams had written in 1790, "[p]roperty must be secured, or liberty cannot exist"; property put in the hands of the poor or dependent would be like "the lamb committed to the custody of the wolf."[42] The Revolution set up a perpetual tension between claims for equality and the demand of independent men that they should be left free to act as they wished. This excluded dependents, including the small number of people who worked for wages, from full citizenship. At the end of the eighteenth century most states required even white men to own some property in order to qualify to vote. In a 1789 sermon a Connecticut minister condemned the practice of slavery and the slave trade but expressed the fear that the system might become a model for treatment of other poor and dependent groups. "We are become so bold . . . as to bid off the poor at a public vendue, and this is become customary in all our towns, and why is it not as likely we should step one step further and sell them for slaves, and in process of time through custom, it will . . . seem as right to sell the poor and helpless for slaves, as it ever was the Africans . . .?"[43]

The Revolution's Effects

CONTEMPORARIES, ESPECIALLY in the many zones that had been subject to fighting or come under coastal bombardment or invasion, stressed the hardships and dislocations that war had produced. Advocates of a stronger central government, too, focused on the crippling financial effects of wartime destruction, currency inflation, and public debt. Alexander Hamilton, chief architect of the new federal funding system of the 1790s, wrote that the Revolution had "destroyed a large proportion of the monied and mercantile capital of the country and of personal property generally." Economic historians, noting that the colonies' prosperity reached a peak as war broke out in 1775, have estimated that per capita income fell sharply between 1775 and 1790. Output may not have returned to its pre-Revolutionary levels for a quarter of a century or more after the war ended.[44]

The realignment of trading patterns consequent upon leaving the British Empire disrupted some sources of profit and income. Independence removed the thirteen colonies from under the British commercial umbrella, and it took time for trading links to be restored or substitute ones successfully developed. The Rhode Island port of Newport, long a prosperous center of slave trading and other commerce, was already being rivaled by its smaller neighbor, Providence, before the war broke out. Newport's capture by the British during the war severely weakened its position, and the town permanently lost its local prominence in Atlantic trade to Providence after the war ended.[45]

Disruption ran inland as well as overseas. Charles County, located on the Potomac River in Maryland, was an example. War and associated economic changes brought to an end the kind of prosperity that the county's planter gentry had grown accustomed to in the late colonial period. Upheavals in tobacco markets, coupled with the difficulties of wartime, led to family bankruptcies and to a lasting depression in the county's economic fortunes. Families and individuals began to seek opportunities elsewhere. The county's population fell gradually but consistently after 1790, so that by 1860 it was reduced by one-fifth. In the late colonial period Charles County, like other prosperous Chesapeake regions, had had a majority white population, though its gentry were served by many of the 40 percent or so who were slaves or free blacks. Now, as its economy and population went into decline, the ratio of blacks to whites in the county rose. In the nineteenth century slaves and free blacks, who were less free than whites to move and take advantage of opportunities elsewhere, became a majority of the population in an area that had become, relatively speaking, an economic backwater.[46]

Farther west, Independence also disrupted older economic patterns by removing imperial barriers to the expansion of white settlement.

Settlement entailed the division of hitherto noncommoditized land. Although this process advanced the creation of land markets, it also fostered the destruction of other markets, especially those arising from existing patterns of trade and cultural interaction between colonists and Indians, across the zones of contact that historian Richard White has dubbed the "middle ground." For Native Americans the effect of the American Revolution was to "transform their contact with whites from trade and interchange across a frontier zone into constant retreat west behind a moving . . . line," as the division of land created a "frontier" where none had previously existed. Trade implied free-flowing movement, but property denoted stasis and territorial exclusion. Trade remained important for Native American societies but now took place in much altered social and political contexts. In 1793 the Shawnee Confederacy's negotiators spurned the federal government's offer of cash for lands to grant to white settlers arriving in Ohio, responding that "money to us is of no value, and to most of us is unknown." The government should instead, they suggested, use it to buy out the white settlers who had appropriated Indian land and to alleviate the inequalities that pressed whites to find new land in the West.[47]

Yet the Revolution also helped unleash a period of relative expansion and economic buoyancy. The white population grew faster in the 1780s than in any decade before or after, and this rapid population increase, particularly the high birthrate, provided one engine of future expansion and growth. Even as many localities faced disruption or decline, others grew significantly or underwent changes that sowed the seeds of later development. The colonial economy had provided a framework that permitted the Revolutionary states to pursue economic diversification and a degree of independence. The war secured political independence. The Constitution guaranteed that the United States would become a common market, free from internal tariffs and trade restrictions. State and federal provisions for the enforcement of contracts, the protection of property, and the collection of debts, together with new monetary and financial policies, all tended to favor commercial interests. The survival of elites, including much of the North's mercantile leadership, guaranteed that there would be people in a position to take advantage of this. Independence had coincided with the publication of Adam Smith's *The Wealth of Nations*, which in time delivered an intellectual blow to European trading systems as powerful as the political and military blows that the rebellious Americans were aiming at empire. Radical exponents of American independence, such as Tom Paine, joined the ranks of those advocating free markets and institutions that could exploit and develop them. Endowed already with an increasing sense of individual self-worth, the heirs to the Revolutionary generation pushed themselves out of the confines of colonial society into new fields, occupations, and regions.

The exigencies of war had called for new efforts in home manufacture and production. In some regions this helped lay the basis for future economic development. The war and the economic crisis that followed it in the 1780s may have contributed to the convergence of prices—and hence the strengthening of market influences—that the historian Winifred B. Rothenberg has traced in parts of Massachusetts in this period. Evidence from New England also suggests that the disruptions of the Revolutionary War and the demands for domestic labor that these created helped further an improvement in women's material living standards that had begun in the 1760s. The demands of war supply and finance, as well as the legacy of indebtedness that the war bequeathed, led to fierce political conflicts but also to creative and original solutions that laid the basis of a new financial system and capital markets. Post-Revolutionary commerce outside the British Empire demanded new patterns of trade while the diversion of Europe into war in the 1790s paradoxically aided the United States by minimizing the effects of the break with Britain. In Salem, Massachusetts, the merchant and shipowner Elias Hasket Derby expanded the business he had inherited from his father, helped reorganize local shipbuilding, and sent ships in the 1780s and 1790s to new trading destinations in the Baltic and the Indian Ocean. When Derby died in 1799 his fortune, rumored to be one million dollars, was among the largest yet accumulated in North America. His house, built overlooking the family's wharf on the Salem waterfront, was among the most expensive in New England.[48]

Union and Region

THE FINANCIAL crises and popular disturbances of the 1780s had, however, emphasized the fissures in the new republic and provoked strong concerns about its ability to survive either class divisions or regional differences. Elite fears of popular unrest or insurrection had helped shape the movement for a new federal constitution in the late 1780s, but the anxieties of mid-decade and the fierce ratification debates that followed underscored the ambiguities of the Revolution's legacy. Regional voting blocs were important throughout the existence of the Continental Congress. Now Antifederalist opinion, especially in the most populous states, such as Virginia, Massachusetts, and Pennsylvania, strongly expressed the notion that the sources of authority in the new nation should remain with the distinctive and diverse states, and thus incorporate the power of regional differences into the political system. Even many leaders who came to support the Constitution had previously despaired of finding a framework for national government. As one of them wondered, "will such a heterogeneous body . . . ever coalesce?" Benjamin Lincoln of Massachusetts, doubtless still smarting at his humiliation at the hands of his South Carolinian supposed allies when they obliged him to surrender Charleston in 1780, contrasted the "enterprising spirit" of the Northern states with a South that he argued had been made "feeble and defenceless" by slavery. In the mid-1780s Lincoln was one of a number of prominent figures who believed that the United States' future would lie in the creation of separate regional governments, making the nation a loose confederation of regions whose differences would then not disrupt the conduct of policy. Lincoln changed his mind only when he read the newly promulgated Constitution. He supported it as a promising compromise between the rigidities of national government and the flexibility of individual state administrations.[49]

Lincoln and other Federalists, however, remained anxious about the ability of the nation to hold together. Benjamin Franklin, in one of his last famous statements, expressed the hope that the Constitution would last but noted that "nothing in this life is certain, except Death and Taxes." Even George Washington wrote of his fears for the nation's future. Much of the sharp political conflict of the 1790s stemmed from anxiety that opponents' opinions or proposals, or even the very existence of political opposition, might destroy the Union. Disagreements arose on foreign and financial policies and around class divisions, but a persistent concern remained the question as to whether disparate regional societies could together sustain a federal political system. Various plans and conspiracies were hatched in the two decades after 1790 to detach the trans-Appalachian West as a separate nation or confederation. After the election of Thomas Jefferson to the presidency in 1800 seemed to indicate their political eclipse, Federalists themselves most often became associated with plans for disunion. In 1803–1804 a group of conservative New Englanders proposed detaching New York and New England to form a separate Northern confederacy. The entertainment of a comparable proposal by Federalists meeting at Hartford to discuss their opposition to the War of 1812 would irreparably stain their party with the taint of treason and help ensure its decline.[50]

Proponents of different views of national policy from the 1790s onward also entertained different views of the character of the nation's development. Historians have long pointed to the divide that emerged soon after the passage of the U.S. Constitution between two of its most prominent promoters, Alexander Hamilton and James Madison. As the historian Lance Banning has recently written, these differences were not so much—as is often assumed—between Hamilton's advocacy of a strong federal government and Madison's conception of a weaker one deferential to the power of the individual states. Both, Banning suggests, accorded power to federal authority but advocated that it should be directed to different ends. Hamilton viewed it as a means by which the United States could emulate Britain's early success on a path that would take it to commercial and industrial development. Madison, along with his ally Thomas Jefferson, sought to avoid the British path by using territorial expansion to guarantee supplies of land that could sustain a rural society of independent freeholders. Commerce, for Madison, would be not so much an instrument of economic development as a means to avoid it. The Hamiltonian vision entailed a pattern of intensive development; the Madisonian, one of extensive growth across the land. American growth and development in the nineteenth century would be rooted in the simultaneous pursuit of both visions.[51]

Federalists such as Benjamin Lincoln contributed to the pursuit of intensive development by seeking to restrain westward settlement and territorial expansion. Among Lincoln's tasks in the 1790s was service as an emissary in an unsuccessful effort to reach an accommodation with the Shawnee Confederacy in the Ohio country, one that would have placed constraints on the rapid process of American emigration and occupation of Indian lands. Madison and Jefferson, on the other hand, helped lay the basis for extensive growth by acquiring further western territory and reducing restraints placed upon whites' pressure to remove Indians from their lands to make way for new settlements.[52]

The Revolution profoundly altered the terms on which American politics and social discourse were conducted, but it also confirmed some directions that colonial society was already taking. It challenged, but did not depose, social hierarchy; and it opened access to additional territory that could satisfy the insistent search for land that had already marked the colonial period. The expansion of national territory would reinforce the effects of the high land-to-labor ratio that had shaped the hierarchies and inequalities of colonial societies. Above all, the Revolution did not erase the strong regional differences that had grown up between the British North American colonies. Rather, it created an arena in which those differences could continue to flourish.

☼ *CHAPTER 3* ☼

Social Change in the Early Republic

T WO YOUNG women from England who arrived in the United
States in 1795 wrote of sighting as their vessel approached New
York "the land of virtue, of peace, and of plenty." For slaves, American
inequality was absolute, but for most of its free members American society was more egalitarian and less divided by contrasts between wealth
and poverty than Britain or much of Europe. A higher proportion of
people owned land or other productive property. Many fewer were
desperately poor or indigent. Although the mansions of wealthy merchants and estates of wealthy planters were easily distinguishable from
the ordinary dwellings around them, let alone from the cabins of the
poor, they did not approach in grandeur or extravagance the great
palaces of European aristocrats. Emigrants and visitors often celebrated this difference from Europe: "The lowest here," reported one
in 1794, ". . . are well fed, well dressed, and happy . . . they stand erect
and crouch not before any man." A Frenchman declared that in the
United States there were no "numerous classes, who . . . do not labour
at all. . . . Their generals distil brandy, their colonels keep taverns, and
their statesmen feed pigs." By the same token some visitors complained of this relative egalitarianism. Servants were hard to find, for
example, and by the standards of Europe's elites were insufficiently du-
tiful or deferential when they could be hired. To both American and
European observers, these circumstances denoted the "middling"
character of American society.[1]

Equality and Inequality

UNTIL THE late eighteenth century, significant numbers of migrants to America were involuntary. They were slaves forcibly transported from Africa or the Caribbean slave islands, for sale particularly in the lower South. Between 1783 and 1819, however, about 300,000 emigrants from Britain and Ireland reached the United States along with smaller numbers from Germany and other parts of Europe. Although the Southern states attracted some of these white immigrants, people were not usually drawn to plantation regions, where the presence of slave labor tended to obviate demand for surplus white workers. Migration was most commonly to the backcountry, where land was available for purchase or rent, and where there was the hope of establishing a livelihood in circumstances of rough equality, if not of comfort. Settled rural regions, even relatively egalitarian ones like New England, however, did not attract large numbers of immigrants because their few requirements for labor could be met locally, land was more expensive, and access to it required local knowledge or connections. The most buoyant demand for immigrants lay in the growing port towns and nonslave staple-crop regions of the Mid-Atlantic, where relative inequality was balanced by the availability of employment for wages. These were the destinations to which most late-eighteenth- and early-nineteenth-century migrants headed.

Leaving Europe for America usually gave these migrants advantages. They need not worry about mass poverty or famine, which could still occur in Europe: even during seasons of harsh weather or crop failure, rural regions of America were usually capable of supporting their populations. And there were other sources of basic security. One was a high incidence of marriage: overall more than 92 percent of white U.S. households in 1790 were male-headed, compared with about 80 percent in England. Birthrates were high, so there were relatively small numbers of single women without access to either property or the support of children. Although widowhood was common, fewer widows than in Europe lived alone without any family support (even so, about one-third of widows relied on some form of public poor relief).[2]

Despite these contrasts with Europe, American society had its own structures of inequality. The most fundamental were rooted in the household system itself, in the differential rights and access to property of husbands and wives, and in the authority men exercised over women, and parents over children. In 1800 only 13 percent of Americans were white men aged twenty-six or over, the group from which the majority of independent citizens were drawn. Some of them, and most of the 87 percent remaining, who included women, children, slaves, and free people of color, were in positions of subordination or dependency.

While these fundamental inequalities applied everywhere, different regional social structures modulated them in distinct ways. The most unequal places were regions with large numbers of slaves, whose enslaved population owned little or nothing, where wealth distribution was heavily skewed in favor of the planter gentry, and where inequalities among whites too were often considerable. Prince George's County, Maryland, for example, had not only the state's highest proportion of slaves, at 52 percent of the population, but also high rates of white farm tenancy. Port towns, where the wealth of commercial elites was juxtaposed with the poverty and marginality of many maritime workers and their dependents, were also places of sharp inequality. Rural regions with freehold land and a wide distribution of property were more egalitarian, though staple export crop areas such as eastern Pennsylvania exhibited more differentials than nonstaple regions like interior New England. In Chester County, Pennsylvania, between 1783 and 1820, the number of "inmate" laborers on farms grew from about one-fifth to more than two-fifths of households.

The land-to-labor ratio remained high, and indeed increased. Between Independence and 1819 the United States gained control over the whole eastern and central portions of the continent below Canada, from the Atlantic Ocean to the Great Plains. Just as the Seven Years' War had expelled the French from Canada, the Revolutionary War largely expelled the British from territory south of Canada. Treaty negotiations in the 1790s and the favorable outcome of the War of 1812 ended any remaining British presence in the Ohio Valley and Mississippi Basin. The Spanish withdrew from the massive Louisiana Territory across the Mississippi, and the French government's sale of it to the United States in 1803 almost doubled America's land area. Native Americans lost any European allies in their efforts to resist the influx of settlers, soldiers, and officials. After American incursions and conflicts with Indians in its territory in the Southeast, Spain ceded Florida and adjacent possessions to the United States by treaty in 1819, adding further to a land area now many times larger than the original thirteen states. The accession of previously unclaimed land well outstripped even the rapid rate of population growth. On one hand, this territorial expansion broadened opportunities for those able to take advantage of it. On the other, it underscored the importance of forms of dependent and unfree labor. For generations only formal coercion, in the form of slavery, or the less formal obligations of household-based organization would be capable of supplying the labor and effort required to open up this land to settlement.

Opportunities and Constraints

FOR MANY men and women who had lived through the Revolution and whose lives drew to a close in the 1820s, the first half-century of American independence was a period of considerable hardship. The financial crises of the 1780s confronted many with debt and the threat of eviction or loss of their land. Thousands found themselves in debtors' prisons or forced onto the goodwill of family, neighbors, or creditors. Relative prosperity in the 1790s and early 1800s was unevenly shared. European wars, the imposition of a trade embargo by the Jefferson administration in 1807, the 1812 war with Britain, and the subsequent reopening of international markets after 1815 all contributed to instability and altered structures of employment. A postwar boom that prompted a flood of imports from Europe, dislocating many American artisans and manufacturers, ended in a financial panic in 1819, which marked the start of the first nationwide economic depression.

One index of the hardships faced by the Revolutionary generation lies in the claims for government pensions submitted by former soldiers of the Revolution when Congress made these available to enlisted men after 1818. The number of initial claims and the impact of the financial panic put immediate strains on the system; pension payments were halted and veterans told in 1820 that they could reapply only by demonstrating severe financial difficulties. Within two years at least twenty thousand former soldiers took the so-called pauper's oath that could qualify them for a federal pension of eight dollars a month. They represented more than one in nine of all patriot soldiers who had survived the Revolutionary War and a considerably higher portion of those still alive by the early 1820s. Men such as Uriah Cross, from Connecticut, who was wounded while serving in the war and later spent forty-five years in at least eight different towns in upstate New York, ended up elderly and—as Cross wrote in his petition for a pension—"destitute of any means of support except that provided . . . by . . . friends." Jeremiah Greenman, who had served throughout the Revolution in the Rhode Island line of the Continental army, and survived wounds and imprisonment by the British, was also reduced forty years later to pleading poverty in order to secure financial assistance. After moving from one place and employment to another, Greenman had settled with his family on a modest upland farm in Ohio. Hampered by age, his old wounds, and small resources, he had little to rely on but his family's support. His land was poor, and he had few possessions other than a few animals and a modest number of household goods. With his wife in poor health, and with his children "not in affluent circumstances," so unable to "contribute towards my support without embarrassing themselves," Greenman was obliged to apply for "the bounty of my Country" . . . "which I fought for and three times bled to regain from Brittish Tyrants." His predicament and those of his fellow petitioners testified to the fragility of opportunity in the post-Revolutionary decades.[3]

This was because, despite their advantages, American societies at the end of the eighteenth century also faced various constraints. Urban dwellers experienced increasing population densities and overcrowding, danger from fires, and exposure to deadly disease. In the Philadelphia yellow fever outbreak in the summer of 1793, between 10 and 12 percent of the population died; among those without the means or connections to find shelter outside the city, the death rate was 20 percent. In outbreaks of the disease in Baltimore in 1794 and 1797, 15 percent of the population died, and the death rate in the crowded waterfront neighborhood of Fell's Point was 25 percent. In the South, free black households were on average twice as likely as nearby white households in the same district to be headed by a female, and most women householders were poor. In rural and urban areas alike, employment for the poor was often intermittent and highly dependent on the seasons or the periodic demands of crops and commercial activities. Sickness or competition from incoming laborers also undermined people's certainty about finding and keeping work.

Recent studies have called into question historians' traditional emphasis on early America's "middling" character, stressing not only the peaks of wealth in many towns and regions but also the extent to which a poor substratum of the population has been undercounted and overlooked. Philadelphia had about 15 percent of its population in poverty. In New York City the number of public relief recipients multiplied six times between 1784 and 1814, faster than the growth of the population, so that the number in poverty reached 20 percent. Rural areas too had their "strolling poor." Often the boundaries between sufficiency and destitution were thin. The Reverend Ezra Stiles Ely, who founded a Presbyterian mission to the poor of New York in 1810, condemned the low prices given to poor widows for doing needlework and the disparities between the wages of the poor and the prices charged by merchants for the goods they produced.[4]

So the early republic's household-based regional societies faced a variety of pressures for change. The late colonial period had been prosperous, producing in many areas average living standards above those in Britain or elsewhere in Europe. But the Revolutionary period brought dislocations as well as new opportunities. Three kinds of pressures in particular placed strains on already settled regions: population growth; the shortage, exhaustion, or maldistribution of available land; and the economic crises associated with the Revolution and its aftermath. These pressures affected all parts of the new republic but varied with the social characteristics of each region.

Pressures for Change

THE 1780S witnessed one of the fastest percentage population increases of any decade in American history, and from 1790 to 1860 population continued to rise by between 28 percent and 31 percent each decade. In the late eighteenth century, with levels of immigration from overseas generally low, the bulk of this increase was attributable to natural population growth. High birthrates and fertility rates, and comparatively low mortality rates, meant that the American-born population rose rapidly. In his inaugural address as president in 1801, Thomas Jefferson alluded to the unseen future of "a rising nation, spread over a wide and fruitful land, . . . advancing rapidly to destinies beyond the reach of mortal eye."[5]

Rapid population growth created an age structure heavily weighted toward youth. Of the nation's white people in 1800, for example, only 31.6 percent—fewer than one in three—were over twenty-five. More than two-thirds of them were close to or below the average age of first marriage and had barely begun to have children of their own. As these people matured, married, and contributed children to the population over the following decades, they created a strong expansionary pressure that would help transform American society.

It was significant too that the societies these people were born into were overwhelmingly rural. About 90 percent of the population in 1790 lived in rural areas, and a large proportion relied on the land for their livelihoods. In rural areas overall family size averaged from 5.0 to 5.6 persons, and was increasing. In Columbia and Greene counties in New York's Hudson River Valley, to take one example, total population rose from 35,000 in 1790 to 61,000 in 1820. Farming regions throughout America faced a potentially severe problem. Landownership, though by no means universal, was widespread. Families were large, population was growing fast, life expectancy for farming families was long, and in most states inheritance laws and custom favored the distribution of real property among families' offspring rather than its inheritance by one child. Given that land was not equally distributed among families, and that the aspiration to divide land among offspring had provided an impetus to accumulate land where possible, even with relatively low overall population densities per square mile, older settled regions of the eastern seaboard soon ran out of unoccupied land.

One result was a decline in average family landholdings. In the countryside surrounding Boston, Massachusetts, where holdings had averaged 120 acres in the early eighteenth century, average farm size had fallen to 43 acres by the eve of the Revolution, and the pressure did not cease. By then, thousands of Massachusetts and Connecticut farm families had fewer than 40 acres apiece. In parts of southern New England where land had been equally distributed in the early eighteenth century, property distribution was becoming markedly unequal by the early nineteenth. In Chester County, Pennsylvania, the ratio of landless laborers to householders rose by nearly 45 percent between 1756 and 1820. In one area of Virginia where over 60 percent of households had owned land in the 1770s, by 1800 the proportion had fallen to fewer than half. Not surprisingly, older-settled areas reflected the strain more than newer ones: in Brandywine Hundred, Delaware, in 1797, for instance, farm sizes averaged 88 acres, of which an average of 64 percent was "improved" for cultivation or pasture. In Appoquinimink Hundred farther south, farms were larger, averaging 240 acres, but only 46 percent of these had been improved. The process of acquisition, improvement, and division of the land had gone further in Brandywine, leaving less time than in newer areas before access to the land became severely limited. Similar patterns and contrasts could be traced up and down the seaboard regions.[6]

Aggravating the problem of gaining access to land was the concern, particularly in regions producing staple crops such as tobacco and wheat, that crop yields were falling, crop diseases spreading, or soil becoming exhausted. Many districts of southern New England that had grown wheat in the late colonial period were obliged to abandon the crop and concentrate on corn, rye, and other grains as "wheat rust" and "Hessian fly" infected the wheat fields. The main Pennsylvania wheat regions were largely spared these infestations until early in the nineteenth century, but their spread did encourage the movement of wheat cultivation elsewhere and the switching of former grain areas into other farming activities, such as dairying.[7]

Further south, tobacco, especially when it was grown continually (without rotation) on larger plantations, was notorious for exhausting the soil and rendering it unfit for successful cultivation after a period of years. The Revolution had disrupted the tobacco trade by cutting off its principal market, Britain, and in the aftermath tobacco cultivation never regained its former preeminence or prosperity. In consequence the Chesapeake's gentry families declined in relative importance, both politically and economically. In Albemarle County, in the Virginia piedmont, the wealthiest 10 percent of the population in 1800 owned almost the same proportion of total real estate that had been held by only 5 percent in 1775. Tobacco cultivation became concentrated on smaller farms instead of large plantations. In parts of eastern Maryland and northern Virginia, landowners in the 1780s and 1790s diversified their farm output, switching their efforts from tobacco to wheat so as to share in the prosperity of the wheat boom that had long benefited Pennsylvania farmers. This shift from tobacco to grain was most apparent in districts within reach of the growing port town of Baltimore, which began to capture some of Philadelphia's rural hinterland and markets for farm exports and manufactured goods.[8]

The shift from tobacco to grain in the northern Chesapeake did not initially lead to a significant decline in slavery. Slaves were put to work in the highly seasonal patterns of wheat cultivation but also used to grow other crops, such as corn, to raise and tend livestock, and to undertake skilled craft work. This gave the region a degree of self-sufficiency and provided many slaves with a basis for developing their own culture and activities. Slaves with access to patches of land on which they could grow garden crops were able to engage in informal trading relationships with poorer whites. Some were hired out to other employers. Gabriel, who became implicated in an alleged conspiracy to rebel in Richmond, Virginia, in 1800, was one such hired-out slave. He had become part of a semi-autonomous milieu of black and white artisans, mariners, and laborers who had little connection with the slaveholding gentry and little deference to its authority. Richard Parkinson, a traveler in the region, was one of several visitors who noted the freedom with which some slaves spoke of the laziness of their masters and of their own right to consume the produce they had raised. When white leaders succumbed to fears of slave insurrection, talk of such kind, and the quasi-independence that crossed color lines, exposed Gabriel and others to suspicion that in this case brought them to their deaths on the gallows. By the first decade of the nineteenth century, many Chesapeake slaveholders were selling surplus slaves or transferring them to land acquired in the piedmont region of Virginia and North Carolina, where they could be put to work raising tobacco on fresh soil.[9]

Three kinds of response to the pressures of population on the land emerged across the eastern United States. Some farmers and planters decided to settle in new regions. In many places individuals moved to find work in towns or in the maritime economy. And in certain regions, households sought to deal with these constraints by intensifying or diversifying their activities. All these efforts would lead to significant social changes.

Migration and Expansion

SEVERAL FACTORS came together in the second half of the eighteenth century to drive American populations beyond the areas of original settlement in the seaboard states. By 1800 about one-fifth of the white population of the United States was settled in frontier regions. Many European settlers had long held a desire for land, and for the personal independence landownership could bring. In some respects the late-eighteenth-century push into new regions merely continued that aspiration. During the pre-Revolutionary period elite investors with influential political connections had sought sizable land grants beyond existing settlement zones, including large territories west of the Appalachians, in the hope of eventually making speculative profits by dividing up this land and selling it to settlers. Conflicts between land-company interests, Native Americans, and British policy for the backcountry had done much to intensify colonial resentment of Britain, and the West became an important arena of conflict during the Revolutionary War. The peace settlement of 1783, by guaranteeing American control of much of the land east of the Mississippi, helped open up to systematic development territory that hunters, migrants, and squatters had already been moving into in significant numbers. The U.S. Constitution, along with the federal land ordinances of 1785 and 1787 that regulated the appropriation of the territory north and west of the Ohio River, set out terms by which newly settled regions could organize themselves as territories and be admitted to the Union as states. The fact that these new regions would acquire equal status with existing states and not become colonies of the seaboard states was itself a spur to settlement. When socioeconomic conditions in older regions led people to seek new ways of securing their livelihoods, the political developments of the 1770s and 1780s by which the United States had laid claim to vast areas far beyond society's current needs provided one basis for addressing them.[10]

Although access to new territory held out promise for prospective settlers, and for the land speculators who hoped to profit from settlement, it did of course create many losers too. Foremost among these were Native Americans, who now faced the full onslaught of a push for their land backed by the military power of state and federal governments. By effectively removing other foreign powers, particularly Britain, from the contest for control of the trans-Appalachian West, the peace settlement had left Indians with only a single government to negotiate with, severely weakening their bargaining power. Although groups like the Shawnee in the Ohio country formed alliances to resist Americans' encroachments on their lands, and achieved some military success in the early 1790s, they were ultimately unable to withstand the force projected against them and had to sign away many of their rights. Many Americans meanwhile took the political arrangements favoring the spread of settlement, the assistance of governments, and the difficulties facing those who resisted as signs that their possession of these new lands was legitimate. Nor were Native Americans the sole losers. Early white traders and settlers, who had established often productive, frequently peaceable interchanges with Indians, found their ways of life swept aside as emigration and settlement became more systematic. White settlers and officials often regarded them as wild or uncivilized for their frontier existence and close connections with Native Americans.[11]

Although the political changes and territorial gains of the Revolutionary period made new land available for migration and settlement, structural conditions within older regions created the impetus for expansion. In late-colonial Virginia, large planter estates and widespread tenancy had already encouraged poorer families, tenant farmers, and servants completing their terms of service to settle in the backcountry by purchasing, mortgaging, or squatting on unoccupied land. Younger sons from planter families attached to the region's traditional practice of primogeniture also sought land in newly opened territory. During the 1770s and 1780s, streams of migrants, both wealthy and poor, settled in and beyond the Blue Ridge Mountains, clearing land and creating farms in what would soon become the state of Kentucky. In New England, meanwhile, the tradition of partible inheritance, in which property was divided among heirs, had also long generated migration and settlement of new land. During the second half of the eighteenth century, many families from Connecticut and Massachusetts moved north to settle land and form new towns in Maine, New Hampshire, and Vermont. From the 1780s onward, as the new political framework opened access to regions to the west, migrations began into upstate New York and to the Ohio Valley. Substantially as a result of in-migration from older settled regions, the population of New York State nearly trebled within twenty years, from 340,000 people in 1790 to 959,000 in 1810.[12]

Settlers' desire for land was more than matched by speculators' visions of the fortunes they could make by providing it. In the aftermath of the Revolution, investors, politicians, and those connected with them vied for the opportunity to purchase or receive grants to lands they hoped to sell at a profit to further investors or to settlers. In Burlington, New Jersey, a group including the ambitious wheelwright and small merchant William Cooper maneuvered to acquire rights to land in New York State that had previously belonged to grandees who had fled to Britain during the Revolution, among them the last royal governor of New Jersey, William Franklin. Cooper's acquisition of land in this Otsego Patent, and his creation there of a central village, Cooperstown, which he conceived as the nucleus of an agricultural settlement, represented one among many possible models of frontier development. Well-connected federal officials, such as Henry Knox, former secretary of war, and Robert Morris, a key figure in Revolutionary finance, embarked on even more ambitious schemes involving tens of thousands of acres of undivided land. Knox built a grand house in Maine, from which he oversaw the surveying and management of his huge landholdings in the region. Morris involved himself in grandiose land speculations along the Appalachian frontier, including the fraudulent acquisition of holdings on the Yazoo River in what later became Alabama. Excitement among investors drove up the imagined values of these lands, or the paper that represented them, during the first half of the 1790s; Morris became notable as the richest man in America. But after 1795, when the deceptiveness of the Yazoo land scheme became apparent, the boom abated. The paper value of land collapsed, and the great speculators like Morris and Knox were caught with borrowings they no longer had the remotest chance of repaying. Along with many others, they ended up in debtors' prison.[13]

For one thing, their hope of holding land and living off rents or unearned income from its sale or lease frequently proved illusory. Even resident land developers like William Cooper faced difficulties enough, though he did not go bankrupt in the crisis. But the big land speculators' failure derived from several problems in addition to their inflated ambition and financial recklessness. Demand for land and pressure for expansion from within existing rural societies was significant, but it was not nearly sufficient to drive all the schemes that were floated to profit from them. There was simply so much land potentially available that individual speculators had relatively little chance to match their visions of wealth by actually selling it. Moreover, although speculation and settlement in much of the area south of the Ohio River and east of the Mississippi (which would become the states of Kentucky, Tennessee, Alabama, and Mississippi) was conducted by private companies, the Old Northwest across the Ohio and around the Great Lakes became the model for government-controlled disposition of the public lands now owned by the new republic.

Government became a party to the settlement of the West for two principal reasons. The first was political. Not surprisingly, as land company prospectors, surveyors, squatters, and purchasers explored, acquired, and settled territory, they often provoked tension with or outright hostility from the Native American groups from whom they had taken it. They then demanded military support or protection from the federal government, or organized state militias for the same purpose. As had occurred earlier on colonial frontiers, backcountry advocates of fierce suppression of the Indians clashed with coastal officials who counseled caution or moderation in Indian policy. The federal Northwest Ordinance of 1787 explicitly stated that Indian lands should be acquired only with consent and by legal means. But such protections as officials sought to provide could not alter the fundamental issue: white settlers were encroaching on western land and obtaining it in increasing quantities. The mechanisms of consent and legal process could be readily manipulated to cover fraud and theft. Indeed, the purpose of establishing the legality of land acquisitions from Indians was not primarily to protect Indians at all but to assure purchasers and subsequent owners that they would have sound title to the land they were acquiring. Within four years of the Northwest Ordinance's passage, federal troops were engaged in the Ohio country trying to suppress the resistance of tribes led by the Shawnee to any policy of white settlement. Federal commissioners, including the former general Benjamin Lincoln of Massachusetts, who sought to negotiate a settlement in 1793, professed sympathy for Indians' rights as against the rapacity and greed of speculators and settlers. But officials like Lincoln were convinced that the Indians were eventually doomed to give way before the onslaught of settlers. Even as they sought to regulate the process, they regarded white society's expansion to the west as inevitable.

The federal government was also deeply involved in western settlement for financial reasons. During the Revolution both the Continental Congress and state governments had used the promise of land to reward soldiers for military service and reduce the burden of government debt. Many soldiers and suppliers had received part of their pay in land warrants, paper promises of access to the one item the government might obtain in abundance. While hardship had obliged many ex-soldiers to sell these warrants, the transfer to the federal government of states' claims to western land, and the federal assumption in the early 1790s of states' debts, redoubled the connection between the federal government and the West. Although the Constitution granted the federal government taxation powers, its efforts to levy direct taxes at the end of the eighteenth century provoked strong, sometimes even violent, opposition. Indeed, other than a short-lived attempt to tax land, houses, and slaves in 1798, and another temporary taxation measure during the War of 1812, there was no federal direct taxation before the Civil War. Federal revenue instead derived from duties and tariffs on overseas trade, but the sale of public lands also became a significant source of government income. In this way the government's need for revenue and interest in national expansion became linked to popular demands for land. Land sales were made at first to private companies but after 1800 also to smaller groups of investors and individual settlers with means. Federal revenue from land sales amounted to only $101,000 before 1800 but then accelerated rapidly, to $4,569,000 from 1801 to 1810, and $16,326,000 between 1811 and 1820. Between 1800 and 1820 almost 18.5 million acres of public lands were sold.

Behind these movements were changes in the perception of land. In older regions, such as southern New England, more people came to see the land they owned not as a possession, conferring status or intrinsic value, but as a commodity that could be traded. Land speculators, acquiring title or claims to "unsettled" lands previously under Native

American control, hoped to profit by reselling it at a higher price or dividing it up for sale to settlers. The federal land ordinances of the 1780s, which laid down terms for the settlement of the Old Northwest, helped systematize the process of commodifying land. They prescribed a standard method of land division whose imprint is plainly visible to this day in the grid-pattern of field boundaries and road systems that stretches from Ohio to the Rocky Mountains.

If the means for bringing about migration and resettlement involved changes in patterns and attitudes, migration often reflected the social structures of the regions migrants came from. For many of the farm families and their offspring who migrated to new regions, the process was an attempt to recreate the kinds of societies and social opportunities they had known back home. Already in the early eighteenth century, Massachusetts farmers had migrated to unsettled regions in eastern Connecticut, buying tracts of land five or ten times the size of their existing small farms. They sought to acquire sufficient land to carve out farms for their own children and to build the kinds of local institutions that existed in their home regions. In the Revolutionary period and after, many of their successors made similar moves to northern New England. Levi Fay of Marlborough, Massachusetts, for example, had lived on rented farms for much of a long career; finally, in 1798, he bought land in Lunenberg, Vermont, and moved his family there the following year. Many of these migrants planned their movement and acquisition of land in company with family members or neighbors. Rather than being a creation of adventuring individualists, the early frontier was an extension of the household-based rural societies of the Eastern states.[14]

New England and New York migrants to western New York and beyond settled most readily in areas where land speculators or land companies were prepared to pursue development policies that suited their needs. In Otsego County, New York, William Cooper initially envisioned building a closely knit colony of farmers and artisans gathered around his settlement at Cooperstown, with his own "manor house" as its symbolic center. He soon realized that most of the people who purchased land from him were New Englanders more interested in setting up dispersed family clusters of farms that spread across his land grant than they were in complying with his own vision of a concentrated, hierarchical settlement. Later migrants to western New York were attracted to the Holland

Land Company's Holland Purchase region because its resident agents were amenable to settlement policies they found appealing—unlike those in adjacent grants, where companies were more concerned with extracting income and fees from purchasers. A circular of 1817 advertising land in Jefferson County, New York, was addressed to prospective settlers from purchasers already satisfied with their dealings with the area's proprietor-speculators. The subscribers to the circular, all farmers from eastern New York or New England, stressed the availability of "generally . . . very good quality and well watered" land, the ability "with a little industry" to produce maple sugar sufficient for each family's needs; the "cheap and convenient" availability of lumber from abundant pinewoods and "the great number of mill seats"; the quantity and fine quality of potashes to be procured from burning off the land, and which "frequently pay . . . for clearing the land"; the "excellence" of the land for a variety of crops; and the high yields of wheat that had been obtained. Recent migrants usually had a strong interest in encouraging others to join them. They did so in this case by stressing the extent to which they could recreate what they had experienced in their previous locations.[15]

Southern yeoman families, too, created new farm settlements just as they had been doing before the Revolution. In the South Carolina backcountry during the 1780s and 1790s, those who did so risked widening the distinctions between the state's coastal and interior regions that had helped cause internal divisions in the late colonial period. Over two decades, however, a mixture of factors helped reduce this potential rift in South Carolina's white society. Because settling interior land always involved significant labor, more prosperous yeoman farmers began to acquire slaves, usually in small numbers, to help with clearing and running their farms. Meanwhile planter families in the seaboard region, seeking new land for their own offspring, also moved slaves into the interior to clear and use land they acquired. After the mid-1790s this increased use of slaves was accelerated by the introduction of cotton cultivation, but it had begun before cotton became a significant product in the interior. Already in 1790, slaves accounted for 18 percent of South Carolina's interior population, and slaveholders were 23 percent of the region's white households. As the proportions of slaveholders continued to rise, and slaves continued to become a larger component of the interior population, marked social inequalities between whites became characteristic of the interior as well as the coast. Old tensions between the backcountry and the seaboard were ameliorated by the emergence of a social structure common to both.

Although migrants to the frontier often hoped for greater social equality than in older regions, frontier settlements often could not produce the kind of egalitarianism that republican theorists and advocates of freehold landholding anticipated. Levi Fay's move from Massachusetts to Vermont did not fulfill all his hopes. As his son-in-law later wrote, having "only acquired property sufficient to purchase his land and move his family there," Fay "consequently . . . was not able to help his children very much, but could only afford them a decent setting out (as it is generally call'd)." In western Pennsylvania by the mid-1780s one-tenth of taxpayers owned one-quarter of all real estate, and more than one in three adult men owned no land of their own. By the 1790s these inequalities had widened further: 41 percent of men were now landless, and the richest 10 percent of landowners held 35 percent of the land. In Otsego County, New York, almost one-quarter of voters in 1795 were tenants rather than landowners; by 1814 that proportion had increased to almost two-fifths, in a population that had meanwhile tripled. New settlements in the upper Susquehanna Valley consisted more of tenants than of independent farmers, and in many cases landlords also controlled local mills and transportation.[16]

Along the Appalachian frontier, relatively poor farm families moved to purchase or squat on backcountry land. In the Augusta-Rockbridge area of Virginia, the Adair family was landless in 1800, like more than half the households in the region. Between 1799 and 1805 they managed to accumulate sufficient means to emigrate and take up land in Ohio. But for many without land who moved west, migration did not improve matters. Kentucky had been settled from Virginia and elsewhere since the Revolution, and in 1792 achieved statehood. The settlement of the state replicated the distinctions in seaboard Southern society. Kentucky was marked by struggles between large and small settlers and by the competing aspirations of land speculators for profits and homesteaders' search for household independence.[17]

Poor migrants' fortunes much depended on where they settled and whether the land they began to farm was sought after by planters and others with the means to displace them. In the fertile region around

Lexington, Kentucky, known as the Bluegrass, wealthier migrants who began to establish large farms in the 1780s and early 1790s succeeded in driving out poorer squatters. Landownership in the Bluegrass became heavily skewed toward wealthy holders as state laws protected the interests of resident land speculators as well as permitting the introduction of slaves. By 1800 slaves constituted one-fifth of Kentucky's population, many of them employed on plantation-like estates growing hemp and other crops for shipment out of the region. For a period the Bluegrass contrasted with the development of the "Southside" that lay to the southwest, an area of smaller farms, many of them held by squatter-settlers who had been able to secure title to the land they worked under a 1795 preemption law. Like many in the uplands of the South, these yeoman farmers grew mixed crops and had access to hunting rights and other resources on open land. Compared with lowland regions, slavery was rare. During the early nineteenth century, however, the introduction of tobacco cultivation also began to commercialize the Southside. Here too the number of slaves and larger farmers grew, and property distribution became more unequal.[18]

Meanwhile the growth of slavery and of large plantations in central and northern Kentucky discouraged many small farmers from settling. Those who had moved there from Pennsylvania or Virginia considered moving across the Ohio River to the territory regulated by the Northwest Ordinance. On one hand, this migration provoked the conflicts with the Shawnee Indians and their allies that between 1791 and 1795 brought war to the Ohio country. On the other hand, it mirrored the class differences that were apparent in the westward movement from already unequal eastern regions. Small farmers sought the opportunity to avoid being overrun by wealthy planters. One group of squatters in Kentucky petitioned Congress for land in Ohio to avoid being made "Slaves to those Engrossers of Lands and to the Court of Virginia," which before Kentucky statehood regulated the terms of land settlement, often in large owners' favor. Among other things, the squatters could hope that the Northwest Ordinance's provision banning slavery north of the Ohio River would discourage large planters from following them and continuing to exploit the competitive advantage of slave labor. And for a time early Ohio was relatively egalitarian. In 1798 it had a higher proportion of landowners among its population than any other U.S. state or territory. But the actions of large speculators meant that even without slavery, Ohio faced growing inequalities. By 1810, 45 percent of adult men were landless, and one-quarter of taxable real estate was owned by a mere 1 percent of taxpayers.[19]

So enthusiasm for western settlement, though driven by a long-standing popular aspiration for land and by the constraints that had emerged in older-settled regions, was often tempered by hard realities. Above all, though the prospect of inexpensive, unsettled fertile land seemed to open opportunities for those who faced constrictions in eastern regions, people's ability to make use of those opportunities was still determined by their resources. Western settlement was most readily an option for those with some means. Slaveholders could do especially well if they were able to deploy their slaves' labor in rapid land clearance and the preparation of salable crops. Nonslaveowning households faced a more daunting task, and poor households especially so. Contemporaries often warned against the exaggerated claims of land promoters or noted the disparity between the hopes of emigrant settlers and the harsh conditions of the frontier. In Baltimore in 1803, a Scottish immigrant observed of newly arrived Highlanders making their way through the port to settle in the backcountry, "[T]hey expected riches and liberty, but found nothing but a struggle to keep themselves alive." The emotional burdens of migration, too, were often unequally shared. Although their experiences varied greatly, women were often seen either as more reluctant to migrate, or as standing to lose more from the breach with family ties than the menfolk who usually controlled decisions about whether and where their households should move. A Philadelphia woman who had left to settle in Tennessee in 1803 was told that her friends "mourn your departure as if you were dead . . . for they never expect to see you again in this world."[20]

Cities and the Sea

OTHER RURAL people, especially young men, migrated not just to find land but to seek out nonagricultural occupations away from home. Jackson Johonnet, born at Falmouth, Maine, around 1774, grew up in what he called a "large and expensive" family. His parents were poor, their farm "small and hard to cultivate," and their circumstances, as he drily noted, were "every way fitted to spare me to seek my fortune." In 1791 he boarded a schooner that took him down the coast to Boston, where he hoped to find work. As it happened, Johonnet did not stay long in the port city. Recruited into the army, he soon found himself fighting on the Ohio frontier, and would obtain brief fame as a survivor of captivity by Kickapoo Indians. But the path he took away from constricted home circumstances to the ocean and the port towns was one often followed by his generation.[21]

During the commercial prosperity of the 1790s the number of jobs at sea grew and would remain substantial for some time. As late as 1820, seamen constituted the nation's largest occupational group except for farmers. Many, like Jackson Johonnet, were sons of farm families who were unlikely to inherit their own land or other patrimony from their parents, or who sought to escape the drudgery of farm life. They joined still larger numbers of recruits from among the populations of port towns and coastal regions, including many for whom opportunities ashore were limited by poverty or prejudice. Of a sample of five hundred Philadelphia seamen who obtained mariners' certificates between 1798 and 1816, for example, 80 percent were wholly or partly illiterate, and 22 percent were African Americans.[22]

Port towns and maritime life had long been the most unequal and class-ridden settings, and this inequality was not reduced as commercial expansion proceeded. Entering service as a seaman usually entailed accepting work in the relatively large, structured organizations that late-eighteenth- and early-nineteenth-century vessels were. Over time, offshore fishing vessels, whalers, and merchant ships tended to grow in size and employ larger crews. Yet recruitment and the manning of vessels in small ports like Salem and Nantucket still followed household-based patterns: kinship was an aid to being taken on, and masters had usually begun their careers as ordinary seamen. But in the larger ports, and with the expansion of crew sizes and the emergence in whaling and long-distance trade of shipowners with several vessels under their control, an increasing proportion of seamen were unlikely to gain advancement to captaincies.[23]

Whaler crews, especially, accepted harsh conditions on voyages that grew in duration. As Atlantic whale stocks were hunted down and captains sought their catches in the Pacific, two- to three-year voyages became common. Whalemen also accepted lower wages than in other occupations, hoping that rich catches would afford them sufficient funds from the shares that were distributed among crews according to status, that they might obtain a stake to set up on land or in a trade of their own. In a republic that valued personal independence, the position of wage-earning seamen who were, while afloat, subject to rigorous discipline was seen as one of "dependency," like that of other wage workers, journeymen, and servants. Partly because he valued commerce more than manufactures, Thomas Jefferson regarded mariners as superior to artisans, but James Madison, reflecting on their harsh, disciplined lives, saw them as members of society least likely to achieve virtue. In many cases, maritime employment was a relatively short-term expedient for young men who hoped to resettle ashore; but numbers of sailors failed to obtain either masters' berths or the means to abandon life afloat. In Philadelphia between 1796 and 1819 about 10 percent of holders of mariners' certificates served at sea for ten years or more.[24]

Like Jackson Johonnet, other migrants from the countryside sought work in the port towns themselves. Larger centers such as Boston, New York, Philadelphia, and Baltimore grew rapidly on the basis of this rural migration, while in the Mid-Atlantic cities in particular, rural migrants joined a growing stream of immigrants from Europe. Baltimore's population doubled in the 1790s. Philadelphia's rose by 25,000 in the same period, almost four-fifths of the increase attributable to in-migration. Estimates suggest that between 1796 and 1800 migration to Philadelphia from the countryside and abroad together ran at an annual rate of 3.9 percent of the existing population. Observers in both cities worried about the increasing number of "masterless poor" and the potential danger to social order they appeared to pose. The passage of vagrancy laws and the creation of almshouses and other institutions reflected elite efforts to regulate this growing urban underclass. As in the Revolution, at times of war the poorer populations of towns became important sources of military recruitment, as Jackson Johonnet found in 1791 when, having arrived in Boston, he was soon persuaded to sign up for military service in Ohio.[25]

Cities were magnets for migrants because, particularly in times of prosperity, they held out good prospects of employment, and their commercial expansion drove the demand for labor of all kinds. Between the early 1790s and 1807 the value of goods imported to New York City multiplied five times and that of goods exported by ten times. The number of resident merchants in the city grew nearly fivefold in the 1790s alone, and other employment in docks and warehouses, at laboring and at hauling goods, in workshops and commercial businesses, grew rapidly to keep pace with the expansion of trade. But smaller ports and river-based trading centers burgeoned as well. New Haven, Connecticut, grew during a boom in the West Indies trade in the 1790s. In 1788 the city had 470 houses and 103 stores; ten years later there were 600 houses and 170 shops. The population of Albany, New York, long a vital trading post near the confluence of the Hudson and Mohawk rivers, and a stopping point for migrants heading west to new land, expanded nearly fourfold between 1790 and 1820, from 3,490 to 12,630. Between 1790 and 1810, those swelling the population of the town included an estimated 9,000 in-migrants from rural areas, many of them from western Connecticut and western Massachusetts, drawn to Albany to seek their livelihoods. In time many moved on to other places, but migration was an important source of the population growth of such smaller towns.[26]

Migration from country to town would also become characteristic of newer regions as they were opened up by farm settlement. A significant facet of the movement to new frontiers was the creation of new towns in the West which were peopled from the older states and from the farming districts around them. Rural migrants also traveled shorter distances, to county seats and village centers in their own regions, swelling the populations of small towns that were scattered across the countryside, finding employment as store clerks or as apprentices in a growing variety of handicraft trades. Often, migration to work at sea or in towns appeared similar to the people who undertook it. Whether they did it willingly or reluctantly, migration could mark a break with familiar patterns of kinship and family support. Gorham A. Worth, who arrived in Albany from the countryside in 1800, aged eighteen, later used in a memoir the notion of going to sea as a metaphor for his new urban career. "Never shall I forget the deep feeling of loneliness that came over me," he wrote, "when the receding headlands of my native bay disappeared in the distance, and I found myself . . . alone on the waters."[27]

Intensification in Rural Societies

EVEN AS these migrations to the frontier, to towns, or to maritime work accelerated during the post-Revolutionary decades, most rural people stayed where they were. Across New England, for example, in the early nineteenth century, on average between 50 and 60 percent of households persisted each decade in the localities in which they were living. (Because those who "disappeared" include those who died as well as those who moved, such figures understate the degree of family continuity.) Although some regions, such as older parts of the Chesapeake and some districts in upland New England, suffered relative stagnation as cultivation and population growth shifted elsewhere, in few places did population actually decline in this period, or farms not continue to be created and cultivated. Nevertheless the majority of people who did not permanently migrate still had to deal with the constraints their societies experienced. They did so by intensifying their efforts to earn livelihoods from the soil and other resources at hand.[28]

Across the Northeast and Mid-Atlantic region, where farm households depended most on family labor, this intensification often took the form of switching to new crops or activities that could raise the incomes or product of the household. In parts of eastern Pennsylvania that had become heavily settled, many farm households took up dairying, using the labor of their female members to process milk into cheese and butter to be sent for sale ultimately in the region's growing urban markets. Similar developments occurred in parts of New England. Starting with some "gentlemen farmers" and the agricultural organizations they created, and disseminated through an emerging agricultural literature and new pattern of farming exhibitions, efforts were made to experiment with and spread information about crops, livestock, and methods of husbandry. During the first two decades of the nineteenth century, fertility rates and population growth in Eastern rural areas remained high, both creating demand for output and supplying labor to meet it.[29]

In the South, where slave labor was available to the farm households who owned it, the processes of intensification were different. They followed the patterns of staple production for export that were already established in the plantation-zone economies. In parts of Virginia, where gentry fortunes had declined after the Revolution with the fall in tobacco markets, elite women joined in the conduct and organization of income-earning activities for their households, supervising slave and servant labor. In the northern Chesapeake regions that had switched from tobacco to wheat cultivation, new techniques included the substitution of plowing for hoeing. New crops, and new balances between crops and livestock raising, also led to new tensions in rural areas: Delaware, for example, faced a protracted struggle after 1816 over attempts—ultimately successful—to close the open range and require livestock to be fenced or tethered to protect crops. In the coastal areas of South Carolina and Georgia, where rice growing had already developed in the colonial period, the emergence of plantations with large slave populations, and the development of water control and planting techniques, ensured the expansion of rice production. The addition in 1803 of the Louisiana Territory to the United States included the region around New Orleans and the Mississippi River delta that would quickly become a center of plantation-based sugar cultivation. But by far the most important development, occurring initially in older regions of the slave states, was the expansion of cotton growing.[30]

Cotton had been raised in the eighteenth-century South, but it was of a particular "long staple" variety that could be cultivated successfully only in coastal areas such as the Sea Islands of South Carolina and Georgia. As they began to settle interior regions more intensively in the 1780s and 1790s, Lowcountry planters sought practical ways of growing cotton inland. The short-staple variety could be cultivated, but it produced intermixed fibers and seeds that were time-consuming and expensive to separate. The development of cotton gins, simple machines to accomplish this task—the best known was invented by a Connecticut mechanic, Eli Whitney, working in Georgia in 1793—made practicable the large-scale cultivation of short-staple cotton. By the turn of the century the expansion of cotton growing had begun dramatically to reshape the South's economy and society.

The intensification of activities in rural societies facing economic constraints was not limited to the introduction of new crops and cultivation methods. Household manufactures were also important. The French visitor Brissot de Warville noted in 1788 that in central Massachusetts "almost all . . . houses are inhabited by men who are both cultivators and artisans." In Farmington, Connecticut, between 1788 and 1790, Eli Woods kept accounts that showed the work he did for others as a clothier, fulling, dyeing, and pressing cloth, and the payments he received in exchange—firewood, grain, and other produce from his farming neighbors. In New Castle County, Delaware, in the 1790s, probate records suggest that just under half of estates included spinning wheels and about 9 percent had looms for weaving cloth. Home textile production retained a position in the region's rural economy that it had held for at least thirty years. But there had been a slight shift in the distribution of these tools; whereas once their presence had been roughly correlated with wealth, now they were more concentrated in wealthy or in poorer families, rather than in those of middling wealth. This suggests that household manufacturing had become an important part of the exchange relationships between households. Work was either done in prosperous families or "put out" to be conducted in poorer ones, so wealthier households were able to draw on their neighborhoods' skills to get work done for them. In Hadley, Massachusetts, Elizabeth Porter Phelps, whose husband owned six hundred acres of farm and woodland, employed some sixty different servants and needleworkers in her household over the half-century before her death in 1812. Of these about half were engaged in producing clothing, most of them young women from families in the locality who expected to work until they were married and then move on to run their own households.³¹

Efforts turned in the direction of manufacturing in all regions, but most particularly in New England where agricultural developments often remained hampered by less fertile soils and more modest commercial markets for crops. Pressure of settlement on landholdings and the difficulty faced especially by poorer individuals and households in making a living from their own resources led to a proliferation of craft occupations, seasonal petty manufacturing, and itinerant working and selling. These activities engaged both men and women in varied tasks and skills. Across the countryside a range of manufacturing activities grew up alongside farming within the structure of the household-based economy. Out of existing rural activities such as blacksmithing, leather working, wheel making, coopering, and milling grew small manufacturers of metal goods, hides, harnesses, shoes, textiles, tools, wagons, furniture, and wooden goods of all kinds. In Ridgefield, Connecticut, around

1800, Samuel G. Goodrich's family could call on the services of a range of local producers. In Massachusetts an overwhelming proportion of the 4.1 million yards of cloth recorded in 1810 was produced in rural households. Horace Greeley later recalled his mother, on their family's rented farm in Bedford, New Hampshire, spinning and weaving a roll of linen from their own farm's flax as late as 1819.[32]

Certain features were common to these manufacturing activities. They were usually adjuncts to farming, and some were linked directly to the intensification of agricultural production. In the Connecticut River Valley of Massachusetts, some farmers began to grow broomcorn, to be manufactured into brooms. After about 1804, when Levi Dickinson of Hadley successfully marketed locally made brooms on a trip to Baltimore, broom making expanded as a seasonal activity in this and neighboring towns. Such activities were often seasonal, and individual manufacturers operated only on a small scale. Manufacturing might be a winter task or carried out by one or more members of a household whose other members were running a farm. Local division of labor or dependence on activity elsewhere was not uncommon. Broom makers bought broom handles from other makers in the hill towns around the Connecticut Valley. Chair and wagon makers sometimes specialized in making particular parts, or relied on itinerant painters to come and finish their work. All such efforts remained closely linked to the activities of farm households. In Sutton, Massachusetts, as late as 1830, 85 percent of the town's workshops were owned by farmers.[33]

But in addition there grew up more specialized activities, often drawing on locally produced materials and concerned with making goods that were not previously available or required for farming itself. Depending on the source of raw materials, skills, and exchange networks, these activities often grew in clusters and became associated with particular localities or regions. In southwestern Connecticut, furniture makers flourished in the rural towns of Newtown and Woodbury—though owing to different levels of skill and different social characteristics, craftsmen in the two towns catered to distinct markets and used different production techniques. Belchertown, Massachusetts, became a center of wagon making. Among towns in Franklin County, Massachusetts, Shelburne and Buckland became known for cutlery, axes, and scythe snaths; Erving for tools; Orange for pails and other woodenware; and Whately for pottery. Other districts featured the making of chairs, whips, leather, straw hats, and other goods.[34]

Whether of agriculture or manufacturing, intensification placed particular burdens on rural women. There were "too many tasks for too few workers" in most rural households, and women often bore the brunt of the extra load. Eighteenth-century economic writers perpetuated a myth that women were underutilized in household-based economies; this was reflected in the claim by Alexander Hamilton in his 1791 "Report on Manufactures" that women and children could be "rendered more useful . . . than they would otherwise be," by being put to work in manufacturing establishments. In fact, women in the early republic faced an increasing range of tasks related both to production and to the reproduction of their families. Child-rearing, cooking, feeding, instructing children, and nursing were prodigious obligations. In 1800 more than one-third of the U.S. population was aged nine or under, and fertility rates were rising. Ideological changes also placed increasing value on cleanliness and on the virtues of "republican motherhood," which charged women with the moral responsibility for raising good citizens. The processing of crops, horticulture, dairying, and the manufacture of yarn, cloth, soap, and other items assumed increasing importance as pressure on households to raise and diversify production grew. Numerous schemes to introduce silk production in America were floated from the eighteenth century on, often to put women and children to useful labor. But, except in regions like eastern Connecticut, where women in farm households were able to make silk-raising and manufacture part of their annual routines, success was scattered or short-lived. "Idle" women and children were, in fact, too scarce. Even in urban areas such as New York and Philadelphia, several attempts in the 1790s to establish manufactories using women and children's labor failed for want of recruits.[35]

Skilled men and women circulated in rural areas to seek work or practice their crafts. Jedidiah Baldwin, born in Connecticut in 1769, was first apprenticed to a clockmaker in the small port town of Norwich, then moved to Northampton, Massachusetts, and then in 1793 established his own workshop in the upper Connecticut River town of Hanover, New Hampshire, on the state's newly settled frontier. Here he had his own journeymen and apprentices, employing up to seven at one time, including young men who circulated in the region, as Baldwin himself had done, to practice their craft. After the trade embargo of 1807 and impending war with Britain disrupted the demand for luxury goods, Baldwin moved from New Hampshire to New York State in an effort to reestablish his business there. Among skilled craftsmen like Baldwin, migration did not just follow common patterns from country-side to frontier or town, but formed a more complex thread of connec-tions through diversifying rural regions.[36]

Three Paths

EXPANSION, MIGRATION, and intensification of production repre-sented three kinds of responses to post-Revolutionary America's social conditions. Many individuals and families took the path their own cir-cumstances dictated, but it is noteworthy that these three paths were not distinct choices. A considerable number of New England and Mid-Atlantic families had offspring who, between them, took all three, and there were indeed many individuals who tried all three at different stages of their lives. The Rhode Island Revolutionary soldier Jeremiah Green-man was an example. After the war he set up a retail business in Provi-dence, doubtless hoping to rise with the revival of commerce in this growing port town. But, like many others, the business failed. Green-man turned to the sea, shipping out as a seaman and in time rising to be-come captain of a seagoing vessel. In 1806, with his sons now grown, he moved the family to land in Ohio. Circumstance left him and his sons on poor farms, leading him to plead a "truly distressing . . . Cituation" when he applied for his war pension in the early 1820s.[37]

The considerable economic and social changes in the early years of the republic were still rooted in the social structures that had taken shape during the colonial period. Important regional differences had en-sured distinctive adaptations to North America's common structural fea-ture: the shortage of labor in relation to land. Although compulsion based on gender, class, and racial inequalities could be found across early America, in New England, the Mid-Atlantic region, and the South dif-ferent patterns of enforced labor had evolved to cope with this shortage. New household-based activities in older regions made use of labor more intensively. Migration to towns and cities from rural regions and abroad reduced labor shortages in certain places. Migration to the west and settlement of new farmland, on the other hand, extended the nation's geography, added massively to the amount of work that needed to be done, and kept labor scarce even in a rapidly growing population. As the historian Alan Taylor has pointed out, between 1780 and 1820 "American settlers occupied, cleared, and farmed more land . . . than in the preceding 180 years of colonization." Dramatic as it was, the size and scope of this expansion helped sustain the key characteristics of social structures in all regions.[38]

The effect of these developments was to reinforce regional differences rather than erase them. This is indicated by the continued unevenness of the nation's labor markets. When the builders of the Schuylkill Canal near Philadelphia ran short of men to hire in the mid-1790s, they decided to look in New England for laborers, but without success. Labor was even scarcer there than in their own region. Rural New England, where wages were relatively high, pursued more intensified activities with intermittent hiring and the household-based labor of women and children. In the Delaware Valley wheat districts, despite generally lower wage rates, seasonal variations in labor demand and supply, coupled with competition for general laborers from farms and the coastal carrying trade, inspired flour millers like Oliver Evans to develop labor-saving devices to reduce the need for hiring. An employer there complained in 1795 that, even though work was sometimes scarce, hired hands were "all masters[,] and must not be told their duty otherwise theyl goe away." Evans's machinery for flour milling, which automated various procedures previously done by hand, attracted considerable notice in the early 1790s. Within a few years of his parading a model of his mill through the streets of Wilmington, Evans found his machinery in use in some one hundred mills on Mid-Atlantic coasts and waterways. Even though labor in the region was relatively plentiful and wages comparatively low, many flour millers favored mechanization as a way of reducing their degree of dependence on a casual, itinerant, or unskilled labor force.[39]

Different regions' paths to growth or development also influenced one another in ways that could deepen the contrasts between them. The intensification of manufacturing activity in the Northeast would quickly lead to that region's emergence as the nation's leading industrial zone.

After 1810, when the value of manufactures produced in the Northern and Southern states still remained roughly comparable, the Northeast would draw away and leave Southern manufacturing behind it. Part of the reasons for this lay in the structure and character of Northern societies, especially in the countryside, but it also rested on the growth of the South—especially the plantation South—as an important market for manufactured goods. As the slave population began to expand and slaveholders devoted more attention to the production of staple crops for export, they sought cheap sources of clothing, shoes, and other basic supplies for their slaves. At first many of these goods were imported from Britain, but by the early nineteenth century small manufacturers in New England and the Mid-Atlantic region were also furnishing such supplies. Men like Arial Bragg of Brookline, Massachusetts, just outside Boston; Moses Combs of Newark, New Jersey; and John Bedford, a master cordwainer in Philadelphia, built up shoemaking businesses in part by supplying "Negro shoes" for the Southern market. For newcomers to the industry, such business could be ideal. The slaveholders who ultimately purchased Bragg's or Combs's shoes were more interested in cheapness than in quality, and the slaves, who had to wear them, had no means of complaining about shoddy goods. As Bragg himself wrote, "little regard [was] paid to the quality either of stock, or work." But the slave-supplies market provided an incubator for the acquisition of greater skill and experience by manufacturers. Shoemakers and others who succeeded in this business often turned to higher-quality, more lucrative work as their abilities improved, and so laid the foundations of industries that would come to supply widespread and growing domestic markets in the decades to come.[40]

New Structures, New Identities

THE THREE-WAY trajectories of America's regional economies—out-migration, migration to towns, and intensification—positioned the United States for a varied pattern of further regional developments as the nineteenth century unfolded. Out of these different trajectories emerged the diversity of the nation's subsequent history. So far, growth and commercial development had occurred essentially within the social frameworks and relationships of the Revolutionary period. By the 1820s, however, new patterns of social structure and identity were becoming apparent.

In one sense these reflected the rapid growth of land area and population. Eleven new states joined the original thirteen during the three decades from 1791 to 1821. The country's total population rose by almost 158 percent between 1790 and 1820, from 3.9 million to just over 10 million. But the age structure of the post-Revolutionary population had been such that some groups had grown more rapidly. In the same period, for example, the number of white males aged sixteen or over increased by 173 percent, from .8 million to 2.2 million. White immigration to the United States, though growing, was still running at a relatively low level and accounted for only about 10 percent of this increase. Natural increase, the consequence of high birthrates and comparatively low mortality rates, was responsible for the bulk of this population expansion.[41]

The nation's growth and geographic expansion were bringing about a shift in the concentration of its activities. Before the Revolution and again up to the 1807 trade embargo and the War of 1812 that followed it, the United States was primarily a seaboard nation with an important focus on Atlantic commerce. Coastal and Atlantic trade indeed remained highly important after peace returned in 1815, but historians have noted a "continental turn" in the nation's economic focus, a shift toward recognizing and exploiting the importance of internal settlement and production. As people settled land in the Great Lakes and trans-Appalachian regions, the center of population shifted westward. The value of American overseas trade—its total exports and imports of goods—increased by 5.6 times between 1790 and 1807, and while its value per capita of population in 1790 had been roughly that at the eve of the Revolution, by 1807 this had trebled. After the resumption of uninterrupted trade in 1815, its total value continued to grow rapidly, and it multiplied more than 11 times by 1836. But its value per capita was much lower than it had been before 1807 and would not resume those levels before the Civil War. At its peak, in 1836, the per capita value of overseas trade was only 63 percent of its 1807 level. Internal production and commercial activities had grown to have more prominent roles.[42]

Democratization

THE CONTESTS during the Revolution between elites and other citizens continued to shape American political culture during the early decades of the republic. The Revolution had challenged the more hierarchical assumptions of the colonial period but did not destroy the notion that some men were better fitted by birth, education, wealth, or accomplishment to exercise leadership over others. Federalists in the 1790s had been the most active exponents of this position, but many of their Democratic-Republican opponents had also subscribed to the concept of a "natural aristocracy" fitted to lead by its achievement of the virtues that would guarantee the republic's safety and stability. So the defeat of the Federalists in the election of 1800, and their subsequent long decline in influence and importance, did not end the tussle between elite and democratic notions of government and citizenry. Gentry rule and hierarchical notions survived. In a slander case before the Massachusetts Supreme Court in 1807, for example, the Federalist chief justice, Theophilus Parsons, ruled against an argument that all citizens were due equal treatment. Evidence of a plaintiff's "rank and condition of life" was admissible in court, Parsons found, "because the degree of injury the plaintiff may sustain by . . . defamation may very much depend on his rank and condition in society." In this case, according to Parsons, "in the manner of gaining subsistence, and in his grade and standing with society," the man who had brought suit "was below mediocrity," and so less likely to be injured by slanders than someone of greater substance.[43]

But claims for "equal rights" and resistance to hierarchical assumptions about status and rank became more common after the Revolution. The story was told in New England of a Congregational minister from Boston who, facing financial difficulties, moved in 1795 to a church in rural New Hampshire where his living costs would be low. But his family's social airs quickly put him at odds with his new parishioners. It became known, for instance, that his household servants ate separately from his family rather than at the same table, as was customary in the countryside. After a few years he gave up and returned to town, to a milieu less intolerant of his "aristocratic" leanings. New concepts, which some historians have called "producerism," distinguished between active producers of wealth and those who lived by the wealth produced by others. They considerably influenced political debate, giving rise to popular claims of allegiance to democratic values and criticism of "aristocracy." Trade societies and artisans' clubs celebrated the virtue of men who worked with their hands and put their skills into production. Men such as these popularized the works and memory of the eighteenth-century scientist and patriot Benjamin Franklin as an emblem of the possibility that workingmen could rise from obscurity to prominence by their own efforts and abilities. Writers such as William Findlay and William Manning condemned the influence of those with "unearned income" and advocated the rights of producers to participate in politics.[44]

The election of 1800 helped unleash a long process of political democratization that resumed the steps the Revolution had taken in this direction. Participation in elections rose rapidly in the first decade of the new century; of the men qualified to vote, record numbers turned out to do so. Significant changes also took place in the qualifications for voters or officeholders. Property qualifications for the franchise were reduced or abolished in many states. In Virginia, James Madison urged a constitutional convention in 1821 to extend the franchise to the propertyless because "there are various ways in which the rich may oppress the poor; in which property may oppress liberty. . . . It is necessary that the poor should have a defence against the danger." There was opposition. An 1821 New York constitutional convention heard from the jurist James Kent, speaking on behalf of upstate gentry, that unleashing the "evil genius of democracy" would hand over power to "men of no property" who would plunder the rich and enable debtors to "relax or avoid the obligation of contracts." Five years later, however, a constitutional amendment removed the last obstacles to white manhood suffrage in the state. After 1829, apart from some surviving restrictions in Virginia and South Carolina, only Rhode Island had not taken the path to universal white male suffrage. The direct influence of religion and religious elites in politics was also reduced. The separation of church and state, pioneered in Jefferson's Virginia and guaranteed at the federal level in the Constitution, not only became an operative principle in newly created states but was extended to older ones as well. When Connecticut and Massachusetts severed their final ties to established churches in 1818 and 1833 respectively, the last vestiges of formal colonial-era connections between churches and government were abolished.[45]

Democratization and disestablishment reflected the ability of white men, including workingmen, to force their way into the political arena. Even as the "politics of the street" that marked the Revolutionary Era was being superseded by the networks of clubs, caucuses, and political meetings associated with the creation of political parties and their domination of politics, new franchise arrangements assured broader popular participation. Criticism of opponents for advocating "aristocratic" privileges—such as in a petition of Delaware tenants and small landowners for the suspension of sheriff sales in 1818—became a frequent feature of political discourse. The election of Andrew Jackson in 1828 marked the emergence of the first "popular" president, born and raised in the mountains and in the West rather than in the world of the old seaboard elites. Jackson's electoral victory marked the success of the contention that the majority of the people, rather than the wisdom of the "best men," was the appropriate safeguard against the accumulation of privilege.

Exclusion

THE "PEOPLE," however, did not in political terms mean everyone. The broadening of political culture in the early decades of the nineteenth century embraced most white men but accompanied a pattern of excluding other groups from such participation or recognition in public life. Since the 1790s, for example, free blacks in Philadelphia and New York had experienced prejudice in the churches that led many of them to withdraw and establish separate black denominations. New Jersey, Rhode Island, and Maine all limited blacks' voting rights. The 1821 New York convention that moved toward universal white male suffrage by reducing property qualifications for voting simultaneously raised the requirements that black males had to fulfill. It is estimated that of almost 12,500 black men in Manhattan in 1826, only 16 met the $250 property requirement that the state constitution imposed. A constitutional reform convention in Pennsylvania in 1838 effectively disfranchised those black males who had until then qualified to vote in the state. Many other signs in the first decades of the nineteenth century indicated a deepening hostility to men and women of color and the closing of economic and cultural opportunities that had briefly seemed available as Northern slavery declined. The Albany town council's 1811 prohibition of the celebration of the black holiday Pinkster; the activities of the English-born New York plasterer William Otter, who went out on "sprees" tricking or beating blacks for fun, and who later worked as a slave-catcher; and the incidence of race riots in towns like Providence in the 1820s and 1830s all denoted enhanced racial divisions in Northern society.[46]

Exclusion by race was accompanied by more subtle patterns of exclusion by gender. Not least because of the limits on their legal standing, women had rarely participated directly in politics; the one state, New Jersey, that had granted the vote to some women property holders abolished the privilege in 1807, just as it was broadening the franchise for men. There is evidence that economic opportunities for women also narrowed. In Bucks County, Pennsylvania, wills made at the end of the eighteenth century were less likely than those of the early colonial period to protect provisions for widows if there were sons to whom resources might be passed instead. In late-eighteenth-century New York and Philadelphia, as many as one-third of trade advertisements in newspapers were placed by women, but this proportion later fell. The "gender gap" between men's and women's wage rates appears to have widened between the Revolution and 1815. Reforms in Philadelphia in the 1820s reduced poor relief other than in workhouses and hence restricted poor women's independent ability to head their own households. Philadelphia widows in the 1820s were engaged in a narrower variety of economic activities than those of their predecessors in the 1790s, suggesting that as household production began to be superseded by other institutions, women's roles became more constricted. Various evangelical churches, set up on relatively informal lines before or during the Revolution, tightened their organizational structures and became formal denominations from the 1790s on; in the process they also required women to accept limits on the roles they could exercise. Just as voting rights and the conduct of political parties gave overwhelming prominence to white men and their "equal rights" as citizens, practices in economic and political life characterized other people as inferior in standing.[47]

Yet the constrictions were not entire. Even as they were excluded from voting, officeholding, or real power, women managed to carve out quasi-public roles in the conduct of political and civic life. Churches too, especially in the revivals known as the Second Great Awakening, became arenas where women had profound influence even as they remained under formal male leadership. In voluntary associations of all kinds, women often played important roles. These organizations came to embody many of the reform movements that would markedly affect public life and political debate in the decades before the Civil War, concerning matters from education and alcohol consumption to the abolition of slavery. It was over slavery, too, that black churches and organizations, and black participation in wider reform associations, would begin to have an effect from the 1820s onward. The English traveler Henry Fearon reported hearing during his visit to the United States in the late 1810s of a man who called at a house and asked a woman servant where her "mistress" was, only to meet the riposte: "I have no mistress, nor master either. . . . In this country there is no mistresses or masters; I guess I am a woman citizen."[48]

That there had been a sea change in popular consciousness was indicated by several events in the 1820s. The Marquis de Lafayette, the French general whose career had begun in the American Revolutionary War, toured the United States in 1824–1825, an aristocrat feted by crowds as a popular hero wherever he traveled in the republic. The fiftieth anniversary of Independence on the Fourth of July 1826 brought the deaths that very day of John Adams and Thomas Jefferson, the only two presidents who were also signers of the Declaration of Independence. Many regarded the extraordinary coincidence as providential, a mark of a generation's passing. Even as universal white manhood suffrage was emerging on the political scene, other groups were beginning to assert their own identities as claimants to participation in the life of the republic. The 1820s saw the first publication of newspapers and periodicals by African Americans, by women, by advocates of the labor movement, even by Native Americans. In one way or another, as winners or as losers in emerging struggles for power, these groups would come to play a significant role in the evolution of American social structures.[49]

Institutional Change and Social Relations

ROOTED AS it was in household structures, the post-Revolutionary economy continued largely to rely, like that of the colonial period, on transactions conducted within the framework of personal relationships. In farming regions, many transactions were carried on between neighbors or kin. Arrangements for obtaining farm labor and household help, or for buying or borrowing items of food or tools, were negotiated locally, mostly among people who had had long-term dealings. Many of these transactions were informal, but when they were recorded they often represented running exchanges of credit and debt, and settlement of accounts over long periods of time. Where transactions took place up or down the social hierarchy, many of the same conditions applied, but there were aspects of patronage and clientage involved. Southern planters constructed political allegiances around their transactions with the yeoman farmers and tenants near their estates. Even in New England, where there was relatively greater equality, political leaders might dispense patronage or favors to clients and expect electoral support for them in return. Exchange dealings between known individuals were regarded as helping ensure the stability and integrity of transactions; dealing with strangers could risk deceit or fraud.[50]

Most long-distance exchanges, between merchants in country towns and port cities, or across the ocean to Europe, were also conducted in ways that sought to replicate the security of face-to-face local transactions. Merchants sought to establish personal connections with those they dealt with, whom they often referred to as "correspondents" and with whom they sought long-term relationships. If their business was large, they might send family members or trusted partners to handle affairs for them in a distant place. Otherwise the conduct and etiquette of commercial relations emphasized the creation of familiarity at a distance, with elaborate personal recommendations and efforts to assure correspondents of good faith and good standing. When difficulties arose, those involved were quick to suspect the breakdown of standards of honesty and integrity. In 1805 the Philadelphia monthly meeting of Quakers deplored a spate of "failures and bankruptcies . . . among us," which it attributed to "engaging in hazardous undertakings out of the counsel and wisdom of truth."[51]

Transactions were linked to networks of personal relationships by the extension of credit. This combination of connections and credit created what the English historian Craig Muldrew has called "an economy of obligations": a complex web of financial relationships that were also personal and depended on the behavior and reputation of those who took part in them. Commercial dealings, especially in towns, at crossroads, and at landing places, often took place in taverns and other gathering points. There was a widespread notion that commerce was sociable. One reason for the growing popularity of the writings of Benjamin Franklin in this period was his emphasis on maintaining one's reputation in an economy formed of chains of personal connections.[52]

The post-Revolutionary expansion of population and thus the number of transactions brought about powerful but subtle changes in these social relations of trade. As the scale and scope of commercial activities increased, crucial changes in the ways they were conducted arose from the complex consequences of trading in a system of personal relationships. On one hand, because personal connections assisted trade and those conducting it, some of the changes reflected efforts to extend the personal character of business. But conducting transactions in a fixed personal framework also entailed risks, not least that obligations might be incurred to people chosen not for their economic or financial abilities but because of a personal connection alone. In some contexts, therefore, personal transactions came to seem constraining, and individuals sought methods for escaping them.

Dealings on credit involved personal obligations from which cash dealings were a liberation. But cash was often a rare commodity, to be conserved for specific uses. Farmers and merchants conducted business on credit, when possible extending the informal mechanisms of personal exchange to create circulating paper instruments. Promissory notes, bills of exchange, and other paper documents circulated regularly among chains of dealers. Legal decisions promoted this circulation. The Supreme Judicial Court of Massachusetts ruled in an 1808 judgment that "the circulation of negotiable paper is extremely useful to trade, as it multiplies commercial credit. . . . Any rule of law, tending unnecessarily to repress this circulation is therefore against public policy." But creating a circulating medium by such means entailed substantial risks for anyone who had signed over (or "endorsed") promissory notes in the process of passing them on from hand to hand. Complex rules governed the liability of endorsers for debts represented by the notes they had signed, and individuals could accordingly be exposed to risks from other people's misfortunes or frauds. Court cases arising out of indebtedness and paper obligations multiplied.[53]

People took various steps to regularize such personal entanglements, to avoid them altogether, or to provide institutional substitutes for them. Advice literature stressed the need for clear written records and communication. As one newspaper editor suggested, "Every man, whether Farmer, Mechanic, or Merchant, who has dealings with the world, ought to know how he stands in relation to it. And in order to do this, he should keep, with precision, honesty, and neatness, a set of account books." But advice was not limited to matters of technique. There was a growing strand of criticism of the attention to personal feelings and connections that had governed transactions but that also seemed to limit success. If someone's debt to you was due, ask for payment, one advice manual suggested. Do not, through "false delicacy" or "indolence," delay seeking it, or "depend on being paid without [asking] for it. . . . [F]ear of giving offence by asking the payment of honest dues, should never be indulged."[54]

Some commentators urged avoidance of personal entanglement whenever possible, other than when sound business calculation would sanction it. "From the commencement of my [career]," claimed the successful Boston merchant and manufacturer Amos Lawrence, "I practised upon the maxim, '*Business before friends.*'" One merchant's manual suggested that the "fair . . . , steady . . . man of business" should "leave to others" the sociable granting of hospitality, frequent loans, or extended credit. After nearly being ruined by the practice, the Philadelphia printer and economist Mathew Carey embarked on a long campaign against excessively endorsing paper for others. By the 1830s, commercial advice literature was replete with the discouragement of giving personal favors, or informal borrowing and lending. "There is no *friendship* in trade," one author claimed.[55]

Men reflected on their conscious efforts to step outside the entanglements of personal connections. James Guild, who left his home in

Tunbridge, Vermont, in 1818 to begin a lonely career as a peddler, left behind what he described as a trail of financial embarrassment and involvement with friends who frequented the village tavern, "content and happy . . . strongly attached to one another, with 'no ambition to shine.'" But relatively few followed Guild's path to economic independence through such individualism. More commonly they sought to create, through institutions, new circles of trust that might offer a degree of security while limiting their obligations.[56]

The spread of freemasonry after the Revolution, from the port towns to smaller inland centers, created new patterns of sociability and fraternity not necessarily connected with kin or neighborhood obligations. Masonic lodges, with their male membership, frequently served as venues for business transactions, at least until an alleged murder in New York State and suspicion of secret organizations fomented a widespread anti-masonic movement after the mid-1820s. Banks had not existed before the Revolution and were founded in very small numbers in the main towns in the 1780s, but they became more common by the early nineteenth century. By 1811 there were almost 90 in the United States, and their numbers then grew rapidly, to nearly 400 by 1818. In New England alone, where there were 15 banks in 1800, 96 existed in 1820, and 324 in 1837. Insurance companies and mortgage lending institutions also grew in number and influence by the 1820s. Banks, issuing notes against their capital and deposits, became circulators of paper money that, though it might be risky and was frequently counterfeited, disentangled its holders from some of the personal connections associated with promissory notes and endorsements.[57]

Banks' functions varied from region to region with different economic and legal frameworks, but an important role for many of them, not least in New England, was to lend money to the men who founded them or their close associates. This pattern of "insider lending" denoted an effort to continue the business of lending to known associates by separating it from older attachments to kin, family, or neighborhood. When Richard Clough Anderson became director of a bank in Louisville, Kentucky, in 1815, his first act was to refuse a loan that his brother-in-law had sought on the strength of their personal connection. Although he was "most friendly and benevolent" and "a kind kinsman [who would] go . . . far to aid a friend or a stranger," Anderson knew that his relative was in financial trouble: "I am so thoroughly convinced that not only all his property will be swallowed by his debts but that his friends who are assisting him must . . . be materially injured in the Shipwreck that I cannot agree to the request." Business considerations and obligations to his commercial partners led Anderson to relegate personal connections to a more private sphere, and to resist his brother-in-law's expectation that kinship might outweigh other calculations. Such decisions marked incremental movements in a long process of disentangling the claims of commerce from the claims of personal obligation.[58]

Self-reliance and Self-control

INSTITUTIONAL DEVELOPMENTS like these were laying the foundations of a commercial economy not primarily rooted in personal connections. An 1830 newspaper article lectured farmers and artisans on the proper way to conduct business: "Let every man take care of himself, and then every man will be taken care of; but when a man entrusts his pecuniary matters to the care of the public, he must make up his mind to starve." This trend toward impersonal business relations was by no means complete, however. While households and individuals remained the focus of most economic activity, personal connections could not fail to remain important. But the emergence of ideas about individual responsibility and the notion of self-reliance came about in conjunction with various other changes. The expansion of population and the volume of transactions played a part, but long-distance and complex dealings were not new in this period and had been handled earlier by personal networks. The effects of population growth and the expansion of settlement did, however, draw attention to the constraints and risks inherent in local, personal dealings, and the apparent opportunities to be gained from breaking away from these. They also suggested the advantages that those with means might gain by pulling out of older patterns of obligation and creating new institutions, such as banks, that they hoped might prove both lucrative and safe from the claims of personal ties.[59]

Accompanying these changes were new concepts about individual standing embodied in the theology of religious revivals and the evangelicalism of the Second Great Awakening. Starting in the 1790s in parts of

the South and the trans-Appalachian West, new religious stirrings revived the lagging fortunes of American Christianity. Established denominations, such as the Baptists and Presbyterians, shared in an upsurge of
religious enthusiasm that also embraced and expanded newer groups, including the Methodists, whose rapid growth in the late eighteenth and
early nineteenth centuries made them the nation's largest denomination.
The spirit of the religious revivals also spread to older-settled regions,
and older churches, and in due course would also become strong in rapidly growing commercial and industrial towns. By the 1830s evangelists
like Charles Grandison Finney, who directed his efforts particularly at
winning converts in urban areas, had become nationally known figures.
Under the influence of the revival, religious observance and church attendance rose from their low points in the Revolutionary period. Denominations proliferated and flourished; new groupings sprang up, and
the more established evangelical sects strengthened markedly.

The varieties and social connections of religious observance and experience also multiplied: there was no single unifying theme to the
process. But one set of changes did underlie the emergence of revivalism, and that was the undermining of older beliefs about religious and
cultural authority. Above all, in the Congregational and Presbyterian
churches of New England, and in parts of the Baptist denomination,
people moved away from the strict Calvinism of much colonial-era belief. From a faith in salvation as the sole gift of God, over which human
action could have no influence, there evolved a range of positions that
placed the responsibility for salvation and the possibility of attaining it
more firmly in individuals' hands. The contention that personal actions
and beliefs could influence the possibilities for salvation passed responsibility for individual souls from God toward those individuals themselves. To many early-nineteenth-century Americans, in different social
contexts, such beliefs provided analogies for understanding the character of social as well as spiritual interactions and responsibilities.

Thus during the decades following the Revolution, the republican idea
of "independence" (as distinct from "dependency") as the basis of citizenship became modified, on one hand by the more democratic notion of
equal standing and equal rights, and on the other by the concept of achieving salvation by personal action. Self-reliance was only one component of
an ideology that also stressed self-responsibility and self-control. This in

turn had two dimensions. The notion of self-control as self-discipline underpinned movements such as that for temperance reform, strongly promoted by evangelicals, which urged individuals to assume control over their own selves by moderating or renouncing the use of alcohol. Similarly, the notion of self-control as self-ownership would shape the call, which became more audible in the 1820s and grew to a crescendo in the 1830s, for the abolition of slavery—that extreme form of dispossession of the self. Underlying these calls were profound distinctions in attitudes to labor and the character of compulsion.

CHAPTER 4

Two Directions for Labor

S LAVERY BECAME an issue for reform as the United States' differ-ent regional societies took increasingly distinct paths. Under the adaptive pressure of the limitations experienced in the late eighteenth and early nineteenth centuries, household-based economies in all re-gions had modified and extended their activities. In some areas these changes reinforced and extended established patterns; in other regions they initiated a process of social transformation. The biggest distinction arose between areas of nonslave labor, where older systems of compelled labor began to decline, and regions of the South that relied strongly on slavery, where coerced labor remained significant.

Some important social and economic characteristics of slave and non-slave societies diverged in this period, setting up an increasingly marked set of contrasts between them. Urban development continued more slowly in the South than elsewhere. Particularly after 1810, manufactur-ing too, though it remained an important feature of many Southern re-gions, did not in most parts of the South keep pace with the scale or scope of developments to the north. Such differences in these features that came to be seen as marks of "modern" societies have often led historians to regard the South as increasingly backward, and its society as relatively slow to change. Following a long tradition, they ascribed this relative backwardness to the persistence of slavery. As a Kentucky physician, Ben-jamin W. Dudley, claimed in 1806, slavery induced "dependency and dis-sipation" among slaves which impaired their capacity for hard work. By mid-century, abolitionist critics of slavery were also pointing to the system's apparent inefficiencies. Many of these analyses rested on the assumption—with roots in eighteenth-century social thought, and seemingly justified by later events—that slavery was not merely inhumane but doomed ultimately to fail and die out.[1]

Various recent historians, however, have sought to qualify the argument that the South was backward. They stress the extent to which the region was actively engaged in developing commercial and other activities. Some accounts have also tended to downplay the effects of slavery on the South, or of slavery's differences from the other forms of labor that were prominent elsewhere in the economy. Meanwhile, historians of slavery itself have done much to emphasize the extent to which it was a system of power, and frequently of barbarity toward its captives. The discussion that follows seeks to put these new conclusions toward a fresh assessment.[2]

The Expansion of Slavery

SLAVERY ENABLED Southern society to participate in the dynamic development shared by other household-based societies in the early United States. The South was not "backward" in the sense of being slow to grow or lacking in dynamic energy, though its commitments to staple-crop production and to the use of slave labor took it in directions that differed from those of nonslave regions. Nor was American slavery inevitably doomed. Its rapid expansion in the nineteenth century suggested the possibility—one that was comfortably assumed by its beneficiaries and regarded with horror by its victims and opponents—that slavery might continue indefinitely. Yet its operations were shaped by the irreducible unwillingness of slaves to consent to their predicament.

Many late-eighteenth-century observers, aware of the injustices and ideological inconsistencies of a republic based on slavery, believed that slave labor would eventually cease to be important, and that the institution would die. They took the abolition of slavery or steps toward gradual emancipation in the northeastern states as signs of progress toward that end. Had production in the South continued to concentrate only on the old staple crops of the colonial period, they might have been proved correct. Tobacco did not need to be grown by slave labor, and many tobacco growers in the upper Chesapeake were shifting to grain crops anyway. In most parts of the North where slavery was not yet illegal by the early nineteenth century, it was dying out even ahead of measures for gradual abolition. As late as 1831–1832 it was possible for members of the Virginia legislature to hold a debate on the future of slavery and to entertain the possibility that it might become extinct.

But its defenders had long reconciled slavery to republican assumptions. After the Revolution, full citizenship was in theory accorded only to those whose personal independence rendered them immune from political pressure or corruption. Slaves, like women, children, and the propertyless, were "dependents," and they were denied rights only in greater degree than those other groups. The republic also protected the rights of property owners, and as democratization for white men eroded property qualifications for the franchise, the entitlement to possess slaves came to be defended all the more vigorously as a property right. Race itself also came to play a more explicit role in the justifications put forward for slavery. People of African descent, so the argument went, were inferior beings who needed enslavement for their own protection. The Virginia political theorist John Taylor defended slavery in the 1820s as a protection for slaves against the poverty, ignorance, and exploitation they would suffer if they were a free but propertyless class.[3]

Such justifications, however, only followed the substantial expansion of slavery in the decades after the Revolution. In practice the extension of tobacco cultivation and the intensification of rice production both created new demands for slave labor. But the South did not remain reliant just on its old crops. The addition of sugar and, above all else, the adoption and expansion of cotton production drove the growth of the slave labor force and the increasing confidence with which it was regarded by its owners as the bedrock of the Southern economy. Between 1790 and 1830 alone the slave population expanded almost threefold. The availability of coerced slave labor for agriculture tied the South even more strongly than before to its staple-crop and export economies. The ability of some slaveholders to sustain plantations (units worked by twenty or more slaves) in many of the most productive districts led to a consolidation of political power across much of the South by members of a planter elite.

Some crops were confined to particular areas. The ready availability of slave labor and the development of water control and planting techniques ensured the survival and development of thriving rice plantations along the South Carolina and Georgia tidewater. Some of these estates became among the largest in the United States, with hundreds of slaves on each. Slave labor was essential not just for growing and harvesting the rice crop but for regulating and maintaining a delicately balanced system of dikes and water flows that irrigated the rice while also protecting the land from inundation by the sea. Similarly, the acquisition of the Louisiana Territory from France in 1803 included a sugar plantation region in the Mississippi delta that also expanded during the following half-century. Large plantations were common there too, together with large slave workforces essential both to the harvesting and to the crushing and processing of sugarcane at mills owned by the planters. Both sugar and rice production involved hard toil in harsh conditions, for which adequate free labor was impossible to hire but which slaves could be compelled to undertake.

By far the most important development in the Southern economy was the expansion of cotton growing, which by the 1850s had become the single most valuable crop not just in the South but in the whole United States. The introduction of cotton gins, which solved the difficulties of growing inland short-staple cotton in the 1790s, unleashed a massive increase in cotton cultivation to provide the raw material for new and fast-growing mechanized textile industries, first in Britain and later in other European countries and the American Northeast. American exports of cotton to Britain alone, which were negligible before 1793, exceeded 100 million pounds' weight by 1815, and more than doubled again to 263 million pounds in 1830. As production boomed, vast acreages were planted with cotton, and new fortunes were created.

Unlike sugar and rice, cotton could be cultivated successfully on small farms as well as large ones. But the need for labor to hoe cotton fields to keep them free of weeds, and for the finicky task of harvesting, meant that yeoman farm families could handle only small acreages of the crop. Advantage went to cultivators who could afford slaves to do this work, so most cotton was grown on slave-worked farms and plantations of various sizes. It was the expansion of cotton in particular that ensured that, far from dying out, slavery would revive. Cotton consigned further generations of enslaved people to lives in bondage.

Cotton cultivation and, to a lesser extent, projects to grow sugar, hemp, tobacco, and other crops with slave labor were the driving forces behind the expansion of settlement after the 1790s into the Southwest. The backcountry of South Carolina had already been settled by a mixture of slaveholders, yeoman farmers, and squatters; cotton reinforced the numbers and power of the slaveholders and created an inland elite. Over the following decades this group colonized and cultivated vast areas in what became Alabama, Mississippi, and parts of Tennessee, and began settlements across the Mississippi River in Arkansas and Texas. In areas like the Macon region in interior Georgia, land was initially opened up and cleared by yeoman farmers who had migrated from the seaboard or moved south from Pennsylvania and the Virginia backcountry. As the more prosperous ones adopted cotton cultivation, buying or hiring in a few slaves each, they began a transformation. With increased cotton production, advantage went to those who could purchase larger acreages and the slaves to work them, and the region began to be dominated by plantation agriculture; by 1840 slaves accounted for half the Macon area's population. Yeoman farmers still remained, but they lost much of their political influence to the more dominant planters. Across the southwestern frontier, initial squatter settlers on speculators' land were undisturbed until the prospect of cotton cultivation made landholders interested in working it. Squatters were then often displaced. They and yeoman farmers might make their way farther west to fresh land if they could, but many remained behind in what grew into plantation districts.[4]

The southwestward expansion of slavery created different kinds of social inequality than those of the seaboard states. Between 1810 and 1840 the combined populations of Georgia, Alabama, and Mississippi increased from about 300,000 (of whom 252,433 were in Georgia) to 1,657,799. Over 40 percent (and in Mississippi, 52 percent) of these people were slaves, many of whom had been moved in chained gangs (known as "coffles") from plantations and slave markets in the coastal states to clear land and create new cotton plantations. The lure of cotton profits, and the drive for the land and labor that could produce them, gave this expansion a particularly hard, grasping edge. Pressure for land in Georgia and Alabama led to unjust state seizures of territory from the Cherokee and Creek nations and, under the Jackson and Van

Buren administrations in the 1830s, to the enforced removal of many thousands of "civilized" Indians to land designated for them in "Indian Territory," which would eventually become Oklahoma.

The Culture of a Slave Economy

THE DRIVE to open new cotton lands caused the sons of seaboard planters to move west to take up land claims. In some cases, as around Macon, Georgia, they bought up or appropriated land that yeoman farmers or squatters had already cleared for agriculture. In other cases, especially in Mississippi in the 1820s and 1830s, they deployed slave gangs that had been assembled from older plantations or acquired in slave markets to break and clear land for cotton. Sons of planters who set out for the Southwest did so both to make profits from cotton and to break with the constraints of family and kinship ties that characterized plantation life back east. They worked their slaves hard to clear land and establish cotton crops, and though they also usually permitted slaves to cultivate their own gardens to help supply their plantations, there is evidence that work routines and discipline were more rigorous than on many older plantations in the Southeast.

Moving slaves into new regions also involved breaking up their families. Because the initial clearing of land made demand heaviest for male labor during the early stages of plantation development, black family life was harder to reestablish than in regions where the ratio of men to women was more even. Whites also faced disruption. Women, accompanying their new husbands to lives on a distant frontier, faced an often wrenching removal from family and kin. Because of the newness of frontier plantation society, the low proportion of white settlers, and social inequalities between planters and nonslaveholding whites, planter women often faced an isolation they had not known back home. The new societies of the cotton South presented both slavery and white life in some of their harsher aspects.

Prominent among earlier interpretations of slave society was the work of the historian Eugene Genovese, who argued that slaveowners formed a noncapitalist, nonbourgeois elite, different from their Northern commercial and industrial counterparts. The class relationships of slavery differed from those between employers and wage earners, Genovese suggested. Planters and slaves were bound by the complexities of their relationship to a pattern he called paternalism. The claims of slaveholders to have responsibilities for their slaves, and the irreducible humanity of slaves themselves, meant that the peculiar fact of holding other people as property placed the planters in an exploitative but noncommercial connection with those they owned. The importance of slave ownership to their social and political status, Genovese argued, combined with this noninstrumental aspect of the master-slave relationship, caused many planters to be devoted to noncommercial concerns. Entrepreneurship was stifled and the relative backwardness of the Southern economy explained. More concerned with reproducing slavery than with maximizing profits, planters sought to avoid risk and put their way of life ahead of commercial considerations.

Later studies have subjected the elements of Genovese's argument to searching scrutiny. In some respects it no longer survives intact, though its central insights about the contradictions arising from holding property in people, about the resistance of slaves to planter authority, and about slavery as a class relationship are still essential to understanding the system. Various authors have argued that masters and overseers were more active and commercially minded in the operation of plantations than was once assumed, and that the cultivation of an "anti-commercial" ethos was an affectation of a powerful planter class anxious to demonstrate its genteel credentials. In regions like the interior of South Carolina, for example, planters adjusted their activities more than once in response to shifts in markets. In the 1780s they began planting tobacco on their newly cleared land, but in the 1810s, as tobacco markets weakened, they switched out of this into cotton growing because British demand was driving prices up. On many plantations, planters and overseers adopted modern practices for overseeing and controlling labor, and for tracking and accounting for their slaves' work and produce. On the sugar plantations of Louisiana, planters were obliged to make complex and sophisticated judgments about investment and the control of resources. They aimed to derive profits not just from the labor of their slaves but from the substantial capital value tied up in sugar mills, crushing machines, and other advanced equipment.[5]

Slavery, then, can appear as a more dynamic system than some older interpretations and the comfortable self-image of many planters would imply. Some studies suggest that this dynamism lay in part in the degree of flexibility in master-slave relations: that the reciprocal relationships that Genovese called paternalism were conducive not to slow-paced production but to a kind of negotiation between parties with distinct interests and incentives, not unlike that between wage earners and their bosses. The distinctions noted earlier between different types of work regimes on farms and plantations often reflected the scope that existed in places for slaves and owners to jockey for position with each other. On smaller farms where slaves were held in ones or twos, they were often working either alongside members of the farm family or left to undertake tasks with a degree of independence. On larger cotton and tobacco plantations, work was usually organized in gangs, under the supervision either of overseers or of slave "drivers" who had been promoted to take this responsibility. Gang systems represented what appeared to be the harshest aspects of slavery: enforced, regimented work under careful supervision embodied not only a tough regime but the assumption that slaves were incapable of working efficiently under other circumstances. Yet gang work might provide the best opportunity for slaves to help one another, if help were needed. The continued prevalence of the task system in rice cultivation, and in other contexts where the nature of the work did not lend itself to large groups or gang supervision, indicated the ability of slavery to accord a limited degree of autonomy to slaves. Accompanying, as it often did, the use of provision grounds (gardens), fishing, and hunting to supplement slave diets, and the possibility of private trading between slaves and others off the plantations, the task system appears to mark the tendency of slave regimes to adapt themselves to circumstances and offer a degree of flexibility within which slaves might find negotiating room.[6]

Power in Slave Societies

YET IF some historians disagree that slavery was inefficient, and have suggested ways in which it frequently offered flexibility, recent studies have also questioned the use of "paternalism" as a governing metaphor for master-slave relationships. Certainly—particularly as it came under scrutiny from its opponents in the 1830s and 1840s—slavery's defenders contended that it offered protective shelter under usually benevolent owners, whose interest in the value of their slaves was itself some sort of guarantee of fair treatment. But evidence from across the range of regions and crop types throughout the South suggests that most of this— even more than the anti-commercial gentility claimed by many planters—was a deceptive (probably also self-deceptive) image. If there was space within which slaves enjoyed a manner of autonomy, it was often slender. "Negotiations" between slaves and their masters or overseers were conducted, if at all, on narrow ground, between parties with widely different access to power and to rights.

Harsh and violent punishments, poor diets, arbitrary power, unhealthy demographic conditions, and other characteristics pervaded the slave system. Benjamin Dudley of Kentucky noted in 1806 that "insufficiency of clothing, and . . . scanty and improper aliment [food]" frequently made slaves susceptible to disease. The fact that in many regions slave populations reproduced themselves and thus grew naturally is now seen as having happened not because conditions were favorable but in spite of poor treatment. In parts of the South these rates of natural reproduction were, in any case, only marginal. Low population densities, which inhibited the spread of infectious diseases and reduced mortality rates, may alone have been a significant factor in enabling slave numbers to grow. Given that slaves were legally bound to their owners, and that owners had wide-ranging (if not totally unlimited) legal discretion to treat them arbitrarily as they pleased, it seems more appropriate to accept the historian Peter H. Wood's portrayal of slave plantations as forced labor camps than as variants of "free" labor institutions.[7]

Even where slaves could make trade-offs, as in the flexibility provided by the task system, the advantages to them were often few. Slaves on rice plantations might obtain a degree more autonomy than those working in gangs in the cotton fields, but they were usually required to do hard, demanding labor, were expected to produce much of their own food, and were as subject as other slaves to degrading and often brutal punishment for infractions. William Dusinberre's catalog of abuses recorded in the plantation records of the rice districts, or Wilma King's evidence of the systematic maltreatment of children, undermine planters' claims to paternalistic solicitude. Frequently their concern for profit from their crops came second only to their anxiety to sustain their power and authority over the men, women, and children they owned.[8]

Considerable research from the 1960s on, including that of Genovese, has helped establish, however, that even within the harshness of most slaves' existence they were able to carve out a degree of cultural autonomy for themselves. This creation of slave cultures may have become more important over time as the number of slaves held in larger units, rather than separately on small farms, rose. The increasing Christianization of Southern slaves during the first half of the nineteenth century also created pockets of cultural autonomy within the confines of the slave system. Even on plantations where white masters insisted on slave attendance at worship or local churches, and where the Word was officially preached with a clear message of personal and racial subordination, the slaves' nighttime, weekend, and backwoods meetings and the circulation of slave preachers enabled many slave believers to acquire from Christian teachings a quite different, oppositional perspective. Above all, these teachings often reinforced the underlying conviction of slavery's fundamental injustice and illegitimacy. Hopes for freedom, the denial of enslavement, the desire for jubilee, the crossing of the Jordan, the delivery from bondage—all took nourishment from religion. Even as many submitted to their enslavement, few accepted it.[9]

Planters and small slaveholders used their coercive power to extract labor from their slaves; wherever they could, slaves attempted to build their own lives and culture within the bounds of enslavement. Ephraim Beanland, overseer on James K. Polk's cotton plantation in western Tennessee, made several complaints to his employer in 1833 that arose from the escapes and other unruliness of the estate's slaves. After Beanland had punished one of them for an infraction, two male slaves ran away. They were being hunted. The overseer was anxious lest Polk should override his own authority when they were recaptured: "I do not want any arrangements made for either of them." At stake in Beanland's view was his ability to coerce the other slaves as well: "I want them boath brought back. If they ain't the rest will leave me also." Misplaced liberality, Beanland implied, had undermined his ability to keep discipline: "your Negroes has traded with white people and bin let run at so lo[o]se

. . . [rein] that I must be verry close [i.e., tough] with them." Notably, though, he was unwilling to assign full blame for his predicament to the slaves themselves. "The[re] is a set of white people that lives close hear [i.e., near here] that would spoil any set of negroes." Like many whites, Beanland could not ascribe the ability to act autonomously to people he regarded as inferior and whom he helped hold captive. Yet there is wide-spread evidence that slaves acted to defend their sense of community, assert their individuality, and resist their bondage.[10]

The ability to acquire a limited degree of cultural autonomy was a source both of solace and of deep anxiety for many slaves. Prominent in slave culture were attachment to marriage and the building of kinship systems. Slave marriage was not legally recognized because it interfered with the absolute property rights of slaveowners, but large numbers of slaves constructed partnerships and family life for themselves within the constraints of the system. Planters tolerated or even encouraged these arrangements because they rightly perceived them as conducive to order and a means for control over their human property. The solaces of family and of life in the "slave community" provided slaves with sustenance in the face of arbitrary power; but they also provided entry points for the cruel exercise of that power when owners found it expedient.

Slaves' fundamental nonacceptance of their captivity, which belied their owners' claims that they were content with their situation, was illustrated not just by the desire for freedom but by the frequent steps that many took to try to achieve it. Recent estimates suggest that as many as fifty thousand slaves each year may have run off from their owners. Of these, only a small handful managed to escape for long. The difficulties of hiding out in swamps or woodlands, of functioning in hostile white societies, or of traveling without means the long distances north to freedom without being caught made permanent escape a relatively rare occurrence. Indeed, many escapes were not intended to be permanent. Slaves ran away to avoid or protest punishment, or to link up with or visit partners and family on other plantations, often nearby. But coupled with myriad small acts of resistance or insubordination, the high incidence of escape reflected slaves' rejection of the circumstances in which they found themselves. Escapes also prompted planters and the white authorities to organize rigorous pass systems and patrols to combat this form of disobedience.

Slave Markets and Slave Families

BUT PLANTERS had another, powerful sanction: the threat to sell a slave away from his or her home or family. Fear of sale and of the breakup of families actively shaped many slaves' lives. Its power to coerce slaves was greatest when slave communities were strong and family ties and children present. It may have exercised somewhat less fear over young men who had not yet formed marriages; they, at least, seem to have formed a measurable segment of those who flouted slaveholders' authority by running away each year. But the variability and changing character of Southern economies gave rise to structural conditions that made slave sale, and the fear of it, a constant presence in the system.

Slavery embodied three conditions that promoted the expansion of slave sales. First, its early stronghold in Virginia now entered a phase of comparative economic decline as old crops became uneconomic, soil was exhausted, and new regions were opened up to the south and west. Second, the expansion of settlement was accomplished, as we saw, partly by squatters and yeoman farm families but also by the movement of slaves into newly opened regions. Finally, the demographic characteristics of some areas, especially the sugar plantations of Louisiana, made them net demanders of slaves because they could not sustain their populations through natural increase. Between 1818 and 1830, for example, these plantations obtained around five thousand slaves each year from the East. Sugar planters, seeking to extract profit from their estates and from the expensive equipment they installed, heavily recruited male slaves for field labor and processing work. The resulting unbalanced gender ratios contributed to the inability of sugar-growing regions to achieve slave population growth and so helped sustain the region's demand for labor from elsewhere. All these factors led to the creation of the antebellum South's most notable institution other than slavery itself: the internal market for slaves.

Over several decades at least one million slaves were moved from older-settled states, first from the Chesapeake and Lowcountry, later from parts of Kentucky, and in the 1850s from Tennessee and Georgia, to new locations west and south. Tennessee, Alabama, Mississippi, and Louisiana, and later Arkansas, Florida, and parts of Texas and Missouri,

were populated with slaves substantially through these forced movements. In the 1820s and 1830s alone, roughly 443,000 slaves were
shifted in this way. About one-third of these slaves were moved in the
company of their owners, as planters established new estates in the West
and assigned slave men and women to settle and develop them. But as
many as two-thirds were sold on the slave market and moved by traders,
either to fulfill orders placed by Western planters with suppliers further
east, or on consignment by Eastern planters for speculative sale in markets where slaves were in demand. Slave trading, in the words of its leading historian, was "the one great entrepreneurial activity in the South."
Networks of slave-trading firms linked large and small towns across the
region. Slave markets and auction houses sprang up, and towns and
countryside alike were dotted with slave jails where men, women, and
children were shackled and confined to await sale or to prevent escape
during overnight stops on forced marches.[11]

Available evidence is ambiguous as to whether slaves were intentionally bred in older regions like Virginia for prospective sale to traders. In
the late 1830s and early 1840s, James Henry Hammond of South Carolina expressed frustration and anger at the slaves on his plantation because disease repeatedly killed young children, spoiling his expectations
of realizing value from the reproduction of his slaves. Hammond,
though, was not necessarily planning to sell slaves; he could hope to save
on purchases as he expanded his plantations. But slaves were sold in a
range of circumstances. Some were sold as punishment for infractions; a
few planters were known to avoid whipping their slaves, instead threatening to sell them if they failed to meet the demands made of them.
Slaves were sold because of changes in planters' plans or fluctuations in
the markets for crops; because planters fell into debt; or because death
led to the breakup and distribution of estate property, which of course
included slaves. Especially under pressure from abolitionist critics of the
effects of slavery on families, some planters made a point of trying to sell
family members together, but they frequently either could not accomplish this or lost control once slaves were in the hands of traders. Family breakups remained one of the lasting indictments of slavery; the fear
and reality of it seared millions of slaves' lives. And the Louisiana sugar
plantations were legendary for their harshness, which gave an added
horror to the prospect of being sold "down the river."[12]

Slave labor was secured wherever it could be obtained, often without regard to the law or individuals' legal status. The newly freed New York slave Isabella Van Wagenen (later known as Sojourner Truth) scored a rare court victory in the late 1820s when she obtained the release and return from Alabama of her son, who had illegally been sold and sent there. William J. Anderson of Hanover County, Virginia, was less fortunate. When his father died in 1816 and his mother could no longer support him, Anderson was bound out as an indentured servant at the age of five. Ten years later his master, a planter, sold him into slavery. Anderson's mother was a free black, so legally Anderson was also free, but this did not save him from shipment to Tennessee or from a twenty-four-year incarceration as a slave before one of his repeated escape attempts at last succeeded.[13]

Slavery and White Society in the South

THE EXPANSION of the plantation system profoundly affected social relations among whites across the South. In many regions, particularly in the mountains and backcountry, plantations were few or nonexistent, and smaller farmers rarely owned slaves. Yeoman farmers, relying on family labor, dominated the social structure of such regions; it was not uncommon, for example, in up-country areas for women to work in the fields. These regions often remained relatively independent of the concerns of plantation districts, placing different demands on state governments and opposing planters on issues such as internal improvements, banking, and tax measures. Areas like upland East Georgia remained relatively self-contained in this way for much of the antebellum period. On parts of the frontier, too, yeoman-dominated communities grew up beyond the edge of plantation developments. Small farmers in Warren County, Mississippi, cleared land quickly by slash-and-burn methods in the 1820s, planning to cultivate new land when soil became exhausted. Many yeoman farm families also moved to Missouri and settled in the same period, rapidly increasing the state's population as they sought to avoid the plantation districts farther east. Missouri farmers, who continued to dominate the state, gave its policies a distinctive anti-developmental character as they attempted to insulate themselves from the financial and market pressures that developed in other regions.

Often, though, yeoman farm settlements accompanied plantation development or were overtaken by them, and planter influence grew. Even in the up-country of South Carolina after 1810, more than 36 percent of households owned slaves, and slaves exceeded 26 percent of the population. The rise in land values as plantations were carved out of new regions made the position of many early-arrived independent farmers precarious, and it was in this context that many "pushed on" elsewhere. In areas like northeast Alabama, where public lands were opened to settlement after 1819, large landowners obtained control of much of the land. On former Creek and Cherokee lands in southern Appalachia, distributed in the 1830s, only about one in five farmers came to own their property.

Across the plantation zone, however, yeoman farm families continued to make their way among their wealthier, more powerful neighbors. In the rice-growing districts of South Carolina, yeoman farmers and their households formed a majority of the white population. Many of these farmers practiced mixed agriculture, but about 45 percent of them also cultivated rice, though probably less intensively than on the bigger plantations, and mainly for home or local consumption. Yeoman farmers in plantation regions often formed client relations with their planter neighbors, creating patterns of political patronage and obligation that represented a significant element in planters' power. There was also a constant overlap between yeoman and slaveholder status. Many small farmers hired in slaves as extra labor when they needed it, and especially during the 1820s and 1830s some become slaveholders in their own right.

Across the South, however, especially where landownership was heavily skewed toward a few wealthy individuals, significant numbers among the nonslaveholding white population could not claim yeoman farmer status. The free rural poor—the vast majority of whom in the deep South were white—had no land of their own and often had fewer opportunities for making a livelihood than their wage-earning counterparts in the North and Midwest. In parts of Alabama and Mississippi, for example, as many as one-third of the white heads of household were landless. Looked down upon by planters, yeomen, and slaves alike, poor whites were obliged to make do with what casual work they could obtain in the interstices of the plantation economy: laboring jobs, usually seasonal, on yeoman farms, or other unskilled, temporary work. The structure of Southern society largely excluded them from stable employment: small farmers needed hired help only intermittently; planters had their slaves to keep occupied, and so had little need for the extra labor of whites. Poor whites found that, by comparison with the North, there were few towns and cities for them to move to and try their luck in, and often fewer employers in transportation or manufacturing to offer alternatives to rural laboring work. Marginal and frequently on the move in search of scarce jobs, the rural poor had little opportunity to exercise political power, even when they could legally vote. Like the poorer farmers of the Appalachian region, most had insufficient means to migrate long distances or to take the risk of cutting themselves off from the family and kinship networks that could help them eke out a living. Their mobility, both social and geographical, was constrained.[14]

Thus although planters represented a small minority of Southern society, their control of land and slaves gave them disproportionate influence, especially among the yeoman farmers and poor whites in their immediate neighborhoods who relied on them for employment or other kinds of patronage. Awareness of the divisions in white society and the possible risks these posed frequently shaped discussions of slavery itself. In some instances, distrust of other whites and belief in the docility and pliability of black slaves led individuals to rely on slaves in preference to the alternatives. A Mississippi planter, Francis Terry Leak, urged a bachelor friend with means to return to running a plantation, arguing that slaves could best be trusted to look after him. Family members, Leak argued, would only be interested in his money, and hired servants could scheme to get themselves a share of his estate. Slaves, on the other hand, knowing they had no hope of gaining legal title to anything he owned, would serve him purely from "affection." At the same time the existence of slavery was seen by many of its apologists as a guarantee of social stability among whites. "The menial and low offices being all performed by blacks," wrote Thomas B. Dew in 1832, "there is at once taken away the greatest cause of distinction and separation of the ranks of [white] society." Hence, Dew claimed, along with many others, there could be a "perfect spirit of equality" among Southern whites. Ideology and self-interest together cemented an attachment to slavery across swaths of white society.[15]

Nonslave Societies in the North

WHILE SLAVERY expanded, making unfree labor more important in its contributions to the American economy and in its significance for the South, nonslave regions to the north were adjusting their degree of reliance on compelled labor. Household production remained central. To that extent, as in the South, the ability of household heads and property owners to demand labor from their own family members remained highly important. But during the early nineteenth century, population growth and the adjustments that accompanied expansion, migration, and intensification of production altered the degree to which Northern economies relied on unfree forms of labor. A lack of data makes estimates conjectural, but by 1820 perhaps one-fifth of the U.S. workforce was employed for wages, a proportion that had almost doubled since 1800. Wage workers were formally free, and their significance for work and production, especially in the North, would continue to grow. Indeed, in the North various forms of unfree labor were by this time declining or coming under scrutiny.

The stream of European immigrants who, since the seventeenth century, had traveled particularly to the Mid-Atlantic and the South to work as indentured servants finally dwindled. Among the last of them were the German migrants who arrived in Pennsylvania as "redemptioners," sold by ship captains to householders to repay the cost of their transatlantic passage and legally bound to work for a period sufficient to pay off their purchase price. Of immigrants arriving at Philadelphia between 1797 and 1812, some 27 percent entered servitude, and in the postwar years from 1815 to 1818 the proportion actually rose temporarily, to about 42 percent. But by 1820 the pattern had altered; the supply of redemptioners dried up, and subsequently the vast majority of immigrants arrived as free laborers. An important reason for the change lay in the scale and character of German communities now established in the United States. Sufficient numbers were now present as farmers or urban proprietors who could assist new migrants effectively without the need for formal servitude. The introduction of regular transatlantic packet ships after 1815 also improved sea communication, making it much easier than before for immigrants in the United States to send remittances to their home communities or arrange informal, kin-based "chain" migrations to bring over and support emigrants. Both factors led to the rapid decline of the redemption system.[16]

Meanwhile in the larger towns and cities, the use of formal apprenticeships to train and supply labor was also declining. Late in the eighteenth century, apprenticeship remained the normal mode of entry to skilled trades, and many young artisans could contemplate becoming masters of their trades. A study of Boston artisans in 1796, for example, suggests a high ratio of masters to journeymen and apprentices in most occupations. But the growth of urban populations and the relative prevalence of poverty helped assure many employers access to labor without the need to rely on legal ties of compulsion. Early trade societies, especially of journeymen who had advanced through formal apprenticeship to obtain their skills, frequently complained of and tried to resist the employment of half-trained or unskilled workers in many artisan trades. At the same time the democratization of white political participation, and the concepts of "equal rights" and producers' rights that it encapsulated, set out new standards for "free" labor against which various other practices and arrangements came to be measured. The printer and economist Mathew Carey remarked in 1826 that it was not acceptable in Philadelphia to strike a servant, black or white, in punishment for an infraction. Household labor, for nonfamily members, was coming to be transmuted into wage labor, with different patterns of authority.[17]

Along the Hudson River Valley, pressure to divide their own estates in the face of family growth and generational change led manorial landlords to tighten their demands on tenants in the 1820s and to abandon their previous leniency toward those who were slow to pay rents. Landlords initiated court actions for debt, increased the proportion of short-term leases that gave tenants little benefit from improvements, expanded their use of sharecropping arrangements, and attempted (unsuccessfully) to take control of timber that grew on common land. In the short run these changes amounted to a tightening of the manorial system's coercive elements, but they also sparked protests that marked the inception of a strong revival of the "anti-rent" sentiment that had challenged landlords in the Revolutionary period. The growing anti-rent movement drew on arguments in favor of "free" labor and against compulsion, and ultimately achieved a significant amelioration of the manorial system in the New York State constitution of 1846.[18]

The ideological climate of equal rights and producerism generated assaults on other practices seen as restricting "free labor." Pennsylvania campaigners condemned imprisonment for debt as "a discreditable remnant of a barbarous system of ancient times, whereby insolvent debtors became the slaves of their creditors, and were subject to all the pains and penalties of slavery." There and in New York and elsewhere they largely succeeded in ending the practice during the 1830s and 1840s. Workingmen campaigned for mechanics' lien laws that could give tradesmen and laborers priority for the payment of wages when an employer went bankrupt. Complaints were heard about wages paid not in cash but in goods at company stores, and the frequency of indebtedness to or by employers who restricted workers' freedom of movement by threatening financial loss. The 1820s witnessed a renewal of the assault on Southern slavery that by mid-century would come to dominate American society and politics. The growth of free black populations in many parts of the North provided a vigorous base for an anti-slavery campaign, and British abolitionists' campaigns against slavery in West Indies colonies provided an international context for a debate over slavery. The rapid spread of evangelical revivalism among Northern churches, black and white, also created a powerful institutional impetus against the sin of human bondage, and provided spiritual and theological underpinnings to notions of individuals' self-ownership and autonomy.[19]

All these developments accompanied a steady increase in the importance of wage labor in the North. Wage work, once regarded as disreputable and as a mark of dependence unless undertaken as a temporary expedient by independent farmers, artisans, or their sons, was beginning a profound shift in respectability. By the late 1840s it would emerge as one archetype of an ideal "free labor" system. Accompanying this, and in part related to the evangelical revivals and their embrace of sentimentalism, was a renewed ideological validation of the family as a social ideal and moral shelter from the world's vagaries and temptations. The respectability of wage work and of family life, added to the long-standing regard for independent proprietorship, underpinned the primary institutions that now governed labor in Northern societies: self-employment;

working for the family in the household; or working for wages. All became construed as part of the fabric of "free labor."

The "Fertility Transition"

ACROSS THE nation, the late eighteenth and early nineteenth centuries had witnessed rapid population growth from natural increase. Among the free population there was a high rate of marriage, and because fertility rates were high, marriages generally produced large families of children. Among slaves, the interests of slaveholders in obtaining the value of children led to the encouragement of breeding and to high fertility there too. During the eighteenth century, however, regional differences had begun to emerge in these high rates of reproduction. These were connected with broader patterns of social change, particularly with differences that were emerging in the importance of households as institutions.[20]

Across the United States as a whole between 1800 and 1860, the average number of live births fell from 7.04 per family to 5.21, a decline of 26 percent. Although this does not immediately appear to be a sharp drop, the aggregate figure masks variations between regions and social groups, some of which were dramatic. Fertility rates fell in all regions but tended to remain higher in the South than in the North, and to fall faster in urban settings and in older-settled rural regions than in frontier areas. The persistence in the South of slavery and of other rural social structures, even as the region expanded geographically, introduced fewer circumstances or inducements for families to alter their reproductive behavior than occurred in the Northeast. Among Alabama's white population in 1840, for example, the ratio of children under ten to females aged between fifteen and forty-nine was 1.85:1. In Connecticut in 1840, by contrast, there were only 0.92 children under ten for every female aged fifteen to forty-nine, less than half the ratio in Alabama. By 1860, except on the frontier, fertility rates in Southern regions averaged between 3 percent and 28 percent higher than in the North.

Even in aggregate, however, the shift was significant. It meant that on average families would give birth to one or two fewer children in the middle of the century than they had at the beginning. Across the white population of the United States as a whole, the proportion of children under five fell from 1,342 per thousand women of childbearing age in 1800 to only 905 by 1860. Households became smaller. Some of the burdens of household work were reduced. By the same token, as children grew up there were fewer of them to contribute labor to the family's activities. Such changes, subtle as they often were, pointed to important shifts in the way societies worked, especially in the North.

Changes in family fertility came about first in older-settled regions, particularly in New England and the Mid-Atlantic states. By 1860 the ratios of children under five to women aged between twenty and forty-four were, respectively, 0.639 and 0.784 in the two regions, significantly below the national average. There had been signs of a fall in family size before the end of the eighteenth century, but this was reversed in some areas, as early-nineteenth-century families averaged over 7 recorded live births. After 1810, however, fertility rates began declining. In Sturbridge, Massachusetts, couples who married between 1780 and 1799 averaged 7.32 children; forty years later, their successors averaged 5.3 children. In Amherst and Hadley, Massachusetts, couples married between 1830 and 1839 had an average of 4.47 live births, by contrast with the 7.12 births averaged by their predecessors thirty years earlier. In about one generation, therefore, fertility fell by more than 37 percent, and the average family had between two and three fewer children than their parents' generation had produced. This process would continue.[21]

Demographers have often connected fertility rates to families' access to resources. An important interpretation of the decline of fertility in New England, for example, attributed it to land shortage. As access to land became more constricted, the argument went, families limited their fertility so as to reduce their need to divide land to provide farms for their sons. By the same token, as access to land became more difficult, couples had to wait longer before accumulating the resources to marry, thus raising the marriage age and reducing the period of marriage during which women were still fertile—hence reducing the average number of children they bore. To a limited degree, the evidence about fertility changes in our period bears out this hypothesis. Marriage ages did rise in the early nineteenth century; some demographers have calculated that about half the reduction in family sizes that occurred before 1850 was attributable to higher ages of marriage for women. Moreover, fertility rates in frontier regions, where access to land was not so constrained, remained higher than those back east.

But more detailed analysis has cast doubt on this argument. Rather than simply adjusting their family size to scarcity, nineteenth-century Americans were bringing about a different kind of social change. If fertility were dependent on resources, we would expect wealthier families to be larger than poorer ones, and some evidence suggests that until the eighteenth century this had been so. But the fertility changes of the early nineteenth century altered that pattern, creating a situation in which family size no longer correlated with wealth, or did so inversely. What kinds of things, then, led husbands and wives to reduce the size of their families?

As noted, higher marriage ages did have an impact on family size. In Amherst and Hadley, Massachusetts, for example, the mean age of first marriage for women, which had been running at below 24 years during the 1770s and 1780s, was consistently over 25 years between 1790 and 1829 and peaked at 27.5 years in the 1830s. But factors other than scarcity of land or access to livelihoods may have played a role in this change. Opportunities for work in cities or settlement in new regions drew young men away from older farming districts, making it harder for women to find marriage partners. In 1830 the five counties of central and western Massachusetts were all among the areas of the state where the ratio of males aged 20 to 29 to females of the same age group was lowest; Hampden County had only 86 men of that age for every 100 women. But women also restricted their fertility in several ways: completing their families earlier (having their last children at younger ages); increasing the birth intervals between children by delaying weaning or practicing sexual abstinence; and in some instances adopting birth-control measures that were beginning to be discussed in popular medical literature. Fertility limitation was therefore to some degree a conscious process, not simply a consequence of access to resources.

Evidence about who limited fertility and where they lived can throw light on the probable reasons for it. Among the U.S.-born white population, by the mid-nineteenth century smaller family sizes were most common among professional and business-owning families, and among the skilled and semi-skilled workforce. These families were more common in the Northeast than in the Midwest or the South, and in urban than in rural areas; and they were more common in districts that gave access to a range of employment opportunities than they were in predominantly farming areas. New Englanders practiced family limitation as urbanization, nonagricultural employment, new institutional access to financial resources, and out-migration altered the fabric of their society and the roles of households within it. This suggests that the change in fertility patterns reflected not access to resources but changes in people's views of the relationships between children, livelihoods, and family strategies. Coupled with these broader social characteristics of smaller families is evidence that women often took the lead in adopting strategies for reducing their rates of reproduction.[22]

In a classic, older, rural pattern, farm families had children both to provide labor for the household and to provide emotional and practical comfort and assistance to other members of their families, especially to parents in their old age. As different opportunities for employment and livelihoods became available through the diversification of rural economies and the growth of urban areas, families began to look at their children in different ways. And as their own sources of livelihood shifted from direct reliance on the land to a greater variety or different sources of income, the availability of family labor to provide for their own needs became less important to some parents. They could invest their emotional and financial resources in fewer children because they might have to rely on them less in old age, and they could be more optimistic that their children could obtain livelihoods for themselves by leaving the land. In this connection it is noteworthy that farm families and those in frontier regions made a later, slower change in their fertility practices, and that poorer families remained more likely than prosperous ones to retain high fertility rates. Children in those circumstances held on longer to their roles of providing labor or income directly for the family than they did among skilled, professional, or proprietary families with other access to livelihoods. Fertility changes were therefore a subtle index of the character of change across different social groups. They marked changes in the functions of households, the increasing status of free labor, and a reduction in the reliance on labor based on deference, unfree status, or social obligation.

Westward Expansion:
Family Aspirations and Restlessness

POPULATION GROWTH and pressures in Eastern societies, together with the aspirations of farm families and other settlers, continued to drive migration west and to swell populations in recently settled territory. New England out-migration, which in the 1800s and 1810s had been heavily directed toward western New York State and the Ontario shore of Lake Erie, in the 1820s and 1830s became more concentrated on Ohio and then Indiana, with substantial movements into these newer regions and then into Michigan. From 1830 on, parallel streams of migrants from Pennsylvania, parts of the South, and Kentucky and Tennessee also settled as far west as Illinois. Meanwhile, farther south, yeoman farmers and slaveholders had settled across the Mississippi. By the 1830s they were campaigning for control of the Mexican province of Texas, where slavery was outlawed but American planters were establishing it anyway. A settler revolt and struggles against the Mexican authorities resulted in the founding of an independent republic of Texas in 1836, strongly influenced by the large landowning planters and ranchers who wanted the land for their own interests.[23]

The speed and character of western migration and settlement contained a number of paradoxes. On one hand it contained mechanisms for social advancement and prosperity, and for the realization of individual ambitions. On the other hand, western settlement was often a collaborative process and not infrequently took settlers and their families into areas where prosperity and social advancement were hard to realize. Men's and women's encounters with new land were, in other words, a complex mixture of innovation with the recreation of older social structures.

Contemporaries frequently noted the apparent restlessness of many settlers in the West and the willingness of families recently arrived in one area to pull up their roots and move on once more to somewhere new. Behind this seemingly frenzied activity lay a variety of causes, rooted in settlers' origins and circumstances. Often enough it reflected a desire to recreate conditions they had left behind in their original homes. "My wishes . . . and my exertions," wrote Isaac Briggs, a Maryland Quaker, as he prepared to move to Ohio in the mid-1820s, "have in view . . . a place where my whole family, for a generation or two to come, may sit down, in *one* neighborhood, in peace, competence, and humble virtue." When Briggs's daughter at length reached her family's new Ohio land, she wrote, "A feeling of thankfulness arose in my heart as I thought, here *is* my home, here *is* an inheritance for my children where they *may* earn their bread [even] if it *is* by the sweat of their brow."²⁴

Early emigrants and more prosperous settlers had advantages over poorer or later-arriving migrants. Data on wealth and geographical persistence confirm the connections between first arrival, prosperity, and the tendency to remain in an area. First settlers often had the choice of the best land or access to water, transport links, or other resources that would benefit them and help sustain their families by enabling them to accumulate or increase the value of property. Propertied families were more likely to remain settled where they were than those with less wealth or with fewer material ties to a locality.

Thus inequality itself was a common mechanism for encouraging further movement on the frontier. Poorer families, those less able to obtain or develop valuable land, were among those more likely to move on to fresh places to settle. The sources of these inequalities often lay in the societies that settlers had left. On the Southern frontier, for example, slaveholding settlers often had substantial advantages over yeoman farm families. They had slave labor to clear land and then raise cash crops; income from crops might then bolster their local credit or enable them to purchase further land. Wealthier settlers, including slaveholders, could also more likely displace squatter-settlers whom they found on their land. A substantial number of out-migrants from newly settled regions were therefore poorer farmers, squatters, or laborers who had been unable to sustain their livelihoods when slaveholding farmers and planters established themselves. Displaced nonslaveholding settlers were prominent among early migrants to the southern tiers of counties in Ohio, Indiana, and Illinois, and to many parts of Missouri. Escaping the inequalities of slaveholding regions and seeking more egalitarian settlements farther west were motives that drew many farm families to newer frontier areas.

On the Southern frontier these motives were also supplemented by the consequences of slave-worked cash-cropping. As in older regions back east, certain plantation crops, including tobacco and cotton, were often quick to deplete the quality even of fertile soil. The haste for income from crops encouraged many farmers and planters to sow cash crops repeatedly on the same land. Methods such as crop rotation or the use of manure or other fertilizers to sustain soil fertility were rarely used in the early nineteenth century. Instead planters acquired new land and moved their slaves and households to it after relatively short periods, again reinforcing the outward thrust of frontier settlement. Others, particularly larger planters, acquired new land simply to expand their successful operations. James K. Polk, who had substantial numbers of slaves on his western Tennessee cotton plantation by the early 1830s, sought more income by redeploying and purchasing slaves to work a new plantation he had acquired and set up in north central Mississippi.

Farther north, where slavery did not exist, the mechanisms for frontier settlement had some parallels with those of the South but also distinctive features. Some migrants, who settled on land acquired from speculators or land companies, found their interests at odds with those of their proprietors and left again to seek better circumstances. William Cooper of Otsego County, New York, found settlers moving off his land in substantial numbers in the 1790s. Later, proprietors like the Holland Land Company attempted to develop policies that would encourage farm settlers to stay and develop the land they were purchasing. But proprietors' policies could not always correct for the effects of other considerations at work.[25]

In many places across frontier regions, land values rose as settlement proceeded and the denser population or connections to towns and commercial centers enhanced the land's desirability or income-earning capacity. Early occupiers or holders of substantial amounts of land found the values of their holdings growing, and the upward shift of land prices was an important factor in overall changes in wealth and wealth distribution during the first half of the nineteenth century. But the price mechanism affected families differently according to circumstances. Those who settled on less fertile or less favorably located land might benefit less readily from rising values. And for the many farm families who had seen moving to new land as an opportunity to realize the ambition to settle their own children on farms, the rise in values provided an impetus that could carry them still farther west.[26]

Critics of Western farming practices noted a tendency for farm families to purchase more land than they needed and to cultivate only small portions of their holdings. But a common reason for doing this was the family's hopes of using Western land to accomplish what they had been unable to do in the East: settle their offspring on farms of their own. Acquiring the largest acreages they could afford might affect their credit and make their financial position precarious, but it was often the best strategy they could adopt to fulfill their family ambitions. The rise in land values had a series of consequences in this context. Holders of only small acreages were often forced out of regions they had settled because they could no longer hope to acquire the land there that they needed for farms for their children. Meanwhile some holders of larger areas of land were motivated by the opening of new regions to trade their holdings in for yet larger acreages closer to the frontier. The desire to settle children on the land, the rise in land prices as regions became settled, and the tendency to regard land as a commodity that could be exchanged rather than as a fixed patrimony to be attached to induced both prosperous and poor farm families to seek out new settlements.[27]

This process, too, contained a set of contradictions. Early-nineteenth-century frontier settlement tended to be across fairly dispersed areas, wherever families could obtain fertile land or title to good land. Soon, though, the need for transportation links and demand for commercial connections led to greater emphasis on localities accessible to water transport. In Kentucky and southern Ohio before 1810, for example, many migrants settled away from rivers, but the emergence of steamboat transport in the Mississippi and Ohio valleys drew new settlers to localities closer to river access and raised the prices of fluvial land. Similarly, in upstate New York, distinctions emerged between the regions lying adjacent to Lake Ontario and the Erie Canal, completed in 1825, and those in the uplands to the south which had poorer access to transportation. Yet over time the demand for land and the desire of families to settle children on the land tended to overcome the limitations of the transport system. By the late 1820s migrants were pushing out onto the prairies of Illinois, taking farm settlement not toward places of commercial interchange but away from them.

Government policy also played a role in encouraging Western settlement and shaping its terms. In several stages between 1800 and the

1830s, democratic pressure in Congress led to the setting of increasingly liberal terms for taking up public land. The price per acre was reduced and the size of minimum purchases cut. Average farm sizes in successive new regions reflected these changes. In Michigan, large parts of which were divided up for settlement after the minimum purchase had been reduced from eighty acres to forty in 1832, farms were smaller and tenancy less common than in Illinois and Indiana, which had been settled earlier on larger acreages. Falling purchase prices and minimum acreages for public land also fueled speculative fevers when periodic "rushes" for new zones occurred. In Gull Prairie, Michigan, land acquired at the government's price of $1.25 per acre when the locality was settled in 1830 had become worth ten times that amount only six years later. Low initial prices and high expectations that values would appreciate led to an especially intense land frenzy. No fewer than 38 million acres of public land were sold between 1835 and 1837; the year 1836 saw the sale of 6 percent of all federal land, and one-fifth of public land sold was in Michigan alone. Even normally staid prosperous Easterners, like the Amherst, Massachusetts, lawyer Edward Dickinson, hungered to get their hands on title to unsettled land. Dickinson's anxiety "to make some money in some way, & if I don't speculate in the lands, at the 'East,' I must at the 'West'," was sharpened by his perception that middling or poorer men, whom he called "mere jacanapes," were riding to fortune on the increase in land prices. Being in on the process was as much a way of preserving the social order as of increasing his own wealth.[28]

Westward Expansion: Individuals and Kin

SUBJECT AS it was to the creation and loss of wealth, to competition for land and other advantage, and to the seemingly restless character of a nation anxious for material advancement, the process of Western settlement was nevertheless connected to existing social structures and relationships. The ability of Southern planters to move onto frontier land as a way of breaking with older family and emotional ties reflected not so much a tendency common to all movement to settle new land but the special opportunities that were afforded to those who controlled slave labor and could use it to achieve a degree of personal independence for themselves. When Southern slaveholders interested in settling in Indiana and Illinois argued in 1823 for the admission of slaves to those states, in violation of the terms of the Northwest Ordinance, they maintained that slave labor would be the quickest means of providing income in a new country and of ensuring the region's rapid development.[29]

Most settlers, however—North or South—were not owners of others' labor and had to accomplish their movement to new land in ways different from planters. In some cases it was possible for yeoman farmers to move away from old ties and start afresh without them, but it was more common for nonslaveholders to rely to some degree on their family ties in order to resettle successfully. Households and families rather than individuals were most commonly at the heart of this important process. As one historian has put it, the settlement of the trans-Appalachian West was not accomplished by "self-made men" but by "family-made men."[30]

Family connections often shaped migration patterns. Young men might be sent west to look for new land or other opportunities, but often they were joined by family members, kin, and sometimes neighbors too. The information they gathered formed a basis for the departure of a wider network of acquaintances. Patterns of chain migration were common, as families who first moved to a new area helped bring their relatives to settle nearby them. Clusters of settlements from different parts of New England, New York, Pennsylvania, and the South remained distinctive features in regions of Ohio and states to the west throughout the antebellum period. Family connections were often the glue by which these regional patterns were fixed. Although evidence from censuses suggests that individuals and families might move frequently, analysis of larger social networks indicates that they often did so within wider social contexts. Family and neighborhood credit and assistance was frequently utilized in setting up new farms. In Michigan and elsewhere there were examples of farms nominally run by one family but actually worked by more than one, as kin or neighbors cooperated to establish their settlements.[31]

The use of family and kin was itself often a mark of social distinction. Wealthy settlers, such as slaveholders in the South, were less likely to make use of them than middling farm families. So too, at the other end of the wealth spectrum, were the poor, who were more likely to be obliged to move according to where they could find work, or access to small plots of land, than to where they could enter a mutual support system based on kinship. In areas where tenancy was common, or where, as in the South, slaveholding prevailed, different patterns of migration helped produce class divisions in the West, based not just on wealth but on the access to social connections and credit that different levels of wealth could allow. Even where in-migrants were from the same general region, distinct patterns of social interaction could remain detectable for years after arrival. Two separate streams of New England migrants, for example, settled the township of Claridon in eastern Ohio after 1810. Even a generation later, the groups maintained distinct social networks and marriage patterns.[32]

New Englanders and other migrants to the Midwest thus assembled a mixture of commercial, family, individual, and communally based institutions that in part reflected the societies they had moved from and in part were adaptations to their new circumstances. Soon, increasing numbers of migrants from Europe heading for land in the West would also mark the landscape with distinctive social patterns. From the 1810s onward, numbers of English migrants sought to settle in farm colonies on newly acquired land in Illinois and elsewhere. Most later English farm settlers, together with a growing number of Canadian migrants into the American Midwest, would follow individual strategies or build limited neighborhood networks not unlike those of New England or Mid-Atlantic settlers. German and, later, Scandinavian settlers were often more concerned to rebuild social and religious communities intact in the Midwest, and relied even more thoroughly on family, kinship, and neighborhood ties to accomplish this. In the settlements of members of the Mormon church, gathered in Ohio, Illinois, and Missouri in the 1830s, with farm families drawn from declining regions of Vermont, upstate New York, and elsewhere, patterns of kinship and religious adherence were also closely woven. All illustrated the potential of the household economy to provide models of social adaptability and change from attempts to secure stability.[33]

Commerce and Towns

THE EXTENSION of rural societies to the West and the changes that occurred in their social structures were also much influenced by urban development. During the eighteenth century the proportion of people living in urban settlements fell, and America became more rural, but this trend was gradually reversed in the early nineteenth century. On average between 1790 and 1840 the urban population as a proportion of total U.S. population rose by about 20 percent each decade, though with a fall between 1810 and 1820. Urban growth reflected both changes in the overall size and activities of the population and the new connections that were being forged between rural areas and commercial centers as the rural population grew larger and more geographically dispersed. In towns of all sizes during this period, commerce and its related functions were the most important activities.

Urban growth seemed most dramatic in the Eastern port cities, which experienced particularly rapid rates of population expansion between 1790 and 1830. Boston, Philadelphia, Baltimore, and New York City all grew, along with smaller coastal towns, though Baltimore and especially New York experienced the most dramatic changes. Philadelphia, though still important, found itself somewhat eclipsed by the rapid expansion of its neighbor cities to the north and south; by 1810 New York had surpassed it as the largest city on the continent. But urban expansion was by no means any longer confined to the older port towns. Inland towns also grew and established themselves. This process was connected with broad changes in the countryside.

On one hand, towns became the predominant focal points of westward migration. Even before new farming regions were settled and cultivated, towns had appeared on major migration and transport routes to cater to the needs of emigrants and to service their new rural hinterlands. Albany, Rochester, and Buffalo in New York; Erie and Pittsburgh in Pennsylvania; Cincinnati, Cleveland, and a host of smaller Ohio towns; Louisville and later St. Louis, and numerous smaller centers on the upper Mississippi River sprang up to provision migrants moving to settle in successive regions of newly opened land. Since the work of Richard C. Wade several decades ago, historians have noted that the archetypal form of "frontier" development, at least in the nonslave and border states, was as much urban as rural, and that these towns placed their marks on the territory that was settled around them. On the other hand, towns in older-settled inland regions also expanded as rural areas diversified their production and became centers of demand for goods and services. Places such as Worcester and Springfield in Massachusetts, and York and Lancaster in Pennsylvania, expanded on the prosperity and needs of the rural areas around them and also became centers of manufacture themselves. In many cases, as at Albany, New York; Hartford, Connecticut; or Trenton, New Jersey, the functions of local urban centers were combined with those of small ports or settler supply centers. In 1811, Timothy Dwight counted twenty-nine different types of manufacture taking place in New Haven, Connecticut. As newly settled farming areas evolved and began to diversify their production, they turned frontier urban centers into the same kinds of mixed-function towns that were expanding in the East.[34]

While many of the speculators who dealt in land for farming were unsuccessful in realizing their dreams of wealth, their possession of land that could support urban development often did lead to wealth or local influence, or both. In small Appalachian towns that were often the first settlements in what became a predominantly rural area, urban landholders tended to form local elites, earning rental income from tenants both in town and in surrounding country areas. In Ohio, small developers such as David Hudson, who had emigrated from Connecticut in 1800, found themselves holding key lots in what became successful small towns. Hudson was able to name the growing settlement he helped found in eastern Ohio after himself, and recruited fresh settlers there from New England. Among various Eastern elite groups, holding land in the West in the hope of speculative gains was an important means of storing wealth. Around Trenton, New Jersey, for example, men such as Richard Stockton and Jonathan Rhea held modest landholdings that scarcely reflected their wealth and influence, but each had substantial interests in Western land as well. Members of the Tappan family from Massachusetts had holdings in various parts of the Western Reserve in Ohio whose value multiplied as settlements developed. A few found themselves owning property on what became big-city sites. There were examples to the contrary, of course. Marc Beaubien, a landowner at the southwestern tip of Lake Michigan in the 1820s, made a habit of giving away parcels of this "mighty lonesome, wet place" at local taverns. Asked much later why he had missed out on the fortune he could have made from owning Chicago, Beaubien explained that "he didn't expect no town."[35]

Although there were other sources of wealth in large urban centers, real property holdings became a significant component of the fortunes of the rich. The most valuable dwellings in Boston in 1798 occupied city lots that averaged fifty-one times the size of those of the poorest dwellings. As population grew, and land values rose, the potential earnings from subdividing such properties were prodigious. An 1846 survey of rich Philadelphians found that at least one in eight had made some or all of their fortunes from city property. Wealthy New York City landowners used their influence to shape the city's physical landscape, pressing for the development of parks and other facilities in locations that would optimize their property values. Even more than in the countryside, the advantages of early possession of urban land could become manifest in growing personal and family wealth.[36]

Whatever their size, towns were centers of diversified activities and occupations. In the slave South too, towns grew up and shared these characteristics of occupational diversity with those farther north. Inhabitants of Vicksburg, Mississippi, for example, by 1860 worked in as many as 193 occupations. Across Virginia, towns such as Charlottesville, Petersburg, and Fredericksburg provided commercial and manufacturing services for the surrounding countryside. But urban growth was slower and generally less significant in the South than in the Northeast and Midwest. The South's largest towns—Richmond, Charleston, New Orleans, and Louisville—all lay at the region's periphery, where its plantation and yeoman farming districts intersected with the main routes of river and ocean commerce. The combination of slave labor and staple-crop production continued, as it had in the colonial period, to create a smaller demand for urban services and functions than did the diversified production and the family- and wage-labor of the nonslave regions. The South's urban population remained a smaller portion of the total than in the North, and the largest Southern towns did not match the Northeast's largest cities.

The emergence of large and small towns as characteristic components of Northeastern and Midwestern landscapes reflected the dispersed character of the functions they fulfilled. Rural areas with mixed-crop and other diversified production created demand for traders and craft manufacturers in local centers. Similarly the demand for provisions and consumption goods that came from both newly settling rural districts and established regions that were achieving a measure of prosperity also supported the position of traders and merchants in dispersed town centers. The shifts in the production strategies of many Northern farm households, noted earlier, were made possible partly by the dispersal of trading functions, and in turn they reinforced local traders' positions. Towns and cities also often became the locations for the institutions—such as banks—that some local households turned to for relief from the limitations and obligations of the local exchange system.

Developments in the plantation South, by contrast, did not fully support or reinforce dispersed trading on the same scale. Shipments of staple goods such as cotton and rice tended to be arranged through specialist agents ("factors") in large port towns. Slaves earned no wages and slender other earnings for themselves, and so provided only limited markets for provisions and manufactures. Many plantations were to a greater degree than Northern farms self-sufficient in their needs for foodstuffs and craft productions, or were themselves centers of local exchange in these items. The character of rural markets, linked to the character of social structures, supported differing patterns of urban development and hence the differences in overall depth and growth of urbanization.

Urban growth accompanied the expansion of commercial functions. The numbers of merchants, stores, ships and steamboats, and banks grew to foster and to measure wider urban expansion. New York City grew rapidly after 1790 in conjunction with an upsurge in commercial activity; its directories listed 248 merchants in 1790 and more than 1,100 a decade later. The scope of its growing hinterland helped the city's merchant class exceed that of Philadelphia in size before the 1807 embargo slowed trade temporarily. But the periods of renewed commercial expansion after the peace of 1815, and again after the recovery from the panic of 1819, continued to drive up the scale of New York's activities. A count of ships in the harbor one day in 1824 found 324 vessels in port; a similar count twelve years later found 1,241 vessels. Such measures were also indices not only of the expanding volume of goods being shipped through New York but of the growth of the labor force necessary to load, unload, provision, build, and repair all these vessels, and to build and supply all the services and facilities that this labor force in turn used. Commercial expansion provided a powerful impetus to city growth that, except in times of slump, produced further gains in commercial activity.[37]

Connections between cities and hinterlands were also fostered by the investment decisions of urban merchants. Throughout the eighteenth century, merchant groups had chiefly pursued overseas and coastal trade, but in the 1790s and increasingly when the 1807 embargo brought to an end the post-Revolutionary commercial boom, they turned their attention to developments in the interior as well. Historians have emphasized merchants' investments in manufacturing, though ventures in transportation and finance were also of broad and lasting importance. Providence, Rhode Island, merchants such as the Brown family sponsored early manufacturing development in the state and had other interests. Zachariah Allen, Jr., who joined his father's Providence mercantile firm in 1801, when he was sixteen, helped turn a business that had previously focused on the West Indies provision trade toward investments in textile manufacturing, machine building, and insurance. The switch from overseas to internal investments was epitomized by the activities of Boston merchants of the Lowell, Appleton, and Lawrence families, who reinvested profits earned from Asian trade before 1807 into substantial textile manufacturing innovations during the War of 1812. Their partnerships, informally known as the "Boston Associates," in the 1820s and 1830s became the most prominent New England manufacturers.

Individual careers also traced the shift of emphasis from sea to land. Nathaniel Bowditch was the son of a cooper from Salem, Massachusetts, who was himself apprenticed as a cooper and then became a mercantile clerk before going to sea on five merchant voyages between 1795 and 1803, rising to become master and part-owner of his ship. Coming ashore again at the age of thirty, he subsequently entered the insurance business, turned his mathematical skills to use as an actuary, and emerged as head of the Massachusetts Hospital Life Insurance Company, a corporation that—despite its name—was notable by the 1820s as the nation's largest lender of mortgages on real estate. Bowditch the merchant's clerk and sea captain turned his career toward financing and profiting from the development of the land.

The expansion of trade and the numbers of merchants also accompanied a growing degree of specialization and the routinization of functions. Merchants in large ports came to specialize not only in particular trades but in categories of goods and stages of the trading process. After the turn of the century it was becoming rare for ship captains to continue their traditional role as traders on their own account, with discretion to buy and sell goods. Merchants now placed these decisions in the hands of agents, who by the 1820s handled most of a ship's commercial business while it was in port. The growth of agency agreements also enabled merchants in large ports to handle trading business elsewhere. The Baltimore merchant house of Alexander Brown built its business during the early expansion of cotton exports by acting as an agent for Southern shippers seeking purchasers in Europe. The growth of the Browns' and others' cotton business meant that Baltimore and New York merchants began to accumulate control of a significant share of cotton exports. The Northern merchants' ability to offer services from their large commercial centers gave them influence over traffic that never came near their own ports, and underscored the implications of the South's comparative lack of large towns.

One reason that New York and its neighbors could gain influence in the cotton trade was that British and European traders handling return cargoes to the United States found better markets for their own export goods in the expanding Northern cities and rural hinterlands than they did in the more constricted markets of the slave South. Hence regional differences imprinted themselves on a wider range of social and economic changes. Merchants intensified their connections with rural regions and developed networks of traders who profited from shipping produce and goods to and from farm families. By the early 1830s it seemed evident to the French observer Alexis de Tocqueville, on his famous American visit, that the nation's best opportunities for profit and wealth lay in commerce.

Social Differentiation

AS RAPIDLY growing centers, towns and cities often came to depend on influxes of migrants from elsewhere. Fertility rates were lower in cities than in the countryside, and there is evidence that mortality rates were higher, especially among the poor. So towns were often unable to grow much by natural population increase. Rural migrants, however, especially young men of limited means, continued to flock to cities and towns, to find commercial, maritime, or construction work. Twelve thousand new-comers arrived in Albany, New York, between 1825 and 1835, many of them young, unmarried men in their twenties, who found work as jour-neymen or laborers. Maritime activities no longer relied solely on coastal communities for labor but drew workers from the rural interior as well. By the 1830s one-fifth of New England whaler crews were from farming re-gions, sometimes to the amusement of other seamen who could not regard them as "proper sailors." When Richard Henry Dana's vessel encountered a Poughkeepsie-based whaling ship off the Chilean coast near Cape Horn in 1834, he noted "one of the lads . . . a thoroughly countrified-looking fellow," who came aboard, "seemed to care very little about the vessel, rig-ging, or anything else, but went round looking at the livestock, and leaned over the pigsty, and said he wished he was back again tending his father's pigs."[38]

The port cities were also receiving increasing numbers of overseas migrants as immigration from abroad began a long upswing after the War of 1812. Already in 1820 an estimated 20 percent of the population of New York City was foreign-born, a proportion that would rise to 50 percent over the next thirty years. Philadelphia continued to be a mag-net for immigrants, and Baltimore and Boston, along with some interior towns, also increased their rate of in-migration from abroad.

By the 1820s it was noted that European immigrants, especially from Ireland, were replacing African-American servants in many New York households. Structural changes in employment underlay tensions be-tween free black populations and urban in-migrants, both American and foreign. A succession of race riots in Providence, Rhode Island, includ-ing the "Hardscrabble" riot of 1824 and the Olney's Lane riot of 1831, were rooted in job competition and in white suspicion of increasing black independence, as African Americans moved from domestic service into their own housing and casual wage work during this period. When seventeen-year-old William J. Brown went looking for a trade in Provi-dence in 1831 he found himself thwarted by a white refusal to let a black do anything "which would elevate us to a free and independent posi-tion." Finally he found a black shoemaker willing to take him on, and he took over the shop when the man died. But he found that he needed sharp skills to avoid being cheated by his customers. One firm for which he supplied shoes tried to trim its payments to Brown by two-thirds, and he prevented this only by keeping a more accurate set of accounts of his own. Elleanor Eldridge, born in the late eighteenth century, undertook household work in rural Warwick, Rhode Island, during the 1812 war, moving from house to house spinning yarn, weaving cloth, washing linens, or nursing the sick. She also lived part of the time with a sister and began to sell on the Providence market the soap they made together. These petty selling activities grew into a more substantial business. Eldridge moved to Providence and established herself as a painter and decorator. She began to accumulate property, supplementing her earnings by renting tenements to poorer neighbors.

Such a progression seems unusual, if not unique, for a woman in the 1820s until we recall that Elleanor Eldridge was black. African Americans were largely excluded from the expanding Rhode Island textile industry; on the other hand, her race exempted Eldridge from cultural constraints on the kinds of work and business that would have affected many white women in the same period. Still, it proved to be her undoing. It is easy to exaggerate the scale of Eldridge's "success"; her income was small, and she was obliged to supplement it with periodic employment away from Providence. Her absence gave enemies a chance to use the legal process to effectively declare her bankrupt and, with the connivance of white lawyers and officials, to seize and sell her property and obstruct her efforts to regain it. Eldridge's race and gender did not mix with her relative independence, and she was reduced to becoming an object of Providence abolitionists' appeals for charity.[39]

Commercial growth expanded the demand for young, male urban labor. By the 1830s New York City had many thousands of clerks and other commercial functionaries, and smaller towns such as Utica, New York, also witnessed a rapid growth in merchants' and store clerks after 1815. Especially in larger cities, many of these young men lived unsupervised in cheap boardinghouses, giving rise to anxiety in some circles about social order and stability. Evangelical reformers and rural observers feared the cities as centers of uncontrolled immorality and vice. A recent estimate has suggested that by the mid-1830s, with a total population of about 270,000, New York City had at least 1,500 and possibly as many as 10,000 prostitutes at work. The publicity given to the murder of the courtesan Helen Jewett in the city in 1835, and the subsequent trial and acquittal of her lover and alleged killer, exposed a shadowy world of sexual bargaining and predation well outside the expectations of "respectable" society.[40]

Even in the colonial period some wealthier residents of Boston and other towns had begun to separate their residences from the tumult and crowdedness of the urban setting. After 1815 this process continued more intently. Between 1816 and 1830 the development of housing for prosperous families at Brooklyn Heights, New York, and its connection by ferry service to Manhattan's commercial district, established what the city's most recent historians have called the "first commuter suburb." Property developments in Philadelphia and at the edge of Boston, together with an increasing interest among urban elites in establishing country residences outside their cities, marked both a tendency toward suburban development and a desire by the wealthy to achieve separation from what they now saw as rough or disorderly crowds of urban dwellers. The continued prevalence and periodic ravages of epidemic disease, such as the serious cholera outbreak in New York in 1832, reinforced this desire.[41]

Most urban dwellers did not have these options and were obliged to crowd into increasingly densely packed working-class districts, or at best obtain modest-sized housing in areas intended for middling families. Poverty and marginality marked the lives of many. Poor women found employment hawking and peddling goods, or working in the grossly underpaid needle trades. For most working men and women, city life brought little relief from the seasonal fluctuations and consequent hardships of the countryside. As the newspaper editor Horace Greeley noted in his memoirs, winter brought hard times to New York as rivers and canals froze up, goods ceased to move, and the cost of coal and supplies rose. "Mechanics and laborers lived awhile on the scanty savings of the preceding Summer and Autumn; then on such credit as they could wring from grocers and landlords, till milder weather brought them work again." If summer brought epidemic diseases, work was again disrupted as thousands who could do so fled to retreats or relatives in the countryside, and much commerce was suspended. The structure and marginality of many urban populations made towns—for reasons different from those in the countryside—areas of recruitment for labor in manufacturing as well as in commerce and its attendant activities.[42]

Social Structures and Manufacturing Growth

BETWEEN 1810 and 1840 there occurred a sevenfold increase in U.S. manufacturing output, most of it in the Northeast, in a belt stretching from the Merrimack Valley in New England to Philadelphia and the northern Chesapeake region. At the start of the nineteenth century most American manufacturing took place in household units, in the shops of urban and rural artisans, or on farms. These regions subsequently saw a rapid increase in other kinds of manufacturing activity: in mills and factories, in urban workshops, and in merchants' putting-out systems that operated in town and countryside. All represented an increase in waged labor in manufacture and tended to concentrate labor in larger units.

Americans skeptical about manufacturing development had long feared this kind of concentration. In the 1780s, Thomas Jefferson had issued a famous warning against adopting the ways of corrupt and impoverished European societies, and advocated a future for America based on farming and commerce, keeping the workshops safely across the Atlantic. By the 1800s, Jefferson and his followers had been obliged to modify their views, but some still adhered to the notion that American manufactures could be conducted on a small scale. A Massachusetts Democratic-Republican, Benjamin Austin, urged Jefferson in 1815 to issue a statement in support of American manufactures, to help "those . . . which have arisen during the late war" achieve "a respectable state of maturity and improvement." Nevertheless, Austin stressed, "*Domestic* manufactures is the object contemplated; instead of establishments under the sole controul of capitalists." Jefferson responded that manufactures should take their place alongside agriculture as a use for surplus labor. His hope was that, as a household-based activity, this could be accomplished without transforming the character of American society.[43]

But in fact manufacturing was growing in a variety of contexts, and control by capitalist proprietors was becoming a hallmark of American industry as it was in Britain and elsewhere. Observers of European manufacturing growth linked it with the presence of large numbers of people without property or other ties to the land, whose need for employment meant that their labor could be harnessed to new activities. While later scholars long ascribed this shift of labor to dramatic changes such as agricultural enclosures (which were seen to drive people from the countryside by removing access to the commons and other sources of subsistence for the rural poor), more recent approaches have stressed the effects of a longer, more complex pattern of changes, including internal migration, population growth, the emergence of industrial by-employments in certain rural locations, the differential effects of enclosures and agricultural improvement on rural regions, and the slow, rather than rapid, emergence of large-scale industrial organizations like mechanized factories. This kind of approach to early European industrialization also holds the key to understanding the origins of American industrial development. From the 1840s on, increasing supplies of labor for American industry would come from large influxes of European immigrants. But important groundwork for American manufacturing was laid before then, in a period when immigration, though increasing, was not yet a primary source of industrial labor. The emergence and character of early industry was instead rooted in the social structure of existing American regions.

The demographic growth of the post-Revolutionary decades produced a substantial increase in the labor supply. The total free labor force in 1800 was 1.9 million; by 1820 it had reached 3.1 million, and by 1840, 5.7 million people. Until the 1812 war period, the pervasiveness of household production had limited the development of larger-scale industrial enterprises, except in activities such as ironmaking and shipbuilding where these had already existed before the Revolution. Most early manufacturing occurred in small urban workshops or in the countryside. The initial importance of rural social structures was sustained even as larger manufacturing enterprises were being developed. Although cities contained significant concentrations of people without property, this was less true of rural regions of New England and the Mid-Atlantic. Manufacturing in these regions did grow out of inequalities but also out of the gender differences within households and the makeshift arrangements put together by farming and marginal families to build their livelihoods.

In New England, population growth and pressure on land had given rise to clusters of craft-based manufacturing activities closely linked to farming and arising out of local exchange, intermittent hired labor, and the division of labor in households. The regular demands of farm work supported blacksmiths, coopers, wheelwrights, and leather workers, and such crafts were widely dispersed across the countryside. But, as noted earlier, more specialized activities also emerged, often using locally available raw materials or employing seasonal or intermittent surplus labor from the farm economy, and with close connections to farm households. In addition to seasonal manufactures, such as the making of corn brooms in the Connecticut River Valley, and part-time production in many farm workshops, there emerged significant industrial developments rooted in these rural social structures.

Toolmaking, chair making, and carriage and wagon making were among activities that grew substantially in rural areas. They either employed a coordinated specialization and division of labor between small workshops that cooperated with one another or, more occasionally, gave rise to larger, capitalized shops and factories where various stages of production were concentrated under one roof. The increasingly crowded population of southwestern Connecticut had access to local resources and to sources of demand in the New York area, and the region became an important center of woodenware, furniture, and metalware production, again initially on a household basis. Among its notable developments were the emergence of mechanical skills and devices for the manufacture of clocks, guns, and other equipment that would help lay the basis for an American engineering industry. Among the facets of this kind of development was the geographical dispersal of manufacturing activity across the countryside, in part to harness sources of waterpower and materials such as wood, but primarily to tap sources of labor.[44]

The dispersed character of the household-based system, and the intermittent supply of labor it produced, spurred the emergence of three features that would become a hallmark of the Northeast's manufacturing: the use of a division of labor to produce simple, component parts that could be assembled into finished products; the beginnings of a degree of standardization of those parts, to make feasible the assembly of pieces provided by different suppliers; and the role of the "manufacturer" not merely as a craft producer with mechanical skills but as a coordinator of work conducted by other people.

So farm workshops became adjunct to and often gave way to larger specialized shops and small factories. Yet production initially based in households did not always directly or entirely come to be concentrated in larger operations. In eastern Massachusetts, shoemaking had begun in the late eighteenth century in various locations, including coastal towns like Lynn where labor was available among former fishing and maritime workers. A division of labor grew up in many households, in which men working on the uppers and other components of shoes gave binding work to their wives or daughters in the household. From the 1820s on, larger shoe merchants, who came to organize the trade, began to distribute binding and other tasks separately, concentrating some activities in their own "central shops" where they could exercise supervision of the work, and sending out binding to be done in rural households across northeastern Massachusetts and southern New Hampshire.

In other instances, household production became the basis for new types of industry altogether. In the early 1820s, Emily Graves Williston, married to a farmer in Easthampton, Massachusetts, invented a process for covering wooden buttons with cloth. Within a few years her development was the basis of a thriving business; her husband, Samuel Williston, put work out at making button molds and covering buttons to rural families in the area, and soon extended his operations into a large firm making buttons, suspenders, and webbing. Such putting-out networks typified regions in the interior of Massachusetts and New Hampshire, where farming remained prosperous but where women and children in rural households also took in industrial work. By the 1830s, according to some estimates, up to forty thousand New England women were at work making straw bonnets, palm-leaf hats, and similar products in their homes. These activities were often not well paid but provided sources of work and income that could be accommodated within the other pressing demands of domestic life.[45]

To explore the effects of social structures on the emergence of larger-scale industrial production, it is instructive to compare developments in the textile industry in two different regions: southern New England and the area centered on Philadelphia. In both cases, textile manufacture was the most prominent early industrial activity; in the early nineteenth century it moved from households into mechanized factories. But the ways in which work was organized in the two regions differed markedly.

In New England between about 1810 and 1830, fertility rates rose to a peak, creating exceptional population pressure on scarce land and on work within households. This pressure effectively increased the labor available to industry as rural households shifted their strategies to abandon their own textile production and find income to purchase cloth. In 1833, Aaron Tufts of Dudley, Massachusetts, noted that household textile manufacture had almost ceased: "Comparatively nothing is done in the household manufactory," he remarked; "a female can now earn more cloth in a day than she could make in the household way in a week." But factory production followed different patterns, matching the varying conditions under which labor could be released from rural households to run it.[46]

Textile mills that operated on the "family" system were established widely across the countryside of Rhode Island, Connecticut, and southern Massachusetts. They recruited poorer rural men, women, and children to live in factory villages, sometimes providing land for men to farm as tenants, and employed women and children in the mills. An early report on one Rhode Island firm found that it had a total of 178 workers: 29 women and 24 men working in the company's mill itself, and another 75 women and 50 men employed as outworkers doing tasks in local farmhouses. By the 1820s the combination of millwork and putting out was in decline in the textile industry, and most tasks became concentrated in the mills themselves.

The disruptions to international trade of the 1807 embargo and 1812 war period encouraged greater investments in American factory textile operations. Most striking were those made at Waltham, Massachusetts, by the "Boston Associates"—merchants seeking more secure profits from earnings they had previously made in trade. Building a large, integrated mill with a substantial capital investment, they soon employed some 260 women workers, according to a contemporary report "principally the daughters of the adjacent farmers." The Waltham system became a model for further successful investments along the same lines, particularly at Lowell, Massachusetts, whose mills from the mid-1820s were soon employing not hundreds but thousands of women workers. Many of these were young women, daughters of farm families especially from New Hampshire and Vermont, where fertility rates had remained higher than in other parts of New England and where many farms were on poorer or marginal land.[47]

The recruitment zones for New England textile workers rarely overlapped; Lowell and Rhode Island mill owners, for example, drew on different regions and different elements of the farm population. And recruitment to these centers was smallest in districts where local manufacturing establishments had grown up instead, or where farming remained most prosperous. Early industrial labor forces, in other words, were found from among quite subtle and precise variations in the structure and character of rural societies.

Comparison with developments in the Philadelphia region illustrates this. In southeastern Pennsylvania and adjacent Delaware, rural economies were obliged to adjust during the 1790s to falling prices in the wheat trade as overall production grew and crops in some regions became diseased. Over the next few decades a division arose between the industrialized Delaware Valley region near Philadelphia and a dairying and mixed-farming region to the west of the city. As in New England, this functional split was rooted in local social structures and inequalities. Population density and pressure on land remained lower to the west, but high population densities in the Delaware Valley provided a surplus of rural labor available to be drawn by manufacturers into workshops and factory villages.

There were some similarities between the early industrial workforces in the two regions. When papermaking establishments near Philadelphia were put out of work by the financial crisis of 1819, about two-thirds of the eight hundred or so people affected were women, mainly daughters of farm families. Similarly, the burning of a cotton mill in the early 1820s on the Patapsco River, near Baltimore, idled one hundred workers, about seventy-five of whom were women, mainly from farms. But it had been more common in Pennsylvania, because of the surplus rural labor generated by wheat farming, for household-based textile manufacture to be conducted by male workers. So industrialization there relied more heavily on male labor than did early New England manufacturing. Combined with the relative prosperity of Pennsylvania farm households that were able to maintain wheat production or switch to dairying, this also meant that rural outwork played a smaller role in the industrialization of the Philadelphia region than it did in New England. By 1830 there were clear contrasts between New England, where women and children formed a high percentage of the early factory labor force, and the Mid-Atlantic region, where the proportion was lower.[48]

Rural surplus labor had long made Philadelphia a powerful magnet for migration. Rural migrants to the city rubbed shoulders with considerable numbers of European immigrants, creating an abundant urban labor market for entrepreneurs to employ. Its combination of migrants and skills made Philadelphia itself a major center of textile production, first in households and workshops, then increasingly in factories. Philadelphia's neighborhoods, including Kensington, Moyamensing, and Northern Liberties, became centers of textile production, initially dominated by male handloom weavers working in their own homes and small shops. In time these shops coalesced into factories owned by local merchants and master weavers. Unlike parts of New England that developed networks of textile firms owned by companies or groups of large investors, Philadelphia remained a center of relatively small proprietary mills. Boston, by contrast, with access to a different kind of labor, did not become a textile city in its own right, though its merchants became powerful investors in the geographically diffused New England textile industry. Even after the expansion of European immigration to New England in the 1840s relaxed many constraints on the urban labor supply, these differential patterns between major cities persisted.

Indeed, for the antebellum period, small manufacturing organizations remained normal. New York City expanded into a major manufacturing center based on small shops owned by artisans or controlled by merchants, producing a wide range of light goods. But some of its industries, especially the production of men's clothing, were transformed in this period. Between 1825 and 1835, clothing merchants organized large networks in the city, centered on small manufacturers' workshops and making heavy use of domestic outworkers for sewing, stitching, and other tasks. As much as some rural areas, city centers became the location for putting-out industries, drawing on and supporting the growing populations of poor families and single women in urban areas. In newer cities too, the clothing trades followed similar patterns. In Cincinnati in 1826 there were thirty-five clothing workshops, employing a total of 132 men and 467 women. By 1841 there had been an expansion and reorganization. Now there were sixty shops, though with only 195 men working in them while another 813 men and almost 4,000 women worked for these shops as outworkers.

Between 1820 and 1840 the proportion of the American population engaged in manufacturing grew from just under 14 percent to nearly 17 percent, but the increase in the Northeast was more pronounced; in Massachusetts the proportion rose from 30 to more than 40 percent. Increases occurred in coastal urban centers such as Baltimore, Philadelphia, New York, and Boston; in rural regions, especially in southern New England and eastern Pennsylvania; and in the newly growing towns and cities that were springing up to serve the farming communities of the new West. The growth of manufacturing was an index of the increasing coordination of activities across urban and rural sectors of the Northeast and Midwest, as markets for agricultural and manufacturing goods became integrated and mutually dependent, and as towns, merchants, and master manufacturers organized links between them.

The recruiting of manufacturing labor, and hence the structure of manufacturing itself, was strongly influenced by existing social structures and by the different ways rural economies, household needs, and patterns of regional and international migration shaped labor's availability. The fitness of recruitment strategies for local circumstances was one of the factors that helped determine the success or failure of a business or industry. Household-based production powerfully influenced the ways manufacturers initially operated. But once they were established, new work processes became dynamic influences. The relationships between employers and workers and the needs of production often conflicted in ways that drove employers to attempt new strategies, which in turn influenced the development of local and regional social structures. In the longer run, particularly in older regions where farming had become especially intertwined with manufacturing, these changes often marked the seeds of decline in household-based industries and the roots of greater industrial concentration.

CHAPTER 5

Crisis and Expansion

T HE SHIFTS in social structure that became evident in the 1820s and 1830s were associated with economic expansion. This was initiated by the slow recovery from the Panic of 1819 and would be brought to a sudden halt by the financial Panic of 1837 and another long period of depression. With greater prosperity came improved prices for farm goods and produce but also increased costs of goods for laborers and families dependent on wages. At the same time entrepreneurs whose businesses had picked up after the 1819 panic tended to take stronger measures to exercise control over their employees. Under these conditions it was not surprising that labor organizations, protest movements, and the first labor periodicals should grow up in the 1820s and contribute by the early 1830s to a burgeoning period of industrial militancy in both craft and factory-based occupations.

In 1826 the radical pamphleteer Langdon Byllesby, in a commentary on the causes and consequences of unequal wealth, noted the implications of social and economic changes. He saw commercial activities becoming generalized and mercantile exchanges being elevated above those between locals and equals. Making commerce a source of profit and relieving the mechanic and farmer of the obligation to exchange among themselves, Byllesby argued, the trader obtained undue wealth without productive labor. Why, he asked, should the merchant be entitled to a greater share of the proceeds of a transaction than the producers themselves received? Byllesby's comment pointed to an important change that was under way, particularly in the North, as the relative positions of merchants, manufacturers, farmers, and laborers were realigned between the 1820s and the 1850s.[1]

New Social Relations in Production

THE GROWTH of manufacturing did foster the emergence of large factories in some regions and industries. Textile mills in Rhode Island and eastern Connecticut and in Philadelphia and environs commonly employed dozens of workers; the larger mills built by Boston capitalists at Lowell, Massachusetts, and other sites employed hundreds and were among the largest organizations of their day. Yet the bulk of manufacturing continued to take place in much smaller craft shops, either in cities and towns or scattered across manufacturing districts in the countryside. Most artisans and industrial laborers were employed in these small units, and social distances between proprietors and workers often remained small. In some occupations, such as printing in small town centers, some machining trades, and construction crafts, the costs of entry to proprietorship were relatively low, and young journeymen could often hope to advance to master's or owner's status. In the Philadelphia construction trades, for example, access to capital and credit enabled many craftsmen to become master builders or achieve equivalent status in specialized trades. Newly emerging crafts, too, like machine building and locomotive building, at first emphasized skill rather than capital and were built up by craft workers who obtained finance or credit to go into business on their own account.

With the expansion of the manufacturing economy, the number of skilled workers also increased. In cabinetmaking in New York City, where some two hundred skilled workmen were employed in 1806, by 1853 there were about eight hundred craftsmen in the trade. In many smaller towns, artisans continued to operate with a degree of autonomy, setting up their own voluntary organizations, fostering a mechanics' consciousness, and using their networks of connections to sponsor or support younger entrants to their trades. Mechanics' ideology during the 1820s and 1830s was still rooted in the post-Revolutionary concept of propertied independence. Mechanics' and trades' associations, and the "middling interest" parties that sprang up in Boston and other towns, urged that property used in the production of goods should be the basis for freedom and equality.[2]

But the small scale of many industrial operations and the continued accessibility in many instances to craft skill or mastership nevertheless masked important changes that were taking place. Although the numbers of skilled workers continued to rise, their proportion in the manufacturing workforce was starting to fall. The two hundred New York cabinetmakers of 1806 controlled their trade. By 1853 the eight hundred skilled craftsmen in the trade were working alongside about four thousand other workers less skilled than they. The introduction of batch production and the division of labor, rooted both in the characteristics of part-time rural manufacturing and in the organizational logic of concentrated workshops and factories, did not so much "de-skill" individual craft workers as alter patterns of work and the social relations that went with them. An industrial world was emerging in which "mastership" and proprietorship were not the presumed aim of most craftsmen; they were achievements to which only a minority could aspire. Of Boston journeymen carpenters in 1790, about 45 percent became masters; by 1825 that portion had fallen to 11 percent. Whether they were employed in small workshops or in larger factories, an increasing portion of manufacturing workers were likely to remain as hired hands. Similar patterns were evident in the maritime economy. Among Essex County, Massachusetts, mariners a smaller proportion advanced from being ordinary seamen to officer's rank in the 1820s and 1830s than had made this progression in the decades following the Revolution.[3]

For those in manufacturing, living arrangements shifted too. The tradition that apprentices or those hired for work would live, or at least take meals, with their employers did not disappear; it continued, especially in rural areas and small towns. But it became rarer in larger towns and manufacturing districts, where separate housing or boardinghouses for workers began to be common. In some cases, apprentices had rebelled against the household discipline of the old system. Master shoemakers in Lynn, Massachusetts, had sometimes whipped their apprentices for poor work or infractions. Joel Munsell, son of a wagon maker in Deerfield, Massachusetts, had been apprenticed as a young man to a printer in the nearby town of Greenfield, but he left when his master insisted on his presence at all family meals. As the number of their workers increased, many employers too withdrew from the conception of the workplace as an extension of the master's household, and established residences separate from their workshops. In New York, Boston, and Philadelphia such separation was frequent by the 1820s. In a smaller city, such as Albany, New York, by 1830 almost two-thirds of the wealthiest 10 percent of households lived apart from their workplaces.[4] Around the large mills built by Boston capitalists in Lowell, Massachusetts, and other towns, company-owned boardinghouses were built to house the young women who were recruited as millhands and known as "operatives" because they worked machines. Seeking to reassure the rural families these women came from, the individual boardinghouses were intended to recreate a household environment under supervision, but they were quite separate from the houses of the mill agents, foremen, and overseers who supervised the workplace. In the fast-growing town of Rochester, New York, distinct middle- and working-class neighborhoods began to emerge in the 1820s. In 1828 the Albany city council commented on the "miserable collection of hovels" that housed many of the town's mechanics and laborers, and where many victims would die in the cholera outbreak of 1832.

Residential separation accompanied a growing separation of functions at work between the activities of production and those of supervision. The distinction had been present in early factories and only grew as factories expanded and became more common. Mill owners installed bells that rang the hours for starting and finishing work, and published "timetables" specifying working hours and the penalties that would be exacted for lateness or absence. But this tighter work discipline also emerged in smaller workshops as master craftsmen expanded their activities, introduced a greater division of labor, and devoted more of their time to organization rather than actual production. A Philadelphia cabinetmaker, Charles James, moved to Cincinnati in 1824, set up his own small workshop four years later, and then switched his efforts from making custom-ordered furniture to turning out cheap ready-made items in batches. As he expanded his output, he began to hire employees to do tasks, such as painting and ornamenting, that he would once have put out to craftsmen in the vicinity. Owners who enlarged their shops hired foremen to supervise work and exercise discipline. A sheet outlining "The Duty of a Foreman of a Printing Office," printed in New Haven,

Connecticut, in 1825, stipulated that the foreman should seek out workmen to hire when wanted, "dismiss them when no longer wanted," "regulate the hours of their work," and "keep them still, sober and peaceable, and attentive to their business, to see that they do not slight their work, [and] that they are obedient to his lawful commands." "In short," the instructions concluded, "he is to be in the view of the Workmen, their Captain and Commander, the same as a Captain of a Ship." And it was the foreman's role, not anyone else's, "to consult and advise with the Owners." Patterns of workplace distinction and authority once unique to maritime circumstances were now increasingly common ashore.[5]

Wage workers were in legal terms "free." They were not legally bound to owners or employers other than by the terms of employment contracts, either implicit or explicit, that they had voluntarily entered into and could choose to abandon. The growth of waged employment marked the passing, in the North, of most forms of "unfree" labor and would become a hallmark of the emergence of a "free labor" system distinct from that of slavery in the South.

There were some exceptions to the disappearance of coerced labor, however. Where textile mills or ironworks were located in rural areas, distant from other settlements, workers frequently depended on supplies from company-owned stores, which often debited them for goods against their credits for wages. These "truck" payments from their stores both reduced companies' need for ready cash and provided a source of profit on the sale of goods. Company stores and truck payments became increasingly common in mining and forestry as these activities developed during the century. In the South, lumber and mining camps often employed numbers of free laborers alongside slaves; in the gold mines opened up at Dahlonega, in northern Georgia, around 1836, for example, three-quarters of the workforce were slaves, but the other quarter were free white laborers. Company stores and truck payments often curbed the effective freedom of workers in such situations. "A factory store is a sponging place," complained Thomas Man of Rhode Island in a protest poem written in 1833; "It is the eel-pot of our sorry race."[6]

Waged employment occurred, moreover, within a legal framework that gave force to employers' efforts to instill and maintain work discipline. Workers were technically obliged to fulfill their contract agreements. In some contrast with the situation in Britain, for example,

American employers almost never sought legal remedy from workers who quit before their contracts had expired; indeed, the ability to leave undesirable employment without legal penalty was a crucial characteristic of "free labor." Yet there remained legal provisions that placed limits on the absolute freedom of workers. First, employers or foremen usually had power to fire them at will. Second, while they were at work, employees were subject to the disciplinary authority of their bosses under the scope of master-and-servant laws derived from English tradition; legally, workers had little remedy for conditions they found intolerable other than to quit the job. Third, though it was very rare for employers to sue workers who quit on them, it was often impossible for employees to recover back wages if they walked out of a job before a contract expired. Most workers were not in a position to sue for their wages, and in some cases that did come before the courts, judges found that failure to perform part of a contract invalidated a claim for any payment in regard to it. Finally, of course, the legal condition of "freedom" took no account of economic means. Having the right to quit at will and being able to afford to do so were quite different matters. As a writer in a Utica, New York, newspaper expressed it in 1832, "I had generally to take up with such wages as my employer offered, and had always to pay him the price he asked, for what I wanted to buy." The emerging social distinctions between workers and employers, which were coming into focus for the first time in the 1820s, gave rise to reflections on the actual character of "free labor."[7]

Labor Radicalism

MECHANICS' IDEOLOGY had stressed the importance and virtue of those who were "producers." It viewed participation in productive labor as the principal basis for earning and for citizenship. Workingmen's advocates such as Philadelphia's William Heighton attacked "aristocratic accumulators" who were not direct producers themselves but who profited from others' labor through trade, the rental of property, or other "unproductive" pursuits. Craft workers arriving from England and Ireland, and settling in growing towns like Paterson, New Jersey, often subscribed to such ideas and lent their weight to the politicization of manufacturing centers. This ideology was reinforced by religious ideals as mechanics came to participate in the evangelical revivals of the Second Great Awakening that swept the Northeast from the 1820s on. Baltimore artisan evangelicals embraced the producerist ideology; there and elsewhere mechanics and laborers invoked a biblical tradition of equality against what they saw as "unrighteous distinctions" in society. In many cities and towns, Methodism proved attractive to craft workers drawn by its emphases on spiritual equality, self-improvement, and self-discipline that fit well with the ideals of producerism.[8]

Yet as the conditions of work changed in the 1820s and 1830s, divisions opened between those who could become masters or proprietors and those who remained wage workers. Along with growing residential separation and the decline of working arrangements based in proprietors' households, these divisions gave rise to anxiety even among skilled craft workers that they were being looked down upon by the middle-class men who owned and controlled their trades. At the very time democratization was giving most white males the vote and bringing them formally into the political sphere, many men were sensitized to the new social divisions they perceived growing around them.

In New York and other towns during the early 1820s, mechanics' organizations began to criticize the Tammany Society and other centers of Democratic-Republican organization and influence as bastions of privilege, fostering the interests of the elite groups that ran urban politics. Across the Northeast, workingmen's parties were organized at the end of the decade in an attempt to convert this opposition into action at the ballot box. In Albany in the late 1820s, the established Mechanics' Society split apart and separate masters' and journeymen's organizations appeared, the latter growing particularly strong among printers and carpenters. Elements of a burgeoning labor movement challenged the power of employers and sought to restore what its advocates saw as an undermining of the independence of craft workers and laborers. Working men and women in several crafts and occupations campaigned or went on strike over issues such as wage rates, hours of work, discipline, and other working conditions.

They also disputed the exercise of control over these things. In 1831, 250 carpenters and joiners in Cincinnati went on strike against a lengthening of the workday by their employers. The following year their colleagues in Buffalo struggled with their bosses over the journeymen's claim to have "ten hours of labor to be called a day's work." When employers insisted that the workday lasted from dawn to dusk, and journeymen walked off the job in protest, master builders resolved not to rehire them. Journeymen masons, too, then lodged their claim for a ten-hour workday. New York City tailors and cabinetmakers struck several times in the early 1830s in disputes over who would set rates of pay (still called "prices") for their work. Workers at a Trenton, New Jersey, factory secured an agreement from owners that they would be paid half in cash and half in "store orders" (credit notes redeemable only in goods at the company store), but then went on strike in protest when the cash share of their wages fell below the agreed level.

Women workers were notable participants in this upsurge of labor radicalism. New York tailoresses went on strike in 1831. Massachusetts shoe binders protested twice during the 1830s against employers who refused to agree on wage rates when they handed out tasks, or cheated them out of wages due. Like many male colleagues, these women claimed "equal rights" to the fruits of their labor. In 1834 and 1836, young women working in the Lowell textile mills went on strike against wage cuts or rent increases in company boardinghouses, campaigning as "the daughters of free men." On the latter occasion they were successful in pushing the companies to rescind changes.

Patterns of militancy among early industrial workers often varied according to their distance from household patterns of organization and production, and to the extent of their continuing involvement in household production. Rural outworkers were least "militant" because they could show discontent in other ways—by refusing to continue to take work, or simply by failing to return materials. Factory workers who were separated from household work, such as the Lowell women in the 1834 and 1836 stoppages, or the English immigrant women at the Manayunk Mills in Philadelphia who established a tradition of militancy, were more likely to take strike action because their working and living arrangements bred solidarity and cohesion, and because they could not so readily turn to household-based work to eke out their livelihoods. In between were women working in the "family system" mills of Rhode Island, Connecticut, and southeastern Massachusetts, who rarely adopted the militancy of their Lowell or Philadelphia counterparts but who used absenteeism and other subtle forms of action to express protest or assert some measure of control over their working lives.

Labor advocates saw factories and the companies that owned them as threats to the equality and independence the producer ideology valued. "The liberty our fathers sought / The factory system sets at nought," wrote the Rhode Islander Thomas Man in his 1833 poem. Journeymen carriage makers in Massachusetts, protesting against the incorporation of a carriage-building company, wrote of their aspirations to become masters of their own shops, to which they perceived the proposed corporation as a threat. "The *many*," asserted a Utica newspaper in 1832, "have become the temporal and local slaves of the few"; productive laborers were "suffering under the malignant influence of an unseen power, that carries with it the *semblance* only of right, and is, in reality, as the Horse-Leech upon his earnings." The New England labor radical Seth Luther argued that society had become divided between "the producers on the one part and the consumers and accumulators on the other," and concluded that producers were not benefiting from their labors equally with those who lived off the work done for them.[9]

A keynote of many 1830s labor protests was the claim that capitalists and master craftsmen were disrupting the harmony and mutuality of a society of independent producers. Their claims were reinforced by the precarious standing of labor unions and militant action before the law. Strikers and unions often faced injunctions and other legal penalties while strike action was usually regarded as a breach of contract, subject to sanctions. Although a landmark Massachusetts court judgment in 1842 would uphold the legal right of trade unions to exist, many other provisions continued to weigh labor disputes firmly in favor of employers and proprietors. And in the shorter term, economic events would also tip the balance against labor.

Slump

THE END of the 1830s and the early 1840s found the American economy once again in deep crisis. The boom of the early 1830s had pushed up prices and, with easy money available on loan from banks, floated a good many speculative schemes. Inflation and banking reforms in the mid-1830s, including the hotly contested decision of Andrew Jackson's administration not to recharter the Second Bank of the United States, were followed by critical shifts in international economic conditions that, as had happened in 1819, provoked a panic in 1837. As one Ohioan recollected, when the banks were forced to suspend specie payments "all varieties of failure naturally followed," and there was great disruption. Scores of banks collapsed. Mercantile firms and small businesses alike were plunged into bankruptcy as debts were called in and the money supply dried up.[10]

All parts of the country were affected by the panic and by the slump that followed and lasted for several years. But the damage was lighter in the South than in the North. Southern cotton growers faced the sudden collection of debts and the prospect of financial ruin, and many in fact failed. In the new regions of the Southwest, where there were few banks, for example, many recently established planters were forced either to abandon their efforts or to turn for financial support to the families they had left behind in the Southeastern states. But the cotton market stabilized quite rapidly. Owners of slaves found they had the labor and the locally produced food supplies to continue production. Although cotton prices remained low for several years, the slave-based economy was able to adjust to these conditions, and it continued to expand.

The North faced greater disruption. The financial panic affected many businesses that had been highly regarded and assumed to be sound. The sudden collapse in 1837 of a poorly constructed building in New York's financial district seemed to some to be a symbol of the city's precarious economic fortunes. Most prominent was the failure of the silk importing firm of Arthur Tappan, one of New York's leading merchants, and a prominent evangelical reformer and philanthropist. Tappan was reported to have gone bankrupt with debts exceeding one million dollars. Commercial operations seemed to be placed in peril, and some individuals never recovered from their failure. A Hudson Valley man plagued by financial misfortune jumped from a third-floor window to his death in 1841, reportedly after having failed in an attempt to shoot himself.[11]

Believers in the doctrine that fortune stemmed from self-discipline and effort, rather than from chance, were shaken by the realization that the fruits of hard work could be so easily wiped out, and that chance often dictated who would be a victim. Newspaper editors and other observers agonized that the panic had resulted from an absence of self-control, as businessmen had succumbed to the temptation to overtrade in pursuit of easy wealth. The Amherst, Massachusetts, lawyer Edward Dickinson, who in 1836 had been tempted to break his own self-restraint to invest in land speculation, pondered like many others the "revulsion" that the financial collapse seemed to indicate, part of it his own lack of self-discipline. Investors did indeed get burned: the writer Caroline Kirkland and her husband had been living in the town of Pinckney, Michigan, which he had been trying to develop as one of its promoters. In 1843 they were obliged to give up and move back to New York, having lost most of the money he had sunk into the project.

The interruption to the financial system affected manufacturing businesses, even those whose products were in strong demand. The firm of R. Hoe and Company of New York, maker of the large printing presses that had been revolutionizing newspaper publishing for some years, was forced into bankruptcy and reorganization. As companies went out of business and factories closed, large numbers of people were thrown out of work. Wages and prices for farm produce fell, so both workers and farm households suffered. A tailor in Cincinnati wrote in 1840 that "our prices [i.e., wages] were so curtailed by our employers that we found it impossible to gain a livelihood." For two months he had been obliged to work for his board only. Many small manufacturers and craftsmen were unable to stay afloat financially without taking out mortgages or going to work for others. A Cincinnati chair maker, Jacob Roll, who had been a master for twenty years, was forced to abandon his own business in 1839 and go to work as a wage earner for one of his rivals. Thousands crowded the relief rolls in each of the large cities. As late as 1844, when the depression was beginning to lift, one New York City charity organization alone gave aid to more than 28,000 people.[12]

Immigration and the Labor Supply

THE DEEP effects of the Panic of 1837 and the depression that followed were felt in changes that altered the direction of Northern society when the economy began to recover. In some ways these changes reconfirmed patterns that had already been apparent in the 1820s and 1830s. As businesses were rebuilt, both large and small organizations remained important: the economy was still constructed around small enterprises, often household or workshop based, as well as larger companies and institutions. Across the nation as a whole, masking great variations in the size of particular enterprises, average manufacturing establishments rose in size from 4.31 workers in 1840 to 7.78 in 1850, and 9.36 in 1860, a 117 percent increase in twenty years.

Had the panic and depression of the late 1830s and early 1840s been confined to North America, it would not have had the profound effects it did on American society. Instead it was an international phenomenon, and so in addition to its influence domestically, the depression also altered the behavior of people in other countries toward the United States. Above all, it helped intensify the flow of immigrants who had been sailing to America in rising numbers, particularly since the 1810s. The influx reached new levels in the 1840s, changing the direction of American society, and particularly that of the North, permanently.

Economic depressions in the United States generally produced a slowdown in the arrivals of immigrants from Europe, and initially the same pattern prevailed this time. From Ireland, for instance, 48,000 immigrants came in 1837, before the impact of the financial panic was apparent; but in 1838 the number fell to 11,000. Word went back across family networks or other channels to discourage so many people from venturing across the Atlantic, for fear of finding no employment when they arrived. But several factors in the late 1830s and early 1840s neutralized this effect. Because the depression was also severe in European economies, especially in the British Isles, some workers and families shut out of opportunities at home took the risk of traveling to North America in the hope of rescuing themselves from difficulty. In 1841 alone about 120,000 people emigrated from Great Britain, many of them to North America. Textile workers from Lancashire, Yorkshire, and Scotland, affected by the closure of mills or displaced by the widespread abandonment of handloom weaving, sought out new opportunities in New England, New York, or Philadelphia. Pottery workers from the English Midlands organized emigration societies in the hope of removing to land in Wisconsin, or of taking up pottery work in the Ohio Valley. Some emigrants indeed succeeded in making a transition from laboring status to landed proprietorship that they could not have contemplated in Britain. John Claxton, a thirty-six-year-old domestic servant, arrived in New York from Liverpool in 1840. Ten years later he was in business as a miller in the town of Whitestown, New York, though without yet having obtained real property of his own. Ten years on again, by moving west, he had achieved that; he now had a farm in McHenry County, Illinois, and owned real and personal estate totaling $2,150. Irish craftspeople and laborers, impoverished by the disruptions in the Irish economy, or having already migrated to England or Scotland only to find continued difficulties there, also headed across the ocean to settlements being carved out by the rising numbers of their compatriots. All this meant that, even as the American economy was floundering in the early 1840s, its supply of labor was being augmented.[13]

Further overseas circumstances soon reinforced this process. The failure of the potato crops in Ireland in the mid-1840s, coupled with vast inequalities in Irish society and the effects of British free-trade policies on the situation, inflicted starvation on huge numbers of poor peasants who had no other food supply or resources to fall back on. Deaths from starvation and disease and the consequent disruption of rent payments led to a further massive displacement of tenants from large Irish estates. For the United States, the results of the Irish Famine were twofold. First, large numbers of men and women who had some means sought to emigrate to escape a collapsing economy. Second, as destitute people were cleared off many estates in Ireland, charitable and government efforts resulted in the shipment overseas of large numbers, simply to remove them from a situation incapable of sustaining them. Irish immigration to the United States jumped massively from the mid-1840s to the early 1850s, running at more than 100,000 in 1847 and as high as 221,000 in 1851.[14]

In other parts of Europe, too, economic disruption and political upheavals helped increase the numbers of families and individuals seeking to emigrate. The most important effects were in parts of the German states. Here the failure of political revolutions in 1848 and the consequent exile of liberals and radicals defeated by political reaction added to a flow of migrants already triggered by the weakening of peasant agriculture in areas such as the Rhineland. Early industrialization in Germany was undermining the household-based proto-industrial occupations of peasant-farming regions. The demand for industrial labor in the United States created perceived opportunities, especially for German mechanics and other skilled workers. Although it was increasing in the 1840s, the flow of German migrants did not peak until 1854, when the number of Germans arriving in the United States, at 215,000, temporarily exceeded that of any other group. German migrants continued to play an important role in the provision of new labor to both urban and rural regions. They were joined by French Canadians escaping similar constraints in Quebec peasant agriculture, and in the 1850s by a small but growing exodus of Scandinavians displaced by limits to rural economies in Norway and Sweden, who sought to create new farm settlements in Wisconsin and Minnesota. Among the migrants from Germany were significant numbers of Jews, who helped swell the total U.S. Jewish population tenfold between 1840 and 1860, to around 150,000. About one-third of Jewish immigrants arrived in family groups. Like Irish and other migrants, Jews settling in American towns and cities began to create religious congregations and community organizations.[15]

The most important effect of these migration flows, from Britain and Ireland, from Germany and Scandinavia, and from Canada, was permanently to reverse the structural labor shortages that had influenced the character and development of the American economy since the colonial period. During the 1840s immigration to the United States reached an unprecedented annual average of 170,000 people, but even this was exceeded in the 1850s when the average reached 260,000 per year. From 1840 to 1855 almost 3.3 million immigrants arrived, and from 1845 to 1855 the number of arrivals was equivalent to 14.5 percent of the 1845 population, the highest proportion in U.S. history. Immigrants swelled the North's working population in particular. Between 1840 and 1850 the proportion of immigrants among the male workforce of the Northern states rose from 29 percent to 38.3 percent, and in another decade would reach 45.5 percent. But in some rural regions, and particularly in larger cities and manufacturing towns, the impact of immigration was even greater than these aggregate figures suggest. In Pittsburgh by 1850, seven of ten manual workers were foreign-born. In New York City, where the foreign-born population already measured one-fifth of the total in 1820, the proportion reached 51 percent by 1855, with 70 percent of the city's wage workers having been born abroad.

Irish and German immigrants contributed to a twofold evolution of the American economy, especially in the free states. Substantial numbers moved to large cities, where they provided manual labor for expansion and skilled work for growing services and manufacturing. Of all immigrant arrivals in the United States between 1840 and 1855, some 68 percent landed at New York City. Although a majority dispersed to other areas, the city's role as a gateway to North America contributed substantially to the expanding immigrant populations of New York, Brooklyn, and adjacent parts of New Jersey. Irish immigrants, by the same token, had augmented the Boston population in the 1840s. Although German and Irish migration patterns overlapped considerably, there were notable distinctions in their distribution. Large numbers of both groups settled in New York and its environs, Philadelphia, Pittsburgh, Cincinnati, St. Louis, and the newly growing city of Chicago, but there were larger Irish groupings in New England, and a greater proportion of German migrants clustered in the Midwest and Great Lakes region.

Irish and German immigrants to these cities and to numerous smaller towns took up work across a spectrum of occupations, from manual jobs to commercial proprietorship, depending on the circumstances of their migration. A greater preponderance of Irish immigrants, including many of those displaced by the Irish Famine of the 1840s, found themselves in laboring occupations; 60 percent of Irish-born males in New York City in 1855 held unskilled jobs. German migrants, coming from a greater variety of backgrounds and under less severe economic pressure, were more likely to occupy skilled crafts or small proprietorships. Especially early on in the process of German emigration, significant numbers of migrants had already acquired literacy, training, or craft skills before they left Germany.[16]

In addition to settling in cities and industrial towns, both Irish and German immigrants moved to rural areas in significant numbers. Irish immigrants in rural areas were by 1850 spread widely, but often quite thinly, across large regions of the Northeast and Midwest. Some obtained farms of their own or were able to become tenant farmers. Irish families were among those who in this period took over New England farms that were being sold by locally born families who were migrating farther west. But many Irish, like their compatriots in the cities, lacked the resources to acquire land of their own. Instead, those who had come from rural areas of Ireland adapted their skills to become laborers and general help on farms that, with the increase in commercial crop production, needed more hired workers. Irish farm-laboring families were among the contributors to a subtle but important shift in class relations in the countryside, which was occurring in both older and newer regions.

German migrants to rural locations also furnished general farm labor, but to a greater extent than Irish immigrants they were positioned to acquire and develop farms of their own. A higher proportion of German than Irish immigrants had held their own farms back home, and those seeking land to farm in America were likely to head to relatively unsettled frontier areas where land was cheaper and opportunities for creating new communities greatest. Significant clusters of German farm families settled in regions such as southeastern Wisconsin and southwestern Illinois, where settlements were being established at the time of their arrival. Smaller numbers pushed on farther, to parts of southern Texas, establishing German farming communities toward the edge of white settlement, such as in the Colorado River region near San Antonio. Missouri and other Midwestern states also received considerable numbers of German rural migrants.

Although now finding themselves in new and unfamiliar surroundings, many of these emigrants aimed to recreate aspects of the rural societies they had left behind in Europe. Family clusters, chain migration, and the establishment of colonies of settlement by particular church congregations were notable features of the efforts of German, Swiss, and Austrian migrants. By 1860, for example, one in twelve of all immigrants from the German state of Braunschweig (Brunswick) were settled in a single county in Missouri. With more resources than most Irish emigrants and with stronger community bonds than many Yankee or English settlers on the American frontier, these groups moved to re-form their European social environments on the frontier. It was a pattern that Scandinavian immigrants to Iowa and Minnesota would also repeat. These "ethnic" farm families in the Midwest were more likely than American-born farmers to stay on the land they had acquired. Their households were also likely to retain aspects of traditional patriarchy and gender roles, and sustain greater inequalities between parents and children, and men and women, than those of American-born families in similar circumstances.

The effects of immigration were strongest in the free states. Although immigrants settled in every part of the Union, they were disproportionately underrepresented in the South, particularly in plantation regions. Throughout the nineteenth century these areas would continue to have some of the lowest proportions of foreign-born inhabitants anywhere in North America. Pockets of immigrant settlement did grow in some Southern towns and, as noted, in frontier regions such as Missouri and parts of Texas. But rural immigrants were rarely drawn in substantial numbers to regions with large slave-labor forces. Most German farm settlements in Texas were in places where slavery was weak. In Missouri by 1860, slaves represented 9.7 percent of the state's population, though the majority of them were concentrated in 36 of the state's 113 counties. None of these 36 counties was within the most prominent areas of German settlement, and all the counties with the greatest share of German-born inhabitants were those with below-average or negligible populations of slaves. Here and across the South, plantation slavery and employment for immigrants did not readily mix. Plantation zones usually filled their labor requirements with slaves; the yeoman farmers and poorer white laborers who also inhabited these zones were available for intermittent or casual labor needs. Such areas presented fewer opportunities to most migrants than those where freehold farming, family labor, or craft production were more prominent. German settlements in Missouri and elsewhere in the South were largely in towns and in rural districts without many slaves. Across the South as a whole, only 5.6 percent of the population in 1860 was foreign-born.

In the Northeast and Midwest the foreign-born proportions of the population were significantly higher, at 19.3 percent and 17.4 percent respectively. Here, in both urban and rural settings, immigrants furnished a substantial supply of new labor at different levels of economic activity and wealth. But while rural immigrants contributed to the extension of the frontier and the labor demands of older farming regions, those in urban and industrial areas extended the labor force for new manufacturing activities, or began to substitute for existing labor forces. Most striking was the progressive substitution of immigrant men and women for the preponderance of Yankee women and children in early

New England textiles and other manufactures. In Lowell, Lawrence, and other centers of large-scale textile production, the proportion of women mill workers began to fall after 1840 and by the later 1850s had declined substantially. At one Lowell mill, where the proportion of foreign-born workers was below 4 percent in 1836, it grew to 39 percent by 1850 and to 62 percent in 1860. Similarly, in the Rhode Island or family-system mills of southeastern New England, immigrants became a growing part of the workforce. In these cases they were in part replacing Yankee women and families whose own social circumstances and opportunities were shifting after the protests of the 1830s and the depression of the early 1840s. Facing poorer wages and harsher working conditions in textile mills than their mothers or elder sisters had twenty years earlier, fewer rural women were attracted to factory work after the mid-1840s, and mill owners sought new sources of recruits. In New England, as immigrants came to fill more jobs, older practices like the maintenance of paternalistic boardinghouses began to fall into decline, because their function of attracting single female workers from the countryside was no longer as relevant. Immigrant workers, now usually settled with their families in poorer sections of textile towns, filled the labor needs of factory owners whose original employment rationales had been adjusted to fit the subtle variations in New England rural social structures.[17]

But immigrants were also extending the size of the industrial labor force. The expansion of textile production in newer centers such as New Bedford and Fall River, Massachusetts, was based on manufacturers' confidence in being able to hire adequate numbers of English and Irish migrant workers to staff large mills. At Fall River by 1850, immigrants represented 59 percent of factory operatives and manual laborers. A comparable pattern emerged after mid-century in the Midwestern regions whose native-born settlers had come largely from the Northeast. In Chicago and other towns, manufacturers were much less likely to recruit women workers than had their predecessors in New England; male workers, many of them immigrants, came to dominate Midwestern industrial workforces.

Nevertheless, even in the new context, mill and factory owners continued to rely on means of recruitment and employment that were rooted in the family and household patterns of their workers. Kinship and local networks still influenced recruitment as existing workers ensured that cousins or sisters came to the notice of foremen and were hired on, usually to be trained to the task by their more experienced friends or relatives. French Canadians migrating to work in large Maine and New Hampshire textile mills built patterns of recruitment and family support that often included leaving children behind in the care of grandparents or other relatives in Quebec. By the same token, immigrant workers were slower to penetrate areas of employment where existing family structures still supported work patterns. In the 1850s in the eastern Massachusetts shoemaking industry, for example, based in towns such as Lynn, Haverhill, and Walpole, employers still relied heavily on women working in rural households to bind shoe uppers for finishing by male workers in central shops. Rates of employment of immigrants in shoemaking consequently remained lower than in textiles until after the Civil War, when the various stages of production came increasingly to be concentrated in factories. In metals and machinery trades, too, like those in southwestern Connecticut, employment remained dominated for the time being by native-born, skilled workers and by farm families doing tasks on a by-employment basis. The links between existing social and household structures and labor organization in particular industries helped determine their accessibility to immigrant workers.

Nativism and Cultural Conflict

TO A large degree, immigrant workers filled positions that had been vacated by native-born workers or created by the rapid expansion of manufacturing as the economy recovered from depression in the mid-1840s. Boston's population alone rose by an average of five thousand a year throughout mid-century. The demands for new construction and other activities that accompanied this growth helped expand employment in the city. Although there were exceptions, conflicts between native-born and immigrant communities in the 1840s and 1850s tended to arise not directly from employment issues, but over wider cultural, religious, and political differences.[18]

Protestant New England, in particular, had long nursed suspicions of Roman Catholicism, rooted in the fierce religious divisions in seventeenth-century England that had fostered the English Revolution and prompted the Puritan migration to North America. Fears of Catholic subversion of the British monarchy became, in eighteenth-century America, qualms about government tyranny and then, through the Revolution, concern over foreign interference with the affairs of the republic. In the late 1820s and early 1830s, virulent anti-Catholic literature from England, which appeared following Catholic emancipation there in 1829, circulated in American evangelical circles and helped fan smoldering resentments into hatred. Targets of anti-Catholic bigotry included newly established and growing communities of Irish immigrants and, notoriously, a convent in Charlestown, Massachusetts, that in 1834 was burned to the ground by a Protestant mob. Further episodes over the next two decades exacerbated the conflict.

Rivalries between Protestant and Catholic fire companies and other civic organizations in Philadelphia fueled serious riots in the early 1840s, including one in 1844 in which churches were destroyed, numbers of people were killed, and military force was required to restore order. The arrival of large numbers of Irish Catholic immigrants, soon followed by the migration of Germans, some half of whom were Catholics, also altered the balance of religious affiliation in some areas and introduced debates over schooling and cultural differences to the politics of several states. Just at the time Northeastern states were introducing common school systems to provide universal elementary education, controversy broke out with the Catholic church over the obligation of Catholic families to use these schools and the right to set up a parallel network of parochial schools that would emphasize Catholic teachings. Schooling debates rocked the politics of New York and Pennsylvania; the 1844 Philadelphia riot had been provoked by Protestant fury at an allegation that the Catholic bishop had disparaged the King James version of the Bible, which many Protestants took literally to be the Word of God.

There was also a growing and long-running divide over alcohol. Although it was not mapped precisely on religious differences, this became an index of cultural persuasion. The evangelical revivals had fostered voluntary movements for temperance that won widespread support (if not always observance), particularly in rural areas. The labor radicalism of the 1830s and the slump following the 1837 panic had prompted many Protestant workingmen to sponsor efforts for total abstinence. The Washington Total-Abstinence Societies that spread rapidly in some cities and rural working communities from 1840 on represented a strong assertion of the view that social equity would proceed from self-discipline and self-restraint. As the depression faded and the Washingtonians lost some of their influence, evangelical-backed efforts to secure legal curbs on alcohol consumption gathered weight. Cultural issues of law and self-control become linked with the political anxieties prompted by the growth of Catholicism.[19]

The influx of large numbers of immigrants had led political parties to organize newly arrived men to vote. Except in Rhode Island, where property qualifications for voting still applied, poverty was not a hindrance to the enfranchisement of new citizens. Democrats, especially in the larger towns and cities, were quick to enroll immigrants as citizens and obtain their votes. The newcomers became an important part of the Democratic power base, often to the fury of Whig opponents who disdained such approaches or expressed frustration at the effects on their political influence. Controversy over measures to restrain the sale and consumption of alcohol reflected allegiances in many localities. Although there were Catholic temperance advocates and organizations as well as Irish and German temperance societies, these could be a minority in their own communities. Democrats, often supported by Irish or German Catholic voters, largely opposed curbs on drinking while the currency of unpleasant stereotypes, particularly of Irish fondness for the bottle, helped fuel Protestant and Whig support for restrictions. From the mid-1840s on, conflicts over alcohol and other issues provoked virulent nativist sentiment among some urban and rural Protestant voters, who urged a longer qualification time for citizenship and conjured up visions of a political system manipulated by priest-led Catholic voters. For a period in the mid-1850s in the Northeast and parts of the Midwest, nativism attained statewide and even national prominence in the temporary success of the American (or Know-Nothing) party, though its efforts to restrict the citizenship and voting rights of immigrant men largely failed.

In larger towns and in the rural Midwest, religion, cultural attitudes, and political allegiances were important aspects of social division as some Protestants sought to make temperance and related values a test of "Americanism" and to restrain or exclude alternative influences. From their perspective, the measure of immigrants' entitlement to participation in politics and culture was the extent of "assimilation" to the norms they claimed as traditional. But many immigrants sought to achieve American citizenship and the loyalties it entailed while also identifying with other religious or cultural traditions. In matters of religion, schooling, and political allegiances—especially to the Democratic party—they wanted to be part of the national fabric without abandoning their own loyalties to community or principle.

Urbanization and Urban Society

ETHNIC TENSIONS also played out against the background of important shifts in the native-born white populations of the North following the Panic of 1837. Aspects of these changes, most visible in towns, were related to the functions and emerging power of urban centers in the national economy. The displacement caused by the panic and depression helped fuel greater migrations to cities and towns from rural localities where livelihoods became harder to sustain. Rural migrants thus joined the streams of European migrants who were swelling urban populations from 1840 on.

The consequent rapid growth of towns and cities transformed parts of the Northeast. In 1790 between 5 and 10 percent of the region's population had lived in urban areas (defined as settlements of 2,500 or more inhabitants). By 1850 this proportion had reached 38 percent in Massachusetts; even in New York State, with its massive rural interior, the figure rose to 19 percent. Ten years later, Massachusetts' proportion had reached 60 percent, New York's 39 percent, and Connecticut's 27 percent; in Rhode Island, the most urbanized state, two-thirds of the population lived in towns.

Towns and cities fulfilled a range of functions, usually shaped by their location and their surrounding regional economies. The port cities of the East Coast remained the chief points of U.S. contact with the Atlantic economy, while Midwestern cities like Cincinnati and Louisville emerged as conduits and suppliers to expanding frontier settlements. As commerce, both internal and external, grew, cities became increasingly important centers for coordinating and handling transactions. In many cases, that coordination included the processing of primary materials into manufactures, so that most large urban areas also became manufacturing centers. In towns like Pittsburgh, where ironworking and other metals trades expanded on the confluence of demand from East and West, manufacturing played a predominant role in the city's economy. Philadelphia's relative decline in commercial importance was more than balanced by the growth of manufacturing there, and the city remained strong in textiles and other long-standing major trades. Boston's involvement in textile production, as noted, was more tangential; in New England this sector was dominated by dispersed rural mill sites and by growing specialist manufacturing towns. But Boston's own manufacturing activities expanded in a range of areas that involved coordinating or supplying a growing demand from wealthy and middling households. New York and its smaller neighbor Brooklyn expanded rapidly on the growth of overseas trade and domestic production, forging large manufacturing centers in clothing, printing, and other trades while also emerging as the nation's leading financial and commercial center.

Commercial connections with their hinterlands and market zones were central to the functions of all cities, and regional economies became the chief determinants of their size and structure. Generally speaking, the larger the city, the more varied were the occupations of the people who lived there or visited. Most striking was the extraordinary range of activity. On New York's Broadway in 1856, Walt Whitman observed the passing of a day's crowd and its succession of different social groups. First came early-morning delivery carts, then construction workers who set out at 5 a.m., then "shop-girls, chatty and laughing or outworn and weary" heading "to many a bindery and tailor-shop, to attics and back-rooms innumerable." They were succeeded by clerks, who were in turn followed by "their employers, merchants and money traders," the last to head to work. During the day the street filled with a kaleidoscope of passersby: women promenading in town, and a mass of beggars, gamblers, paperboys, dandies, glass menders, tradesmen, country louts, policemen, militia companies, funerals—all surging up and down the wide street "in an undistinguishable and hopeless confusion." From their docksides and warehouses to their main streets and manufacturing districts, cities presented a picture of continual bustle and movement. City growth added to this impression. Between 1830 and 1870, for example, and within the 1830 boundaries of their city, Bostonians built more than sixteen thousand new dwellings, more than trebling the area's housing stock and averaging almost eight new houses a week throughout the period.[20]

One tradition in social studies has been to portray cities as unstable environments in which individuals remain strangers to one another. On the face of it, the restlessness of urban populations would seem to underscore that view. Historians have confirmed the impression of contemporary observers that cities were places of great movement. Individuals traveled in and out at astounding rates; persistence over extended periods was often limited, and when combined with the comings and goings of traders and visitors, the populations of cities like Boston could appear to turn over completely within relatively short periods. In comparison with the seemingly less anonymous countryside, cities appeared as centers of social distance and remoteness for those who lived in them.

But it is important to qualify this impression that cities were merely agglomerations of strangers. Patterns of social connections within them were often strong, just as they were in the countryside. Churches, voluntary organizations, and work activities all created networks within which individuals and families developed and maintained ties. Migrants to cities from the countryside often had contacts or family connections they followed and sustained, and many overseas immigrants established similar contacts. Migrants from home and abroad often followed common patterns in the evolution of their urban experience. Boardinghouses, many of them specializing in particular ethnicities or regional groups, were a frequent first recourse for single men or families moving into a city. Contacts might then be made with co-workers, and housing arranged by groups of unrelated men or families connected with occupation or workplace. Urban experience was often shaped by previous circumstances. A group of emigrants from an estate in County Clare in Ireland sustained rental accommodations in one of New York's poorest neighborhoods as they adapted to life in the city and continued to use their older social ties as a means of mutual cooperation and support. According to one observer, "whole streets in East Boston were the domains of towns or groups of towns in Maine or New Hampshire," from which migrants had arrived to work in the neighborhood's shipyards.[21]

Local attachments of this kind played a significant role in town formation. They also figured in the creation of suburbs at the edges of cities, which became communities not just of residences but of local occupations and services that recreated urban functions on a smaller scale, geographically distinct from city centers. The village of Jamaica Plain on the outskirts of Boston, for example, between 1840 and 1850 shifted from being predominantly a farming community to a suburban area as its agricultural population fell from two-thirds to one-third of the total. But a recent study of this shift also noted the mixture of middle-class, artisan, and laboring occupations that grew up there in the process, and the lending patterns and networks of association, including taverns and voluntary organizations, that emerged.[22]

Even so, just because they were not always anonymous places did not mean that cities were models of friendly egalitarianism. Harsh living conditions and social divisions made them highly unequal, more so than nonslave rural regions and as much (in a purely quantitative sense) as many plantation districts. Wealth distribution was more uneven in urban areas than in most rural regions, so as urban populations expanded, inequality grew with them. In the United States as a whole in 1860, the richest 1 percent of the population controlled 29 percent of total personal wealth. In urban areas, however, the top 1 percent owned 45 percent of total wealth. This discrepancy in part reflected the commercial and exchange functions of towns and cities: part of the wealth held there was controlled by the movers and shakers among their commercial elites. But the discrepancy also reflected the depths of poverty and lack of resources among portions of the urban populations.

In Boston, 1 percent of the population held 65 percent of aggregate wealth recorded in tax lists in 1860, and the richest 10 percent held more than 95 percent of recorded wealth. The remaining 5 percent of wealth was held by the middling 40 percent of the population, and the bottom half of the city's population had none at all. Although tax records are, for various reasons, imperfect reflections of wealth distribution, they offer a rough indication of the ways property and resources were owned. Across the U.S. population as a whole in 1860, about 30 percent of free nonfarming men owned real estate—usually the homes they lived in; a similar proportion held true in four medium-sized cities studied by Michael Katz. In larger East Coast cities, however, the proportions were usually smaller than this. In Philadelphia about 13 percent of men owned their own homes, and in crowded, poorer city neighborhoods the proportion could be much smaller. In New York City's Fourteenth Ward in 1850, for example, only 125 of 3,700 household heads (3.3 percent) owned any real estate at all. Various studies also suggest that native-born urban dwellers were more likely to own property than immigrants. In Boston in 1860, 46 percent of New England–born residents were taxed on some real or personal estate, considerably higher than the 31 percent for the city's population as a whole. In-migrants from other regions, and particularly the foreign-born, had lower rates of access to wealth and property.

Those with little or no access to property usually lived in overcrowded, mean, often unsanitary conditions. Early public health reports on East Coast cities like Boston drew attention to the serious health hazards of poor, packed, insalubrious tenements, the apartments often crammed into small spaces in back courts with little access to air, light, and water. Mortality data suggest that adult death rates rose between 1840 and 1860 as poor urban populations increased and harsh disease environments probably grew too. Infant mortality rates in cities were also considerably higher than in most rural areas. In the Northeast, urban fertility rates rose above those in the countryside, largely as a reflection of the size of urban immigrant populations among whom fertility had yet to begin falling. Across American society, mean life expectancy and the average heights of adults—further measures of a population's well-being—both declined in the period while the share of the population receiving some kind of assistance rose by 76 percent in the 1850s. Even in sound financial times, urban poverty reached significant levels. In Boston during 1853, a good year for business, 26,000 people were on some kind of poor relief, including one in ten of all children under fourteen. The following year, 1854, marked a brief period of depression. Philadelphia officials estimated that 700 people were begging on the city's streets, which were also home to some 1,800 vagrant children.[23]

Low wages for male laborers and fluctuations in the availability of much unskilled employment accentuated these conditions. While labor advocates and middle-class ideology fostered the ideal of the "family wage," with which a male breadwinner could support his family without assistance from other members, this was an unreal prospect for most working-class men and women. Women and children were usually involved in income-earning activities as part of or in addition to their household responsibilities: taking in outwork sewing for clothing manufacturers, or operating their homes as boardinghouses for other laborers and their families. Taking in lodgers and boarders often fitted with other household obligations for women and provided more regular income than could be obtained by taking on wage work outside the home. The demand for and supply of boarding places in working-class households contributed to the crowding of many urban neighborhoods. But women also undertook a whole variety of functions, from working as domestic servants and laundresses to running their own eating places or other small businesses that sold goods.

Class Divisions

THE CONTRASTS between these circumstances of the poor and the vast wealth of the larger cities' richest citizens attracted the notice of writers skeptical of the directions urban life was taking. Exponents of the wage system trumpeted the opportunities for saving that careful and economical living could achieve for poor people, and the press repeatedly published examples of men and women who had saved out of their earnings. But when a Dedham, Massachusetts, newspaper claimed in 1847 that a woman factory worker there had worked for forty years and accumulated two or three thousand dollars in savings, the New York editor Walt Whitman exclaimed: "To be shut up in a cotton prison for forty years—only to support life during that time, and save a paltry pittance at the end of it!" Manufacturers, he pointed out, could "make" that kind of sum in a week. Philadelphian George Lippard, writing in his 1864 novel about New York, *The Empire City*, noted the contrast between its "huts and palaces," often directly juxtaposed, where "lofty mansions and miserable huts stand near each other." "The great wealth of the great city," Lippard declared, "was only a Golden Shroud, mocking the misery and wretchedness which it could not hide."[24]

In the 1840s journalists seeking to measure and report on the wealth and influence of their cities' richest residents established a tradition of subjecting urban elites to critical appraisal. Awareness of the existence of great fortunes was emerging in the boom and bust of the 1830s and 1840s, and as elite groups such as the families who dominated Boston society, or who rivaled one another for control in New York, grew more prominent. The term "millionaire" was first coined around 1840; Moses Yale Beach, who compiled a collective biography of wealthy New Yorkers, estimated that the city already had 10 of them in 1845, and the number would grow to around 115 by 1860. Beach, with his contemporaries in other cities, traced the origins of these and smaller fortunes to the commercial, financial, and industrial activities that were either centered in the cities or fostered by them.

These journalists sought to understand whether wealth had been generated by self-made men who struggled up from poverty, and in many cases they found this to be so. But they also noted two other phenomena that gave them pause in contemplating the future of a supposedly egalitarian republican society. One was the influence of inheritance, the other was the effect of rising real estate values as cities grew. In an 1846 compilation on the holdings of Philadelphians with estates of $50,000 or more, 121 of 942 individuals for whom details were available were listed as having wealth derived wholly or partly from real estate. In New York, Moses Beach wrote of the nation's richest man, John Jacob Astor (whose wealth he put at $25 million), that though his operations in the fur trade and other businesses had certainly been valuable, "the greatest source of his wealth has resulted from the increased value of real estate consequent on the continued growth of the city." Astor had landholdings in frontier Missouri, Wisconsin, and Iowa, but New York City property was his greatest investment. By buying up the mortgages of others held on city land, Beach claimed, Astor could benefit both from the rise in values and from frequent foreclosures for nonpayment. Abner Forbes and J. W. Greene, in their 1851 compilation on the wealthy of Massachusetts, concluded that "many of [Boston's] existing fortunes have been created without the slightest effort, or participation even, on the part of the present holders, by the rise in the value of real estate."[25]

Other commentators noted or lamented the apparent effects of increasing class divisions. Churches and other organizations that had once catered to constituencies across class were criticized when they appeared to step toward greater exclusivity. Reverend Stephen Olin, the president of Wesleyan University, condemned the rich of New York and other towns in 1846 for constructing new, "magnificent churches in which sittings are too expensive for any but people of fortune." "Instead of associating themselves with their more humble fellow Christians, where their money as well as their influence and counsels are so much needed," Olin charged, they were intent on creating comfortable places of worship that owed more to the standards of the wealthy drawing room than the tradition of Christian egalitarianism. Observers of the Astor Place theater riot of 1849, in which a New York crowd protested the presence of an English rival to a popular American actor, saw it as a symbol of social division. The *Philadelphia Public Ledger* claimed that the riot revealed "an opposition of classes" between elitists and the majority, that "leaves behind . . . a feeling that there is now in our country . . . what every good patriot has hitherto considered it his duty to deny—a *high* class and a *low* class." Successive riots in the city in the 1850s were often blamed on the poor, but in 1855 the editor Horace Greeley attacked the rich for their greed, and New York's populist mayor, Fernando Wood, provoked outrage among the wealthy in 1857 when he asserted that "those who produce everything get nothing, and those who produce nothing get everything."[26]

A New Middle Class

BUT WHILE divisions between rich and poor grew wider in the 1840s and 1850s, they were masked to some extent by the continued expansion of the modestly prosperous proprietary, professional, and trade groups that made up the urban and small-town middle class. During the 1850s the prominent Massachusetts editor Samuel Bowles, of the *Springfield Republican*, wrote of "the great middling interest class," who "work with their hands, who live and act independently, who hold the stakes of home and family, of farm and workshop, of education and freedom." He urged them to oppose the Northern "aristocrats" and Southern slaveholders who constituted the nation's wealthy elites. Yet Bowles's appeal to a group who "work with their hands . . . and act independently" was only a partial description of the composition of this class in the aftermath of the Panic of 1837. Bowles's language harked back to an earlier phase in which direct "producers" were their own proprietors and could be contrasted with "nonproducers." Many such people did, of course, still exist. But by mid-century the middle class was also being augmented with new groups whose relationships to manual work and skill, and to proprietary ownership, were subtly different from those of previous decades.[27]

The ranks of "professional men," especially lawyers, physicians, and the clergy, had expanded steadily since the Revolution. While there were about 1,800 clergymen in 1800, for example, by 1845 there were almost 40,000 who more or less formally occupied the roles of pastors or preachers. But it was the expansion of commerce that produced the most notable growth in the numbers of nonmanual, nonproprietorial workers. When in 1826 the Philadelphia printer Mathew Carey published advice to European emigrants who were contemplating moving to the United States, he suggested that such nonmanual workers would find little opportunity because their places were already taken up with Americans. Laborers who crossed the Atlantic would find work in plenty, Carey suggested, building roads and canals, but shopkeepers and clerks should be discouraged from migrating because "there is at all times a superabundance" of such people. As cities and towns grew, however, their commercial activities recruited larger numbers of clerks and functionaries. The 1840 Census counted more than 57,000 retail stores in the United States, of which almost 58 percent were in New England and the Mid-Atlantic region. But many "middling" occupations were dominated by small proprietors who, until the Panic of 1837, expanded along with inflationary prosperity and with confidence in their standing as "independent" republican citizens.[28]

The events of the 1830s and 1840s by no means eliminated this group, and they continued to accumulate in numbers and social significance. But two circumstances helped alter the composition of the middle class. First, a reorganization of capital that began with the emergence of new railroads, factories, and financial systems in the 1830s increased demand for clerical and equivalent types of labor that were not manual crafts but were mainly hired rather than independent in status. The effects of the 1837 panic speeded these institutional shifts, particularly in the North, emphasizing the role of corporations and large investors, and introducing commercial innovations such as credit reporting and new accounting methods. Second, the panic's upheavals, and the many bankruptcies it triggered, undermined the confidence of some independent proprietors that they could sustain their own way in business. Failure rates remained high after the early 1840s. Some contemporary accounts suggested that as many as nine of ten businesses would fail over a twenty-year period. In Columbia County, New York, between 1843 and 1849, half the businesses either failed or left the area within five years. In Hampshire County, Massachusetts, the rate of failures was lower but may still have reached 50 percent over the years between 1843 and 1861, in addition to those whose owners removed or died during the period. As recovery from the panic spread during the mid-1840s, many individuals sought more secure alternatives to self-employment. With the growing demand for employed nonmanual labor, these men and their sons emerged to supply it.[29]

Factories required machine tenders. Railroads and other construction activities needed labor to build them and produced a heavy demand for manual workers to operate and maintain them. But all these organizations also needed administrative staff. Corporate-owned factories employed managers or agents who might or might not have investments in the business but were primarily acting on behalf of the owners, not for themselves. These men hired clerks and bookkeepers to help run the business and keep track of materials, labor, and finished goods. Railroads required managers and superintendents, station agents, clerks, train conductors, and other functionaries. Railroad companies were not only organizations of unparalleled size but by their nature were geographically dispersed in an unprecedented manner, so new business and bureaucratic methods were needed to manage them effectively.

Broader commercial developments also created demand for new types of workers. The simple expansion of banks and multiplication of mercantile firms required more clerks and officers to run and supervise them, and the quantity of such work in large cities created clerical jobs on a large scale—in brokerage firms, insurance, and other activities. In New York City by the mid-1850s, it is estimated, there were almost 14,000 mercantile clerks alone. Across New York State, meanwhile, the number of retail stores, urban and rural, had grown from an estimated

12,207 in 1840 to just over 23,000 in 1855, many of which provided clerical employment. The growth of nationwide markets in manufactured goods also produced new methods of selling and dispatching products to distant purchasers. From the 1830s to the 1850s there emerged the "drummer" or traveling salesman, whose task was to arrange for the sale of goods from manufacturers to regional wholesalers, or from wholesalers to retailers. By the eve of the Civil War there were tens of thousands of such men. In New York City by 1855, in a total population of about 630,000, about 30 percent lived in households supported by these "new middle class" occupations.[30]

As the historian Edward Balleisen has suggested, the dangers of personal financial failure and the shattering experience of bankruptcy during the depression encouraged many men to seek salaried positions that could provide security without great financial risk. Balleisen concluded that access to such employment was "crucially influenced" by "family connections and class position." Recruitment to nonmanual employment was initially skewed toward the American-born, the sons of farmers and of urban or small-town tradesmen whose businesses were most disrupted by the 1837 panic, and who could use local knowledge or personal connections to seek out newly created jobs. Of the five sons of Elijah W. Carpenter, a physician in the rural town of Bernardston, Massachusetts, two were placed in traditional artisan apprenticeships with a firm of cabinetmakers in the nearby county seat of Greenfield. But neither of them went into the trade they had been taught. One, Edward J. Carpenter, went into business for himself as a newspaper agent and periodical dealer; his fellow apprentice and three other brothers all found work from the expanded demand for nonmanual employees, two as retail clerks and two as conductors on the New York Central Railroad. Family contacts, kinship, and neighborhood all contributed to the finding of clerical and other employment, just as they had earlier guided men and women to apprenticeships and clerical positions in stores. The result was that new immigrants, or members of ethnic groups without the same connections, were for the time being disproportionately excluded from the expansion in such work. Without the same networks of social contacts as their American-born neighbors, immigrants had to rely on finding manual wage work. The forging of ethnic divisions in a new class structure was under way.[31]

Meanwhile another group of men was using economic expansion to find more independent work for themselves in the opportunities presented by growing urban centers. Many men once bankrupted by the panic remade themselves as "brokers," dealing in a range of paper financial instruments, acting as agents for insurance companies, and handling sales of urban and suburban real estate. William Bassett of Lynn, Massachusetts, after failing as a shoe manufacturer in the early 1840s depression and trying unsuccessfully to restart as a retail grocer, reemerged as such a "broker," handling all the functions just mentioned. In Bassett's case, however, this proved to be a step toward other things. Local contacts and knowledge enabled him to run successfully for office in Lynn's new city government in the early 1850s, and to secure a salaried position as "cashier" in one of the town's banks. It was the armies of men like Bassett and the Carpenter brothers who, as clothing styles changed with shifting job functions in the mid-nineteenth century, brought about the emerging distinction between "blue collar" or manual, and "white collar" or nonmanual work—an enduring mark of class distinction in America that has lasted in language and consciousness ever since.[32]

Evidence indicates that in many parts of the country these new "white-collar" workers were able to achieve a measure of prosperity and social advancement. In mid-nineteenth-century Boston, clerks were the most likely among wage-earning groups to be able to accumulate property; skilled manual workers who did so usually took longer and expended more effort. Elsewhere by 1860 a significant proportion of nonmanual employees owned some real estate, usually the houses they lived in, and many had more personal estate than many farmers. In a small town like Jacksonville, Illinois, a measure of white-collar success was the extent to which members of this group remained residents in the town over a period of years. Whereas overall persistence rates here in the 1850s were between 20 and 30 percent, men in white-collar occupations were, at 47 percent, considerably more likely than average to remain in town, and they accounted for about three in four of the men who did so.[33]

As white-collar occupations demonstrated some success in providing stability and modest prosperity, so methods of gaining access to them began to evolve. Courses or curricular programs in mercantile skills had been taught in some academies and secondary schools since at least the start of the century, but the 1840s and 1850s witnessed the emergence of formal institutions that specialized in such training. Mercantile or business colleges sprouted in the main commercial cities. One early example was Folsom's Mercantile College, established in Cleveland, Ohio, around 1848. A few years later Folsom's formed the model for a college in Buffalo that would grow into Bryant and Stratton business colleges, a significant chain of such institutions. Among the students in Folsom's business courses in 1855 was the sixteen-year-old son of a modestly prosperous family that had lived in various rural areas and small towns in upstate New York before moving west to Cleveland in 1853. This student would demonstrate that, for an exceptional few, the new route through commercial training, clerkships, and into business partnership could lead toward more than prosperous security. His name was John D. Rockefeller.

Two Elites

THE EMERGENCE of a new middle class in the commercial towns of the North and Midwest was in some respects matched by a similar development in the South. In small Southern commercial centers such as Charlottesville, Virginia, and Vicksburg, Mississippi, similar patterns of mercantile clerkships and comparable occupations also grew in number and importance in the 1840s and 1850s. To some extent also, employment in new corporate concerns like railroads expanded in the South as they did elsewhere. But although the character of this expansion was similar across regions, its scale was not. Southern towns remained fewer in number and generally smaller in proportion to total population. Southern commercial enterprises and transport developments remained on a smaller scale and less thoroughly developed than in the North. The range of financial and commercial services offered by the major Northern cities was rarely matched in the South; indeed, Northern businesses made significant inroads in the handling and financing of Southern exports and imports. Just as with the smaller scale of Southern manufacturing, the more modest size of the Southern white-collar middle class reflected key differences in social structures between the regions.[34]

Central to those differences were patterns of elite power and authority. Crucial to those patterns, in turn, was the availability of labor and—since agriculture and rural occupations continued to predominate in the South—labor's relationship particularly to the land. Slaveholders in the South controlled labor that produced profits and wealth for them directly from the cultivation of crops. Most slaveholders owned only one or a handful of slaves, but the minority of larger slaveholders who established and ran plantations emerged as the chief figures in the economies and politics of the slave states. Their ownership and control of slaves gave planters the means both to be the only significant group in American society to make large profits directly from cultivation, and the only important landed group to exercise effective political influence in their own states and in national government. Even in areas of the South where slavery was relatively weak, the ethos of a planter aristocracy could hold sway. The Ohioan William Cooper Howells, whose family moved across the Ohio River to Wheeling, Virginia, in the mid-1830s, recollected that even though there were only fifty or so slaves in the town, "the old slaveholding families exerted a great deal of control over the place, and they affected [i.e., copied] the manner and prejudices of the slaveholding part of the state." In plantation districts, both in older and newer-settled parts of the South, this control by slaveholders was even more palpable.

Outside slave-plantation regions the relationships between landownership, labor, and power were different from those enjoyed by planters. Because their access to labor power was limited and their ability to cultivate land therefore more subject to constraints, most family farmers were not able to generate great prosperity from farming. Farming remained a combination of a business and a way of life that was sustained less by its lucrativeness than by the hope and belief that it could provide comfort and security for farm families and their offspring. As had been true since the colonial period, wealth and power evolved in nonslave regions not from the direct control of the land and its production but in the shipping, processing, and marketing of farm products, in the sale of goods to farm families in return, and in the financing and organizing of the range of commercial and other functions that complemented the farm economy. Successful creation of wealth in the North and Midwest lay to some extent in profits from the trading-up of land prices during the course of settlement, but in the long run it derived to a greater degree from shipping, transporting, and supplying goods than from growing crops. While slave regions' elites were planters, in non-slave regions they were merchants, bankers, in some cases manufacturers, and in many cases the lawyers who constructed the commercial system and worked at making it function. Although the mid-century economist Henry C. Carey could assert that "the landowners of the world are the great capitalists," and "the exchangers are the small ones," he quickly noted that it was the "exchangers . . . and their machinery [who] absorb the chief part of the profits of the land." As Langdon Byllesby had remarked in the 1820s, middlemen seemed to receive a disproportionately large share of profits from the labor of others. Just as slaveowners in the South profited from the work of their slaves, commercial elites in the North profited from the productions of multitudes of farm families and small craft producers.[35]

These different means of earning profits also created different relationships to political power. In the South, the historian Francis Parkman would write in the 1860s, the "slave oligarch" was taught to hold and defend his "place of power and peril" by participating in both political and economic leadership. In the North and Midwest this connection between wealth and politics was weaker. By the time of de Tocqueville's tour of the United States in the early 1830s, it appeared that a substantial divorce between economic and political leadership had taken place in Northern states. Most merchants and financiers, Tocqueville suggested, did not participate directly in politics. Instead, lawyers had emerged as a group who frequently took their places in political institutions, and with the emergence of well-organized party politics were often represented in an emerging group of professional politicians. Parkman, who identified himself with the social elites of Northeastern cities, followed Tocqueville in noting that wealth and politics had become separated. "[T]he best instructed classes," Parkman claimed, were distinct from the "swarm of professed politicians," whom he looked down upon and distrusted. Drawing on an argument that reached back through Tocqueville to the Federalists of the turn of the century, Parkman asserted that in the North, "worth and character had withdrawn from public life," leaving it to be conducted by "mediocrity." Other contemporaries reflected on this perception. "Whoever may hold the reins of power," claimed *Hunt's Merchants' Magazine*, a leading commercial journal, in 1856, merchants "really rule. . . . The counting-house should be conscious of its nobility, and . . . zealously labor . . . to compel all the world to acknowledge the virtue and value of its lessons."[36]

Two Paths to Growth

NOT ONLY did the two kinds of elite groups—South and North—have different relationships to labor and politics, they also came to hold different notions of economic development. Since Hamilton's financial plan of the early 1790s and the fierce disputes of that decade over the desirability of closer trade links with Britain or with France, political opinions had divided over economic policies and over government's role in economic life. Advocates of a more interventionist, developmental process, associated with the "American system" of the Kentucky politician Henry Clay, had crystallized in the 1830s into the Whig party. Exponents of greater laissez-faire, of downplaying federal involvement in the economy, and of emerging provincial commercial elites, were from the 1820s to the 1840s often aligned with the Jacksonian Democratic party. Although there was a greater degree of Democratic support in the South and a greater degree of Whig adherence in the Northeast, party affiliations around these elements of developmental policy crossed sectional and social divisions before the mid-1840s. There were many planter Whigs and more Northern merchant Democrats. During the 1840s, however, a crucial realignment of political allegiances was becoming apparent. As we shall see in the next chapter, this realignment was primarily connected with the emerging debates over slavery. But it had other dimensions too, not least because slave and nonslave regions and their respective elites were beginning to reach differing views on other aspects of the nation's economic and political development. These views, also rooted in elites' relationships to slavery, labor, and commerce, helped align divisions over slavery itself, and slavery's extension, with divisions over national policies for the extension of the economy.

Among the early observers of this debate, the Pennsylvania economist Henry C. Carey in the late 1840s put his finger on some of the critical consequences of having slave and nonslave societies operating in parallel under the same political system. Carey's argument was not at first directly concerned with slavery, but he noted in 1847 that there were distinctions between economic trends that led, on one hand, to the dispersal of settlements over the landscape, and, on the other, to what he called the "concentration" of social and economic activities. Dispersal was generated by the tendency of agricultural-based societies to occupy larger and larger areas of land. Both the desire among farm families for land for legacies to provide to their children, and planters' search for land that could be worked by their slaves, created an expansive pressure that resulted in the distribution of population over wide areas and the dispersion of economic activity. Concentration, which Carey favored, was accomplished by the more intensive cultivation of land, by the diversification of activities in farming regions, and by the close connection between farming, manufacturing, and commerce that he argued would best foster prosperity. Recognizing a mounting tension between these two paths to economic growth, Carey sought to promote what he called a "harmony of interests" between agriculture, industry, and commerce.[37]

As events would turn out, however, the interests of America's two principal elite groups, Southern planters and Northern merchants, would continue to generate tension between these two approaches to growth. By 1854, Henry Carey himself would associate expansion and concentration directly with regional differences: "Northern men seek no enlargement of territory, but they desire to render productive what they have. . . . Southern men seek additions to their territory, but they do not seek to render productive what they have." While planters continued to promote the concept of extensive development across the land, many members of commercial elites came to favor policies that would promote the more intensive development of existing regions, hence increasing their productivity and potential commercial profitability. During the late 1840s and 1850s these divisions over patterns of economic development became associated with divisions, first, about national expansion and, second, about slavery itself. In the process, the differences between elites and between patterns of economic growth became instruments of regional and sectional division.[38]

CHAPTER 6

From Regional Differences to Sectional Divide

T HE TRANS-APPALACHIAN population of the United States, which had already reached 2.4 million in 1820, continued to grow rapidly, to some 15 million by 1860. The calculated geographical center of U.S. population, which in 1820 had lain about forty miles from Washington, D.C., by 1860 was in Pike County, in southeastern Ohio. Henry C. Carey's writings after 1847, advocating economic consolidation and diversification, appeared in the context of a sharp national debate over this expansionism.

The 1844 presidential election took place as the American leaders of independent Texas, strongly influenced by the republic's slaveholding planters, were petitioning for admission to the Union as a state. Many New Englanders and upper Midwesterners, including supporters of the abolition movement, opposed Texas annexation on the grounds that it would add a slaveholding state and potentially increase the power of the South in national affairs. The Whig party's candidate for the presidency, Henry Clay of Kentucky, also opposed annexation and had the support of considerable numbers of mercantile and financial leaders who favored curbing the Union's territorial expansion. Carey's arguments for consolidation, and for the more intensive development of existing U.S. territory, were directed partly at this group who, as merchants rather than landholders, were likely to benefit more from an intensification of production and markets than from the continued expansion of low-density,

labor-extensive settlement across the land. Although he was no abolitionist, Carey shared with many Northerners a fear that Texas annexation and expansionist policies would aggravate a blossoming conflict
over slavery that, until the early 1830s, had been kept largely under
wraps. Pursuing his ideal of a "harmony of interests" between the agricultural, industrial, and commercial aspects of society, Carey and many
Whigs advocated intensified development as a means of achieving prosperity without conflict over who could occupy what land.

Expansion and Consolidation

ONE HISTORIAN has described the 1844 election as the first to present voters with "an explicit and unequivocal choice between expansion
and consolidation," between the development of "an agrarian frontier or
a trading commonwealth." The Democratic candidate chosen to oppose
Clay for the presidency that year was James K. Polk, who owned slaves
and cotton plantations in his home state of Tennessee and in Mississippi,
and who advocated Texas annexation and national expansion. The elec-
torate was finely balanced, and the support that Clay could normally
have expected in New England, New York, and the upper Midwest was
weakened by the candidacy of James G. Birney for the anti-slavery Liberty party. As it turned out, the contest hinged on a narrow victory for
Polk in New York State that tipped the election's final result to the expansionist side.[1]

Clay and Polk each drew support from across the nation. Clay, himself a Southern slaveholder, received backing from plantation districts
like the Louisiana delta and parts of the Georgia and Alabama cotton
belt. Polk received slaveholders' support too, especially in Mississippi,
North Carolina, and parts of Georgia and Virginia. Prominent planters
like James H. Hammond of South Carolina had contemplated moving
to Texas in hope of growing more profitable crops and of losing fewer
slaves to disease than in the lower South. But Polk was also well backed
in several regions where yeoman farmers predominated: in much of
Arkansas and Missouri, in the Louisiana backcountry, in parts of the Appalachian uplands, and in southern Illinois, where many emigrants from
the South had settled. Polk's expansionist policies drew on the two

groups' aspirations: slaveholders' desire for more land for the plantation economy, and small farmers' wish for land to be available for the creation of family farms. Whereas Clay had urged consolidation as a means of averting political conflict, Polk and his followers trumpeted expansion as a way of overcoming the economic constraints that would, they argued, inevitably overtake a growing population.

This long-running expansionist argument, which Polk had first articulated in a graduation speech at the University of North Carolina in 1818, appealed to those who had traditionally benefited from it. New lands, Polk had then suggested, echoing Thomas Jefferson, would "overcome caprice and scarcity." Democratic publicists in the mid-1840s returned to these themes, added new rationales for expansion, and at the same time implied that the process was inevitable. As the Irish-American editor John L. O'Sullivan most famously put it, "our manifest destiny [is] to overspread the continent allotted by Providence for the free development of our multiplying millions." This invocation of providential patriotism helped obscure a fundamental dispute over alternative roads to national prosperity.[2]

The consequences of Polk's electoral victory in 1844 soon confirmed Whig apprehensions that expansion would provoke conflict. Texas annexation, accomplished in 1845, was quickly followed by pressure for further acquisitions and for a hard line against both Mexico and British territorial claims in the Pacific Northwest. Oregon, already being settled by American emigrants, was quite soon secured for the United States without a struggle with Britain, but deliberate American provocations in the Rio Grande Valley created a pretext for war with Mexico in 1846. Anxious lest territorial acquisitions from Mexico extend the domain of slavery still farther, many New Englanders and upper Midwesterners voiced fierce criticism of the war. A retired newspaper editor in Massachusetts reflected the opinion of many like him when he wrote in his diary in May 1846:

> Contractors, jobbers, speculators—all sorts of men but honest ones, may make money out of this contest, but the others will have to pay all, and the poor soldiers will lay their bones on the banks of the del Norte or other places, and be forgotten and unknown. . . . It is called patriotism to make war on others who are feeble, and to attempt the conquest

of large territories, when in fact, it is downright knavery, robbery, and plunder.

Opponents of the Mexican War would help foster a new, anti-slavery Free Soil movement that backed efforts such as the congressional Wilmot Proviso of 1846 to prohibit the expansion of slavery into the newly acquired territories and to sustain the integrity of the Missouri Compromise of 1820 that had limited slavery's extension.[3]

Notwithstanding the opposition to it, the Mexican War and its promises of fresh land to occupy were broadly popular. About 100,000 men volunteered to serve in the army. The short-run political losers from these developments were the Whigs, who found their efforts at neutrality over slavery eroded from underneath them. As Clay had feared, further westward expansion let slavery loose as the predominant political issue of the period. The ideology of "free soil," aimed at restricting the expansion of slavery, would in time prove more potent than the more radical abolitionist position in bringing about a severe sectional division. Within a decade and a half, the competing pro-slavery and free-soil versions of expansionism and extensive growth would force the major regions of the United States into antagonisms resolvable only by war. Henry Carey's hopes—that a focus on "concentration" and intensive development could avoid sectional antagonism and promote harmony—would lie in tatters.

Why the South and the North Were Different

SLAVEHOLDERS AND their alliance with farmers keen on expansion proved to be the power behind the greatest addition of territory to the United States since the Louisiana Purchase of 1803. To be sure, the South did not uniformly pursue "extensive" agricultural expansion. Some parts of the region took different paths. Local developments before the Civil War in the west Georgia up-country, for example, created a more diversified economy, producing a variety of crops and produce for market, than in the more traditional up-country region lying to its east. Some parts of Virginia had achieved a degree of diversification in responding to the Panic of 1837, and there were also indications of diversification and manufacturing developments in parts of Texas and the Southwest frontier. Nevertheless the revival of international markets after the depression of the early 1840s produced an upswing in prices for the South's principal plantation crops. This had the effect of sustaining or reviving traditional production patterns and underscoring the pressure to find more land, especially for cotton cultivation.[4]

Parts of the South Carolina backcountry that had suffered population decline in the 1830s were revived by the increase in cotton prices in the 1850s. Although soil and climate conditions posed geographical limits to the extension of cotton growing, the expansionary context and prosperity of mid-century confirmed many Southern regions in their attachment to existing crops. Many white Southerners "stuck with their staple crops and used slave labor if they could afford it," and some recalled the observation of the South Carolina nullificationist Robert J. Turnbull (1775–1833), who had written that the plantation states were an exception to the general rule "that domestic manufactures is the true policy of nations." Some evidence indicates that farmers and planters in the Southern states had become less self-sufficient in manufactures by the 1850s than they had been a generation before. On the Watson farm in Louisa County, Virginia, the weaving of cloth ceased with the death of the family matriarch in 1849, and the slave Jim, who had done the weaving, no longer counted it among his tasks. By 1850 some observers were becoming alarmed at what they saw as an excessive Southern dependence on Northern manufactures. As a Boston-born Arkansan, Albert Pike, graphically expressed it to the Southern Commercial Convention in New Orleans that year, "From the rattle with which the nurse tickles the ear of the child born in the South to the shroud which covers the cold form of the dead, everything comes from the North." Southerners' graves, Pike averred, were "filled with Southern soil," but the soil was "pulled in by Northern spades and shovels."[5]

Historians have frequently argued that slavery itself was a barrier to economic diversification in the South. They have suggested that profits from staple crops were higher than in manufacturing, and that Southern leaders feared a growth of manufacturing that would place large concentrations of slaves in urban environments. They have also argued that slaveholders were less enterprising than their Northern counterparts, and more concerned with maintaining the social order and political culture sustained by slavery than with pursuing economic "progress" or modernization. Yet such conclusions pose a puzzle. The Southern economy, and planters' wealth, grew healthily in the mid-nineteenth century. Moreover, considerable manufacturing did take place in the South, and most of those who worked in it were in fact slaves. By the 1850s between 150,000 and 200,000 slaves, about 5 percent of the total, were in industrial occupations. Although one in five of these slaves were hired out to manufacturers by their owners, the other 80 percent were owned by the companies or individuals they worked for. So the question seems to be not "Why was there so little industry in the South?" but "Why was there not more of it?" Why was expansion, rather than diversification, the predominant characteristic of the Southern economy?

Much of the answer lies in the character and interests of the main Southern elites. They were significant owners of land and were successful at profiting from the use of slaves in crop production. Not only did having slaves enable them to profit directly from cultivation, but the value of the crops they raised helped sustain the rising value of new land acquired in anticipation of being brought under cultivation. Slaveholders were especially well placed to obtain profits from these increasing land values because they controlled and directed the labor necessary to clear land and bring it into production. Expanding the area of land to be made available helped keep land prices low at the frontier and optimize the returns to investing slave labor in improving uncultivated acreage. It was not cotton profits alone but the connection between crop returns and land values that persuaded so many Southern planters to pursue their single-crop strategies. The price rises of the 1840s and 1850s merely confirmed the tendency. The South Carolina rice planter James H. Hammond had once advocated diversification but now abandoned the effort to achieve it on his estates and instead added to his plantations' acreage. The contrast with the Northern elites' relation to land and labor could not have been more profound. Northerners were unable to control farm labor directly. For them, profits and any realization of improved property values could only come from diversification.[6]

A recent comparative study of two counties on either side of the Mason-Dixon Line, one in Pennsylvania, the other in the Virginia piedmont, provides important insights into the distinctions that were emerging between slave and nonslave regions. Its author, John Majewski, suggests that there were no important differences between local Virginian and Pennsylvanian economic elites insofar as the pursuit of "progress" was concerned. As much as their more northerly counterparts in Cumberland County, Pennsylvania, the planter-connected leadership of Albemarle County, Virginia, sought to promote transportation and financial improvements, especially railroads and banks. In their intentions they were no less enterprising than the Pennsylvanians. But the two groups faced different constraints on their ability to achieve their aims, constraints that Majewski largely attributes to the different scale of the markets in their respective regions. The Pennsylvania merchants and civic leaders were well connected with commercial and financial institutions in Philadelphia, with which their town conducted constant trading back and forth. Local sponsors of railroads and other development schemes found it relatively easy to attract outside capital and to link up to longer-distance networks of trade and traffic. Virginia railroads, on the other hand, were more likely to be locally financed and to conduct business within a smaller region; outside capital and trade was harder to obtain. While Chambersburg, Pennsylvania, and Charlottesville, Virginia—the respective county seats—served roughly comparable hinterlands, Chambersburg's market and disposable income were larger and thus provided a level of business that would attract the investment and connections that could support improvements. Albemarle County developments were left behind because a smaller market generated less investment and activity.[7]

Yet while Majewski's explanation is clear enough, it needs a further step to be completed. Why did otherwise similar trading centers have markets of such different size and value? A large part of the answer lies in their respective regional social structures. In 1850, 52 percent of Albemarle County's population was enslaved, and Albemarle was one of thirty-seven Virginia counties where the slave population equaled or exceeded half the total. A degree of self-sufficiency on plantations, coupled with the severely limited purchasing power of slaves—who were usually paid no wages and given cheap supplies—dramatically curbed the size of markets and hence of the commercial and transport functions needed to serve them. Southerners may not have been any less "enterprising" than their Northern cousins, but they had harnessed themselves to a social system that took them on a different path. This had consequences.

A further condition that shaped the distinct paths of Northern and Southern societies after 1840 was their differing relationships to the long-standing labor shortages that had shaped American development since early European settlement. Because labor scarcity in the face of abundant land resources had placed a premium on access to coerced or compelled labor, the South had theoretically long enjoyed an advantage compared with the North. Whereas nonslave regions had largely to rely on family and wage labor, and other forms of coerced labor had declined, the South had access both to family and to slave labor. Until the 1830s this advantage prevailed. But the events of the 1840s reversed the situation. Northern societies, both urban and rural, were attracting increasing numbers of immigrants. As immigrant numbers grew, the Northern labor shortage receded. Particularly in cities, and most especially on the East Coast, employers could often count on the ready availability of manual labor, and wages—particularly for general "unskilled" labor—fell in relation to prices. The South, by contrast, faced an opposite trend. As a region that proved comparatively much less attractive to immigrants than the North, it was much less able to take advantage of the upsurge in immigration that marked the 1840s and 1850s. Instead, as the nation's land area expanded and new regions like Arkansas and Texas were opened up to plantation agriculture, demand for slaves to work there rose substantially. About 60 percent of slaves living in Southwestern states had been traded on slave markets rather than brought west by their owners. Demand for slaves began to outstrip supply, and their prices in slave markets rose. This too would have consequences for Southern society. Economically, as well as politically, the annexation of Texas, the expansionary policy of the Polk administration, and the expansion of the plantation zone would exact a high price from the planter elites who sought to obtain their fruits.

Missouri: Two Systems in Conflict

IF THE contrast between Pennsylvania and Virginia illustrated one aspect of the distinctions between American regions, newer-settled areas to the west also presented significant variations in their social systems. One example was Missouri, a slave state admitted to the Union in 1820.

It came to mark a juxtaposition not primarily between slavery and non-slave systems but between a yeoman-based rural economy and an urban economy with which it was not well integrated. In Missouri, extensive and intensive approaches to American development came into direct rivalry with each other.

Like other areas of the lower Mississippi Valley, Missouri had attracted planters and their slaves in the 1810s and 1820s when settlement was being established. But partly because of its location, and partly because planters' interest was at that time concentrated more on Alabama and Mississippi, Missouri—like Ohio, Indiana, and Illinois—also proved attractive to nonslaveholding small farmers who had migrated from the margins of plantation society in older regions of the South. Despite some commercial development and the growth of St. Louis as a significant trading center, Missouri's workforce was 84 percent agricultural in 1840. Slavery was by now in decline in the state; from 15 percent of the population in 1840, slaves fell to only 10 percent in 1860. Missouri's yeoman farm population gained increasing political influence, which it exercised in substantial votes for Polk and expansion in the election of 1844. Missouri became a center for farm families who were seeking shelter from the vagaries of the marketplace and an opportunity to remake the more traditional lives they had left behind. Both the Southern yeoman households who dominated the rural population and the considerable number of German rural settlers who joined them sought to sustain household production and limited involvement with commercial markets. Their comparative self-sufficiency insulated many Missouri farmers at the outset of the 1837 panic. But the state's largely unregulated banking system soon ran into financial trouble and embroiled Missouri in a long depression that lasted into the late 1840s. Burned by their experience with banks, Missouri voters exercised extreme skepticism at further commercial developments and managed to restrain the number and size of financial institutions for the rest of the antebellum period.[8]

This anti-developmental strategy, however, came into stark contrast with a commercial revival in St. Louis that began in the mid-1840s. Several factors boosted St. Louis's economy. The revival of cotton production and hence of river traffic increased its business with the Mississippi. The growth in Western settlement, and especially in overland emigration to the Far West, placed the city in the front line for supplying migrants, and St. Louis became an important crossroads and staging post for both North-South and East-West traffic. Local boosters promoted the city and its prospects in the light of national territorial expansion, holding out the vision of a great metropolis that would grow to match in scale and wealth anything the East Coast might offer. Indeed, in just five years between 1845 and 1850, the population of St. Louis grew by 120 percent, making it, with eighty thousand inhabitants, the nation's eighth largest city. Among the many who came were two types of migrant in particular. Immigrant workers, from Ireland and especially from Germany, moved to St. Louis to seek construction and skilled jobs, which were readily available as the city expanded. Alongside them came large numbers of commercial and professional migrants, many of them from New England and the Mid-Atlantic region, who set out to establish in St. Louis the kinds of commercial systems that had already evolved in Eastern cities.[9]

These Eastern commercial and professional migrants played an important role in St. Louis's growth in the 1840s and early 1850s. They brought capital with them from Boston or New York and were able to take advantage of access to information, credit, and networks of connections superior to those available to their counterparts from Midwestern centers. They profited for a time on the congruence of river and emigrant trade that St. Louis attracted. But the city failed to develop a strong commercial relationship with its own hinterland. The weak banking system and limited market connections of many small farmers in Missouri did not generate the kind of demand or flow of capital that made possible strong urban-rural exchanges in other Northern and Midwestern states. Yankee merchants in St. Louis operated to an extent distantly from more local traders, who were less able to get credit than they were, and who suffered higher rates of commercial failure.[10]

Although its yeoman farm economy, rather than slavery, was the main cause of Missouri's limitations as a rural market, the growing debate over slavery encouraged many Yankees in St. Louis to leave the city when hard times hit again in the commercial slump of 1857. The passage of the Kansas-Nebraska Act in 1854, the outbreak of a civil war in Kansas two years later, and the Supreme Court's Dred Scott decision in 1857 (in a case originally heard in St. Louis), all sharpened animosities between Northerners and Southerners. Like merchants in various centers, many of these men had not acquired property in St. Louis, and many felt themselves to be visitors rather than permanent residents of the city. Many moved to other places less inhospitable to Yankees. Chicago, in particular, became a notable beneficiary of this development. It had a larger, more developed hinterland, with which commercial ties were increasing, and it lay at a safer distance from the political fault lines between slavery and freedom. Meanwhile a substantial urban craft and laboring workforce had grown up in St. Louis. German workers in particular among these groups had ethnic links with their compatriots in the Missouri countryside, but neither had strong connections with the state's majority farming population or with its pro-Southern ideology. With their allegiances to the Union often stronger, these social groups in and around St. Louis would become the basis of important political divisions in the state with the approach of the Civil War.[11]

Texas: Extending the Plantation Zone

IF MISSOURI represented the juxtaposition of two regional systems and tested the ability of Northern commercial capital to operate without a strong sense of place, the new regions opened up by the expansion of the 1840s also marked the working out of three different models of development. Texas, already being settled by Americans while it was still a province of Mexico in the 1820s, appeared as an extension of the plantation and yeoman farming societies that had already spread across the South. Oregon, being opened to settlement by overland emigrants in the early and mid-1840s, began as another extension of the household-based farming societies of the Northeast. California, the first and most important of the Mexican provinces acquired by victory in the war of 1846–1848, would turn out not to replicate societies back east but instead to represent new social formations and a new set of extensions of Northern commercial capital.

Texas attracted a range of traders and settlers. As elsewhere, promoters billed its available land as a potential paradise for small farmers: "Any man with 500 dollars can become an independent farmer, and with industry and economy may . . . have a good home for his family . . . ," wrote one. As already noted, German farming communities sprang up in the eastern and central parts of the state. But Texas also became a westward extension of the cotton plantation zone, and the predominant influences in much of settled Texas were the interests of cotton planters and slaveholders.[12]

American settlers had acquired Texas land under the Mexican government. After obtaining independence in 1836, slaveholding interests used their influence in the new government to secure legal dispossession of many of the remaining Mexican estate owners, or *hacendados*. In alliance with small farmers, they passed populist laws favoring settler landowners and disadvantaging land speculators, but then conspired with absentee investors to form land rings to accumulate large holdings. By 1860, 26 percent of Texas farmers were landless. After Texas joined the United States, the process of building the plantation zone continued. Between 1850 and 1860 the slave population of Texas grew more rapidly than the free population, trebling in size. Slaves came to account for 30 percent of the total population. By 1860, in thirteen counties in the northeastern, eastern, and coastal sections of the state, the slave population exceeded 50 percent of the total. Despite the overall variety in its rural social structures and the introduction of some economic diversity, Texas remained dominated by agriculture. Manufactures expanded in some centers, but in common with other plantation regions Texas retained a low rate of industrial investment per capita.[13]

The dispossession of older landholders in Texas and other parts of the Southwest that had belonged to Mexico laid the basis for the creation of a Hispanic labor force which would be employed for wages in farming, ranching, and mining from mid-century on. But the Anglo population was itself fractured by class divisions comparable with those in other zones where plantation and yeoman farming mixed. Zachariah Ellis Coombes, a Kentuckian whose family had moved to Texas in 1843, ran the school at the Brazos Indian reservation in northern Texas during the late 1850s, and evoked in his letters and diary contempt for members of the elite and their manners. Although his own position as a teacher enabled him to be treated as "aristocracy" in a small community, he distanced himself from what he called the "dignitarys and aristocrats who would not . . . condescent so much as to eat with a laboring man and have wished me to lay aside my plain democratic ideas of equality among respectable men." Remarking that he came "of a plain, straight forward, plain spoken family," he had evidently offended those with more pretensions: "In conversation . . . I took occasion to give my ideas of what constituted a polite gentleman, which I said consisted in acting the hypocrite to everybody." Class distinctions among the white population denoted a society of sharp inequalities.[14]

Oregon: Extending the Family-farm Frontier

OREGON, BY contrast, offered some settlers the prospect of sustaining an egalitarian society based on household production and independent landholding. Opened in the early nineteenth century to fur trappers and traders, the Oregon territory was also by the 1830s being visited by missionaries keen to convert its indigenous populations to Christianity. Prominent among them was a Presbyterian couple, Marcus and Narcissa Whitman, who proselytized among the Cayuse and Nez Percé Indians. By the 1840s two new considerations were in play. Oregon was claimed by Britain, and American settlers and officials sought to resist British annexation. In the nation at large there was also increasing interest in migration to the Far West. Helping encourage one thousand migrants to reach Oregon in 1843, the Whitmans hoped both to strengthen U.S. claims to the region and to initiate a pattern of family migration that could provide Oregon with a settled American population. Their efforts, and those of others, would soon pay off, but the Whitmans would not live to see it. The arrival of white families seeking land sharply increased tensions between settlers and indigenous peoples. Fearing dispossession, and following an outbreak of measles in their villages, Cayuse warriors attacked the Whitmans' mission station in November 1847, killing fourteen inhabitants and capturing forty-seven. The Whitmans were among the dead.[15]

Nevertheless the settling of territorial disputes between Britain and the United States prompted a demand for Oregon land, and a substantial migration began. The American population, at first mostly concentrated in the fertile Willamette Valley, numbered about 5,000 in the mid-1840s but grew steadily. Migrants, chiefly from the border regions of the Midwest, were primarily concerned to establish family farms, and the Oregon Territory's administration promoted in-migration by allocating land to settlers on favorable terms. The process helped drive out local Indians, and territorial law provided other measures for elevating the rights and opportunities of white settlers over those of the small number of Pacific Islanders, blacks, and others who had also come to Oregon. In 1852 alone an estimated 12,000 migrants arrived from the Eastern United States. Despite the creation of some large landholdings, Oregon remained predominantly a settlement for family farmers who hoped to carve out sufficient holdings to support themselves and provide land for their offspring, as they had done back east. By 1860 Oregon had more than 5,600 farms, of which more than 93 percent were smaller than 500 acres. Many settlers had moved in family and neighborhood groups from the central part of the continent, seeking, as one historian has put it, "not a totally new life but a better old one." Like everywhere else, Oregon's settlements were marked by inequalities, but these were often less pronounced than in older regions or other new settlements.[16]

California: New Social Models

BEFORE THIS pattern had become established, some Easterners thought Oregon would become "the seat of Empire" in the Far West. A writer in the magazine *DeBow's Review* in 1846 suggested that Oregon's most fertile districts were "the Eden spots of Western America," and that by contrast California, to its south, would remain "arid and infertile" and comparatively unimportant. But events were soon to disprove this prediction. California's acquisition by the United States in 1848 coincided with the discovery of gold in rivers of the Sierra foothills east of Sacramento by American and European settlers who had already entered the region in modest numbers during the 1840s. The news of the gold strike, when it eventually reached the East Coast, was characteristically greeted as evidence of the providential character of American annexation, and touched off an unprecedented rush for riches. Between 1848 and 1853 some 250,000 people migrated to California from various points of origin.[17]

During 1849 tens of thousands of Easterners and Midwesterners, mostly young men, many of them from farm families, set out by sea or land for the long journey to the goldfields, all hoping to make their fortunes. By the time most American migrants to California arrived, they were already behind thousands of others who had flocked to the region from various parts of the Pacific: from Mexico and Chile, from Polynesia, even from Australia. These circumstances set a number of terms for California's early history. It was a polyglot society, almost unprecedented in its social and ethnic variety. Wrote Mary B. Ballou from the goldfields, where she and her husband kept a store and boardinghouse, "I am among the French and Dutch and Scotch and Jews and Italians and Swedes and Chinese and Indians and all manner of tongues and nations but I am treated with due respect by them all." Still, notions of racial hierarchy and of national claims to possession gave many arriving Americans the right in their own minds to push aside those they regarded as inferior, and to assert their own claims instead. Furthermore, as the California Gold Rush gathered weight it acquired practical and mythical implications for other parts of American society, giving California a unique position in the popular imagination.[18]

To many the Gold Rush appeared as an opportunity for advancement in a still poor society. Early gold-mining techniques, based on panning or simple placer methods of separating gold from the riverbed silt where it was found, seemed to combine the wonders of alchemy (turning dross into gold) with the virtues of producerism (hard work would have its reward). Young men who set out for the goldfields faced enormous physical challenges, both on the journey to California and after they arrived, which those who survived could regard as a test of manhood. To some degree the search for riches, and the accomplishment that success in the goldfields might bring, appeared to conform to ideals of individual striving and opportunity. Many migrants to California emerged from the kinds of social dislocation and disruption that had already spurred young men in particular to migrate within older-settled societies in the East. Yet there were also many aspects of the preparation and conduct of the Gold Rush that reflected the social networks and patterns of cooperation in which many Americans were embedded. Although it attracted young men pursuing visions of wealth and adventure, it drew particularly from regions and groups where kinship and neighborhood networks could sponsor gold seeking. Among the pioneers of the California goldfields, and instrumental in establishing early techniques of gold prospecting and extracting, were Mormons, supported by close familial and communal ties. In the East, meanwhile, family and neighborhood networks were instrumental in raising funds to finance groups of prospectors. Men organized emigrant companies, or traveled to California in groups based on local patterns of connection and affiliation. Even though many of these groups had dissolved by the time they reached the actual mining districts, they played a crucial role in organizing the effort to get there. Moreover, gold digging itself was in many respects a cooperative venture, and returning gold seekers frequently had to face the expectations of the kin and neighborhood sponsors they had left behind.

Often those expectations were not met. There were, of course, many aspects of Gold Rush California that would have violated most rural communities' sense of propriety and virtue. Mining camps were raucous, sometimes dissolute places. Their populations were heavily male. Women connected with them were often—in others' estimation, and frequently enough in reality—associated with prostitution and other debauchery. Too commonly, also, prospectors had little luck finding gold, or lost or traded away what they did find in expenses, drink, or entertainment. Many Eastern households hoping that modest riches from the goldfields might lift their burden of debt or help realize family ambitions were disappointed. Enough gold seekers did return with wealth and enough fortunes were made that the allure of gold remained a strong motivation for other rushes to newly discovered fields in the decades that followed. But for most people the impact of the Gold Rush was stronger on the imagination than on the pocketbook.

Indeed, for several reasons, individual gold seekers and the men in the mining camps were not the primary beneficiaries of the Gold Rush. First, unlike farming, which promised the potential for repeated income from property, mining produced only a onetime gain from the land. Labor in mining did not cultivate the land but destroyed it. Miners secured wealth from the goldfields only if they were lucky in obtaining a good claim on which to work, and then only for as long as gold remained to be found there. Once they exhausted one claim, they could continue to get returns only by securing another. The very scale of the Gold Rush, which put tens of thousands of men into the early riverbank goldfields, ensured that easily found gold was rapidly discovered and removed, and that finding new claims increased in difficulty. The phase quickly passed in which ordinary men, organized only to cooperate with one another, could find gold by hard work. Many forty-niners returned to the East without having covered their expenses, let alone struck their fortunes.

Better prospects for gold-mining profits lay with larger, more highly capitalized organizations. As early riverbank claims were exhausted, exploration for gold turned to more capital-intensive methods. Hydraulic mining involved constructing elaborate water flumes and apparatus to wash out huge quantities of riverine soil, screening it for the minute proportions of valuable gold it might hold. The costs of obtaining rights to land for this purpose and constructing the equipment to do it lay far beyond the means of most individual miners, and hydraulic mining became the province of larger-scale capitalist companies. Such mining still required heavy labor, though, so companies hired men for wages to do the work required; as wage earners, these men had no stake in the gold they recovered. While these firms pursued hydraulic mining, others began quartz mining—digging and drilling into quartz rock formations to extract gold-bearing ore that then had to be crushed. Although the costs of the mining itself were often lower than in hydraulic extraction, advantages went to firms that invested in crushing equipment and that could control the production of gold or hire workers to extract ore for them. Once the first flush of the Gold Rush had passed, California mining became a significant locus of waged work and capitalized industry; by 1852 about 100,000 miners were at work in the goldfields. Once again, individual miners were rarely in a position to make gains from these arrangements. Even many investors in these companies found themselves without profits to pocket. One man involved in river bar mining claimed in 1852 that of thirteen ventures within five miles of his place, only two had produced much return for their owners, and several had been complete failures.[19]

This man was also a storekeeper. Even during the early months of the Gold Rush, the fortunes made by a small proportion of miners in the placers had been more than outweighed by the significant returns achieved by commercial operators in the goldfields, in San Francisco, and in other supply centers. San Francisco had already been established as a modest port and trading center when, in 1848, word came of the gold discoveries on the American River inland. Within days, it was said, the town emptied, and as fresh ships arrived in the port they too were deserted and stranded as all able-bodied men took off to search for gold.

Soon, however, shrewd observers noted that as the influx of prospectors from the Pacific and then from the East grew, their opportunities for profit would lie more readily in supplying goods than in digging for gold themselves. Merchants organized supply stores in San Francisco, moved to locations near the goldfields, or extended credit to partners to set up groceries and other supplies for miners. Among the influx of Easterners in 1849 and after were also individuals with capital or partners in East Coast mercantile firms whose purpose was to profit from the prodigious demand for goods that the Gold Rush generated. Just as merchant elites back east had based their prosperity on trade with farming and manufacturing hinterlands, so early California merchants sought to profit from their trade with the goldfields.

On the strength of these commercial developments, San Francisco and smaller towns grew rapidly. Soon San Francisco would be the seventh-largest city in North America and, in ways tailored to California's circumstances, was replicating the commercial, financial, and transportation organizations that had already come to dominate Northeastern and Midwestern cities; half its population had been born outside the United States. So sought after were clerkships in San Francisco businesses during the 1850s that families were prepared to advance loans to firms in return for employing their sons, effectively as apprentices, to secure them an entry point to the new middle class. Within a short time of its explosive growth as a mercantile center, the city was duplicating not only the functions but also the social structures of Eastern commercial centers. Despite the difficulties of communication, close ties were established between West Coast and East Coast businesses. After leaving the U.S. army in 1853, William Tecumseh Sherman, who as a military officer in California during the Mexican War had played a role in the establishment of an American administration and in the communication of news of the gold strikes, became the San Francisco agent of a St. Louis banking firm. When this branch closed in the 1854 slump, his firm reassigned Sherman to New York City, though not long after his arrival there the 1857 panic forced the bank to fold.[20]

Other arrivals in California took their eyes away from gold mining to consider the potential of the state's rich land resources. James L. L. Warren moved from Brighton, Massachusetts, in 1849 and set up first as a merchant in the goldfields before moving his business to Sacramento and then to San Francisco. As the state's farming economy developed, he came to specialize in agricultural and horticultural supplies, and also edited a farming periodical. Under Spanish and then Mexican rule, substantial areas of land had been granted to *californio* landholders and were held in large estates. Just two hundred Spanish-Mexican families owned as many as fourteen million acres between them, an average of seventy thousand acres per family. The Treaty of Guadalupe Hidalgo, by which Mexico ceded California to the United States in 1848, guaranteed these landholdings under Mexican law. But American figures, such as the explorer and adventurer John Frémont, had already acquired large holdings of land under these Mexican grants before the late 1840s, and new arrivals came to obtain more. Many early American landholders in California were rich investors seeking large profits from increased land values; some were already millionaires. By the 1850s also, American squatters had settled on land in northern California and contested the rights of the existing owners. Over time, and by various means, substantial acreages were transferred from Mexican to American ownership, forming the basis for a distinctive agricultural economy. As was also happening in Iowa and other parts of the Midwestern frontier, large accumulations of land were being used to form substantial farms, particularly as cattle ranches or to grow wheat; other cultivators developed viticulture and vegetable growing. The supply of labor in California, which included displaced Native Americans, *californios*, and Gold Rush miners from various backgrounds, enabled large wheat farms, using hired labor, to become an established part of the central California landscape.

Although they all developed varied social structures, each of the new regions opened to settlement in the 1830s and 1840s exhibited a dominant pattern that became its hallmark. Texas extended plantation slavery. Settlers in Oregon aimed to transplant small-scale family farming and, particularly in the temperate areas of the state, largely succeeded. In their own ways, Texas and Oregon each reflected existing patterns in older rural regions of the United States. California, however, presented something new: a combination of mining, commerce, and agriculture that marked not the older patterns of East Coast or Midwestern societies but the tendencies toward which these societies were evolving. American settlement in California had begun on a wave of enthusiasm for the populist possibilities of wealth creation by gold mining. But the exigencies of mining and supply, and the patterns of landholding in the region, all furthered the emergence of a wage labor system, both in mining and in agriculture. Standing beside the owners of mining companies and large farms, both of whom employed wage workers, were the emerging commercial elites of San Francisco and other growing towns, who had transplanted the Northeastern insight that fortunes were to be made as readily from handling goods as from producing them. Smaller landed proprietors, who had retained their majority position in Eastern societies, appeared to be squeezed out of the picture.

Small farmers did exist, however, in California as elsewhere. And some, during the 1850s, debated the future of the California land system in a way that explicitly drew the state into wider debates about slavery and freedom. California had been admitted to the Union in 1850 as a free state, but observers worried that its patterns of wealth and property holding would nonetheless lead to oligarchy. By 1854, James L. L. Warren's *California Farmer* was advocating the establishment of small farms and attacking large ranchers and their efforts to displace settlers from the land. By 1860 only about 5.6 percent of farms throughout the state exceeded five hundred acres in size, and most of these were concentrated in fifteen of California's forty-four counties. New Englanders, such as the Massachusetts nurseryman John Quincy Adams Warren, who visited California in 1861, argued for breaking up large *ranchos* into smaller farm units.[21]

Even as wage labor was emerging as a dominant aspect of Northeastern and Western societies, advocates of small farming, small proprietorships, and craft trades used their ideals as the measure for a criticism of slavery. J. Q. A. Warren suggested that California, with its large wheat farms and cattle ranches, was reproducing "all the evils of the staple-crop economy of the South" other than slavery itself. The *Petaluma Journal* in 1860 published a call for the creation of fifty-acre farms in California, to avoid the emergence of an "English or Dixie aristocracy." Large "bonanza farms," the paper claimed, were no better than slave plantations. An article in the *Napa Reporter* also advocated small farms, because large estates and staple crops were "incompatible with free labor." Indeed, the disparities within American society largely became reduced in debates of this period to comparisons between slavery and "free labor." While proprietorship and the independence it promised served as the model for free labor, the realities of wage labor would give advocates of slavery a weapon to criticize it in turn. Even as California's economy expanded and diversified, it became embroiled in the key national debate about labor.[22]

Freedom and Slavery

TO UNDERSTAND the power and significance of this invocation of "free labor" (and the related concept of "free soil" as slave-free territory for free labor to inhabit), it is useful to review the evolution of concepts of slavery and freedom over the preceding decades. Before the American Revolution, political writers had condemned as potential enslavement measures or circumstances they feared would constrain individuals or society. British taxation and administrative measures, the revolutionaries had claimed, would "enslave" Americans. Over time other conditions also became regarded as tantamount to slavery. Campaigners against imprisonment for debt, for example, argued throughout the early nineteenth century that putting debtors in jail was subjecting them to a form of slavery. Temperance reformers argued that alcohol enslaved those who consumed it. In its metaphorical sense, "slavery" could refer to any circumstance or behavior that connoted an absence of independence.

At first these metaphorical uses of the concept of slavery to criticize other political or social evils bore little direct relationship to the ways in which chattel slavery itself was understood. Although strenuous objection to property in humans emerged in the Revolutionary period, and many Americans expressed their opposition to chattel bondage, to those who were not themselves enslaved the "peculiar institution" could appear little different from other forms of dependency. Unfree labor was common in the late eighteenth and early nineteenth centuries. While slaves were distinct from servants, apprentices, children, or married women, because of the permanence of their condition, the racial basis of their subjection, and the severe discipline they could be subject to, they were not alone in being considered not fully citizens. Wage workers too, in this period, were regarded as dependents: by virtue of obligations to their employers, they were not fully capable of exercising their own discretion.

Early-nineteenth-century social changes and the erosion of various other forms of unfree labor brought slavery to prominence as a particular kind of institution, one that to its opponents, both slave and free, was a paradigm of social evil. The abolition of property qualifications for voting in many states accorded white men, in particular, equal standing with one another as citizens regardless of their wealth or background. The opening of new economic opportunities, the growth of markets, and the influences of romanticism and evangelicalism all contributed to a shift of understanding about social relationships. Now there was less emphasis on concepts of hierarchy and rank and more on the character of individuals. Protestant evangelicalism emphasized individuals' personal relationships with God and stressed individual faith and effort in the achievement of salvation. Under these circumstances, "slavery" came to seem less a condition of dependency than one of the absence of self-ownership or self-control. To be enslaved no longer meant just to be in a subordinate position; it also connoted a lack of ability to take responsibility for one's own actions or future. Debtors and alcoholics could be said to suffer "enslavement" because, either through lack of self-discipline or misfortune, they were not fully in control of their own lives. While addiction to alcohol and other aspects of loss of self-control became subject to widespread movements for the reform of individuals and their redemption, radical advocates of abolishing chattel slavery argued for its destruction as a unique social evil.

As the movement for immediate abolition of slavery gathered weight in the North and Midwest in the 1830s, it provoked fierce political resistance. Southern politicians secured measures to prevent abolitionist literature from being circulated to the South through the federal mails, and also imposed a "gag rule" in Congress that prevented anti-slavery proposals from being debated or petitions received. Opposition within the North was strong too. Abolitionist lecturers frequently faced hostile mobs, and churches that allowed them to make speeches were attacked or sometimes even blown up in protest. The main political parties, each reliant on cross-sectional support, remained anxious to sustain a tacit agreement to keep slavery off the political agenda; only the expansionary moves of the 1840s and the emergence of anti-slavery political parties altered this state of affairs. Meanwhile, though, important battles over slavery had been taking place within the churches, and it was here that abolitionists first made important inroads into the complacency with which white society contemplated black slavery. During the early 1840s debates in all the largest Protestant denominations—Methodist, Baptist, and Presbyterian—led them to divide their Southern branches, which continued to uphold slavery, from their Northern branches, which criticized or condemned it. When the slavery debate finally began to drive the nation itself into two parts, slavery proponents recalled this religious division. "The public opinion of the North," complained the South Carolina secession declaration of 1860, "has given to a great political error the sanction of a still more erroneous religious sentiment."[23]

The retreat of other forms of coercion and the rapid expansion of chattel slavery made the contrasts between slave and nonslave systems increasingly stark. In addition, the expansion of the wage labor force, and subsequently of a salaried middle class, compromised the Revolutionary Era ideal of "independence" based on landholding and small proprietorship. Once, only farmers and other property holders were "free." Now, as depression and immigration undermined older ideals in the 1840s, various types of labor—landholding, wage working, and salary earning—became assimilated to a new concept of "free labor." Wage workers, once regarded as subservient and dependent, were elevated and redefined. A slave was a person owned by someone else; slaveowners were condemned for holding slaves against their will. Among men at least, everyone else—merchants, manufacturers, farmers, craftsmen, and wage earners—belonged to the category of "free" laborers, deemed able to exercise their own will. "There is a fair amount of equality among men here," wrote laborer Johann Pritzlaff from a Northern state to his family in Germany in 1842: "everyone is his own master." Slavery's proponents shored up their defense of it by invoking white racial superiority and the need for social order, but in doing so they helped drive deeper the conceptual wedge between slavery and freedom. "Free labor" became the new social and political ideal; the only debate was over who should have access to its benefits.[24]

The growing political conflict over slavery and its expansion in the 1840s and 1850s tightened further the association between wage labor and "freedom." Just as the Revolutionary generation had appropriated the concept of the "freeborn Englishman" to assert that they would not be "slaves" to political tyranny, Northern wage workers were quick to assert their rights by distinguishing themselves from Southern slaves. They readily accused employers who displeased them of plotting to enslave them. In 1847 a young man called Omar Morse agreed to work as a farm laborer for "old Harry Backus," a merchant, manufacturer, and landowner of Brockport, New York. Morse soon decided that he had chosen the wrong employer and likened his position to that of a slave: "I was supposed to be the nigger and he the master." Complaining that he was treated like a "brute," and that "no man that is endowed with a proper sense of his manhood will submit to any such regulation," Morse told Backus he would not accept his treatment. "I told him I had my papers to show that I was a free man—had never been sold into bondage and no white man less than sixteen feet between the eyes could ever make a slave of me." He walked off the job, reflecting that "it might do in countrys further South but up in the free state of New York all men whether rich or poor had certain rights and . . . would maintain their rights whether congenial to the moneyed aristocracy or otherwise." To Omar Morse and thousands of other workingmen, slavery was a paradigm of confinement against which they measured their own manhood and their own conception of their rights. Some women workers, too, used the contrast with slavery to assert their rights and to claim the privileges of free laborers in the workplace. Meanwhile other advocates of free soil and free labor regarded it as a guarantee of manhood and condemned slaveholders as effeminate fops. A tract promoting settlement in Minnesota in the early 1850s declared that the territory displayed "none of the langour and debility . . . that turn men into feeble women, in the harvest field, as they have south of us." In Minnesota "Labor . . . stands up firmly on its legs . . . and drives things through."[25]

Yet though male wage labor achieved the status of full respectability as "free labor" in the 1840s and 1850s, many contemporaries noted that material circumstances placed real bounds on practical "freedom." Differences between occupations and widening disparities in the distribution of wealth curbed the exercise of freedom. A sample of farmers in 1850 were found to have on average eighteen times the mean wealth of a sample of laborers; by 1860, after prices had risen but wages lagged behind, a similar comparison showed a difference of fiftyfold. Differentials between artisans and nonmanual workers also widened in the 1850s.

The most basic limits to freedom were poverty and need. In 1854, a peak year for German immigration, Martin Weitz arrived in New York City from Hesse-Darmstadt to find many of his compatriots destitute, unable to find work because they spoke no English. The following year, after he had at last been hired as a weaver in a Connecticut mill, Weitz wrote his father that "last winter sometimes I just wanted to jump into the water, if you don't have a job in America it's a terrible thing." Unemployment reached unusual levels in the slumps of 1854 and 1857, and poverty with it. In 1855 almost 6 percent of the entire population of New York State was classified as state paupers; Massachusetts and Pennsylvania also had large numbers of adults and children on poor relief. Walt Whitman estimated that there were 15,000 unemployed workers in New York and Brooklyn in the fall of 1857 and that the number would rise to 25,000 over the winter. Low wages made life a struggle for many in any case. A Massachusetts visitor to New York City in October 1857 lamented the condition of "so many who have *even with work* had to struggle to get along and support their families." The 1850s witnessed a new anxiety about cities and manufacturing towns as centers of poverty. A New York author worried that eighty villages in the state had lost population in the 1840s while cities like New York, Brooklyn, and Buffalo had expanded rapidly. Urging a reform of rural life to hold back the flow of people to the cities, he sought to restrain what he saw as increasing dangers from the poverty of a "free" working class.[26]

To bolster their own position, apologists for the South and for slavery put forward a similar critique of free labor. "We have ventured within these cotton prisons," one wrote, "where in every revolving wheel, and the atmosphere of the confined rooms, we have had nothing but . . . the lust of the miserly economist, and the soulless taskmaster." Authors such as George Fitzhugh, in his books *Sociology for the South* (1854) and *Cannibals All!* (1857), argued that Southern slaves were better off than Northern wage workers because they were, he claimed, taken care of in childhood, old age, and sickness, and were not left to find means of survival in the vagaries of the employment market. Hired hands had none of these assurances, and their basic poverty and reliance on employment for support for themselves and their families made their freedom merely illusory. They were, argued Fitzhugh and others, dependent on their employers for the incomes that sustained them, and so were no better able than slaves to resist their employers' authority. To Fitzhugh and others, including labor critics in the North, Northern workers were in fact "wage slaves."[27]

Southern apologists went further, justifying slavery not merely because of what it supposedly provided for workers but on account of its superiority in maintaining social order. Fitzhugh and his colleagues argued that social inequalities and distinctions were inevitable—there would always be a bottom-rung or "mudsill" class who were irretrievably condemned to poverty and subordination. Better, they argued, that this class be kept in restraint by the bonds of slavery, and better that they be held distinct by the marks of race and color than be "free" workers, liable to upset the social order with protest and rebellion. White workers in the South, Fitzhugh and others asserted, achieved a measure of real freedom through their contrast with slaves and through the social standing their race and status gave them in a slave-based society. "Free" workers in the North, they argued, were in fact enslaved, despite their whiteness and their legal freedom, because of the absence of a confined "mudsill" class into which they could not fall.

Advocates of free labor in the North refuted these assertions. The abolitionists among them fiercely condemned the conditions in which slaves were held and worked to undermine the pro-slavery myth that slaves were well cared for and contented. They cataloged punishments and abuses, which were also testified to by escaped slaves in numerous published narratives. They added moral condemnations of the violation of family life in the South, both through the sexual exploitation of female slaves by their masters and through the terror of the slave market and its perpetual threat of family separation. The publication in 1852 of Harriet Beecher Stowe's novel *Uncle Tom's Cabin* conveyed to a large white audience in the North sharp images of slave family life irreparably torn by the slave system. In its evangelical roots, its sentimentality, and its appeal to Northern women, Stowe's book did more than any other single work to carry the anti-slavery message beyond the circles of abolitionist sympathizers.

Although it did so subtly, Stowe's work was also among many that upheld by comparison with slavery the widely proclaimed virtues of free labor, above all through its conferral of personal autonomy. Free labor advocates charged that Fitzhugh and the apologists for slavery were wrong to claim that social ranks or classes were fixed. Social mobility, they asserted, assured the rise of men and women from the bottom of society to positions of comfort or respectability; any who failed to make this rise were themselves at fault. Such arguments provoked divisions even among abolitionists. "Poverty is not slavery," the radical Bostonian abolitionist leader William Lloyd Garrison had written. But others, including Garrison's own close colleague Wendell Phillips, saw a kernel of truth in the criticisms of "wage slavery": that poverty was not necessarily due to personal failings, and that it did produce real constraints on the men and women who endured it. Yet whether free labor was perceived as an ideal to be striven for or as a working system with clear virtues, its attributes and its differences from slave bondage came to stand for the distinctions between North and South. As the political crises of the 1840s and 1850s advanced, complex regional differences became resolved into sharp contrasts in social structures.

From Diversity to Sectionalism

HAD IT not been for the existence of slavery, the mounting political conflicts around it, and the contrasts with freedom that slavery threw into relief, it would have been conventional to regard the mid-nineteenth-century United States as a grouping of regional societies with their own distinct characteristics. There was no national currency. Agriculture and manufacturing were organized in regional clusters. Even the new railroads that were being built from the 1830s to the 1850s, linking centers of economic activity and reflecting the needs of commercial centers, did not form a nationally integrated network. Rather, they were a set of regional systems based on different track gauges and separated from one another by the need to transfer goods and passengers whenever two lines built to different gauges met up. These regional barriers to easy movement were not merely between North and South. The Southeast and newly settled areas of the Southwest were separate from each other, but the upper South, which was separate again, connected through as far as Pennsylvania. Railroads in the North and Midwest were divided into several separate groupings: New England and much of New York formed one, and the Midwest west of Ohio another; but Ohio and its connections, southern

233

New York, and New Jersey each had track gauges distinct from the others and from those of adjacent regions. This situation did not alter substantially until the 1860s. Until then, social and economic activity was still being conducted on a regional rather than a national scale. Divisions between North and South were not the only or predominant ones.[28]

Moreover there were many significant North-South interconnections. Large numbers of Northern merchants and manufacturers were involved in the cotton market and cotton manufacture, and depended on the South not only for their supplies but for business connections and markets. Migration had taken many Northerners south to live; one estimate suggests that by 1860 about 360,000 Northern-born individuals were living in the South. Through marriage or business expansion, considerable numbers of Northern families had kin and property connections in the South. Henry Watson, Jr., born in Connecticut in 1810, visited Alabama as a young lawyer in the early 1830s. He shuttled between New England and the South for a period before settling to practice law in the Alabama town of Greensboro, married there, and purchased a cotton plantation that by 1860 included over nine hundred acres and more than a hundred slaves. Richard J. Arnold, from a leading Rhode Island commercial family, acquired a plantation in Georgia through marriage in 1823. By 1858 he owned four cotton and rice plantations and almost two hundred slaves, in addition to property and commercial interests in his home state. Southern merchants and planters, too, frequently traveled to the North. They arranged transactions in the large commercial cities or vacationed in the tourist resorts that were springing up by Northern lakes, mountains, and ocean beaches, offering relief from the humidity and torpor of the Southern summer climate. On occasion, abolitionists made issue with these visits, encouraging slave servants who accompanied their owners to break for freedom, or helping those who attempted to do so. Some such cases ended up in court when slaveholders launched prosecutions for interference with their property. More broadly, as the abolitionist and free-soil campaigns continued, opponents of slavery criticized the complicity of Northern manufacturers and merchants in the slave system. A division between "conscience Whigs" advocating curbs on slavery, and "cotton Whigs" who favored avoiding the subject, produced one of the first cracks in the political party system whose realignment in the 1850s would mark the shift from regionalism to sectionalism.[29]

The Compromise of 1850, by which Southern lawmakers accepted California's admission to the Union as a free state in return for the passage of a much-tightened Fugitive Slave Law, reflected the hope of many Americans, North and South, that the dispute over slavery could be resolved and put away. There remained in the North substantial opposition to anti-slavery agitation, augmented by the Democratic party's recruitment of many immigrant voters who saw no reason to make common cause with black slaves in the South. Yet Northern commentary on the slavery controversy during the 1840s and early 1850s, while urging compromise and resolution, frequently conveyed indifference or hostility to the Southern whites who resisted reform and insisted on their right to own slaves. In 1850, Francis Parkman claimed that "a great union party is forming" in response to the Fugitive Slave Act, and that it would be "in opposition to the abolitionists and the southern fanatics." Parkman evinced antipathy to slaves, Southern property rights, and abolitionists in equal measure: "I would see every slave knocked on the head before I would see the Union go to pieces," he wrote, "and would include in the sacrifice as many abolitionists as could conveniently be brought together."[30]

Northern frustration with Southern power and influence in the U.S. government was reinforced during the 1850s not only by political events but also by evidence of the continued strengthening of slavery and the plantation system. Cotton, sugar, rice, and tobacco production all expanded, as did the geographic area of plantation agriculture and the total population of slaves. As the expansion of settlement in Texas and the Southwest created fresh demand for slaves, the prices they were sold for increased. By the late 1850s the total value of slaves held in the South exceeded the total capital invested in transport, manufacturing, and banking throughout the United States. As the cotton boom reached its height, South Carolina's James H. Hammond declared that "Cotton is King . . . No power on earth dares to make war upon it." Despite its rapid diversification, especially in the North and Midwest, the nation's largest capital investment continued to be in slave labor. With cotton in the lead, the South was the largest producer of U.S. exports. Cotton alone accounted for three-fifths the nation's exports by value in 1860, and other plantation crops also contributed. The twelve richest counties in 1860 were all in the South. The South as a whole, had it been a separate economy, would have been the fourth most prosperous in the world. More than half of all slaves worked in cotton, and about three-quarters of agricultural slaves lived in cotton-growing districts; tobacco, rice, and sugar between them employed another 25 percent of agricultural slaves. When cotton prices reached peak levels, yeoman farmers in some regions of the South also produced the crop without slave labor, but their output fell off in slump years, suggesting that they were marginal to the cotton economy, only called on when necessary. Slave-grown crops and the farm and plantation owners who controlled them held preeminent power in the South's economy and hence enjoyed disproportionate influence in American society.[31]

Slavery and Society

FROM THE early expansion of slavery in the colonial period, owners of slaves had substantial legal power to enforce their authority, including discretion to punish slaves summarily for disobedience, resistance, or escape. Although slaveholders or overseers were occasionally prosecuted for excessive punishment leading to the death of a slave, such prosecutions were rare. One state court even held that a master's killing of his slave could not be murder because a conviction for murder required proof of intent, and no man would intentionally destroy his own property. Any community constraints against excessive brutality were tempered by a strong reluctance to interfere in a slaveholder's own business. Slaves therefore had little protection against the arbitrary will of their owners. State laws provided, moreover, for public legal assistance to slaveholders when slaves' infractions exceeded their own power to control. For generations, information about slave runaways had been advertised in newspapers and in public places on the assumption that white citizens and law officers would help identify and return escapees. Backing this public assistance were pass systems, night patrols, sheriffs' posses, and state militia units which could all be mobilized to restrict slaves' movements, inquire into slaves found traveling, seek out and capture runaways, and be ready to suppress signs of revolt. Repression of serious slave resistance was usually successful. Few significant revolts occurred after the Nat Turner rebellion of 1831 in Virginia. As the historian Winthrop D. Jordan demonstrated in a discussion of shadowy indications of uprisings in Mississippi in the 1850s, if rebellions did occur, word about them barely got out. Slave resistance continued in the form of work stoppages and slowdowns, property crimes, and the steady incidence of runaways.[32]

After the Turner rising and the increase in Northern abolitionist activity during the 1830s, Southern systems of police were tightened. Nevertheless the passage in some Northern states of laws giving a measure of protection to escaped slaves helped prompt an upsurge of runaways, particularly from the border states, where slaves faced shorter journeys to the state line or to the Ohio River that separated them from freedom. In localities where slave and free states adjoined one another, such as along parts of the border between Pennsylvania and Maryland, there was frequent traffic in escapees and much discreet effort, particularly in communities of free blacks, to assist fugitives. To many slaveholders, the possibility of escapes and the complicity of Northern states appeared to threaten the security of slave property, and Southern politicians began calling for enforcement of the constitutionally mandated federal statute requiring the return of fugitive slaves with legal assistance. The new Fugitive Slave Act of 1850 was the price the South extracted for its fears for the future of slavery.[33]

In reality, though, the incidence of escapes to freedom in the Northern states or in Canada had been much too slight to weaken the slave system. The number of runaways did increase in the 1840s, but in most parts of the South the severity of the patrol system continued to make permanent escape highly difficult. Slavery exerted formidable power over its subjects. Many Northerners, however, perceived the Fugitive Slave Act as an extension of slavery's influence into their regions. The act's provisions, overriding personal liberty laws in states like Pennsylvania that had protected escapees, and compelling the assistance of Northern law officers in the return of slaves, produced considerable resentment in the white North and great dismay in Northern black communities. The law threatened not only actual runaways who had reached freedom but also free blacks who might be kidnapped and legally committed to slavery by slave catchers and corrupt officials. The increasing financial value of slaves in the South only exacerbated these dangers.

In the South too, slaveholders faced a measure of resentment at their growing influence. Planter hegemony had never been unchallenged from within white society. Different regions of the South evolved markedly different social structures, with varying proportions of planters, yeoman farmers, poor whites, and slaves. Most regions were marked by inequalities, not just between slaveholders and slaves but among whites as well. These inequalities had shaped Southern political development. Political support for the Jacksonian Democrats against the emergent Whigs in the 1830s and early 1840s followed patterns traceable to class and wealth, though with different alignments in upland and lowland regions, and in the upper and lower South. Political insurgencies by yeoman farmers periodically challenged planter elites in both old and newer states. South Carolina, where the rice-planter elite used its influence to exclude many white farmers and laborers from politics, was the least democratic state in the Union by the 1850s, three decades or more after voting reforms had opened up the franchise in most other states.

The expansion of slavery and the relative scarcity of slaves by the 1850s deepened these inequalities within Southern white society. Until mid-century the price of slaves had usually tracked the price of cotton. Now the two diverged, and slave prices rose regardless of fluctuations in the returns that could be anticipated from their labor. Only the wealthy could continue to purchase slaves in the market. Although the actual number of slaveholders grew by 10 percent in the 1850s and the number of planters (those owning twenty slaves or more) by almost 23 percent, the proportion of Southern white families who owned slaves fell as the price of slaves increased. In 1830, 36 percent of white families across the South had owned at least one slave; by 1850 this proportion had fallen to under 31 percent, and by 1860 it had fallen even further, to just over 26 percent. Owning slaves and controlling the products of slave labor were important sources of wealth, so as these became less equally distributed, overall inequalities of wealth grew. Measures of farm size, landownership, wealth holding, and slaveholding all indicate growing inequality between 1850 and 1860 in cotton-growing regions. By 1860 the white South was more socially divided than it had ever been. The expansion and power of slavery, which its defenders claimed was an instrument of white democracy, had instead become an instrument of white inequality.[34]

Households and Southern Cohesiveness

DESPITE THESE growing inequalities, the South remained for the most part a cohesive political region. The principal reason for this was the calculus of race, which served in many circumstances to override class differences among whites. Pro-slavery advocates trumpeted the advantages for whites of living in a society where they shared a status, however unevenly divided, that made them distinct from the racially determined underclass below them, and into which they could not fall. Southern intellectuals were also quick during the 1840s and 1850s to propagate new notions of white racial superiority that were beginning to emerge in the transatlantic development of so-called scientific racism. Recent studies suggest that these ideas not only emphasized the supposed inferiority of people of color but also embraced increasingly self-conscious concepts of "whiteness" as an identity linking ethnic groups of European descent. Ownership of slaves in itself came to be seen by some as an indication of true whiteness, and concepts of white identity may have differed in plantation and nonplantation regions of the South, where rates of slaveholding diverged widely.

Racial ideologies and white racism, however, do not provide a sufficient explanation for the willingness of nonslaveholding whites to support their richer slaveholding leaders. Notions of white supremacy were entertained by a wide variety of Americans, including (in the North) some supporters of the free-soil movement and (especially in the upland South) yeoman farmers who, when the Civil War began in 1861, would prove loyal to Unionism rather than to planter-led secession. An additional connection tying nonslaveholders to their planter neighbors was a conception, based only partly on race, that their social positions were comparable because they shared the position of household heads. Small farmers and planters alike stood as patriarchal rulers over the dependents in their families, their wives and children, and (if they had them) slaves and hired workers as well. This shared identity as family patriarchs was acted out in the political arena as planters and farmers together took part in the rituals of elections and county government.[35]

Even in the rice-plantation districts of coastal South Carolina, where social and political inequalities were wider than in most parts of the

South, their status as masters of their own households gave planters and yeomen a mutual affinity that bridged the gaps in wealth and social standing that separated them. Amidst the region's large rice plantations, yeoman farmers made up a significant proportion of the white population. Their farms were interspersed with the holdings of their wealthy neighbors, and networks of patronage and mutual assistance helped bind farmers and planters together. Planters granted mortgages, loaned money or supplies, and in other ways fostered patterns of obligation that—while not breaching yeomen's "independence"—forged ties that sustained political and social cohesion. Yeomen provided labor services, served in the patrols and militia units that policed the slave system, and frequently voted for their patrons at election time. Many planters in fact regarded themselves as "farmers" and fostered this sense of shared identity with their less prosperous neighbors. In other parts of the plantation South, where social inequalities were less pronounced than in the rice swamps, similar patterns of mutual affinity were also established. So as planters became more distinct from yeomen in terms of wealth, and came to assert the common interests they had with each other in guarding slavery against opponents, they could draw on their affinity with yeomen in order to claim that they spoke for the South in general. To some Northerners too, as well as many Southerners, slavery's character as a household institution placed it beyond criticism. In his first annual message to Congress in 1857, President James Buchanan claimed that "the relations between master and slave . . . are 'domestic institutions' . . . limited to the family . . . and are entirely distinct from institutions of a political character."[36]

Households and Northern Egalitarianism

YET WHILE planters proclaimed their commonality with yeoman farmers and used the patterns of the household economy to sustain social inequality, Northern rural supporters of free-labor ideology were using their experience of the household system to reach opposite conclusions. To free-soilers, the modest family farm rebutted slaveholders' claims to share equality with their poorer neighbors. Because it relied on a tyrannical class relationship and enabled the accumulation and cultivation of large landholdings, slavery seemed to them a threat to the ideal of equality. As the journalist Walt Whitman wrote in 1847, the extension of slavery into territory annexed from Mexico would place a few thousand "polished" slaveholding aristocrats in a position to dominate "the grand body of white workingmen." Free-soilers attacked the power of the South's planter aristocracy and advocated policies, such as Homestead laws providing free public land for settlers, which they hoped would extend the domain of small-scale farming. Their perception that slavery would create aristocracy wherever it spread, and that slaves would provide unwelcome competition for free laborers, animated their fierce resistance to any further extension of slavery into the Western territories. Many Southern yeomen perceived slavery as a guarantee of their notional equality with planters, but large numbers of their Northern and Midwestern counterparts saw it as precisely the opposite: a threat to the notional equality among themselves.

As farm settlement proceeded across the Midwest, hallmarks of a prosperous, relatively egalitarian rural society appeared. By comparison with many parts of the South and of Europe, landownership was widespread. In many rural areas more than half the household heads owned their own farms. Farm holdings were also, on average, modest in size: owner-occupied family farms, rather than large estates, predominated. In some newly settled areas, such as in Iowa in the 1850s and 1860s, Eastern investors did create large "bonanza" wheat farms worked by wage labor, but over time many of these would fail and be broken up into smaller units. Although there were regional variations in rates of tenancy, overall in the Northern states by 1860 only 16 percent of farms were rented. Indeed, part rental of farms often complemented owner occupancy, as farmers rented extra fields, rented out parts of their land for which they had no use, or rented land for their sons as a step toward ownership. In most rural areas the distribution of landownership in 1860 continued to be most strongly correlated with age. Farmers accumulated land during their lives, disbursing it again as their children grew up so as to secure livelihoods to the next generation. With land and the means to acquire it available, many farm families in the Midwest were able to achieve their principal aim of securing for themselves and their children the resources for independent living.[37]

Some Midwestern farmers also replicated the social patterns of older rural areas. Settlers arrived in family groups, or where they had family or neighborhood contacts. Neighborliness provided sociability as well as practical assistance with the tasks of farm making. Sometimes these patterns marked an attachment to agricultural traditionalism. Amish farmers in Iowa, for instance, did not pursue maximum farm output or productivity but instead restrained output in order to foster a balanced community, placing community needs and the provision of land for the future ahead of immediate returns. Some German Lutheran groups also stressed the gathering of a community above the pursuit of family or individual ambitions.

Cooperative practices were also put to use to enhance output. Modest-sized Midwestern farms were often too small individually to justify the acquisition of new machines, such as mechanical reapers, but evidence from farmers' account books shows that they cooperated with neighbors to acquire equipment that was shared between households, using careful scheduling and swapping of labor. Cooperation fostered progress as well as traditionalism. In Homer, Iowa, in 1858, J. H. Williams stressed to his son the importance of family cooperation in farming: "to farm alone[,] productive as the land here is, will not do. But for us to act in union, and concert, carrying on Merchandising agriculture and the stock business . . . united, would with due and intelligent care be a *success.*"[38]

Midwestern farming did not, however, rest purely on the classless egalitarianism that these patterns imply. Inequality and class divisions also arrived with settlers on the frontier. Studies of new farming areas from Ohio to Utah note the advantages enjoyed by early settlers, who could secure access to the best land, wood, and water supplies, and also to the likely sites of future town developments; these advantages showed up in wealth data over several decades. Squatters who had obtained land owned by others secured their rights under the 1841 Preemption Act, which gave them up to 160 acres of federal land they had occupied and improved. But there were frequent conflicts with speculators and landowners who disputed these rights. Many settlers had insufficient means to set up farms without resort to borrowing. A leading study of Midwestern farming suggests that by 1860 the minimum costs of starting an 80-acre farm were three times the annual wages of the average

Midwestern worker, and that 40 percent of wage workers would have been unable to raise the means even for a 40-acre farm. Economic historians have debated the implications of the fact that large numbers of farmers took out mortgages to finance their activities. Older historians tended to stress the burdens this placed on them; more recent studies see the mortgage as an opportunity for families of limited property to invest in a future livelihood. Certainly they faced large risks; one scholar estimated that between 30 and 40 percent of mortgaged farmers had to face foreclosure and the forced sale of their property. Omar Morse, having moved west from New York State in the late 1840s, acquired a succession of farms in Wisconsin and Minnesota over a period of twenty years, each of which he lost when the mortgage was foreclosed for nonpayment. The effect of these financing arrangements was to draw farmers more closely into the commercial networks centered on Midwestern towns and cities, which purchased and processed their farm output and sought to supply them with manufactures and other goods in exchange. Many small farmers failed to keep pace with the fluctuations of markets and the demand for returns. Those who succeeded were the ones who gave the Midwest its reputation for prosperity.[39]

Successful farmers gave the Midwest its apparently classless, egalitarian character, but the work of farm making required labor that was often beyond the ability of families to provide for themselves, or even to provide for each other through cooperation. Hired laborers filled the gap. The creation of a family farming system in the Midwest depended on the existence of a market for wage labor. Young men moved around from job to job. Farmers with sons or time on their hands hired themselves out to work. Poorer families migrated with the seasons to follow the harvests, woodcutting, sod breaking, and other tasks that could employ them temporarily before they moved on again. Calvin Fletcher, an Indiana farmer, reckoned that in 1846 one in three of the state's voters were "tenants or day laborers or young men who have acquired no property."[40]

Many Midwesterners argued that this growing pattern of wage work did not constitute the creation of a permanent hired underclass but that working for wages was a step on a ladder of progress toward independent proprietorship. Most famous among exponents of this common view was the former Whig and Illinois lawyer and politician Abraham

Lincoln who, both before and after his successful candidacy for the presidency as a Republican in 1860, recounted it as an article of faith: wage work was merely a temporary condition. As Lincoln would put it in his annual message to Congress in 1861, "the prudent, penniless beginner in the world, labors for wages awhile, saves a surplus with which to buy tools or land for himself; then labors on his own account another while, and at length hires another new beginner to help him." In another version, the young man labored for wages one year, rented land another, and proceeded to acquire land of his own, to which he soon hired another young man to help him work. As is suggested by the correlation between age and wealth that still applied in many Northern rural districts, many men had followed patterns something like this. Yet Lincoln's claim in notes for a speech in 1859 that seven-eighths of Indiana's farm output was raised "by the hands of men who work upon their own ground" was in a literal sense exaggerated. Taking the farm economy in isolation, the emergence of a permanent laboring class in the 1850s was hard to trace. But a large number of floating, mobile, casually employed hired men and women thronged the towns and cities of the Midwest to find work in occupations that, though they were located off the farm, were nevertheless closely connected with the agricultural economy. Taking account of these workers makes it clear that permanent wage work was becoming an essential characteristic of the freehold farm system.[41]

Yet the small-proprietor *vision* of the Midwest as a land of modest family farms was in political terms highly significant. It contributed a crucial component of the free-soil argument and helped turn inside out the South's assumption of identity between large planters and small farmers. As he addressed farmers and other groups at numerous meetings across the Midwest in 1859 and 1860, Lincoln signaled that the Jeffersonian mantle of the independent landholder had fallen onto his own shoulders. Stopping the expansion of slavery would be the only way to protect the small farmer from being overtaken by aristocratic planters who exploited the labor of others. In a speech to Wisconsin farmers, Lincoln proclaimed the superiority of a society of modest, family-worked farms that practiced "the art of drawing a comfortable subsistence from the smallest area of soil"; such a society "will be alike independent of crowned-kings, money-kings, and land-kings."[42]

The two visions, the Southern one of identity between farmers and planters, and the free-soil one of an egalitarian society of family farmers untroubled by interference from planters or their slaves, each adapted the realities of a household-based rural economy—but reached radically different conclusions. The differences helped turn the debate on slavery into a wedge between North and South, and to turn the discussion of regional variety into a conflict over sectional difference.

The Logistics of Political Collapse

BY 1854 the Pennsylvania economist Henry C. Carey could write of the divisions that had already emerged between North and South: in education, in the churches, and in agricultural and political conventions, some of which were already contemplating the division of the Union. Political division was fast following. Southern political conventions had already canvassed the possibility that states might secede from the Union to protect their interest in slavery. Pro-unionists on both sides of the North-South divide blamed political opponents for aggravating tensions: Northerners criticized secession talk in the South while Southern Democrats blamed Northern abolitionists and free-soilers for provoking secessionist proposals. Slavery lay beneath the fundamental social and political distinctions that drove the two sections apart. Without slavery, there would have been no Southern planter class, the only significant landed elite in American society that exercised political power. In the absence of slavery in the North, farmer occupiers of the continent's abundant land had relinquished effective economic power, and a measure of political influence, to groups such as merchants, bankers, manufacturers, and the lawyers who served them, who had driven and benefited from economic diversification.[43]

Slavery also skewed the South's commercial involvements. Although the use of slave labor enabled the region to become the nation's largest earner of export income, it also curbed the development of the consumer markets that were emerging as an important element of economic diversification in nonslave regions. Most slaves exercised little or no market influence themselves. Even the "slave economies" that grew up around slaves' gardens and other kinds of independent production and marketing, especially in districts where the task system left slaves with time to work for themselves, were not integrated into wider market patterns. They constituted only a limited sphere of economic autonomy for those who took part in them.

Political ideas and apprehensions were also tied to these differences. Prominent among the arguments advanced by Southern advocates in the 1850s were those concerning their anxiety that the South, for all its wealth and economic sway, would be overtaken and eclipsed by a larger, more diversified North. Some Northern figures with close ties to the South, like the powerful Boston cotton manufacturer Amos Lawrence, saw Southern diversification as a means of averting political conflict. Chiding the South Carolina radical Robert Barnwell Rhett in 1849 for his state's "childishness in their fears that our northern agitators can harm them," Lawrence argued that the South should endeavor to set up spinning mills to process the cotton it grew. Some Southern writers also urged renewed efforts to diversify the Southern economy, but their prescriptions were constrained by the growing political impossibility of advocating anything that might seem to interfere with slavery or call its efficacy and legitimacy into question. Others feared that the South would shrink in size and power, that the black population would grow faster than the white, and that the South would face encirclement by a dynamic, incompatible Northern society. In older parts of the South, especially on the seaboard, leaders were concerned with the continued out-migration of people to newer-settled regions. As the South became more assertive in national politics in the 1840s and 1850s, its politicians fretted that the process of national expansion they had helped foster by annexing Texas and pursuing the Mexican War would, paradoxically, end up weakening their position.[44]

These anxieties help explain the fierceness with which Southern leaders insisted that the geographical spread of slavery should not be placed under legal or constitutional limits. From their opposition to the Wilmot Proviso of 1846 on, they and their allies exercised a growing vigilance over theoretical threats to the limitation of slavery. When the Illinois senator Stephen A. Douglas proposed his "popular sovereignty" principle in the early 1850s (that decisions about slavery should be left to popular votes in new territories), it appeared brilliantly contrived to secure Southern aims by enlisting a sufficient degree of Northern support. But Douglas faced Southern critics fearful that the principle would work against them. Even so, the contests over the Kansas-Nebraska Act of 1854, which embodied the principle, reflected Southern insistence on pursuing it and Northern anti-slavery anxiety that it would permit unlimited scope for the expansion of slavery. The Supreme Court's 1857 decision in the Dred Scott case, which did remove limits to the legal transportation of slaves, marked a severe setback for the free-soil position, underscored by the Court's overturning of the 1820 Missouri Compromise.

But to Southern advocates of the freedom to keep slaves, a Supreme Court decision in a society that was becoming numerically weighted against them seemed an insufficient guarantee. By pressing their demands for a constitutional amendment to embody the findings of the Court, Southern radicals took their cause too far, even in the opinion of Northerners who sympathized with them. Pressure for such an amendment was one of the factors that split the Democratic party at the end of the 1850s and created the political divisions that would lead to Southern secession from the Union when the free-soiler Abraham Lincoln was elected to the presidency in 1860. The exercise of Southern influence in federal decisions, both legislative and judicial, divided the Northern majority that had once complied with slavery against abolitionist attacks. It drove Northerners in the direction of the abolitionist camp even as many of them denied this was where their sympathies lay.

On both sides of the sectional divide, observers objected to the wider social and economic implications of the systems they opposed. Southern planters came to see Northern economic diversity as a threat to their interests, and disunion from the North as a way of staving it off. Writing a year after his state's declaration of secession, South Carolina's James H. Hammond reflected that in supporting it he had "wished to be *Independ[en]t* of [the North] . . . its corrupt and ignorant Politicians, and its Capitalists, who have built up and would continue to sustain its Commerce, in Manufactures, its whole Mercantile and Financial System, *at our cost*, and in the Union *in despite of us*. I wished of all things to be free of this grinding bondage in all its parts." At the same time the Vermont free-soiler John W. Phelps was arguing that slavery represented a threat to white labor, and particularly to the immigrant poor, who were obliged to compete against the "easy circumstances" of Southern slaves and "are often distressed by want."[45]

In an essay published in 1863, entitled "Aristocrats and Democrats," the New Englander Francis Parkman mused that "it was a strange union that linked us to the South. . . . Strong head and weak body against strong body and weak head; oligarchy against democracy." Parkman was contrasting the engagement of Southern social leaders in politics with the division between "the best instructed classes" and the "swarm of professed politicians" in the North. His diagnosis of the differences between two systems had its roots in their contrasting social structures. Both Phelps and Parkman, though supporters of the Union, wrote in terms that suggested it now lay in the past. "The strange union" was surely broken, not just by the war that was now raging but by the long-standing differences that had turned into stark incompatibilities. In the depths of conflict in 1863, reunion seemed to many people to be something far from inevitable.[46]

✿ *CHAPTER 7* ✿

The Civil War:
Two Kinds of Revolution

T HE ELECTION of Abraham Lincoln to the presidency in November 1860 signaled the division of the United States into two hostile sections, North and South. Lincoln was the first successful presidential candidate of the new, free-soil Republican party and the first elected president to have received no Electoral College votes from one of the major regional sections of the Union. The South's secession and the long, bloody civil war it precipitated were the immediate results of political breakdowns and the failure of compromise. But those breakdowns and failures in turn were reflections of deeper regional divisions within the United States and the effects of social processes on those divisions. For economic, cultural, and political reasons, slavery and the conditions for its future existence had precipitated conflicting regional patterns into two broad camps. Slavery and "free labor" had become central defining themes that, on one hand, helped drive the South into substantial unity and opposition to the Union and, on the other, had helped bind otherwise different Northeastern and Midwestern regions together in the Union's defense. Regional differences, instead of producing balance and cohesion—as Democrats and Whigs of the 1830s had hoped they would—had become the sources of a disastrous split.

In both sections of the country the Civil War's social consequences were mixed and, to a degree, paradoxical. The conditions faced by the

Confederacy and its eventual defeat ensured that slavery would be destroyed. The institutions and relationships that secession aimed to defend were laid in ruins, along with many aspects of the plantation economy. This was a permanent, revolutionary social change. Yet the circumstances of Emancipation ensured that it would not end unfreedom or coercion in the South. During postwar Reconstruction, the freed slaves' hopes for economic and political freedoms would be dashed and new systems of inequality and segregation constructed. The South underwent a revolutionary change that ended up being much less far-reaching than might have been expected.

In the North, meanwhile, war seemingly brought few radical social changes. Northern social structures seemed broadly the same after the war as before. Secession removed political obstructions to various free-soil policies and permitted the continued westward extension of freehold, household-based farming. Yet the war also, more subtly, helped concentrate tendencies already evident beforehand—toward social division, the creation of distinct middle and working classes, and the emergence of corporate ownership of industry and finance that would further the urban and industrial transformation of the country in the later nineteenth century. In the North, subtle change had long-term revolutionary consequences.[1]

The White South's Hubris:
Society and Secession

UNDERLYING THESE changes and paradoxes, antebellum social structures had powerful effects on the onset and conduct of the war itself. Apologists for the South often denied after the war that slavery had been the conflict's main cause, and their influence on national opinion and historiography was such that for much of the century following 1865, the extent of slavery's responsibility for the Civil War was a subject of serious debate. Few historians now doubt its fundamental role. Most point out that other causes for the war that were offered instead—commitment to states' rights or to a "Southern way of life," economic differences between the sections, or differences over aspects of economic policy, such as tariffs—were themselves traceable to social differences of which chattel slavery was a fundamental part. Southern leaders' objections to tariffs on manufactured goods, for example, derived from their section's heavy reliance on staple agricultural exports, a facet of a slave-based plantation system. The states' rights principle, defense of which became the chief slogan of the white South after the war, referred particularly to the "right" of states to permit the ownership of slaves. The notion of a "Southern way of life" was another emblem of white supremacy, evoking nostalgia for a period in which some human beings were the property of others.[2]

The irony of Lincoln's election and the South's reaction to it, indeed, was that Lincoln himself and his moderate free-soil Republican supporters had no intention of interfering with the right to own slaves in the states where slavery existed; they wished only to restrict its extension into new Western territories. States' rights were safe in their hands; all they sought to restrict was the individual rights of slaveholders to own human property wherever in the United States they chose, and to uphold the rights of nonslave states to exclude them. Some Southerners asserted that soil exhaustion caused by wasteful cultivation methods required the opening of new territory to slavery. Many more, frantic about the threats to slavery they perceived, confused free-soil ideology with outright abolitionism and ignored the distinction between the two positions. Condemning Lincoln as an abolitionist, they precipitated the war that alone would turn him reluctantly in that direction.

Recent accounts of antebellum Southern attitudes have not merely exposed the underlying dominance of slavery in these issues but have also attempted to resolve the apparent paradox of the South's opposition to Lincoln by redefining its traditional emphasis on states' rights. Instead of adopting a defensive position to secure such rights, Leonard L. Richards and others have argued, the South pursued secession when it perceived that it had failed in using its control of federal power to extend slavery. Buoyed by cotton profits and the wealth in slaves that rose sharply in the 1850s, a self-confident Southern elite pursued national expansion and sought to impose its own terms on the rest of the nation. When Lincoln's election marked the unambiguous rejection of that strategy, secession seemed, to politicians and their supporters determined to preserve slavery, the most logical alternative. Yet secession, by bringing on war, achieved exactly the opposite of what its proponents intended. Within four years the nation's most valuable property was free, and its wealthiest and most powerful social institution had been thoroughly wrecked.[3]

Late in March 1865, as the Civil War was at length drawing to a close, a procession of black residents of Charleston, South Carolina, paraded to celebrate the imminent Northern victory and their own liberation. With them came a cart bearing a coffin marked with slogans, including "Slavery is dead" and "Sumter dug his grave on the 13th of April, 1861." Better than many historians in the decades to come, Charleston's freedpeople grasped that the destruction of slavery had proceeded from secession and from the South's decision to open the war by attacking Fort Sumter. Secession had not undermined slavery immediately, but the Union's determination to resist secession and the South's determination to fight to defend it proved to be slavery's undoing. As their slaves perceived, the South Carolina leadership's choice in April 1861 to pursue war rather than forgo secession would be its fatal error.[4]

White Southerners, even planters, were by no means unanimous in advocating secession. Wealthy planters in Natchez, Mississippi, argued against breaking with the Union. Voters in Louisiana were divided 52 percent in favor to 48 percent against calling delegates to a secession convention, and pro-Unionists could count sugar planters among their number. Nevertheless, decisions by the Southern states to secede from the Union, and then to form or join the Confederacy, were directly influenced by the strength of slavery and by the power of a preponderance of planter leaders to shape events. Following Lincoln's election in November 1860, South Carolina took little more than a month to resolve to secede. Of all the states it had the highest proportion of slaves (57 percent) among its population. In January 1861 the five states with the next-highest proportions of slaves also declared their secession from the United States: Mississippi (55 percent), Florida (44 percent), Alabama (45 percent), Georgia (44 percent), and Louisiana (47 percent). By the end of that month every state whose slaves were more than two-fifths of its population had left the Union. Texas (30 percent) shortly followed, making the southernmost tier of states a solid secessionist bloc from the Sea Islands to the Rio Grande.

Already there were intimations of impending disaster. The French abolitionist and religious writer Agénor de Gasparin, in a book on the prelude to the Civil War published in 1861, noted that the South, by seceding, was abandoning its best guarantee of social order—the North. Secession, he reasoned, would induce a slave insurrection in the South. The Southern leadership would be "left alone in the presence of its enemy"—the planters' own slaves. Referring to the great Haitian slave revolt of the 1790s, whose memory haunted slaveholders throughout the Western Hemisphere, de Gasparin predicted that the South would face a massive uprising, "a St. Domingo carried to the tenth power." Events would prove him wrong in detail but correct in principle.[5]

The Texas secession convention, meeting in March 1861, was addressed by George Williamson, who had been sent as a commissioner by the neighboring state of Louisiana to persuade Texas to follow the path of secession and join the Confederacy. Even though his own state had only narrowly supported secession, Williamson set out the argument for it in clear terms, stressing the similarities between Louisiana and Texas. "Louisiana looks to the formation of a Southern confederacy to preserve the blessings of African slavery." "Both states," he noted, "have large areas of fertile, uncultivated lands, peculiarly adapted to slave labor; and they are both so deeply interested in African slavery that it may be said to be absolutely necessary to their existence, and is the keystone to the arch of their prosperity." Secession and confederacy were essential, Williamson argued, to defend slavery against the indifference of the federal government and likely assaults on it by abolitionists. Should Texas not secede, Williamson claimed, "the people of Louisiana would consider it a most fatal blow to African slavery. . . . The people of the slaveholding States are bound together by the same necessity and determination to preserve . . . slavery." Texas's decision to join the Confederacy seemed to vindicate Williamson's argument.[6]

In the next tier of states to the north, however, slavery was not as prominent, and voices of caution, and of support for the Union, were raised from regions where yeoman farming predominated and planters had less influence. Secession in these states came about more slowly, and in response to the press of events rather than the enunciation of principles. On April 14, 1861, South Carolina troops opened fire on the federal Fort Sumter in Charleston harbor, aiming to capture it before the Union could resupply and reinforce its garrison. These opening shots of the Civil War sharpened the secession debates in the remaining slave states, prompting four more of them to join the Confederacy. In every one, divisions between slaveholders and nonslaveholders, and between plantation and nonslave regions, shaped the temper of debate. Many white Virginians were torn between their attachment to slavery and their perception of the benefits of the Union. At a convention in early 1861, for example, John B. Baldwin had praised slavery as "a blessing alike to the master and the slave . . ., to the nonslaveholder and the slaveholder," but he advocated adherence to the Union because that alone could guarantee the possibility of expansion. Another Virginia Unionist, Alexander H. H. Stuart, warned that secession would undermine slavery by "surrendering the guarantees of the Constitution, and substantially bringing down the Canada frontier to the borders of [the state]." But the state's slavery advocates, urged on by their colleagues to the south as the war began, passed a secession resolution on April 17, 1861, that was ratified by referendum five weeks later. Arkansas and Tennessee passed secession measures in early May; North Carolina was the last to secede, more than a month after war had begun. Sharply divided between strong plantation districts and significant regions of yeoman farming, North Carolina managed to stay intact in the struggle that followed. But Virginia's breach with the United States provoked its own internal secession as the state's upland, northwestern counties with small slave populations broke away to rejoin the Union and—as West Virginia—to achieve separate statehood in 1862. Mountainous, nonslave eastern Tennessee also remained loyal to the Union, though any question of its separation from the slave regions of the state was rendered moot in 1862 when the Union army occupied much of Tennessee.[7]

The correlation between involvement in slavery and willingness to secede from the Union was borne out in the four remaining slave states. In these "border" states, where slavery was weakest, political divisions were sharp enough to keep them from joining the Confederacy, although Southern sympathizers in Kentucky and Missouri passed secession resolutions that never went into effect. Instead the border states became emblematic of what many white Americans came to see as the tragedy of the Civil War: families whose members were divided by sectional principle and obliged to fight one another. In Maryland, for example, two-fifths of military recruits served with the Confederacy and three-fifths with the Union forces, reflecting the state's deeply divided loyalties. Indeed, throughout the United States there were families whose kin and marriage connections crossed sectional lines. A Connecticut woman, Katherine Hubbell, had married a Georgian a year before the war began. The brother of the prominent Massachusetts editor and politician John Gorham Palfrey was a sugar planter in St. Mary Parish, Louisiana. In Georgia the family of the British-born actress and writer Fanny Kemble was divided when her slaveholder husband Pierce Butler sided with the Confederacy and his wife and daughter remained loyal to the Union. But it was the border states, especially Kentucky and Missouri, that were most deeply divided. War, and the principles for which it was fought, cut across many ties of kinship and neighborhood.[8]

In Missouri, antebellum social divergences laid the basis for violent conflict during the war. As in many slave states, large plantation owners, who held much of the best land in the Missouri and Mississippi valleys and who owned slaves in substantial numbers, also exercised substantial political power. The majority of Missouri landholders, however, were small farmers without slaves, who had come to depend on the slave system for the various means by which they made their livelihoods. Yet in-migration to the state during the 1850s, and particularly the expansion of St. Louis as a trading and manufacturing center, had markedly increased the numbers of Missourians who had no attachment to slavery and relied on their own or hired labor. Among them were growing numbers of German and other immigrant farmers, craft producers, and merchants. Advocates of secession found themselves outnumbered by Unionists, and many took to guerrilla tactics to support the Confederacy. Among Missouri Unionists, however, there were also deep splits over the question of slavery. Pro-slavery Unionists at first prevailed, but during the war the number of anti-slavery Unionists in Missouri grew, their ranks augmented in part by runaway slaves. The state enacted a statute for the gradual emancipation of slaves in mid-1863, before growing anti-slavery sentiment and the pressure of events resulted in a constitutional convention in January 1865 that agreed on measures for immediate emancipation.

Social Structures and the Conduct of War

AGÉNOR DE GASPARIN'S assessment in 1861 of the viability of a separate Confederacy was pessimistic. Even if the North should choose not to resist the rebellion, the French observer predicted, an independent slave South would run into trouble. It would become prey to quarrelsome divisions among its states. Across the first six states to secede, the population was almost equally divided between free people (mainly white) and black slaves. The fear of revolt and the task of holding slaves in subjection would be burdensome. Slaves would continue to escape, de Gasparin wrote, but with the United States now divided and the Union no longer constitutionally obliged to recognize slaveholders' property rights, these runaways would find secure refuge not just in Canada but in the Northern states too. Sustaining its slave labor force would oblige the Confederacy to reopen the international slave trade, provoking powerful opposition and probably military intervention from Europe and the North. So even without Union opposition, de Gasparin concluded, the Confederacy would fail because its success required a state of peace which its efforts to maintain slavery would inevitably undermine.[9]

As war began, many circumstances seemed to favor the North. In 1860 the Northern states held 70 percent of the U.S. population, 90 percent of its manufacturing output, six times as many banks and bank branches as the South, twice its railroad mileage, twice its number of pack animals for military transport, and four times its output of wheat. Of major manufacturing products, the North's output in textiles was seventeen times that of the South, in boots and shoes thirty times, in pig iron twenty times, in guns thirty-two times, and in railroad locomotives twenty-four times. Both in size and in organization the North appeared considerably better fitted to fight the war that the South's secession had brought on. This advantage revealed itself especially in military recruitment. No one, of course, anticipated that the war, once started, would last for four years and claim the lives of more than 620,000 soldiers from both sides. But it was clear that the Confederacy, with 9 million inhabitants, almost 4 million of them enslaved, could run out of soldiers sooner than the Union, with its population of 22 million.

Comparison of the means of recruiting soldiers to fight in the Civil War with those employed eight decades earlier in the Revolutionary War reflects some of the important social changes that had taken place in the interim. In the Revolution, military leaders had had no regular army to turn to; all recruitment was voluntary. The situation in 1861 was not very different. The few thousand regular army officers put themselves forward for federal or Confederate service according to their sectional loyalty, forming the backbone of the senior officer corps on both sides. But the force of sixteen thousand regular enlisted men was mostly retained by the union for frontier duty and played little part in the Civil War. Instead, men were recruited through state volunteer militias, and state regiments made up the bulk of the armies on both sides. Patterns of recruitment differed, though, from those in the Revolution.

Recruitment methods in the early stages of the war were geared to older patterns of small armies and relatively short-term enlistments. Early recruitment was frequently conducted locally as units on both sides were formed of young men who often enlisted together. A man's comrades would often be the men with whom he had spent the previous July Fourth holiday. As the war wound on, and units were reorganized or decimated by casualties, connections between recruitment and locality weakened; on both sides, military service became a more "national" experience. With the growing demand for soldiers, lengths of service tended to grow too. A Boston laborer, Brown P. Stowell, for example, enlisted twice during the war, first for ninety days, the second time for two years—though he spent much of his second hitch in a Confederate prison camp. Over time the war made substantial exactions on the populations of both sides. More than two million men, including 40 percent of Northern males between eighteen and thirty-five, served in the Union army or navy; among those at the younger end of the age range the proportion of participants was higher. Overall about 35 percent of Northern men of "military age" served. In the South, with its much smaller white population, the corresponding rates were higher: about 61 percent of men eligible for military service enlisted, including about 80 percent of young men in their late teens and early twenties.[10]

The Civil War achieved the scale it did in part because the social structures of both North and South permitted the initial recruitment of large numbers of soldiers without inevitably disrupting the core activities of their respective economies. As in the Revolution, a rush of volunteers on both sides enthusiastic for service eased recruitment efforts at the war's outset, and this initially provoked anxieties about maintaining food supplies. Pennsylvania farmers fretted in 1861, for instance, that sudden labor shortages and the requisition of wagons and livestock for military use "may seriously affect the next year's crop." But even when early battle casualties had banished this initial urge to enlist, social conditions helped make the flow of Civil War recruits more stable than in the Revolutionary War. In the Confederacy, poorer families from yeoman farming districts did face the prospect of losing crucial farm labor to military service. As one Georgia farmer wrote to his wife from his unit in Virginia in the spring of 1862, when it had become clear that he would not be home for that year's planting season, "you must be man and woman both while the war lasts." Across the South, though, the existence of a significant poor white population of relatively marginal, casual laborers enabled army recruitment to be sustained well into 1862 and 1863. In the North, likewise, the presence of large American-born and immigrant wage-earning groups in both industrial and agricultural regions also enabled recruitment to continue on a voluntary basis for the first two years of the war.

During the Revolutionary War, troops mustered into provincial and state militias had often been reluctant to serve far from home, not because of a localist mentality so much as because their labor was essential to the household-based agricultural economy that was the source of food supplies. Civil War recruits were more willing to serve at considerable distances from home, and their absence had a slighter economic effect than it would have had two generations earlier. In rural regions of the North, farmers were less likely to serve than their sons or poorer members of the population. In commercial centers, artisans, white-collar workers, and the unskilled were available in considerable numbers. Plantation agriculture in the South was still carried on by slaves, enabling many young white men to enlist for service. In the North, manufacturers recruited immigrant workers to tend machines, and farmers began to invest substantially in labor-saving machinery to assist with tasks previously done by hand. Before the war, some farm laborers had opposed mechanization: when Daniel Edwards, a farmer of Little Genesee, New York, bought a mowing machine in 1858, a group of local boys took it and dumped it in a pond. Within three or four years, however, the boys would have been in the army and no longer around to protest a machine's threat to their laboring jobs. All told, about one-third of the North's agricultural workforce saw military service.[11]

Still, there were limits to each side's ability to recruit soldiers. Casualties in battle and from disease mounted. Neither side, particularly the

South, had inexhaustible reserves of men prepared to volunteer. By April 1862 the Confederacy had passed its first conscription law, which was later strengthened. That August the Union imposed a draft on states that failed to meet recruitment quotas, and the following March it enacted its own conscription law. The war was beginning to have severe effects, not only in terms of human losses but on each side's ability to sustain itself economically and socially. Here, as pressures mounted, Northern society and resources began to prove more powerful and resilient than Southern.

Local recruitment efforts, using bounties to entice men to enlist, were preferred to employing the draft, and in the end relatively small numbers of Northern enlistees were drafted rather than "volunteers." The town of Jacksonville, Illinois, ran out of enthusiastic volunteers in the summer of 1862 and began to offer small recruitment bounties. By 1865 these bounties had reached five hundred dollars, though with them the town was able to fulfill the quotas demanded of it without recourse to the draft. Modern research has modified a long-standing perception that Union recruitment relied heavily on putting newly arrived immigrants into the army. Foreign-born men did serve, but not in full proportion to their numbers in the population; they formed about 30 percent of men of military age in the Northern population but only one-quarter of Union recruits. After a brief decline at the beginning of the war, European emigration to the United States almost resumed its peak rate during the early 1860s, virtually all of it headed to the North. As men volunteered or were conscripted into federal service, foreign skilled and unskilled workers were available to replace them. Immigration did not directly fill the ranks of the army, but it did ensure that the North did not run out of labor. Lacking the North's attractiveness to immigrants, the South had no comparable resource to call on.[12]

Women and War

AS IN the Revolution, both Union and Confederate economies relied substantially on women's and family labor to maintain production on farms and in homes while men were absent on war service. Women's labor made an essential contribution to the war effort on both sides. But there were important variations from North to South in the character and impact of women's participation, and there has been substantial debate as to the wider significance of women's wartime activities. In the rural North, where household-based independent farming predominated, women had already assumed important responsibilities; wartime exigencies were in some respects merely an extension of this. In that large proportions of Northern farmers (unlike their sons, or hired laborers) remained on the land instead of joining the army, household patterns of work were altered less in gender terms than in the need to adapt to a shortage of help. Some economic historians credit women and children's more intensive work on farms during the war with raising the overall level of farm productivity during the 1860s.[13]

Northern women, especially from middle-class and working families, also became involved in growing numbers with war-related organized activities—serving as nurses or auxiliaries in hospitals, or under the auspices of the United States Sanitary Commission, founded to promote clean and healthy conditions in Union army camps. Lori Ginzburg, among others, has interpreted women's service in large public organizations as a step toward equivalence with men's employment and service outside the home, and has argued that it set the scene for women's postwar involvement in social reform activities. More recently, however, Elizabeth Leonard has questioned the transformative impact of women's wartime public service. They were engaged, she has suggested, in fields such as nursing that were already regarded as "women's" tasks, and the middle- and upper-class women among them largely resisted pressures to centralize organizations like the Sanitary Commission, preferring to maintain local bases for arranging women's public participation. Economic historians too, reviewing the patterns of men's and women's employment after the war, have suggested that wartime public service had only a limited influence on later notions of gender roles. New employment patterns that appeared further on in the nineteenth century were more the product of longer-term changes than of the war itself.[14]

In the South, both on farms and on plantations, the higher proportions of male recruitment into army service created substantially more female-headed households. Farm women and planters' wives took on wider tasks and responsibilities than they had been accustomed to. On plantations this often included direct supervision of slaves. Again, historians have debated the impact of these circumstances. Some have argued that wartime roles were merely a traditional extension of women's activities, others that they undermined accustomed Southern assumptions about gender and race. One writer has suggested that as Southern farm women took over their families' farms, and (because cotton exports ceased) shifted from staple crops to household manufactures and providing for their own needs, they belied menfolks' assumptions about women's dependence and their own independence. Returning from war, often with injuries, many Southern men found their patriarchal presumptions reversed, or at least challenged. Yet most Southern women appear to have regarded the defense of hearth and home as their main objective, and returning men often embraced this notion as part of their retrospective understanding of the causes of the war. In this case, as in the North, the effect was to mute or suppress significant challenges to attitudes about patriarchy.

Southern women's public service was also less highly organized or regimented than that in the North. Although institutions comparable to the Sanitary Commission were important, Southern women's contributions to wartime work were often more individualized than collective. Cultural taboos (associated with slavery and race) against rendering personal services also restrained many upper-class women from volunteering for public work as nurses, a task they undertook only in private households, with male accompaniment, or left to more "masculine" lower-class women.

"A Rich Man's War and a Poor Man's Fight"

MILITARY SERVICE on both sides came to be characterized by class differences and class resentments, though again these operated differently from South to North. In the South, yeoman farmers and poor whites from nonslave regions on the margins of the Confederacy were less likely than their cousins in plantation districts to be recruited for Confederate service, and some protested against draft laws compelling them to fight. Class resentments curbed their participation; partly for this reason, over 30 percent of eligible men in the Confederacy did not enlist or obtain exemptions. In plantation districts, however, where planters and poorer farmers and laborers lived in close proximity, networks of patronage, neighborhood, and obligation helped compel participation. Nevertheless there is evidence that Confederate soldiers were in relative terms more prosperous than their Union counterparts, fighting as they were to defend the property in slaves that they insisted on upholding. On the other hand, Confederate recruitment policy reflected the desire that plantations and their slave populations be properly overseen: one son of each slaveholder with twenty or more slaves could gain exemption from military service. This privilege for the planter class prompted widespread resentment.

Northern military recruits tended to be less prosperous than nonrecruits. Again, though exemptions could effectively be purchased by the practice of paying for a substitute instead of serving, at three hundred dollars, roughly the annual earnings of a day laborer, this privilege was obviously well beyond the means of the poor. Among Northern professional and white-collar groups there were higher rates of purchasing substitutes or paying commutation fees than among farmers or laborers. The growing wage labor market, the importance of casual labor in many contexts, and the high level of geographical mobility among poorer workers all favored military recruitment from among these groups without disabling local networks or economic activities. Resentment that this was "a rich man's war and a poor man's fight" characterized opinion on both sides.

In some instances this resentment boiled over into violence. After local drafts were introduced under the federal Militia Act of 1862, crowds resisted recruitment in parts of the Midwest. In some townships in the Pennsylvania anthracite region, women mobilized to protest against army recruiters. In New York City in July 1863, resistance to the draft, led by Irish unskilled workers who resented both black access to employment and the three-hundred-dollar commutation fees that exempted wealthier men from service, produced several days of serious riots. More than a hundred people, many of them black, were killed and over one million dollars' worth of property destroyed in one of the most serious civil disturbances in American history. Union troops, including units that had just been at the battle of Gettysburg, were hurried to New York to suppress the riots. The fear of insurrection that the draft riots inspired across the North revealed lines of class and ethnic suspicion or resentment. In the rural town of Hatfield, Massachusetts, for example, Yankee townsmen established patrols to maintain order and especially to keep watch over the local population of Irish and French Canadian farm laborers, present in large numbers to work at haying and harvest. Faced by strikes of miners in the coalfields of northeastern Pennsylvania, coal operators played on anxiety about draft resistance to induce the federal government to send troops to suppress the unrest. Heavy punitive action followed, together with efforts to root out members of a secretive Irish organization, the Molly Maguires, who were alleged to be fomenting resistance.[15]

As the Civil War dragged on over three and then four years, and as morale sagged, the number of desertions from both armies rose. An estimated 200,000 men deserted from the Union army alone, equivalent to about 10 percent of its total enlistment. The South had more than 100,000 desertions, representing perhaps 12 percent of its army's total strength. But in view of its smaller population and weakening military position, desertion became a more serious matter for the Confederacy than for the Union. Hardships at home, particularly for the many men who served from poor counties, were a strong incentive to desert; some, especially from yeoman farming districts short of labor, left the ranks around harvest time and other seasons when farm work was most pressing. Military defeat helped undermine Confederate morale, especially among nonslaveholding whites. Near Savannah, Georgia, the former slave Nancy Johnson found herself sheltering Confederate deserters toward the end of the war. They "came to our house & we fed them," she testified. "They were opposed to the war & didn't own slaves & said they would rather die than fight."[16]

Political Division and Cohesion

THROUGHOUT THE first three or more years of war, however, the North experienced more serious disunity or division than the white South. Given its relative demographic and economic disadvantages, the Confederacy's best hope of success was to discourage the North from pursuing the war against it. Early Southern military successes in 1861 and 1862 at first seemed capable of pushing the Union to negotiate for peace but in fact failed to do so. Confederates' hopes of foreign inter-vention in their favor also came to nothing. Political divisions in the North, though, fueled more sustained expectations of a settlement to the conflict. Many traditional Democratic voters withheld their support from Lincoln's administration, and some were openly opposed to fight-ing the war. Especially in areas that had received settlers from the South, these views were reinforced by feelings of consanguinity with Southern kin or by notions of white supremacy. Ohio, Indiana, and Illi-nois were strongly divided as racism, ethnicity, and political allegiances reinforced one another. In Jacksonville, Illinois, differences between lo-cal Republicans and peace Democrats divided public life in the town; there was, for instance, no unified July Fourth celebration there for the duration of the war.[17]

But the North held together despite its divisions. Union victories at Gettysburg and Vicksburg in early July 1863 marked the end of Con-federate hopes that it might use military success to sue for peace or even stave off a Union invasion of the Southern heartland. Although that in-vasion proceeded slowly, its effects at length both shattered the South and neutralized political disunity in the North. The Union capture of Atlanta in the autumn of 1864 was followed by Lincoln's success in the November presidential elections against his Democratic rival and for-mer general, George B. McClellan. Although McClellan did win sup-port in some border states, the southern tier of the Old Northwest, and in cities with a strong Democratic presence, Lincoln's defeat of his can-didacy marked the demise of the peace Democrats' hope for a negoti-ated end to the war. Sherman's march to the sea and Grant's armies' breakthrough to Richmond and other centers in Virginia rapidly fol-lowed. Little more than five months after Lincoln's reelection, the Con-federacy had been defeated.

The White South's Nemesis: War and the End of Slavery

THE HUMAN cost of the Civil War to both sides was huge. The 620,000 soldiers who died of wounds or disease still amount to more than all the U.S. military deaths in all the nation's other wars combined.

Across the nation, scores of thousands more were maimed or disfigured for life. One-sixth of Union troops and one quarter of Confederates lost their lives. Of 133 men from Deerfield, Massachusetts, for instance, who fought in the war, 34 were killed. The overall death rate, equivalent to almost 2 percent of the total U.S. population in 1860, was roughly double that suffered in the American Revolution. Among men, and among the most relevant age groups, death rates were much higher. About 8 percent of all white males between 13 and 43 were killed, but whereas in the North that rate was about .6 percent, in the South it was three times higher, at 18 percent, or more than one in six of the age group. The Union's demographic and economic advantages made this great price, considered in a structural sense, bearable: though it incurred many losses, it did not undermine itself by doing so. The Confederacy, by contrast, could not sustain its losses. As the war progressed, it was forced to suffer not only death and destruction but the undermining of its own society.[18]

Above all, the war destroyed the institution the Confederacy had been formed to sustain: chattel slavery. From the perspective of slavery's defenders in 1860, the rapid defeat and destruction of the system within five years would have seemed trebly surprising, if not ironic. We have already noted that the proponents of secession took steps to break away from the United States in response to the election of a free-soil Republican, Abraham Lincoln, who had neither the intention nor the power to impair slavery in the states where it was legal. In determining to prosecute the war against the Union when Lincoln's administration made it clear that secession would not be tolerated, Southern leaders upheld their own sense of strength and righteousness but introduced two further vital conditions that would, together, ensure their defeat. Because they were fighting against a politically divided North, early Southern military successes increased Lincoln's reliance on his Radical Republican and abolitionist supporters and forced him, reluctantly at first, to make slavery a military issue in the war. Furthermore, by resisting the Union to the extent of obliging its armies to invade the Confederacy in order to defeat it, Southern leaders enabled their own slaves to take a hand in destroying slavery. Slaves' most potent weapon against their enslavement had always been escape, but in most of the antebellum South permanent escape from bondage had been very difficult for slaves to accomplish. By provoking a

Northern invasion, however, the Confederacy introduced to thousands of slaves the circumstance that could most make their escape feasible: the presence of a Union army close by.

Lincoln, faced in 1861 and 1862 with weak Union military performance and deep political divisions, found himself obliged to turn to the political elements that could offer the war crucial support. Confronted by opposition from Northern Democrats and others urging peace with the South, Lincoln was drawn toward greater reliance on politicians who were most resolute for war, including Radical Republicans adamant that slavery should be destroyed. Slaves and slavery became central to his strategy. Faced with a South that had so far successfully stood up to the tests of war, Lincoln took steps to undermine it at its weakest point, announcing and then implementing the Emancipation Proclamation, made effective on January 1, 1863, which freed slaves belonging to supporters of the Confederacy. Mindful of continued Northern opposition to abolishing slavery and of Union slaveholders' property rights, Lincoln contrived Emancipation as a military necessity rather than a political act. The result was what one black abolitionist called "a halfway measure, which purports to give freedom to the bulk of the slave population beyond the reach of our arms," while keeping in bondage "those whom alone we have present power to redeem." While Radical Republicans criticized Lincoln for the proclamation's shortcomings, they acted to ensure that the moment became symbolic of a crucial shift in the North's war aims. This was no longer a war just to restore the Union but a war to abolish slavery. The logic of Emancipation would from now on corrode the shackles of slavery, North and South.[19]

For one thing, proclaiming slave emancipation enabled the North to capitalize on its demographic strength while emphasizing the South's social weaknesses. Within months, pressure from radicals persuaded the administration to recruit black soldiers for the Union army (black sailors already served in the navy). From the summer of 1863 on, the growing presence among Union ranks of regiments of free blacks and former slaves represented both an increase in military power and a symbol of the war's new cause. Black troops were not treated equally with whites. Their regiments remained segregated, they were led by white officers, their recruitment bounties were lower than those for white enlistees, and they were paid less than whites, creating special difficulties for many free black families who lost wage earners through military recruitment. Yet by the war's end, more than 200,000 African Americans had served with the Union forces, about 10 percent of total federal strength; in proportion to blacks' presence in the free population, this was a significantly higher participation rate than among whites. The war experience would be a vital element in black Americans' developing sense of citizenship in the years to follow.[20]

Recruiting black soldiers also secured the North an advantage that the South could scarcely seek for itself. Although its population of more than 3.9 million slaves enabled the Confederacy to function by guaranteeing a measure of food and other supplies while many white men were fighting, political and ideological constraints hampered the Confederacy's ability to mobilize slave labor directly for war purposes. Despite recruitment crises as the war continued, Southern leaders dared not contemplate recruiting or conscripting slaves to fight. Not only might arming slaves lead to the mayhem they most feared, it would also be a contradiction of the very things the South was fighting for. Enlisting slaves to fight could only carry with it the promise of freedom, so putting slaves in the army would undermine the very institution it was seeking to uphold. Only in the last weeks of the war, when the Southern manpower shortage became desperate, were slaves for the first time conscripted to serve in unarmed roles as laborers constructing military defenses. This impossibility of using a large part of its population for war purposes was one of the Confederacy's fundamental contradictions, and a significant factor in its defeat.

Slaves themselves, meanwhile, were acting to dismantle the system that shackled them. War conditions helped them. Recruitment into the Confederate army drew off manpower that had been used to patrol and enforce the slave system. From early in the war, whenever Northern forces entered plantation districts in the South, slaves took the opportunity to escape behind federal lines. Iwen, a slave in Montgomery County, Maryland, walked off his owner's land and found refuge in nearby Washington, D.C. Such escapees, mainly from Virginia and Maryland, helped swell the capital's black population by three times during the war. From 1862 on, in northern Virginia, in Tennessee, and on the South Carolina Sea Islands, which were recaptured by Union forces, slaves escaped from captivity and took refuge with soldiers. Especially before the preliminary Emancipation Proclamation, this was not welcomed or countenanced by government or army officials. Some slaves met with racism and hostility; some were forced back to their homes or handed over to owners who came looking for them. But some white soldiers, especially from regions with strong anti-slavery traditions, protected refugee slaves even when they were ordered not to. The owner of Iwen, the Montgomery County slave, followed him to Washington and received permission from federal officers to recapture his man and take him home again. But Iwen was perhaps fortunate to have taken refuge with the Tenth Massachusetts Infantry, whose men drove his owner off. When the slaveholder returned and was about to seize Iwen to take him away, "a large crowd got around . . . and knocked him about throwing small stones and dirt at him and otherwise ill treating him and finally driving him out of the camp without . . . his Negroe." Under pressure from the escapees, and representations by their own troops, officers were increasingly obliged to relent and permit them to stay. In an absurd formulation, reflecting the anomaly of slaves' legal status as humans who were also property, the government determined that they would be classified as "contrabands of war," as property that had been stolen—or in this case that had stolen itself—from the enemy.[21]

Seeking to protect their interests, especially as the military tide turned against the South in 1863, some slaveholders attempted to move their slaves into areas where escape and flight would be made difficult. Large numbers of slaves were forcibly moved (or "refugeed") to Texas, for example, in the hope of placing them as far as possible from federal forces. By inducing the Union army to enter the South to suppress the rebellion, Southerners had effectively shortened the distances that escaped slaves had to traverse. In many cases this made feasible the escapes of whole slave families that would previously have been impossible to accomplish. During Sherman's army's campaign to capture Atlanta and its subsequent marches through Georgia and the Carolinas in 1864 and 1865, thousands of slaves left their plantations and took their freedom by following in the army's wake. Prominent among the effects of Sherman's march, with its sixty-mile-wide band of destruction across the countryside, was this self-liberation of the South's captive labor force in the heart of the plantation economy. The war altered the geography of slavery, putting tens of thousands of slaves within reach of freedom by their own actions.[22]

Not all slaves waited for federal forces to reach their region, nor was their resistance limited to escaping. At Oklona, in central Mississippi, shortly after the Emancipation Proclamation, Confederate scouts captured numbers of escaped slaves, some of whom had armed themselves. Those with arms were court-martialed and, if found guilty, hanged; but others caused consternation to their captors by refusing to give their owners' names. Octave Johnson, born about 1841, had been raised in New Orleans and trained as a cooper. By the time he was fourteen, his mother was sold away by his owner, and in 1861 Johnson himself was sold to a planter in St. James Parish, Louisiana, for whom he worked at his trade by the task rather than in a gang system. But Johnson angered the overseer by staying in bed after the morning bell, "because I was working by task," and ran away into the woods to avoid the inevitable whipping. He remained there for eighteen months, about four miles from the plantation house. He was not alone. By the time he left the woods there were about twenty other male slaves and ten women hiding out with him. This small maroon community sustained itself by hunting and gathering, and by exchanging game meat for cornmeal with house and plantation slaves. But the escapees were themselves being hunted. Hounds unleashed to search for them had to be evaded. On one occasion, Johnson claimed, he had to jump into a bayou to escape a pack of dogs and got away only when the dogs were attacked by alligators in the water. In due course Johnson abandoned the woods and made off to a Union military camp at New Orleans. After being employed there and becoming an officer's servant, he enlisted in the army himself.[23]

On Canoochie Creek, near Savannah, Georgia, Nancy Johnson took her freedom when the Union army occupied the neighborhood. During the war her mistress had made her weave cloth for sale to the Confederate army, work for which she was unpaid, and she had to use her nighttimes to spin and weave for her own family's needs. Now that she was free, she determined to get away from home despite her former owners' insistence that she stay and work for them. Like many newly freed slaves, Johnson went away for a period but then returned. Her former mistress asked if she "would now behave and do her work." Johnson replied "no . . . I came to do my own work." When the woman again asked her to come back to work for her, Johnson "told her no that I was free," and the woman said, "be off then & called me a stinking bitch."

Slaves and masters came into conflict not just over their own affairs but over the war itself. When some Confederate fighters stopped at his plantation near Somerville, Tennessee, in 1864, Bartlet Ciles ordered his slave, Archy Vaughn, to feed their horses. Vaughn obeyed, but too slowly for his master, who promised to whip him as a punishment. To avoid the lash, Vaughn escaped at night with his master's old mare and set out for Union lines. But he was captured and returned to Ciles, who took him into the woods, tied him up, castrated him, and lopped off part of an ear. For some other slaves too, liberation came at a price. Among the slaves on Potter's Plantation, near Savannah, Georgia, was a dairy-woman called Mary Jess, who had been allowed special privileges. In addition to her regular task work, she had been permitted to raise poultry and cattle, to keep a garden, and to sell her stock and produce to earn money for herself. When Sherman's troops came through the district late in 1864, Mary Jess's property was among the things they seized, and eventually Mary Jess was awarded $130 in compensation by the federal government, about one-fifth of what she had claimed.[24]

Reconstruction in the South:
From Freedom to Coercion

IN 1861, Agénor de Gasparin had speculated about the future of Southern society once, as he predicted was likely, the Confederacy had been rejoined to the Union. In common with most observers, the issue of race dominated his assessment, and he shared the assumption widespread among whites that social and racial integration would be neither feasible nor desirable. Still, he claimed, the example of the British West Indies, where slavery had been abolished in the 1830s, suggested that prosperity and peace would be possible, even if racial division and separation were to continue. But he also noted the more pessimistic prediction of his French predecessor Alexis de Tocqueville that abolition in the South would lead to a struggle for power between the races and result in the oppression of the other by whichever group obtained the upper hand. In the event, it was Tocqueville's prediction that proved to be the more prescient. The abolition of slavery, formally accomplished by the passage of the Thirteenth Amendment in 1865, offered the possibility of revolutionary change in Southern society, but it soon became clear that racial oppression and separation, rather than coexistence, would mark the postwar South.[25]

The end of the war found many parts of the former Confederacy in economic ruin. The neglect and loss of labor occasioned by the war would have caused damage anyway. But in addition, across wide swaths of the plantation zone, Union military policy had laid waste farms and plantations, their crops, and much of their productive equipment. War had destroyed millions of dollars' worth of property across the eleven states, and the region's overall production was a fraction of its prewar value. More than 200,000 soldiers in the Confederate forces had been killed or died of disease during the war, and tens of thousands more were maimed or disabled. Having lost 18 percent of their white males aged thirteen to forty-three, the Confederate states were left disproportionately short of active adult men. Immigration to the South continued to be low, so replenishment from that source was slow. In accounts of his Southern travels for a Boston newspaper in 1869, the writer Russell H. Conwell began with descriptions of the wreckage of battlefields and of bones and metal fragments still scattered on battle sites and burial places—potent images of the South's physical destruction and human losses.[26]

Such destruction apart, the South also faced revolutionary social change. The emancipation of slaves ended the system that had provided the wealthiest white planters and more prosperous farmers with their labor force. Slaves had run away, enlisted, been killed or died of disease, and were then finally emancipated by government fiat. Often they then showed their true feelings to their former owners. Mary Jones, whose family owned a large plantation with hundreds of slaves in Liberty County, Georgia, was just one among many planters who lamented that "the servants that used to faithfully . . . wait around us are (many of them) dead or scattered or sadly and willfully changed." The Louisiana sugar planter William T. Palfrey expected that "the labor element at the south, to be derived from the former laborers, is gone forever, to any useful or practical extent." In five cotton states alone, slaves had before the war represented over $1.6 billion of invested capital, or 45.8 percent of total wealth. Emancipation wiped out that wealth, together with the access to labor and credit that it represented for its owners. Land values fell too, partly because it seemed no longer likely that income-earning crops could readily be produced, and partly because impoverished planters and other landowners glutted the land market as they tried to sell property to raise cash. Many planters faced unaccustomed poverty and the prospect of financial ruin. "When you sit down to a full and dainty meal or lay your head on your soft and downy pillow . . .," wrote William Palfrey bitterly to his brother in Massachusetts, "do not let your thoughts revert to the condition of those who are reduced . . . to the slender crust and the hard couch of poverty." Together, the physical destruction of war and the dismantling of slavery unraveled the South's plantation economy. Even in 1870, five years after the end of the war, total Southern output had reached only three-fourths of its 1860 value. Average annual income per capita in the South returned to its 1860 level only around 1890, but by then it was only half the national average, compared with 75 percent in 1860.[27]

Yet the difficulties faced by planters, farmers, and their families paled beside those faced by most of the 3.9 million newly freed slaves. As the Northern black leader Frederick Douglass noted, Emancipation had brought them legal freedom but nothing else. It left most of these millions of men, women, and children without food, shelter, or property, and without the means to acquire these except by their own labor. Lincoln had evidently assumed that freedpeople would work for wages, but during the war many slaves and their allies in the North had subscribed to the hope that the destruction of the Confederacy would lead not just to the end of slavery but also to a fundamental redistribution of landed property in the South. The dream that this could provide every ex-slave family with "forty acres and a mule" was widely shared. According to some Radical Republicans, giving former slaves the land they and their forebears had been compelled to work for generations without pay would compensate for the theft of their labor, solve the problem of subsistence, and lay the foundations of a stable society of independent small farmers.[28]

Southern leaders, along with most Southern whites, had other ideas. In the immediate aftermath of war, racism and economic necessity combined to set them on an attempt to rebuild their economy and ways of life along lines familiar to them. The period of Reconstruction after the war in the South was dominated politically by struggles over the terms on which the former Confederate states should be readmitted to the Union, the extent to which former slaves would be granted full rights of citizenship, and the degree to which political control would return to the elites who had dominated Southern society before the war.

In their first efforts to reassert control, many planters in the summer of 1865 attempted to rebuild the plantation system using their existing black labor force. They sought to operate their plantations in the way they had been accustomed, except that they would pay wages to their former slaves for working in the gang or task systems that were in operation. In circumstances where wage payments were impracticable, because planters had no access to cash or credit, they attempted various makeshift arrangements, including "squad share" systems on some large plantations, in which gangs of ex-slaves would work in return for a share of the crops they raised. Many planters also sought to continue the systems of discipline and punishment they had practiced as slaveowners. A Virginia planter, John Hartwell Cocke, even tried to persuade his former slaves to agree to work on contract for him on the same terms as before Emancipation—an arrangement for voluntary bondage that was overturned by federal officials after freedmen complained.[29]

Planters' efforts immediately encountered difficulties. Although for want of any alternative some former slaves accepted the arrangements planters imposed on them, large numbers of them simply refused to work on such terms. Many rejected the plantation system and the attempts to restart it. In the short term, tens of thousands used their newly gained freedom to leave their old plantations and move elsewhere. Many traveled to find members of their families who had been dispersed under slavery or in the chaos of wartime. Tens of thousands married, taking the earliest opportunity to secure legal recognition of relationships that slavery had formally denied them. Often, because of sales by planters or the dislocations of war, partners had to move to get together again. Many other former slaves simply moved because they could now do so, and took the first opportunity to escape the influence of their former owners. Others who stayed in one place exercised their rights as freedpeople to refuse to follow the orders of planters. By rejecting planters' authority, they began to influence the future course of the

Southern economy. They also undermined the paternalist assumptions of many former slaveholders that their human property had been content in its bondage.[30]

To counter the influence of former slaves using their newfound freedom, planters used their connections in an effort to compel them to work. President Andrew Johnson's administration readmitted former Confederate states to the Union during the summer of 1865 on terms that minimized the penalties imposed for having rebelled. Under this mild regime of presidential Reconstruction, newly reconstituted states passed draconian laws, known as the Black Codes, restricting the rights of movement of former slaves, creating provisions for arresting and jailing indigent travelers as vagrants, and seeking to compel black men and women to stay in one place. Fixed there, unable to travel, freedpeople would have little choice but to accept the terms and conditions that local planters dictated. As they had under slavery, white patrols and vigilante groups attempted to enforce these efforts by intimidation and terror. Black resistance was sufficient, however, to stall these efforts. Many ex-slaves refused to accept contracts for work, or protested at failures by planters to honor their obligations; planters' difficulties obtaining cash to pay wages, for example, undermined the trust even of the more willing freedpeople, who came to suspect that planters were deceiving them. Added to this, during 1866 and 1867 the refusal of Radical Republicans in Congress to accept Johnson's policies led to the dismantling of presidential Reconstruction, the dismissal of the first state governments, and the scrapping of the Black Codes.

From early in the war, some black leaders and Radical Republicans had advocated the distribution of land to freedpeople as the most appropriate means of constructing a stable society in the South once slavery was ended. In the South Carolina Sea Islands, recaptured from the Confederacy by Union troops in 1862, former slaves were put to work for wages on plantations under white supervisors. Arrangements were later made to divide land into plots for cultivation by individual black farmers. At Davis Bend, on the Mississippi River, military officers oversaw the division of plantation land into individual small farms for ex-slaves. On the coastal strip of South Carolina, Georgia, and northern Florida that was captured by Union troops in early 1865, General Sherman's Field Order No. 15 also provided for the partition of lands for settlement by freedmen.

Hopes were high that these examples could be followed across the South. Northern advocates of land redistribution believed it could achieve a double purpose. It would destroy the economic basis of planters' political power, thus neutralizing the groups that in some states had spearheaded the movement for secession. It would also turn a slave-based society into what they took as the ideal model for a republic: a society of small landed proprietors. The Pennsylvania congressman Thaddeus Stevens, one of the leading advocates of land redistribution, noted that the abolition of a planter class would benefit poorer whites as well as newly freed slaves. How, he asked, could "republican institutions . . . exist in a mingled community of nabobs and serfs; of the owners of twenty-thousand-acre manors with lordly palaces and the occupants of narrow huts inhabited by 'low white trash'?" For the legacy of slavery to be erased, Stevens argued, "the whole fabric of southern society must be changed." Land reform would be the means of doing so.[31]

For a short while after the end of the war there were signs that these hopes for Southern land reform might be fulfilled. The creation of the federal Bureau of Refugees, Freedmen, and Abandoned Lands (the Freedmen's Bureau) held out the promise of forty-acre plots to be made available by lease. In South Carolina and Louisiana the distribution of plots to former slaves was under way in the summer of 1865. But these steps were soon obstructed by the politics of presidential Reconstruction. White Southern property owners, restored to influence under the Reconstruction measures, quickly found sympathetic Northern allies to help them reverse the changes that were in train. Under pressure from figures such as Barnwell Rhett, the son of South Carolina's leading secessionist, the Freedmen's Bureau rescinded its measure for land distribution in the Sea Islands in September 1865, only two months after announcing it, and Radical Republican bureau agents there and in Louisiana were dismissed from their posts. Former slaves at Edisto Island, told that they would have to relinquish their plots, protested and thwarted plans for an alternative wage-paying plantation by refusing to stay in the area if they could not keep the land they had been allocated. At Davis Bend and other sites, redistributed land was also confiscated from ex-slaves and returned to its former owners.

Planters and their white allies in the South adamantly refused to accept land reform, primarily to resist the possibility that former slaves might obtain a basis for social equality. J. Quitman Moore, a Mississippi planter, expressed fear of what he called "black agrarianism," ex-slaves' aspiration "to become *landholders* and *tenants* and not *hirelings*"—in other words, to achieve a degree of independence. Many ex-slaveowners were hostile to their former slaves, whom they condemned for "ingratitude" in seeking their own terms for freedom. Most probably also believed that freedpeople were incapable of looking after themselves or their land properly, and eagerly absorbed reports of failures or shortcomings in free-labor and land-reform experiments. But white Southerners' influence was enhanced by the extent to which Northerners and federal officials shared their views. Racism and prejudice caused many federal military officers in the South to deny that former slaves could successfully operate as farmers without white supervision. Some observers in the North supported land reform only as an expedient to keep former slaves on the land; the *New York Times* argued in June 1865 that if freedpeople were not settled where they were, they would crowd to cities, including those in the North. But most Northern politicians were reluctant to accept land-reform policies that appeared to interfere with property rights; at most they were prepared to see blacks resettled on lands that had been "abandoned" (usually in the disruption of war) and hence no longer under clear ownership. Other Northern observers, keen to see efficient staple-crop production restored rapidly in the South, saw land reform and the creation of a black small-farmer class as an obstruction to rebuilding the Southern economy. The Boston merchant Edward S. Tobey, writing in 1865, urged the employment of ex-slaves as wage workers on government-owned plantations, to restore cotton exports and secure a supply of gold currency earnings.[32]

The reversal of presidential Reconstruction by Radical Republicans in Congress in 1866 and 1867 temporarily deposed the newly restored Southern leadership and gave rise to new hope for measures that could permanently settle former slaves on just terms. This phase of congressional or Radical Reconstruction did have a considerable impact. Black men were enfranchised across the South and quickly helped elect governments and legislatures that in many states included black representatives and senior officials for the first time. The Freedmen's Bureau and charitable agencies sent teachers into many areas of the South and established schooling for former slaves and their children. Passage of the

Fourteenth Amendment to the Constitution in 1868, confirming that ex-slaves were citizens and guaranteeing all citizens equal protection of the law, and of the Fifteenth Amendment in 1870, upholding the right to vote regardless of color, had been pressed by radicals in Congress to protect freedmen's rights. Renewed efforts at land reform, with the passage of a Southern Homestead Act in 1866, attempted to provide access to land on generous terms comparable to those offered on the Western frontier by the 1862 Homestead Act.

By private or government action, in limited ways, aspects of the vision of a black freeholders' democracy were sometimes achieved. By the early 1870s an estimated 5 percent of rural black families in the South did own their own land. In some areas, such as the former rice-plantation districts of the Southeast coast, black proprietorship was quite common and was often an extension of the system of provision grounds that had been made available to slaves under the task system. Elsewhere, such as in plantation districts of Alabama, a small number of former slaves were allocated land of their own by planters; recent research has suggested that these were often planters' blood relatives, born from sexual relationships between planters and female slaves. But the vast majority of former slaves remained unable to obtain land of their own. Planters and Northern opponents of land redistribution continued to resist interference with property rights. Most Republicans, including radicals, also regarded these rights as sacrosanct and hesitated to meddle with them; they rejected the arguments of some abolitionists that redistribution would merely be just compensation for generations of slaves' unremunerated labor. "Abandoned lands" and other sources of land for redistribution under the Southern Homestead Act remained scarce. During the 1870s even radical supporters of this measure gave up defending it against assaults in Congress, and ultimately the act lapsed.

Tenancy and Sharecropping

HAVING SUBSTANTIALLY resisted plantation wage labor but failed to obtain significant land reform, former slaves found themselves compelled by 1867–1868 to accept other means of earning their livelihoods from the land. Some had been so reduced to desperate measures that they had no bargaining power at all. A Kentucky freedman, Robert Tomson, having been jailed at Louisville for killing his employer's hog to get food, sent a letter to his old master asking to be taken back to work for board only, "as long as you want me" and "without one cent of money" in wages. But many former slaves were able to oblige landowners to break up their plantations into smaller farming units, though they could not force them to relinquish ownership. Instead, depending on their own means and local circumstances, they accepted tenancy or sharecropping agreements with planters. Tenants rented land for cash payments each year, earning the income for this by selling their crops in the marketplace. But a large proportion of former slaves did not have sufficient means of their own to become cash tenants. Needing to hire not just land but tools, seed, and livestock too, hundreds of thousands of former slaves became sharecroppers, working a portion of the landowner's land in return for a greater or smaller share of the annual crop. In some areas, again, sharecropping arrangements were an extension of the old task system; elsewhere, when there were no alternatives, ex-slaves reluctantly accepted it in preference to working in gangs.[33]

Freedpeople's preference for sharecropping or tenancy over working for wages was rooted in the relative independence it provided from direct white supervision. It also enabled ex-slaves to operate as family units. In many cases, freed slave families began to conduct themselves along what had become traditional gender roles in farming societies, dividing labor between men who worked in the fields and women who undertook primarily household and domestic tasks. Especially in cotton-growing regions, this removed from field labor many women who had, under slavery, been obliged to work as field hands. Some contemporaries attributed a short-term fall in productivity in cotton growing partly to this switch, and some economic historians have agreed. Other scholars have noted that the change had mixed implications for members of black families. The creation of traditional family life, often hard to sustain under slavery, was a prize many had sought. Still, the association of black men more exclusively with crop-raising and marketing, coupled with their political enfranchisement under Radical Reconstruction, marked a shift in the gender balance of power, often to the disadvantage of women. Even in cases where gang labor continued for a period, women's work appears to have been used as a kind of bargaining chip with planters. On the Barrow plantation in Georgia, which operated a squad-share system until the mid-1870s, male ex-slaves could exert some pressure on their landlord by deploying or withholding the labor of women in their families.

Planters became advocates of sharecropping or tenancy as alternatives to gang systems not least because these reduced the opportunity for ex-slaves to exercise such power. As with independent farming, sharecropping or tenancy placed many of the risks of cultivation largely on the family unit, displacing it from landowners. With the spread of sharecropping and tenancy, many black families did indeed gain the use of "forty acres and a mule," but the forty acres did not belong to them and, if they were sharecroppers, often the mule was not theirs either. Freedpeople, by resisting plantation wage work, completed a revolution in Southern agriculture that had begun with their liberation from slavery, a revolution that in many districts occurred in an astonishingly short period of time. Yet the failure of land reform ensured that this change remained substantially under the control of white planters, landowners, and merchants, and not of former slaves themselves. Even at the height of Radical Reconstruction, white Southerners were taking steps that would in time reinstate the effective coercion of black labor. Slavery had gone and was not reintroduced, but the patterns of power that now emerged in Southern society replicated many of its facets. The revolution was arrested in mid-course.

The Postwar Southern Economy

IN ECONOMIC terms, the destruction of slavery and its replacement by new labor arrangements made some activities difficult or impossible. Many of the great rice plantations of the South Carolina and Georgia coasts fell into decline after the Civil War. Without a large slave labor force there was insufficient labor to work the rice fields and to operate and maintain the earthworks and water channels that ensured the cultivation system's delicate balance. Exceptions included the Georgia plantations of the Rhode Islander Richard J. Arnold, who invested capital from his commercial interests to pay wages to former slaves to raise rice, and who by the time of his death in 1873 became one of the world's largest rice farmers. But most planters had no access to the sources of capital that Arnold used, and were unable to follow his example. Rice production continued mainly as a small-scale activity on small farms. The end of slavery also disrupted sugar production in Louisiana. Although in this case the creation of sharecropping and other measures to control labor helped ensure the supply of workers for harvesting and grinding, and the industry did not decline, it took until the 1880s to rebuild sugar production to its prewar levels.

Tobacco and cotton cultivation adapted more easily to the new labor systems. Although tenancy and sharecropping removed planters from direct supervision of production, they could nonetheless exercise control over labor, often in an increasingly rigid way. Because most sharecroppers and tenants had few resources of their own, landlords or the provision merchants who supplied workers' goods and food over the year achieved a stranglehold on their activities. Most cultivators' legal position was that of laborers, not of landholders, and that gave them little protection. Landlords could evict them after the annual contract ended, or use their legal power as owners to restrict tenants' movements and effectively tie them to the land. Debts run up at the store for goods provided over the year were set against the earnings from crops raised. If, as was common, a tenant's share of the crop was insufficient to cover this debt, he and his family were held in a form of debt peonage, under legal obligation to remain on the land until they were no longer wanted. Poverty and their legal obligations made many black families dependent on the decisions of the landlords or merchants who controlled them.[34]

Although there was something of a struggle for power between landlords and merchants after the Civil War, because many impoverished planters found themselves under the financial thumb of provisioners, the effects for sharecroppers and tenants were similar. As cotton production increased again, and as it found its way onto world markets that had already been forced to adapt to the cotton famine of the Civil War period, supply exceeded demand and prices fell. The mid-1860s marked, in any case, a peak in the growth rate of world demand for cotton; from then on producers were shipping raw cotton into softening markets. Merchants and landowners, only interested in the crops from which they could earn cash, nevertheless compelled their tenants to raise cotton, and as the price declined they sought to make up for losses by insisting on greater output. This drove increasing numbers of sharecroppers into greater debt, and greater poverty. Stories abounded of tenant farms whose cotton fields reached right to the walls of the croppers' cabins. Land that could have been used for gardens and vegetable patches was put into cotton cultivation, further increasing tenants' dependence on provision merchants for their food supplies, and further adding to their indebtedness.

In consequence, the patterns of landowning and tenant farming in the post–Civil War South contributed as much as slavery had earlier to an overall rigidity in the region's economy. Unlike the farming areas of the North, many of which diversified over time as farmers made their own decisions about what to grow, much of the South remained locked in the production of staple crops for export to other regions and nations, in part because cultivators were obliged to produce what their landlords or provision merchants demanded. The abolition of slavery did not alter this fundamental characteristic of the South's activities, and it would be the mid-twentieth century before substantial change came to many Southern farming regions. Despite the efforts of promoters of a more modern "new South," the plantation zone in particular remained heavily agricultural and comparatively undiversified. By the 1880s, prominent observers such as Henry Grady were bemoaning the weakness of the South's manufacturing industries and the region's persistent dependence on other parts of the United States and on foreign suppliers for many of its requirements. In a famous lecture at the end of that decade, Grady echoed the image employed almost forty years earlier by Albert Pike at the Southern Commercial Convention— of a funeral in which only the body itself and the soil it was buried in were supplied by the South. Having enumerated the products, from the corpse's clothes to the coffin and headstone, that all came from manufacturing centers in the Midwest and Northeast, Grady voiced a lament for "that country, so rich in undeveloped resources," that "furnished nothing for the funeral except the corpse and the hole in the ground and would probably have imported both of those if it could have done so."[35]

The Yeoman South

THIS ECONOMIC rigidity also influenced another distinction that had survived from slavery: the differences between upland and lowland parts of the South. Upland areas, dominated by white freehold or tenant farming, continued to have smaller black populations and to operate in ways distinct from the principal plantation regions. But upland farmers were not unaffected by the broader economic changes of the post–Civil War period. Increasingly they were brought into the sphere of market production. Land and hunting laws closed off access to the open range, obliging smaller farmers and poor families to seek their livelihoods in wage labor or small-scale market production. As New Englanders had discovered in the late eighteenth and early nineteenth centuries, greater engagement in markets led to social changes. In parts of the upland South, such as in Alabama and Georgia, where there had been high rates of landownership among white yeoman farmers before the Civil War, tenancy and evidence of poverty became more common as farms came to rely more heavily on producing for market. White tenancy in the cotton states grew between 1860 and 1880. In more northerly parts of Appalachia between 1850 and 1870 the proportion of families without land rose from 30 percent to 50 percent. It was no coincidence that in the piedmont and upland regions of the Carolinas and Georgia, textile manufacturers—many of them based in New England—established new mills from the 1870s on, bringing a new phase of industrialization to the rural South. By setting up in these areas, mill owners sought access not only to water, fuel, and cotton supplies but to a rural labor force like that they had recruited in the North in the 1820s and 1830s. Appalachian land, lumber, and mine owners discouraged independent landownership by farmers so they could more readily recruit wage laborers for their own operations. Tenancy and company villages became characteristic of the region.[36]

The enduring rigidities in the postwar Southern economy and society were not purely the results of economic circumstances. It might have been expected, for example, that with falling cotton prices, planters and provision merchants would have promoted agricultural diversification, using their power over tenants to oblige them to vary the crop regimes on their holdings. One reason they did not was political. The exercise of power had as much to do with controlling a population and labor force of former slaves as it had to do with economic objectives. The legal and economic conditions of tenancy and sharecropping were reinforced by the political and social conditions in which they operated.

Radical Reconstruction, with its steps toward education for ex-slaves and extension of the franchise to black men, seemed at first to reflect the aspirations of former slaves to achieve full recognition as independent citizens. Even in the absence of land reform, education and the vote offered the promise of political protection and the prospect of future opportunities. But racism, bitter political rivalry, and systematic intimidation ended up destroying many of the frameworks for black self-advancement and drove away the individuals and institutions that could help sustain them.

Black enfranchisement considerably extended the influence of the Republican party in a region in which, because of its anti-slavery stance, it had not achieved much political purchase before 1861. Democrats' hostility to increased Republican power after the war was closely mapped on white hostility to black participation or advancement. Local white leaders in many areas of the South sponsored the activities of the Ku Klux Klan and other secret terror societies, and launched overt political attacks on Reconstruction state governments. These they accused of corruption and of being the puppets of Yankee do-gooders and federal officials—"carpetbaggers" who had intruded from the North. As a Tennessean wrote in the 1870s, the South was "languishing under the corrupt influence of the General Government," and "disfranchised under the accursed system of reconstruction" in which "a parcel of irresponsible adventurers were elevated to high positions."[37]

The origins of the Ku Klux Klan reflect not simply the hostility between North and South, or between planters and their former slaves, but also the antagonisms within Southern society between yeoman farmers and poor whites, on one hand, and wealthier whites on the other. The politics of race and of class were entwined. The Klan was founded in 1866 in Pulaski, Tennessee, an area dominated by small farmers and white laborers who had themselves faced disruptions as a result of war. Here and in other nonplantation areas such as parts of northeastern Mississippi, whites faced competition for work from former slaves. The intimidation and terror they employed was directed both at driving blacks out of their districts and at punishing large planters who had sought to employ them. In urban centers too, such as Baltimore and New Orleans, white workers went on strike to drive black laborers out of employment as shipbuilders and longshoremen, and to force proprietors to hire white-only workforces.[38]

But the campaign of terror acquired the broader purpose of reasserting white control over Southern politics and suppressing many aspects of blacks' autonomy. Intimidation and murder drove black men and white Republicans from the polls and threatened independent black farmers who sought to exercise economic freedom. This period too, according to the historian Martha Hodes, witnessed the emergence of white hostility to interracial sexual encounters and made the fear of a black threat to white womanhood a potent incitement to racial violence. The combination of these issues drove freedmen and their supporters out of politics, making the protective clauses of the Fourteenth and Fifteenth Amendments and the later Civil Rights Act of 1875 dead letters, and reinstating racial and hierarchical divisions in Southern society. The result, after Reconstruction ended, would be the establishment of formal policies of racial segregation and black disfranchisement, and the rise of lynching as a tool of intimidation and control. The revolution wrought in the South by the abolition of slavery was stopped in its tracks and thrown into reverse.[39]

The Postwar North:
Toward Revolutionary Change

AS THE South moved from revolutionary upheaval toward the reinstitution of racial and economic constraints, the North was set on an opposite trajectory. The Civil War did not provoke such profound changes in the North as the abolition of slavery did in the South, but it confirmed and accelerated trends that had been apparent since at least the 1840s. While the South's economy was destroyed or disrupted by war, the North's was boosted: the Union states' total output in 1870 was 40 percent higher than it had been a decade earlier. In the postwar decades, American society continued its expansive growth across the continent and sustained the well-established tradition of dispersed, extensive settlement. But to an even greater degree the period marked the nation's turn toward intensive and concentrated development, increasing urban populations and manufacturing output, and a deepening reliance on immigrant workers and their descendants to provide the additional labor needed to accomplish these developments. At the same time the influence of commercial and financial elites, and the power of commercial organizations over both the extensive and concentrated portions of the economy, was enhanced. And in the inequalities and conflicts these changes created lay the sources of protest movements that would play an important role in later-nineteenth-century culture and social consciousness.

Fueled by population growth, the continued aspiration for land, the provision of public land free of charge to settlers under the Homestead Act of 1862, and the extension of railroads to the West, the expansion of American agriculture continued unabated during and after the Civil War. Between 1860 and 1870 the rural population of the United States increased by a quarter. Indeed, the scene was being set for what would become an excessive overexpansion of farming into arid regions that could not appropriately sustain it, spurred by an extraordinary but often sincerely held belief that cultivation of the land would alter climate—that "rain follows the plow." Until the 1880s more than half the total U.S. workforce was employed in farming, and throughout the late nineteenth century the agricultural sector continued to expand in absolute size and value of output. In 1870 there were already 2.66 million farms, 37 percent more than in 1860. By 1900 the total number of farms had more than doubled again. In newly settled regions like Kansas, Nebraska, and the Dakota Territory, the number of farms multiplied by eight times; even in New England they continued to increase. Output of major staple products, such as wheat, cotton, and cattle, also doubled or tripled, but evidence from regions dominated by smaller farms suggests that farm output also became more diversified as markets and transportation developed, and as such farming became more commercialized. Part of the increase in farm output stemmed from rising investment in agricultural equipment and machinery, but it was also attributable to the increased efforts of women and children on farms necessitated by the war. This renewed emphasis on the use of family labor remained a feature of smaller farms across the North and Midwest in the postwar decades.[40]

To some extent, as had been the case in new regions before the Civil War, this surge in agriculture also involved an expansion of large farming units and of the employment of wage laborers in agriculture. Large "bonanza" farms growing wheat continued to be opened up on the prairies and Great Plains, and in California. Cattle ranching on the high plains and in Texas also involved large land areas and substantial workforces of hired *rancheros* and cowboys. By 1870 hired hands accounted for almost 37 percent of all individuals working in U.S. agriculture. But the postwar period also witnessed a continuing increase in the number of family-run farms. In the 1870s the expansion of farming and farm output coincided with an economic depression and initiated a long downward trend in prices for many commodities. This reinforced the importance of smaller farm units and turned the later nineteenth century into the heyday of North American household-based farming. By 1890 wage workers represented only one-quarter of the farm labor force, and farm families the other three-quarters. As in the past, many individuals continued to see farming as a source of family security. The German immigrant Johan Bauer, who had come to the United States from Baden in 1854 and first found work in manufacturing, later farmed in Illinois and acquired land in Missouri. Worried about "the frequent and often sudden changes in circumstances" he encountered, Bauer determined to avoid the "danger of losing what you've acquired with great trouble and effort." So, as he wrote in 1868, he had begun "to invest . . . in land. . . . I thought in times of confusion, land remains a refuge & with some effort and work I can always feed myself and my family." By 1880, Bauer owned 125 acres.[41]

But this extensive expansion, and the family strategies that Bauer and thousands of others pursued to accomplish it, increasingly depended on the articulation of commercial links between agriculture and more intensive kinds of development. These intensive developments, in the growth of cities, industry, and commerce, were the most striking hallmarks of later-nineteenth-century American society. The change could be measured at many levels. Some individuals, as in the past, decided that farming was not for them, but did so from observation of what was going on around them as well as from personal taste. Jerry Remington, a Union officer, wrote to his family during the Civil War that "of all kinds of labor that of the hands gets the least pay. . . . Body and sinew the world over are cheap." He resolved not to follow his father into farming.[42]

Although it would be almost 1920 before a majority of Americans lived in urban areas, the expansion of towns and cities that had begun in the North continued even more rapidly after the Civil War. In 1870 there were already twenty-five cities with populations of fifty thousand or more; by 1900 there would be seventy-eight. The inflow of migrants from rural areas and from overseas to cities and manufacturing areas fueled a rapid expansion in industrial production. Meanwhile capital investment flowed to increase the size of many manufacturing establishments and extend mechanization. In 1840 about 70 percent of U.S. capital stock had been represented by farm improvements; machinery contributed only about 5 percent. By 1900, despite the massive expansion of the farm sector, farm improvements were contributing only one-third of capital stock, and machinery more than one-quarter. This shift was a measure of the change in emphasis from extensive to intensive forms of production that had accelerated particularly after the Civil War.

By 1870 the United States was already the world's largest economy, and by the end of the century, measured by average product per capita, it had become the sixth most prosperous of the world's economies. By the mid-1890s the value of its manufacturing output alone, which had ranked fourth in the world in 1860, had grown almost to equal the combined production of its three nearest industrial rivals, Britain, Germany, and France. It was also the world's largest producer of most leading minerals and a significant exporter of grain and other agricultural produce. During the nineteenth century as a whole, the value of U.S. exports abroad rose from 3.2 percent to 15 percent of total world trade. As American manufacturing and agricultural exports grew in value, the United States ceased after the 1870s to run the annual trade deficits that had been usual until that time. An enthusiastic English observer, writing in 1881, exclaimed that "ten years in the history of America is half a century of European progress. Ten years ago the manufactures of America were too insignificant for consideration in the Old World. Today England herself is successfully rivaled by American productions in her own markets."[43]

The wage-earning workforce in industry continued to grow rapidly. By the 1880s the number of workers in manufacturing, mining, and transportation permanently exceeded the workforce in farming. The number of independent businesses in manufacturing, mining, or commerce rose from an estimated 427,000 in 1870 to 1,111,000 thirty years later—a massive extension of entrepreneurial effort. These industrial and commercial developments also accelerated the nation's overall prosperity. The average overall rate of U.S. growth in income per capita was about 25 percent faster between 1870 and 1890 than it had been over the previous fifty years, even taking into account the destruction of war and the persistent poverty in much of the South. But regional differences were persistent. By 1880 mean income per capita in New York, Massachusetts, and Rhode Island was roughly three times that in Virginia, the Carolinas, and Georgia.[44]

These developments also reinforced the prewar tendency for inequalities to sharpen within regional societies as well as between them, as profits and power accrued most readily to owners of commercial, industrial, and financial institutions rather than directly to the owners or cultivators of land. Many Union officers contemplated commercial careers after leaving the army. Rutherford B. Hayes advised his younger military aide William McKinley in 1866, "My notion of the place for a young man is a fine large growing town anywhere, but would prefer a new town in the West. . . . With your business capacity and experience I would have preferred railroading or some commercial business. A man in any of our Western towns with half your wit ought to be independent at forty in business." The wartime North had seen the emergence of a cohort of prosperous merchants and manufacturers who had made their fortunes by supplying military requirements. Doubts as to the quality and value of some of their goods led them to be popularly referred to as the "shoddy aristocracy," after cloth made from waste woolens that itself acquired a reputation for poor quality. Although economic historians have suggested that contemporaries exaggerated the power and wealth of Union contractors, there are grounds for noting the influence of a generation of commercial figures, many born in the 1830s, who did not fight in the war but instead built commercial fortunes that would swell in the postwar economy. Most prominent among this group would be the young Cleveland, Ohio, commission merchant John D. Rockefeller, who during the war built up not only a provisioning supply business but also key holdings in the emerging oil industry, which was first established in western Pennsylvania.[45]

The activities of Rockefeller and his business partners after the war, employing ruthless competitive methods to drive out or consolidate with numerous rivals in the oil business, and securing effective control of the region's oil refining and shipment, became legendary examples of the concentrating power of capital in the rapidly growing late-nineteenth-century economy. The use of corporate forms to raise large amounts of capital and to shelter business investments in a whole range of industries, from railroads and mining to manufacturing and raw materials processing, marked the emergence of large corporations as widespread, powerful institutions. Their efforts to drive out competition and secure quasi-monopoly control of their industries would create one of the most controversial areas of business regulation in the late nineteenth and early twentieth centuries, with lasting effects on American society and government. The fortunes to be created from conducting and financing corporate activities were sufficient to continue the process of wealth and income inequality that had been present for decades. The late-nineteenth-century historian Henry Adams would later describe the post-1865 milieu as "a banker's world." Studies of social elites confirm that great wealth and power in America now lay in commercial, industrial, and financial activities, not on the land itself. Supplementing these organizations and great fortunes was the continued growth of a substantial, nonmanual "white-collar" middle class, now identified by the badge of its most distinctive male clothing.

By convention and often in reality, nonmanual workers were distinguished from their often poorer manual colleagues by the latter's "blue-collar" overalls or work clothes. By 1870 some two-thirds of the total U.S. workforce were employees rather than proprietors, independent farmers, or self-employed, and in manufacturing states like Massachusetts and Pennsylvania the proportion was higher still, 75 percent or greater. The growth of a manufacturing workforce, sustained as before the Civil War with continuing supplies of immigrants, increased the importance of friction between workers and their employers, particularly in an unstable and competitive economic environment. The conflict between labor and capital became the central social issue of the late nineteenth century.

Organizations like the Providence [Rhode Island] Association of Mechanics and Manufacturers continued their prewar promotion of the "presumed harmony of interests" between employers and waged employees in manufacturing trades, and even grew in membership during the 1860s and 1870s. But later the group went into rapid decline as the growing distinction between manual and nonmanual occupations and the barriers to advancement within firms rendered obsolete old assumptions about the ability of employees to progress to proprietorship. Only skilled workers in some circumstances could continue to hope for such advancement.[46]

Moreover the abolition of slavery helped remove the ideological yardstick by which "free labor" had, before the Civil War, been compared with its opposite. While some erstwhile abolitionists, including the prominent radical William Lloyd Garrison, considered their work done with the passage of the Fifteenth Amendment, others, such as Garrison's ally Wendell Phillips, joined a growing campaign of support for the rights of workers in the face of their employers' power. Labor unions, revived during and after the Civil War, mounted strenuous efforts to overcome the legal disadvantages that free-labor ideology entailed for workers. Regarding workers as individual contractors for the use of their own labor, the law, often restated by court judgments, presumed contractual relationships to be equal that were in fact often highly unequal. Efforts to improve wages and curb excessive working hours—manifest in a growing but unsuccessful campaign for an eight-hour working day—ran into serious difficulties in the 1870s, as vigorous opposition from many employers combined with a severe economic depression beginning in 1873 to weaken many workers' positions. The German-born Missouri farmer Johan Bauer noted in 1874 that "the Americans are too proud to believe that in many ways there is as much poverty and misery as in other countries." Faced with cuts in real wages and worsening working conditions, organized labor in a number of industries, such as mining and railroading, grew increasingly militant. A series of widespread and disruptive strikes on the nation's railroads in 1877 both culminated these reactions to economic setbacks and set the stage for further decades of often violent labor conflict.[47]

But the growing power of commercial and industrial capital affected not only workers. It also altered the conditions under which many farmers, especially in the Midwest and prairies, and in parts of the South, could operate in the context of expanding national markets for their crops and produce. Before the Civil War many Northern farmers had achieved a degree of balance between local patterns of exchange and interactions with distant markets. In the postwar economy, farm debt and the increasing importance of national and international markets for most produce altered farmers' sense of relative autonomy and made them more dependent on dominant commercial organizations. Particularly in single-crop regions, such as the Midwestern wheat belt and parts of the cotton South, where absence of diversification obliged farmers to rely heavily on the fortunes of their main crop, they faced conflicts and disputes with railroads, merchants, and shippers, and with the banks that held mortgages or other debts against them. In response they formed cooperatives and protective organizations such as the Patrons of Husbandry (also known as the Grange), to try to pool their power, retain some influence in expanding markets, and lobby for reforms. In the 1880s and early 1890s the farmers' movement would grow into a vociferous political campaign, spearheaded by the People's party, or Populists, which flourished briefly between 1892 and 1896. Workers' and farmers' movements alike condemned the "new slavery" that, as one Populist orator put it, kept "the producing classes in thrall to the wealthy."

A symbol of the shift in power and influence that subordinated extensive agricultural developments to the intensive, diversified activities of manufacture, finance, and transportation could be found in the memoirs of the New York–born farm laborer Omar Morse, who for several decades from the late 1840s had struggled to establish himself and his family as farm owners on a succession of smallholdings in Wisconsin and Minnesota. Constantly obliged to work for wages to keep up with mortgage payments, and repeatedly forced to sell out and try again because of crop failures, illness, or financial reverses, Morse doggedly pursued landownership, "hoping some day to be more independent and better able to make . . . my family more comfortably provided for." By the 1880s, now a widower in his sixties, Morse still clung to his dream of independence on the land by urging his son, Manley, to join him at farming. Manley, however, having watched the losing contest, pursued a different course. Over his father's opposition, he became a skilled craftsman and settled down to work for wages in the car-building shops of the Northern Pacific and Burlington railroads.[48]

1877: A Rulers' Compromise in Historical Perspective

THE YEAR 1877 proved to be a turning point, North, South, and West. Railroad strikes across the Northeast and Midwest gave rise to the most violent clashes between workers, government, and employers to date, and led to far-reaching steps by government and capital to resist labor's influence. Republican party weakness in the presidential election of 1876 had led party managers to execute a deal with Southern congressmen that would secure support for the nominated candidate, Rutherford B. Hayes, in return for concessions to the South. As a consequence, once the Hayes administration took office the next year, federal troops were withdrawn from their final posts of occupation in the South, signaling that the North's efforts to reconstruct the South had ended. Meanwhile the stunning defeat of George Armstrong Custer's cavalry at the hands of the Sioux at the Battle of the Little Big Horn in 1876 marked the high point of Indian resistance on the Great Plains and initiated a fifteen-year campaign to subjugate Western tribes, destroy their livelihoods, and complete the conquest of their lands. These events marked three important strands in American social development. They were not, in a direct sense, connected, and were certainly not the consequence of concerted action or policy. But they did represent both continuities with the past and a convergent set of views about the relationships between property, work, and opportunity in American society.

Developments in the postwar South, as noted, left most African Americans excluded from the economic, social, and political gains that the overthrow of slavery had caused them to hope for. Native Americans too had always, from the founding of the republic and before, been explicitly excluded from citizenship. Not merely had they frequently and repeatedly resisted European incursions into their continent, but Anglo-American law and ideology had largely defined indigenous peoples as outside the body politic. The expansion of white society therefore entailed the destruction or removal of Indians rather than their incorporation. The campaigns on the Great Plains that culminated in the massacre at Wounded Knee in 1890, and the forcing of the last independent Native American groups into reservations, marked the final stages in a three-centuries-long effort to control the continent and bring to the West both the expansionary and intensive-development strains nurtured in Eastern societies during the nineteenth century.[49]

Assaults on labor unions and the persistence of "free labor" ideology in the Northeast and Midwest also marked the continuation of decades of assertion of the rights of property over those of labor. They were part of an effort to ensure that capital would sustain its control over an increasingly large and powerful workforce. Employers frequently secured the assistance of government in upholding their positions in disputes with workers. When the federal military occupation of the South ended, there were more federal troops deployed in Pennsylvania against strikers than remained in the entire former Confederacy. Troops were also sent in 1877 into the formerly slaveholding city of Baltimore, Maryland, to quell labor disturbances. A growing proportion of the industrial workforce, too, was foreign-born. As at times in the past, nativist sentiment bolstered capital's assertions of the rights to act in its own interests.

Many of these conflicts—between whites and Native Americans, between whites and African Americans, and between "American" capital and an immigrant-based wage labor force—appeared to be formed around race or ethnic divisions. But there were also critical class divisions that determined their character and ferocity. Each contained at its heart conflicts over the terms of access to property, resources, and the labor of others—in other words, to the terms on which men and women could secure their livelihoods and seek opportunities for themselves and their children.

For at least a century, white settlers and land speculators had sought to justify to themselves and their countrymen the occupation of Native American land, not simply by force of arms but by force of ideology. Native peoples were "savages," not by their actions or temperament so much as by the way they organized their societies. Their lack of private property, their reliance on hunting, their assignment of agricultural tasks to women, and particularly their communal ways of life were presumed to justify their exclusion and expulsion to make way for people with more "civilized" social institutions. The conquest of the "West" and its division into private property holdings gave rise to the means of establishing European-style social structures, with their ability through family or class relations to enable the control and direction of labor.

The importation and deployment of slave labor in the colonial period had been one means by which settlers with means throughout the British American colonies had sought to address the continent's built-in labor scarcity. But the economics of slavery worked most favorably for them in places where staple crops could be grown for overseas markets; consequently slavery grew with the plantation economies of the South but became weaker in the diversified regions of the North and in the commercialized port cities. Southern society, however, rested on the social dynamics of white property and slave labor. Although the Civil War destroyed slavery and changed the relationships between the South and the rest of the United States, the persistence of powerful planter elites helped ensure the reimposition of racially based labor controls in the Reconstruction period. But these divisions were class based as well as merely racial. The disfranchisement of black voters in the 1870s and 1880s also affected many poor whites, who were no better able than their black counterparts to overcome the barriers to opportunity that planter-dominated societies imposed on them. White farmers and laborers in areas of the South not dominated by plantations also faced increasing class divisions of their own, either between landlords and tenants, as in parts of Appalachia, or between farmers, laborers, and capitalists, as market production led increasing numbers of farmers and their families into the wage labor market in the later nineteenth century.

The Hayes compromise of 1877 underscored the hegemony of the rights of property over those of labor. Work itself did not convey rights, except insofar as these were the subject of contracts between employer and employee. The fruits of labor might lead to accumulation and the purchase of property that would convey certain rights, but the ability to do this was assumed to be a measure of personal capacity and worthiness. Northern employers and Southern landowners alike in the late nineteenth century controlled the labor of men and women to whom they had contractual ties but no further social obligation. Efforts to organize unions, or to protest conditions, were viewed as impairments of contract that could in some cases justify draconian action. Those in employment were subject to increasing restraint. Although workers had the freedom to quit their jobs, the law granted employers autocratic power over them in the workplace. Labor historians have noted the struggles that took place over the control of tasks in industry, as heavy investment in machinery and new management techniques undermined the old saying that "the boss's brains are under the workman's hat." Like earlier patterns of extensive growth, the massive concentrations of industrial power and output that placed the American economy ahead of other, international competitors by the end of the nineteenth century were built on effectively coerced labor. Informal power was exercised over legally "free" individuals.[50]

The compromise of 1877 brought together several strands of the elites' efforts to overcome the divisions of the Civil War. Political expediency and race consciousness certainly contributed to the emerging climate in which, by late in the century, white Union and Confederate veterans could meet at Blue-Grey Reunions, where they were urged to "remember the battles, not the fight," and where mention of slavery as a cause of the war, or black participation in it, was suppressed. But it also represented efforts by increasingly self-conscious national and regional elites to bury their own conflicts in the interest of pursuing their older goals: the control and subjection of a labor force.

Yet these efforts, though partially successful, were still subject to social-structural constraints of the kind that had characterized American society since the colonial period and that we have been considering throughout this book. The labor and farmers' movements challenged elites with claims to rights and arguments for reforms that set terms for political struggles and debates into the early twentieth century. The Populists even achieved a moment of alliance between white and black farmers, tenants, and sharecroppers in parts of the West and South that briefly overcame the hardening barriers of race. Although transportation improvements and the expansion of markets were propelling an increasing degree of integration across the national economy, regional social structures and other distinctions continued and remained important. Economic development in the last quarter of the nineteenth century remained uneven from region to region, and important measures such as manufacturing output, property values, interest rates, inventiveness, and levels of literacy continued to vary in patterns that would have been recognizable from before the Civil War.[51]

Finally, the changes brought about in nineteenth-century society still had a relatively weak effect on patterns of authority and dependency within families and households. Although many changes, including the fertility transition, public education, rising literacy rates, and romantic sentimentalism, had altered relationships between men and women, parents and children, most households did not lose their character as centers of paternal authority. Legal reforms, such as changes in divorce laws and the passage of married women's property acts in many states, undercut some of the rigidity of doctrines such as *couverture* that had largely occluded married women as individual legal persons. By the 1870s women could vote in a few states, and campaigns for an extension of the franchise to all women were gathering weight. But relatively few women could yet exercise the independent citizenship that these developments pointed to, and it would be 1920 before women in general achieved the basic political rights that most white men had won by the 1820s. In terms of access to sources of wealth, opportunity, and power, most families and households remained unequal in the late nineteenth century; parents had authority over children, but men also retained distinct advantages of many kinds over women. Even though urbanization and industrialization, the rise of consumption, and changes in the character of public life had altered the economic and social position of households, their inequalities would continue to shape society and social developments as they had in the past.[52]

Notes

Chapter 1. Households and Regions at the End of the Colonial Period

1. Carole Shammas, *A History of Household Government in America* (Charlottesville, Va., 2002), p. 31. My own arguments, especially in this chapter and the next, owe much to Shammas's book. See also Mary M. Schweitzer, *Custom and Contract: Household Government and the Economy in Colonial Pennsylvania* (New York, 1987).

2. Cornelia Hughes Dayton, *Women Before the Bar: Gender, Law, and Society in Connecticut, 1639–1789* (Chapel Hill, 1995), p. 147.

3. Dayton, *Women Before the Bar*, chapter 3.

4. John Fitch, *The Autobiography of John Fitch* (Philadelphia, 1976), pp. 34–43; Shammas, *A History of Household Government*, p. 47; Dayton, *Women Before the Bar*, pp. 154–156.

5. *Winchendon v. Hatfield*, 4 Massachusetts Reports, 123 and 129 (1808).

6. J. Hector St. John de Crèvecoeur, *Letters from an American Farmer* (1782; reprint ed. Harmondsworth, England, 1981), p. 268. On land abundance and labor coercion, see Evsey D. Domar, "The Causes of Slavery or Serfdom: A Hypothesis," *Journal of Economic History* 30, no. 1 (March 1970): 18–32; [John Adams], *Discourses on Davila. A Series of Papers on Political History. Written in the Year 1790* (Boston, 1805) [Shaw-Shoemaker no. 7831], p. 91.

7. Jeanne Boydston, *Home and Work: Housework, Wages, and the Ideology of Labor in the Early Republic* (New York, 1990), pp. 19–24; Shammas, *A History of Household Government*, p. 35.

8. Quotation from the indentured servant William Moraley, in Susan E. Klepp and Billy G. Smith, ed., *The Infortunate: The Voyage and Adventures of William Moraley, an Indentured Servant* (University Park, Pa., 1992), p. 89. With its meaning somewhat changed, the phrase was adopted as a title for the influential study by James T. Lemon, *The Best Poor Man's Country: A Geographical Study of Early Southeastern Pennsylvania* (Baltimore, 1972).

9. Jacques Pierre Brissot de Warville, *New Travels in the United States of America* (1788; translated ed., London, 1792), p. 213.

10. Lucy Simler and Paul G. E. Clemens, "The 'Best Poor Man's Country' in 1783: The Population Structure of Rural Society in Late-Eighteenth-Century Southeastern Pennsylvania," *Proceedings of the American Philosophical Society* 133, no. 2 (1989): 234–261; statistics are on pp. 239 and 248–249, t. II.

11. Thomas M. Doerflinger, "Rural Capitalism in Iron Country: Staffing a Forest Factory, 1808–1815," *William and Mary Quarterly* 59 (2002): 3–38.

12. Thomas M. Doerflinger, *A Vigorous Spirit of Enterprise: Merchants and Economic Development in Revolutionary Philadelphia* (Chapel Hill, 1986).

13. Sharon V. Salinger, "Artisans, Journeymen, and the Transformation of Labor in Late-Eighteenth-Century Philadelphia," *William and Mary Quarterly* 40 (1983): 62–84.

14. On the household-based textile industry in Pennsylvania, see Adrienne D. Hood, "The Material World of Cloth: Production and Use in Eighteenth-Century Rural Pennsylvania," *William and Mary Quarterly* 53, no. 1 (January 1996): 43–66; Hood, *The Weaver's Craft: Cloth, Commerce and Industry in Early Pennsylvania* (Philadelphia, 2003).

15. Richard R. Beeman, *The Evolution of the Southern Backcountry: A Case Study of Lunenburg County, Virginia, 1746–1832* (Philadelphia, 1984), p. 33; John Selby, *The Revolution in Virginia* (Williamsburg, 1988), esp. p. 24.

16. Allan Kulikoff, *Tobacco and Slaves: The Development of Southern Cultures in the Chesapeake, 1680–1800* (Chapel Hill, 1986), p. 338, table 37.

17. Selby, *The Revolution in Virginia*, p. 24; "Wealth Distribution in St. Georges Hundred, 1797," Delaware Department of Transportation, Archaeology Project, http://www.deldot.net/static/projects/archaeology/augustine_creek/tables.html (consulted November 2002); Joseph Doddridge, *Notes on the Settlement and Indian Wars of the Western Parts of Virginia and Pennsylvania* (Wellsburgh, Va., 1824) [Shaw-Shoemaker no. 15990], pp. 174–180, quotation from p. 180.

18. On New England's relative equality, see Brissot, *New Travels in the United States*, p. 132–133.

19. Timothy Dwight, *Travels in New England and New York*, ed. Barbara Miller Solomon, 4 vols. (Cambridge, Mass., 1969), I: xxxiv. Charles Gleason, Diary and Record, 1798–99, Miscellaneous Manuscripts Collection "G", Box 2, folder 8, American Antiquarian Society, Worcester, Mass.; Daniel Scott Smith, "'All in Some Degree Related to Each Other': A Demographic and Comparative Resolution of the Anomaly of New England Kinship," *American Historical Review* 94, no. 1 (February 1989): 44–77, especially p. 51, table 1.

20. Jackson Turner Main, *Society and Economy in Colonial Connecticut* (Princeton, 1985).

21. David B. Mattern, *Benjamin Lincoln and the American Revolution* (Columbia, S.C., 1995), p. 19; Joanne Pope Melish, *Disowning Slavery: Gradual Emancipation and "Race" in New England, 1780–1860* (Ithaca, 1998), pp. 15–16.

22. On regional wage differentials, see Gloria L. Main, "Gender, Work, and Wages in Colonial New England," *William and Mary Quarterly* 51 (1994): 50. On

the destinations of emigrants from the British Isles, see Bernard Bailyn, *Voyagers to the West: A Passage in the Peopling of America on the Eve of the Revolution* (New York, 1986), p. 209.

23. Robert A. Gross, "Culture and Cultivation in Thoreau's Concord," *Journal of American History* 69 (June 1982): 42–61; Brissot, *New Travels in the United States*, p. 127; Laurel Thatcher Ulrich, "Wheels, Looms, and the Gender Division of Labor in Eighteenth-Century New England," *William and Mary Quarterly* 55 (1998): 3–38, data on pp. 6–10.

24. Gary B. Nash, *The Urban Crucible: Social Change, Political Consciousness, and the Origins of the American Revolution* (Cambridge, Mass., 1979); Ulrich, "Wheels, Looms, and the Gender Division of Labor," p. 10.

25. On maritime labor, see *Report of the Secretary of State on the Subject of the Cod and Whale Fisheries* (Philadelphia, 1791) [Evans no. 23911]; Elaine Forman Crane, *Ebb Tide in New England: Women, Seaports, and Social Change, 1630–1800* (Boston, 1998), pp. 11–20; data on female-headed households is on p. 16.

26. Daniel Vickers, *Young Men and the Sea: Yankee Seafarers in the Age of Sail* (New Haven, 2005), pp. 96–130.

27. See Richard R. Beeman, *The Varieties of Political Experience in Eighteenth Century America* (Philadelphia, 2004).

28. Marjoleine Kars, *Breaking Loose Together: The Regulator Rebellion in Pre-Revolutionary North Carolina* (Chapel Hill, 2002).

29. Franklin's predictions and their variants are discussed in Robert V. Wells, "The Population of England's Colonies in America: Old English or New Americans?" *Population Studies* 46 (1992): 85–86.

30. T. H. Breen, *The Marketplace of Revolution: How Consumer Politics Shaped American Independence* (New York, 2004); the quotation is from (Hartford) *Connecticut Courant*, February 4, 1765.

31. On the influence of the Seven Years' War on British policy in North America and colonial reactions, see Fred Anderson, *The Crucible of War: The Seven Years' War and the Fate of Empire in British North America, 1754–1766* (New York, 2000).

32. Anthony McFarlane, *The British in the Americas, 1492–1800* (London, 1994), provides a useful comparative perspective on the position of the thirteen colonies.

33. On Britain's legacies to the colonies' regional variety, see David Hackett Fischer, *Albion's Seed: Four British Folkways in America* (New York, 1989). Gadsden is quoted in Richard Walsh, *Charleston's Sons of Liberty: A Study of the Artisans, 1763–1789* (Columbia, S.C., 1959), pp. 35–36. On the "rights . . . of Englishmen," see Eric Foner, *The Story of American Freedom* (New York, 1998), p. 13.

34. Marc Egnal, *A Mighty Empire: The Origins of the American Revolution* (Ithaca, 1988).

35. See Richard L. Bushman, *The Refinement of America: Persons, Houses, Cities* (New York, 1992).

36. Adam Smith, *An Inquiry into the Nature and Causes of the Wealth of Nations* (Edinburgh, 1776), book 4, chapter 7, part 2.

Chapter 2. Change and Continuity in the American Revolution

1. These themes are discussed in Rhys Isaac, *The Transformation of Virginia, 1740–1790* (Chapel Hill, 1982), and T. H. Breen, *Tobacco Culture: The Mentality of the Great Tidewater Planters Before the Revolution* (Princeton, 1985).

2. The Philadelphia example is from "A Mechanic," *To the Tradesmen, Mechanics, Etc., of the Province of Pennsylvania*, broadside, December 4, 1773 ([Philadelphia, 1773]) [Evans no. 13041].

3. On New York, see Edward Countryman, *A People in Revolution: The American Revolution and Political Society in New York, 1760–1790* (Baltimore, 1981); on Philadelphia, Richard A. Ryerson, *The Revolution Is Now Begun: The Radical Committees of Philadelphia, 1765–1776* (Philadelphia, 1978).

4. Eric Foner, *Tom Paine and Revolutionary America* (New York, 1974); Steven Rosswurm, *Arms, Country, and Class: The Philadelphia Militia and "Lower Sort" During the American Revolution, 1775–1783* (New Brunswick, N.J., 1987).

5. On Massachusetts, see Robert A. Gross, *The Minutemen and Their World* (New York, 1976), and Gregory H. Nobles, *Divisions Throughout the Whole: Politics and Society in Hampshire County, Massachusetts, 1740–1775* (Cambridge, England, 1983).

6. On New York, see Barnet Schecter, *The Battle for New York: The City at the Heart of the American Revolution* (New York, 2002), and Richard M. Ketchum, *Divided Loyalties: How the Revolution Came to New York* (New York, 2002). On the Whartons, see Alan Taylor, *William Cooper's Town: Power and Persuasion on the Early American Frontier* (New York, 1995), p. 64.

7. Mary Beth Norton, *The British-Americans: The Loyalist Exiles in England, 1774–1789* (Boston, 1972).

8. Thomas Paine, *Common Sense* [1776], ed. Isaac Kramnick (Harmondsworth, England, 1976), p. 120; *The American Crisis*, December 19, 1776.

9. Hal T. Shelton, *General Richard Montgomery and the American Revolution: From Redcoat to Rebel* (New York, 1994), pp. 133–150.

10. On the difficulty of recruiting soldiers in rural societies, see Peter C. Mancall, *Valley of Opportunity: Economic Culture Along the Upper Susquehanna, 1700–1800* (Ithaca, 1991), pp. 152–153.

11. Charles P. Neimeyer, *America Goes to War: A Social History of the Continental Army* (New York, 1996), stresses the marginality of long-term enlistees. On mutinies, see [Jeremiah Greenman] *Diary of a Common Soldier in the American Revolution, 1775–1783: An Annotated Edition of the Military Journal of Jeremiah Greenman*; ed. Robert C. Bray and Paul E. Bushnell (De Kalb, Ill., 1978), p. 222; Israel Evans, *An Oration, Delivered at Hackinsack, on the Tenth of September, 1780, at the Interment of the Honorable Brigadier Enoch Poor, General of the New Hampshire Brigade* (Newburyport, Mass., 1781) [Evans no. 17150], p. 26; and James Kirby Martin, *Benedict Arnold, Revolutionary Hero: An American Warrior Reconsidered* (New York, 1997), p. 425.

12. On privateering, see, for example, *Instructions to the Commanders of Private Ships or Vessels of War, which shall have Commissions or Letters of Marque and Reprisal, issued in Congress, April 3, 1776* ([Philadelphia, 1776]) [Evans no. 15137].

13. The paragraphs that follow have been aided by Sylvia R. Frey, *Water from the Rock: Black Resistance in a Revolutionary Age* (Princeton, 1991).

14. David Waldstreicher, *Runaway Americans: Benjamin Franklin, Slavery and the American Revolution* (New York, 2004); Rhys Isaac, *Landon Carter's Uneasy Kingdom: Revolution and Rebellion on a Virginia Plantation* (New York, 2004).

15. Greenman, *Diary*, p. 213, entry for July 9, 1781.

16. Mechal Sobel, *Teach Me Dreams: The Search for Self in the Revolutionary Era* (Princeton, 2000), p. 118; [Joseph Plumb Martin] *Narrative of Some of the Adventures, Dangers, and Sufferings of a Revolutionary Soldier* [1830] in James Kirby Martin, ed., *Ordinary Courage: The Revolutionary War Adventures of Joseph Plumb Martin* (St. James, N.Y., 1999), pp. 141–142.

17. See Carol Berkin, *Revolutionary Mothers: Women in the Struggle for Independence* (New York, 2005), pp. 35–41.

18. On the eighteenth-century Ohio Valley, see Michael N. McConnell, *A Country Between: The Upper Ohio Valley and Its Peoples, 1724–1774* (Lincoln, Nebr., 1992); R. Douglas Hurt, *The Ohio Frontier: Crucible of the Old Northwest, 1720–1830* (Bloomington, Ind., 1996); and Eric Hinderaker, *Elusive Empires: Constructing Colonialism in the Ohio Valley, 1673–1800* (Cambridge, England, 1997).

19. David Ramsay, *Ramsay's History of South Carolina from Its First Settlement in 1670 to the Year 1808*, 2 vols. (1858; reprint edition, Spartanburg, S.C., 1959): I, 252–267, quotation on p. 266.

20. Mattern, *Benjamin Lincoln*, p. 54.

21. Barbara Clark Smith, "Food Rioters and the American Revolution," *William and Mary Quarterly* 51 (1994): 3–38.

22. Philip Schuyler to George Washington, July 15, 1775; Richard Montgomery to Robert R. Livingston, and Richard Montgomery to Janet L. Montgomery, both October 10, 1775; all quoted in Shelton, *General Richard Montgomery and the American Revolution*, pp. 79, 106, 117.

23. Alfred F. Young, "George Roberts Twelves Hewes (1742–1840); A Boston Shoemaker and the Memory of the American Revolution," *William and Mary Quarterly* 38, no. 4 (October 1981): 562.

24. Jackson Turner Main, "Government by the People: The American Revolution and the Democratization of the Legislatures," *William and Mary Quarterly* 23 (1966): 391–407.

25. Taylor, *William Cooper's Town*, pp. 16–29, 57–85; Bowdoin quote in Stuart Bruchey, "Economy and Society in an Earlier America," *Journal of Economic History* 47 (1987): 308–309; Lucy Knox to Henry Knox, Boston, 1777, at Digital History, http://www.digitalhistory.uh.edu/documents/documents_p2.cfm?doc=278 (consulted May 27, 2005).

26. Edward C. Papenfuse, *In Pursuit of Profit: The Annapolis Merchants in the Era of the American Revolution, 1763–1805* (Baltimore, 1975); James B. Hedges, *The Browns of Providence Plantations*, 2 vols. (Providence, 1968).

27. Terry Bouton, "A Road Closed: Rural Insurgency in Post-Independence Pennsylvania," *Journal of American History* 87, no. 3 (December 2000): 855–887.

28. Quotations are in Mattern, *Benjamin Lincoln*, pp. 168, 170.

29. Thomas P. Slaughter, *The Whiskey Rebellion: Frontier Epilogue to the American Revolution* (New York, 1986); *Report of the Commissioners, appointed by the President of the United States of America, to confer with the Insurgents in the Western Counties of Pennsylvania* (Philadelphia, 1794) [Evans no. 27977]; Paul D. Newman, *Fries's Rebellion: The Enduring Struggle for the American Revolution* (Philadelphia, 2004).

30. Alan Taylor, *Liberty Men and Great Proprietors: The Revolutionary Settlement on the Maine Frontier, 1760–1820* (Chapel Hill, 1990), pp. 112–114.

31. Alfred F. Young, ed., *Beyond the American Revolution: Explorations in the History of American Radicalism* (De Kalb, Ill., 1993), pp. 330–331; Michael Merrill and Sean Wilentz, ed., *The Key of Liberty: The Life and Democratic Writings of William Manning, 'A Laborer,' 1747–1814* (Cambridge, Mass., 1993).

32. David Thomas Konig, "Jurisprudence and Social Policy in the New Republic," in Konig, ed., *Devising Liberty: Preserving and Creating Freedom in the Early American Republic* (Stanford, 1995), p. 195.

33. Loretta Valtz Mannucci, "The Look of Revolution: Presentation and Representation in the American Revolution," in *The Languages of Revolution*, Milan Group in Early United States History *Quaderno* II (c. 1988), p. 27, available at Vanderbilt University, "Quaderni Online" http://www.library.vanderbilt.edu/quaderno/ (consulted May 24, 2005).

34. See Gary J. Kornblith and John M. Murrin, "The Making and Unmaking of an American Ruling Class," in Young, ed., *Beyond the American Revolution*, 27–29.

35. Thomas Jefferson wrote to John Adams on October 28, 1813: ". . . I agree with you that there is a natural aristocracy among men. The grounds of this are virtue and talents."

36. Gary B. Nash, *Forging Freedom: The Formation of Philadelphia's Black Community, 1720–1840* (Cambridge, Mass., 1988).

37. Melish, *Disowning Slavery*.

38. Shane White, *Somewhat More Independent: The End of Slavery in New York City, 1770–1810* (Athens, Ga., 1991).

39. Rutledge, Pinckney, and Madison are quoted in Jan Lewis, "The Problem of Slavery in Southern Political Discourse," in Konig, ed., *Devising Liberty*, pp. 266, 272. On Washington, see Henry Wiencek, *An Imperfect God: George Washington, His Slaves, and the Creation of America* (New York, 2003).

40. Lucy Knox to Henry Knox, cited in note 25, above. Abigail Strong is quoted in Norma Basch, "From the Bonds of Empire to the Bonds of Matrimony," in Konig, ed., *Devising Liberty*, pp. 228–229. The argument that the Revolution did not alter family, marriage, or household arrangements that were taken to be "natural forms of subordination" is made by Shammas, *A History of Household Government*, chapter 3, and esp. pp. 65–66, 71, 79.

41. *Turner v. Estes*, 3 Massachusetts Reports, 317–319 (1807).

42. Adams, *Discourses on Davila*, p. 92.

43. Samuel Fish, *The Rights of the Poor Defended* (Norwich, Conn., 1789) [Evans no. 21825], p. 18.

44. Bruchey, "Economy and Society," p. 308.

45. John S. Gilkeson, *Middle-Class Providence, 1820–1940* (Princeton, 1986), pp. 13–14.
46. This paragraph summarizes the account in Jean B. Lee, *The Price of Nationhood: The American Revolution in Charles County* (New York, 1994).
47. Alan Taylor, "Land and Liberty on the Post-Revolutionary Frontier," in Konig, ed., *Devising Liberty*, pp. 103–104.
48. On wartime manufactures, see James A. Henretta, "The War for Independence and American Economic Development," in Ronald Hoffman, et al., ed., *The Economy of Early America: The Revolutionary Period, 1763–1790* (Charlottesville, Va., 1988), pp. 45–87.
49. Benjamin Lincoln to Rufus King, February 11, 1786, quoted in Mattern, *Benjamin Lincoln*, p. 158. On the geopolitics of federations, see D. W. Meinig, *The Shaping of America: A Geographical Perspective on 500 Years of History. Vol I: Atlantic America, 1492–1800* (New Haven, 1986), pp. 338–370, 385–395; on early U.S. discussions of confederations, see Cathy Matson and Peter S. Onuf, *A Union of Interests: Political and Economic Thought in Revolutionary America* (Lawrence, Kans., 1990), pp. 91–97.
50. On regionalism, see Kevin M. Gannon, "Escaping 'Mr. Jefferson's Plan of Destruction': New England Federalists and the Idea of a Northern Confederacy, 1803–1804," *Journal of the Early Republic* 21 (2001): 413–443.
51. Lance Banning, *The Sacred Fire of Liberty: James Madison and the Founding of the Federal Republic* (Ithaca, 1995), pp. 58–65.
52. Mattern, *Benjamin Lincoln*, pp. 200–205.

Chapter 3. Social Change in the Early Republic

1. Quoted in Michael Durey, *Transatlantic Radicals and the Early American Republic* (Lawrence, Kans., 1997), p. 218; M. Michaux, quoted in *Republican Spy* (Northampton, Mass.), November 19, 1806.
2. Daniel Scott Smith, "Female Householding in Late Eighteenth Century America and the Problem of Poverty," *Journal of Social History* 28 (1994–1995): 83–107, especially p. 86.
3. Greenman, *Diary of a Common Soldier*, pp. 293–296; see also Vernon A. Ives, "Narrative of Uriah Cross in the Revolutionary War," *New York History* 63 (1982): 279–294; and Constance B. Schultz, "Revolutionary War Pension Applications: A Neglected Source for Social and Family History," *Prologue* 15 (1983): 103–114.
4. Paul A. Gilje and Howard B. Rock, ed., *Keepers of the Revolution: New Yorkers at Work in the Early Republic* (Ithaca, 1992), p. 250.
5. Thomas Jefferson, First Inaugural Address, March 4, 1801, Yale Law School, Avalon Project, http://www.yale.edu/lawweb/avalon/presiden/inaug/jefinau1.htm (consulted May 24, 2005).
6. David B. Danbom, *Born in the Country: A History of Rural America* (Baltimore, 1995), p. 56.
7. Dwight, *Travels in New England and New York*, I: 31.
8. Paul G. E. Clemens, *The Atlantic Economy and Colonial Maryland's Eastern Shore: From Tobacco to Grain* (Ithaca, 1980).

9. Douglas R. Egerton, *Gabriel's Rebellion: The Virginia Slave Conspiracies of 1800 and 1802* (Chapel Hill, 1993).

10. Allan Kulikoff, *From British Peasants to American Colonial Farmers* (Chapel Hill, 2000), pp. 283–284, discusses the significance of frontier settlement by the end of the eighteenth century; see also Malcolm J. Rohrbough, *The Trans-Appalachian Frontier: Peoples, Societies, and Institutions, 1775–1850* (New York, 1978).

11. Taylor, "Land and Liberty on the Post-Revolutionary Frontier"; Richard White, *The Middle Ground: Indians, Empires, and Republics in the Great Lakes Region, 1650–1815* (Cambridge, England, 1991).

12. On primogeniture, see Danbom, *Born in the Country*, p. 53. On New England land sales, see *Eastern Lands for Sale* (Boston, 1788) [Evans no. 21244].

13. Bruce H. Mann, *Republic of Debtors: Bankruptcy in the Age of American Independence* (Cambridge, Mass., 2002).

14. Levi Fay is referred to in Rena L. Vassar, ed., "The Life or Biography of Silas Felton Written by Himself," *Proceedings of the American Antiquarian Society* (October 1959): 136.

15. Taylor, *William Cooper's Town*; *We the Subscribers, Inhabitants of the Towns of Brownville, Le Ray, and Wilna, Jefferson County, N.Y.* (Watertown, N.Y., 1817) [Shaw-Shoemaker no. 40427], Broadside Collection, American Antiquarian Society, Worcester, Mass.

16. On South Carolina, see Rachel N. Klein, *Unification of a Slave State: The Rise of the Planter Class in the South Carolina Backcountry, 1760–1808* (Chapel Hill, 1990); Fay quote: see note 14, above. R. Eugene Harper, *The Transformation of Western Pennsylvania, 1770–1800* (Pittsburgh, 1991). On Otsego County tenancy, see Taylor, *William Cooper's Town*, p. 438, table 15.

17. On the Adair family, see Gerald W. McFarland, *A Scattered People: An American Family Moves West* (New York, 1985).

18. This discussion is based on Stephen Aron, *How the West Was Lost: The Transformation of Kentucky from Daniel Boone to Henry Clay* (Baltimore, 1996).

19. The quotation is in Andrew R. L. Cayton, *The Frontier Republic: Ideology and Politics in the Ohio Country, 1780–1825* (Kent, Ohio, 1986), p. 4. On landownership, see Lee Soltow, "Inequality Amidst Abundance: Land Ownership in Early Nineteenth Century Ohio," *Ohio History* 88 (1979): 133–151, and Hurt, *The Ohio Frontier*, p. 175.

20. Quoted in Durey, *Transatlantic Radicals*, p. 237; Annette Kolodny, *The Land Before Her: Fantasy and Experience of the American Frontiers, 1630–1860* (Chapel Hill, 1984), p. 94.

21. *The Remarkable Adventures of Jackson Johonnet, of Massachusetts* (Walpole, N.H., 1795), pp. 3–4.

22. Simon P. Newman, *Embodied History: The Lives of the Poor in Early Philadelphia* (Philadelphia, 2003), pp. 105–106.

23. Vickers, *Young Men and the Sea*, p. 199.

24. Madison's views are cited in Paul A. Gilje, "The Meaning of Freedom for Waterfront Workers," in Konig, ed., *Devising Liberty*, p. 110.

25. Newman, *Embodied History*, pp. 41–42.

26. New Haven data is from Christopher Grasso, *A Speaking Aristocracy: Transforming Public Discourse in Eighteenth Century Connecticut* (Chapel Hill, 1999), p. 463; David G. Hackett, *The Rude Hand of Innovation: Religion and Social Order in Albany, New York, 1652–1836* (New York, 1991), pp. 68–69.

27. Quoted in Hackett, *The Rude Hand of Innovation*, p. 57.

28. Hal S. Barron, *Those Who Stayed Behind: Rural Society in Nineteenth Century New England* (Cambridge, England, 1984); Christopher Clark, *The Roots of Rural Capitalism: Western Massachusetts, 1780–1860* (Ithaca, 1990), chapter 3.

29. Joan M. Jensen, *Loosening the Bonds: Mid-Atlantic Farm Women, 1750–1850* (New Haven, 1986); Catherine E. Kelly, "'The Consummation of Rural Prosperity and Happiness': New England Agricultural Fairs and the Construction of Class and Gender, 1810–1860," *American Quarterly* 49 (1997): 574–602.

30. Cynthia A. Kierner, *Beyond the Household: Women's Place in the Early South, 1700–1835* (Ithaca, 1998); David J. Grettler, "Environmental Change and Conflict over Hogs in Early Nineteenth-Century Delaware," *Journal of the Early Republic* 19 (1999): 197–220.

31. Brissot, *New Travels in the United States*, p. 127. Eli Woods, Day Book, 1788–1790, Library of Congress; Elizabeth Phelps, Diary, Porter-Phelps-Huntington Family Papers, Amherst College Archives, Amherst, Mass.

32. S. G. Goodrich, *Recollections of a Lifetime, or Men and Things I Have Seen*, 2 vols. (New York, 1857), I: 27. Horace Greeley, *Recollections of a Busy Life* (New York, 1868), p. 26.

33. Nora Pat Small, "The Search for a New Rural Order: Farmhouses in Sutton, Massachusetts, 1790–1830," *William and Mary Quarterly* 53 (1996): 69.

34. Edward S. Cooke, Jr., *Making Furniture in Preindustrial America: The Social Economy of Newtown and Woodbury, Connecticut* (Baltimore, 1996); J. Ritchie Garrison, *Landscape and Material Life in Franklin County, Massachusetts, 1770–1860* (1991; new edition, Knoxville, Tenn., 2003).

35. Martin Bruegel, "Work, Gender, and Authority on the Farm: The Hudson Valley Countryside, 1790s–1850s," *Agricultural History* 76 (2002): 1–27; "too many tasks," Jean Gordon and Jan McArthur, "Living Patterns in Antebellum Rural America," *Winterthur Portfolio* 19 (1984): 184; Stuart W. Bruchey, *Enterprise: The Dynamic Economy of a Free People* (Cambridge, Mass., 1990), p. 144, notes the failure of a manufactory at Hell Gate, New York, in the early 1790s. See also Nancy Folbre, "The Unproductive Housewife: Her Evolution in Nineteenth Century Economic Thought," *Signs* 16 (1991): 463–484.

36. Baldwin's story is in Peter Benes, ed., *The Bay and the River, 1600–1900* (Boston, 1982), p. 44.

37. Greenman, *Diary of a Common Soldier*, p. 301.

38. Alan Taylor, "The Great Change Begins: Settling the Forest of Central New York," *New York History* (July 1995).

39. Brooke Hunter, "'The Prospect of Independent Americans': The Grain Trade and Economic Development During the 1780s," *Explorations in Early American Culture* 5 (2001): 260–287.

40. On Bragg, see Joyce Appleby, *Inheriting the Revolution: The First Generation of Americans* (Cambridge, Mass., 2000); on Combs, see Susan E. Hirsch, *Roots of the*

American Working Class: The Industrialization of Crafts in Newark, 1800–1860 (Philadelphia, 1978); on Bedford, see Andrew Shankman, *Crucible of American Democracy: The Struggle to Fuse Egalitarianism and Capitalism in Jeffersonian Pennsylvania* (Lawrence, Kans., 2004), p. 162.

41. On immigration, see Hans Jürgen Grabbe, "European Immigration to the United States in the Early National Period, 1783–1820," *Proceedings of the American Philosophical Society* 133 (1989): 190–214, esp. p. 191.

42. Trade statistics are from U.S. Department of Commerce, Bureau of the Census, *Historical Statistics of the United States: Colonial Times to 1970* (Washington, D.C., 1976).

43. *Larned v. Buffington*, 3 Massachusetts Reports, 546–555 (1807).

44. Gordon S. Wood, *The Americanization of Benjamin Franklin* (New York, 2004), chapter 5.

45. Quotations in Konig, "Jurisprudence and Social Policy in the New Republic," p. 196, and Edwin G. Burrows and Mike Wallace, *Gotham: A History of New York City to 1898* (New York, 1999), p. 513.

46. On African-American cultural hopes, and their dwindling, see Shane White, *Stories of Freedom in Black New York* (Cambridge, Mass., 2002); on William Otter, see Sobel, *Teach Me Dreams*, pp. 97–103. Gilkeson, *Middle-Class Providence*, pp. 19–22, discusses the growing distance and tensions between white and black populations in that town.

47. On the declining business involvement of women, see Claudia Goldin, "The Changing Status of Women in the Economy of the Early Republic: Quantitative Evidence," *Journal of Interdisciplinary History* 16 (Winter 1986): 374–404; on the gender gap, compare Main, "Gender, Work, and Wages in Colonial New England," with Claudia Goldin, "The Gender Gap in Historical Perspective," in Peter Kilby, ed., *Quantity and Quiddity: Essays in United States Economic History* (Middletown, Conn., 1987), p. 143.

48. Henry Fearon, *Sketches of America* (1819), quoted in Gilje and Rock, ed., *Keepers of the Revolution*, p. 254.

49. On Lafayette's visit, see Lloyd S. Kramer, *Lafayette in Two Worlds: Public Cultures and Personal Identities in an Age of Revolutions* (Chapel Hill, 1996), p. 214.

50. Jon Butler, *Becoming America: The Revolution Before 1776* (Cambridge, Mass., 2000), p. 70, notes: "friendship created trade, and ethnicity and religion provided the touchstone of personal relations and, often, business arrangements."

51. The quotation is from David W. Maxey, "Samuel Hopkins, the Holder of the First U.S. Patent: A Study in Failure," *Pennsylvania Magazine of History and Biography* 122 (1998): 3–37. On business relationships, see Cathy Matson, " 'Damned Scoundrels' and 'Libertisme of Trade': Freedom and Regulation in Colonial New York's Fur and Grain Trades," *William and Mary Quarterly* 51 (1994): 389–418.

52. Craig Muldrew, *The Economy of Obligation: The Culture of Credit and Social Relations in Early Modern England* (New York, 1998); see also Clark, *The Roots of Rural Capitalism*, chapter 3, and Naomi R. Lamoreaux, "Rethinking the Transition to Capitalism in the Early American Northeast," *Journal of American History* 90, no. 2 (September 2003).

53. 4 Massachusetts Reports, 161 (1808).

54. *Hampshire Sentinel* (Amherst, Mass.), November 24, 1830.

55. William R. Lawrence, *Extracts from the Diary and Correspondence of the Late Amos Lawrence* (Boston, 1855), p. 31; Mathew Carey, *Autobiography* (1833–1834; reprint ed., Brooklyn, N.Y., 1942), p. 42.

56. "The Travel Diary of James Guild," *Proceedings of the Vermont Historical Society*, n.s. 5 (1937): 250–313.

57. Steven C. Bullock, *Revolutionary Brotherhood: Freemasonry and the Transformation of the American Social Order, 1730–1840* (Chapel Hill, 1996).

58. Naomi Lamoreaux, *Insider Lending: Banks, Personal Connections and Economic Development in Industrial New England* (Cambridge, England, 1994); Alfred Tischendorf and E. Taylor Parks, ed., *The Diary and Journal of Richard Clough Anderson, Jr., 1814–1826* (Durham, N.C., 1964), pp. 42–43.

59. Quotation: *Hampshire Sentinel*, November 24, 1830.

Chapter 4. Two Directions for Labor

1. Benjamin W. Dudley, *A Sketch of the Medical Topography of Lexington and Its Vicinity* (Philadelphia, 1806), p. 12.

2. A summary of recent work on slavery is Stanley L. Engerman, "Slavery and Its Consequences for the South," in Engerman and Robert E. Gallman, ed., *The Cambridge Economic History of the United States*, vol. II, *The Long Nineteenth Century* (Cambridge, England, 2000), pp. 329–366.

3. Taylor is quoted in Jan Lewis, "The Problem of Slavery in Southern Political Discourse," in Konig, ed., *Devising Liberty*.

4. Joseph P. Reidy, *From Slavery to Agrarian Capitalism in the Cotton Plantation South: Central Georgia, 1800–1880* (Chapel Hill, 1992), esp. pp. 20–30.

5. On the mechanization of processing on large sugar plantations, see Frederick Law Olmsted, *A Journey in the Seaboard Slave States, with remarks on their economy* (New York, 1856), pp. 667–671; Richard Follett, *The Sugar Masters: Planters and Slaves in Louisiana's Cane World, 1820–1860* (Baton Rouge, 2005).

6. On the task system, see Larry Hudson, Jr., *To Have and to Hold: Slave Work and Family Life in Antebellum South Carolina* (Athens, Ga., 1997), and Timothy J. Lockley, *Lines in the Sand: Race and Class in Lowcountry Georgia, 1750–1860* (Athens, Ga., 2001).

7. Dudley, *A Sketch of the Medical Topography of Lexington*, p. 12. Peter H. Wood, "Slave Labor Camps in Early America: Overcoming Denial and Discovering the Gulag," in Carla Gardina Pestana and Sharon V. Salinger, ed., *Inequality in Early America* (Hanover, N.H., 1999), pp. 222–238.

8. William Dusinberre, *Them Dark Days: Slavery in the American Rice Swamps* (New York, 1996); Wilma King, *Stolen Childhood: Slave Youth in Nineteenth Century America* (Bloomington, Ind., 1998); see also William Dusinberre, "Commentary," in Winthrop D. Jordan, ed., *Slavery and the American South* (Jackson, Miss., 2003), pp. 139–146.

9. Michael P. Johnson, "Denmark Veysey and His Co-Conspirators," *William and Mary Quarterly* 58 (2001): 915–976, attributes apparent evidence of a slave

conspiracy in Charleston in the early 1820s to rumor, based on "the heresies widespread among black Charlestonians: that blacks hated both slavery and whites, that slaves should be free, that blacks could be equal to whites."

10. Herbert Weaver, ed., *The Correspondence of James K. Polk*, 9 vols. (Nashville, 1969–): II, 190.

11. Walter Johnson, *Soul by Soul: Life Inside the Antebellum Slave Market* (Cambridge, Mass., 1999).

12. John B. Boles, *Black Southerners, 1619–1869* (Lexington, Ky., 1983), p. 225; James H. Hammond, *Secret and Sacred: The Diaries of James Henry Hammond, a Southern Slaveholder*, ed. Carol Bleser (New York, 1988), entries for March 7, August 1, September 5, November 2, November 5, 1841. On the fear of sale to the Southwest, see Joan E. Cashin, *A Family Venture: Men and Women on the Southern Frontier* (New York, 1991), p. 49.

13. [William J. Anderson] *Life and Narrative of William J. Anderson, 24 Years a Slave* (1857); see Sobel, *Teach Me Dreams*, pp. 119, 124.

14. Charles C. Bolton, *Poor Whites of the Antebellum South: Tenants and Laborers in Central North Carolina and Northeast Mississippi* (Durham, N.C., 1994); Wilma F. Dunaway, *The First American Frontier: Transition to Capitalism in Southern Appalachia, 1700–1860* (Chapel Hill, 1996), pp. 73–82.

15. Leak and Dew are quoted in Jan Lewis, "The Problem of Slavery," pp. 289, 291.

16. Farley Grubb, "The End of European Immigrant Servitude in the United States: An Economic Analysis of Market Collapse, 1772–1835," *Journal of Economic History* 54 (1994): 794–824.

17. Gary Kornblith, "Artisan Federalism: New England Mechanics and the Political Economy of the 1790s," in Ronald Hoffman and Peter J. Albert, ed., *Launching the "Extended Republic": The Federalist Era* (Charlottesville, 1996), pp. 249–272. M[athew] Carey, *Reflections on the Subject of Emigration from Europe* (Philadelphia, 1826), p. 11.

18. Reeve Huston, *Land and Freedom: Rural Society, Popular Protest, and Party Politics in Antebellum New York* (New York, 2000).

19. *A Memorial of Citizens of Philadelphia to the Senate and House of Representatives of the State of Pennsylvania* (Philadelphia, 1830), Broadside Collection, American Antiquarian Society, Worcester, Mass.

20. The discussion on the fertility transition that follows has been guided by Lee A. Craig, *To Sow One Acre More: Childbearing and Farm Productivity in the Antebellum North* (Baltimore, 1993), and Maris A. Vinovskis, *Fertility in Massachusetts, from Revolution to Civil War* (New York, 1981).

21. Nancy Grey Osterud and John Fulton, "Family Limitation and Age at Marriage: Fertility Decline in Sturbridge, Massachusetts, 1730–1850," *Population Studies* 30, no. 3 (November 1976): 483, table 1; Clark, *The Roots of Rural Capitalism*, pp. 134–139.

22. Craig, *To Sow One Acre More*; on women and reproductive authority, see Susan E. Klepp, "Revolutionary Bodies: Women and the Fertility Transition in the Mid-Atlantic Region, 1760–1820," *Journal of American History* 85, no. 3 (December 1998): 910–945.

23. On migration across the U.S.-Canadian border, see John J. Bukowczyk, et al., *Permeable Border: The Great Lakes Basin as Transnational Region, 1650–1990* (Pittsburgh, 2005), pp. 26–27.

24. Emily Foster, ed., *American Grit: A Woman's Letters from the Ohio Frontier* (Lexington, Ky., 2002), pp. 14, 37 (emphasis in original).

25. Taylor, *William Cooper's Town*; Charles E. Brooks, *Frontier Settlement and Market Revolution: The Holland Land Purchase* (Ithaca, 1996).

26. Mary E. Gregson, "Wealth Accumulation and Distribution in the Midwest in the Late Nineteenth Century," *Explorations in Economic History* 33 (1996): 524–538.

27. See Virginia E. McCormick and Robert W. McCormick, *New Englanders on the Ohio Frontier: The Migration and Settlement of Worthington* (Kent, Ohio, 1988); Robert Leslie Jones, *History of Agriculture in Ohio to 1880* (Kent, Ohio, 1983), p. 40, discusses reasons for "extensive" rather than "intensive" land use.

28. Susan E. Gray, *The Yankee West: Community Life on the Michigan Frontier* (Chapel Hill, 1996); Edward Dickinson to Emily N. Dickinson, September 7, 1835, in Jay Leyda, *The Years and Hours of Emily Dickinson*, 2 vols. (New Haven, 1960), I: 30.

29. Ellen Eslinger, "The Evolution of Racial Politics in Early Ohio," in Andrew R. L. Cayton and Stuart D. Hobbs, ed., *The Center of a Great Empire: The Ohio Country in the Early Republic* (Athens, Ohio, 2005), p. 86.

30. On farm settlement, see Jeremy Atack, Fred Bateman, and William N. Parker, "Northern Agriculture and the Westward Movement," in Engerman and Gallman, ed., *The Cambridge Economic History of the United States*, vol. II, esp. pp. 308–311; on families and farming, see Gray, *The Yankee West*, pp. 12–14 and chapter 4.

31. For examples of migrations based on family cooperation, see Foster, ed., *American Grit*, passim; William Wycoff, *The Developer's Frontier: The Making of the Western New York Landscape* (New Haven, 1988), pp. 106–107, 116; and McFarland, *A Scattered People*, passim.

32. Robert A. Wheeler, "Land and Community in Rural Nineteenth Century America: Claridon Township, 1810–1870," *Ohio History* 97 (1988): 101–121.

33. On regional streams of migrants to the Midwest and their continued distinctiveness, see Peirce F. Lewis, "The Northeast and the Making of American Geographical Habits," in Michael P. Conzen, ed., *The Making of the American Landscape* (New York, 1990), pp. 80–103, esp. p. 81; on Canadian migration to the Midwest, see Bukowczyk, et al., *Permeable Border*, pp. 45–50.

34. Dwight, *Travels in New England and New York*, I:37.

35. On David Hudson, see McFarland, *A Scattered People*, pp. 71–77; on the Tappans, see Bertram Wyatt-Brown, *Lewis Tappan and the Evangelical War Against Slavery* (1969; reprint ed., New York, 1971), p. 129; on Beaubien, see Donald L. Miller, *City of the Century: The Epic of Chicago and the Making of America* (New York, 1996), pp. 57–58.

36. Carole Shammas, "The Space Problem in Early U.S. Cities," *William and Mary Quarterly* 57 (July 2000): 505–542; *Memoirs and Auto-Biography of Some of the*

Wealthy Citizens of Philadelphia, With a Fair Estimate of their Estates (Philadelphia, 1846); Roy Rosenzweig and Elizabeth Blackmar, *The Park and the People: A History of Central Park* (Ithaca, 1992).

37. Burrows and Wallace, *Gotham*, p. 435.

38. Richard Henry Dana, Jr., *Two Years Before the Mast: A Personal Narrative* (1869; reprint ed., New York, 1964), p. 36. Margaret S. Creighton, *Rites and Passages: The Experience of American Whaling, 1830–1870* (Cambridge, England, 1995), p. 43.

39. Gilkeson, *Middle-Class Providence*, pp. 19–20; William J. Brown, *The Life of William J. Brown, of Providence, R.I.; With Personal Recollections of Incidents in Rhode Island* (Providence, 1883), reproduced at History Matters, http://historymatters.gmu .edu/d/6537.html (consulted November 29, 2004); [Frances H. Green] *Memoirs of Elleanor Eldridge* (Providence, 1838). On black communities, see James Oliver Horton, *Free People of Color: Inside the African American Community* (Washington, D.C., 1993).

40. Patricia Cline Cohen, *The Murder of Helen Jewett: The Life and Death of a Prostitute in Nineteenth-Century New York* (New York, 1998).

41. Burrows and Wallace, *Gotham*, p. 450.

42. Greeley, *Recollections*, p. 87.

43. *National Utility in Opposition to Political Controversy: Addressed to the Friends of American Manufactures* (Boston, 1816), Broadside Collection, American Antiquarian Society, Worcester, Mass.

44. "Manufacture of Clocks in New Haven," *Hunt's Merchants' Magazine* 33 (May 1855): 644–645.

45. Williston's story is told in Abner Forbes and J. W. Greene, *The Rich Men of Massachusetts* (Boston, 1851), pp. 143–144, and in W. S. Tyler, *A Discourse Commemorative of Mrs. Emily Graves Williston* (Amherst, Mass., 1885).

46. *Documents Relative to Manufactures in the United States*, 22nd Cong. 1st Sess., House Exec. Doc. no. 308 (1833) ["The McLane Report"], I: 69.

47. Mathew Carey, *Essays on Political Economy* (1822; reprint ed., New York, 1968), p. 478.

48. Ibid.

Chapter 5. Crisis and Expansion

1. Langdon Byllesby, *Observations on the Sources and Effects of Unequal Wealth* (New York, 1826).

2. *The Middling Interest* ([Boston], n.d.), Broadside Collection, American Antiquarian Society, Worcester, Mass.

3. Vickers, *Young Men and the Sea*, p. 119.

4. Joel Munsell's story is recounted in Hackett, *The Rude Hand of Innovation*, p. 57.

5. *The Duty of a Foreman of a Printing Office* (New Haven, 1825) [Broadside Collection, American Antiquarian Society, Worcester, Mass., facsimile of an original at the Connecticut Historical Society, Hartford]. On work discipline as a substitute for personal authority over unfree labor, see David Montgomery, *Citizen Worker: The*

Experience of Workers in the United States with Democracy and the Free Market During the Nineteenth Century (Cambridge, England, 1993), p. 55.

6. The Dahlonega example is given in Dunaway, *The First American Frontier*, p. 273; Thomas Man, *Picture of a Factory Village* (Providence, 1833).

7. *Co-operator* (Utica, N.Y.), March 6, 1832.

8. Heighton is discussed in Ronald Schultz, *The Republic of Labor: Philadelphia Artisans and the Politics of Class, 1720–1830* (New York, 1993), pp. 222–228.

9. Man, *Picture of a Factory Village*; Utica Co-operator, March 6, 1832.

10. William Cooper Howells, *Recollections of Life in Ohio, from 1813 to 1840* (Cincinnati, 1895), p. 192.

11. The building collapse is described in [Philip Hone] *The Diary of Philip Hone, 1828–1851*, ed. Allan Nevins, 2 vols. (New York, 1927), I: 245–246, and the suicide in *New York Weekly Tribune*, November 6, 1841.

12. Edward J. Balleisen, *Navigating Failure: Bankruptcy and Commercial Society in Antebellum America* (Chapel Hill, 2001), pp. 98–99; Steven J. Ross, *Workers on the Edge: Work, Leisure, and Politics in Industrializing Cincinnati, 1788–1890* (New York, 1985), pp. 25–28, 48–50.

13. For Claxton, see Joseph P. Ferrie, "The Entry into the U.S. Labor Market of Antebellum European Migrants, 1840–1860," *Explorations in Economic History* 34 (1997): 295–330.

14. Kerby Miller, *Immigrants and Exiles: Ireland and the Irish Exodus to North America* (New York, 1985).

15. On Scandinavian migration, see Jon Gjerde, *From Peasants to Farmers: The Migration from Balestrand, Norway, to the Upper Middle West* (Cambridge, England, 1985); on Jewish migration, see J. Sarna, *American Judaism* (New Haven, Conn., 2004).

16. Ferrie, "The Entry into the U.S. Labor Market," pp. 295–330.

17. Thomas L. Dublin, *Women at Work: The Transformation of Work and Society in Lowell, Massachusetts, 1826–1860* (New York, 1979); see also J. I. Little, "A Canadian in Lowell: Labour, Manhood and Independence in the Early Industrial Era, 1840–1849," *Labour/Le Travail* 48 (Fall 2001).

18. Grace Palladino, *Another Civil War: Labor, Capital, and the State in the Anthracite Regions of Pennsylvania, 1840–1868* (Urbana, Ill., 1990), pp. 66–73.

19. See Theresa Anne Murphy, *Ten Hours' Labor: Religion, Reform, and Gender in Early New England* (Ithaca, 1992).

20. Walt Whitman, "New York Dissected, IV: Broadway," *Life Illustrated*, April 12, 1856, reprinted in Walt Whitman, *New York Dissected*, ed. Emory Holloway and Ralph Adimari (New York, 1936), p. 119.

21. Tyler Anbinder, "From Famine to Five Points: Lord Lansdowne's Irish Tenants Encounter North America's Most Notorious Slum,"*American Historical Review* 107 (2002): 350–387. On residential concentrations of in-migrants, see Peter R. Knights, *Yankee Destinies: The Lives of Ordinary Nineteenth-Century Bostonians* (Chapel Hill, 1991), chapter 1, esp. p. 34.

22. Alexander von Hoffman, *Local Attachments: The Making of an American Urban Neighborhood, 1850–1920* (Baltimore, 1994), pp. 3, 19.

23. On stature and mortality rates, see Clayne L. Pope, "The Changing View of the Standard-of-Living Question in the United States," *American Economic Review* 83, no. 2 (May 1993): 333; Michael R. Haines, "The Population of the United States, 1790–1920," in Engerman and Gallman, ed., *The Cambridge Economic History of the United States*, vol. II, *The Long Nineteenth Century*, pp. 143–206; and Michael R. Haines, Lee A. Craig, and Thomas Weiss, "The Short and the Dead: Nutrition, Mortality, and the 'Antebellum Puzzle' in the United States," *Journal of Economic History* 63, no. 2 (June 2003): 382–413. On the rise of assistance for the poor, see Robert A. Margo, "Wages and Labor Markets Before the Civil War," *American Economic Review* 88, no. 2 (May 1998): 54.

24. Walt Whitman, editorial in *Brooklyn Eagle*, June 17, 1847; George Lippard, *The Empire City* (1864), p. vi.

25. Forbes and Greene, *The Rich Men of Massachusetts*, pp. 36–37.

26. Olin quoted in Edward K. Spann, *The New Metropolis: New York City, 1840–1857* (New York, 1981), p. 228; the Astor Place riot quotation is in Eric Lott, *Love and Theft: Blackface Minstrelsy and the Making of the American Working Class* (New York, 1993), p. 66.

27. Bowles quoted in Gilkeson, *Middle-Class Providence*, p. 60.

28. Carey, *Reflections on the Subject of Emigration from Europe*, p. 23.

29. Martin Bruegel, *Farm, Shop, Landing: The Rise of a Market Society in the Hudson Valley, 1780–1860* (Durham, N.C., 2002), p. 137; Clark, *The Roots of Rural Capitalism*, p. 217.

30. Burrows and Wallace, *Gotham*, p. 726f.; Boydston, *Home and Work*, p. 69. On the growth of bureaucratic organizations, see Alfred D. Chandler, *The Visible Hand: The Managerial Revolution in American Business* (Cambridge, Mass., 1977); on "drummers," see Timothy B. Spears, " 'All Things to All Men': The Commercial Traveler and the Rise of Modern Salesmanship," *American Quarterly* 45 (1993): 524–557.

31. Edward Balleisen, *Navigating Failure*, esp. chapter 7; Christopher Clark, "The Diary of an Apprentice Cabinetmaker: Edward Jenner Carpenter's 'Journal,' 1844–45," *Proceedings of the American Antiquarian Society* 98 (1988): 303–394.

32. On William Bassett, see Christopher Clark, *The Communitarian Moment: The Radical Challenge of the Northampton Association* (Ithaca, 1995), pp. 194–195, 257 n.21.

33. Don Harrison Doyle, *The Social Order of a Frontier Community: Jacksonville, Illinois, 1825–70* (Urbana, Ill., 1978), pp. 95, 101.

34. John D. Majewski, *A House Dividing: Economic Development in Pennsylvania and Virginia Before the Civil War* (Cambridge, England, 2000); Christopher Morris, *Becoming Southern: The Evolution of a Way of Life, Warren County and Vicksburg, Mississippi, 1770–1860* (New York, 1995).

35. Byllesby, *Observations*, pp. 36–54, esp. p. 43; Henry C. Carey, *The Past, the Present, and the Future* (Philadelphia, 1847).

36. Francis Parkman, "Conservatism," *Boston Daily Advertiser*, October 17, 1862, in Wilbur R. Jacobs, ed., *Letters of Francis Parkman*, 2 vols. (Norman, Okla., 1960): I, 156; *Hunt's Merchants' Magazine* 35 (July 1856): 55–56.

37. Carey, *The Past, the Present, and the Future*; Henry C. Carey, *The Harmony of Interests* (Philadelphia, 1872).

38. [Henry C. Carey] *The North and the South* (New York, 1854), p. 15.

Chapter 6. From Regional Differences to Sectional Divide

1. Wayne Cutler, "Introduction," in Cutler, ed., *North for Union: John Appleton's Journal of a Tour to New England Made by President Polk in June and July 1847* (Nashville, 1986), p. xvii.

2. For Polk's remarks at Chapel Hill, see Cutler, "Introduction," pp. xix–xx; O'Sullivan's remark appeared in *United States Magazine and Democratic Review* (July–August, 1845).

3. Sylvester Judd, Diary ["Notebook"] no. 4, Forbes Library, Northampton, Mass., entry for May 14, 1846.

4. David F. Weiman, "Farmers and the Market in Antebellum America: A View from the Georgia Upcountry," *Journal of Economic History* 47 (1987): 627–647. On Southern manufacturing compared with that in the Midwest, see Kenneth L. Sokoloff and Viken Tchakerian, "Manufacturing Where Agriculture Predominates: Evidence from the South and Midwest in 1860," *Explorations in Economic History* 34 (1997): 234–264.

5. Turnbull quoted by Douglas R. Egerton, "Markets Without a Market Revolution: Southern Planters and Capitalism," in Paul A. Gilje, ed., *Wages of Independence: Capitalism in the Early American Republic* (Madison, Wisc., 1997), p. 55; Watson Farm Diary, entry for May 10, 1858, Watson Family Papers, Manuscripts Division, University of Virginia Library, in Michael Plunkett, ed., *Afro-American Sources in Virginia: A Guide to Manuscripts* (Charlottesville, 1995), at http://etext.lib .virginia.edu/plunkett/530.jpg (consulted November 2004); Albert Pike, remarks to the Southern Commercial Convention, New Orleans, 1850, quoted in Fletcher M. Green, *The Role of the Yankee in the Old South* (Athens, Ga., 1972), p. 121.

6. On Hammond, see Drew Gilpin Faust, *James Henry Hammond and the Old South: A Design for Mastery* (Baton Rouge, 1982), chapter 6.

7. This paragraph and those that follow draw on Majewski, *A House Dividing*.

8. This discussion relies heavily on David Thelen, *Paths of Resistance: Tradition and Dignity in Industrializing Missouri* (New York, 1986).

9. Jeffrey S. Adler, *Yankee Merchants and the Making of the Urban West: The Rise and Fall of Antebellum St. Louis* (Cambridge, England, 1991).

10. Ibid., pp. 83–84.

11. Ibid., pp. 111–142.

12. J. D. B. DeBow, *The Industrial Resources, etc., of the Southern and Western Returns of the Census of 1850*, 3 vols. (New Orleans, 1852–1853), I: 328.

13. Randolph B. Campbell, *An Empire for Slavery: The Peculiar Institution in Texas, 1821–1865* (Baton Rouge, 1989); on landlessness in Texas, see Charles C. Bolton, *Poor Whites of the Antebellum South*, p. 82.

14. Zachariah Ellis Coombes, *The Diary of a Frontiersman, 1858–1859*, ed. Barbara Neal Ledbetter (Newcastle, Tex., 1962), pp. 12–13.

15. James P. Ronda, *Astoria and Empire* (Lincoln, Nebr., 1990), esp. pp. 302–336; Gordon B. Dodds, *Oregon: A Bicentennial History* (New York, 1977), esp. p. 59; see also Clifford M. Drury, *Marcus and Narcissa Whitman and the Opening of Old Oregon*, 2 vols. (Glendale, Calif., 1973).

16. Dodds, *Oregon*, pp. 60–70, quotation on p. 62. See also Malcolm Clark, Jr., *Eden Seekers: The Settlement of Oregon, 1818–1862* (Boston, 1981), statistics on p. 262.

17. "Oregon and California," *DeBow's Review* 1 (1846): 64–69. On the gold discoveries as an indication of Yankee superiority, see Abraham Lincoln, "Second Lecture on Discoveries and Inventions [February 11, 1859]," in Roy P. Basler, ed., *The Collected Works of Abraham Lincoln*, 8 vols. (New Brunswick, N.J., 1953), III: 358. The discussion of the California Gold Rush in this and the following paragraphs is drawn from Stephen Schwartz, *From West to East: California and the Making of the American Mind* (New York, 1998), and Malcolm J. Rohrbough, *Days of Gold: The California Gold Rush and the American Nation* (Berkeley, 1997).

18. Mary B. Ballou, *"I Hear the Hogs in My Kitchen": A Woman's View of the Gold Rush*, ed. Archibald Hanna (New Haven, 1962), reproduced at History Matters, http://historymatters.gmu.edu/d/6512.html (consulted November 29, 2004).

19. On worsening conditions for miners in the 1850s, see Jeremiah Starr, *A California Adventure and Vision* (Cincinnati, 1864), and compare p. 41 with pp. 67 and 85. [J. M. Letts] *California Illustrated: Including a Description of the Panama and Nicaragua Routes. By a Returned Californian* (New York, 1852), chapter 19. For one example of a capital-intensive mining venture in the later 1850s, see Pamela Herr and Mary Lee Spence, ed., *The Letters of Jessie Benton Frémont* (Urbana, Ill., 1993), p. 188.

20. F. Halsey Roger, " 'Man to Loan $1,500 and Serve as Clerk': Trading Jobs for Loans in Mid-Nineteenth Century San Francisco," *Journal of Economic History* 54 (1994): 34–63; Michael Fellman, *Citizen Sherman: A Life of William Tecumseh Sherman* (New York, 1995), pp. 51–65.

21. Paul W. Gates, ed., *California Ranchos and Farms, 1846–1862: Including the Letters of John Quincy Adams Warren of 1861* (Madison, Wisc., 1967), pp. xi, 59, 61.

22. Gates, ed., *California Ranchos and Farms*, pp. 15, 41–59.

23. Agénor de Gasparin, *The Uprising of a Great People: The United States in 1861*, translated by Mary L. Booth (New York, 1862), p. 87, quotes the South Carolina declaration.

24. Johann Pritzlaff, 1842, in Walter D. Kamphoefner, Wolfgang Helbich, and Ulrike Sommer, ed., *News from the Land of Freedom: German Immigrants Write Home*, translated by Susan Carter Vogel (Ithaca, 1991), p. 306.

25. "The Autobiography of Omar H. Morse," in James M. Marshall, *Land Fever: Dispossession and the Frontier Myth* (Lexington, Ky., 1986), p. 42; T. Wesley Bond, *Minnesota and Its Resources* (New York, 1853), p. 31.

26. Martin Weitz, 1855, in Kamphoefner, et al., ed., *News from the Land of Freedom*, p. 342; Walt Whitman, editorial, *Brooklyn Daily Times*, October 21, 1857.

27. The quotation is from "Modern Philanthropy and Negro Slavery," *DeBow's Review* 16, no. 3 (March 1854): 270.

28. Douglas J. Puffert, "The Standardization of Track Gauge on North American Railways, 1830–1890," *Journal of Economic History* 60 (2000): 936.

29. William Pratt Dale, "A Connecticut Yankee in Antebellum Alabama," *Alabama Review* (January 1953): 59–70; Charles Hoffman and Tess Hoffman, *North by South: The Two Lives of Richard James Arnold* (Athens, Ga., 1988).

30. Francis Parkman to Charles Eliot Norton, Boston, November 10, 1850, in Jacobs, ed. *Letters of Francis Parkman*, I, 79.

31. Hammond's speech in the U.S. Senate, March 4, 1858 was reprinted in *Selections from the Letters and Speeches of the Hon. James H. Hammond, of South Carolina* (New York, 1866), pp. 311–322. On the wealth of slaveholders and the comparative value of property in slaves in 1860, see James L. Huston, *Calculating the Value of the Union: Slavery, Property Rights, and the Economic Origins of the Civil War* (Chapel Hill, 2003), p. 26, table 2.1; p. 28, table 2.3; p. 30, table 2.4.

32. Winthrop D. Jordan, *Tumult and Silence at Second Creek: An Inquiry into a Civil War Slave Conspiracy* (Baton Rouge, 1993).

33. On the struggle to assist runaways along the borders of free and slave states, see Thomas P. Slaughter, *Bloody Dawn: The Christiana Riot and Racial Violence in the Antebellum North* (New York, 1991).

34. Shearer Davis Bowman, *Masters and Lords: Mid-Nineteenth Century U.S. Planters and Prussian Junkers* (New York, 1993), p. 159.

35. This paragraph and the one following are based on Stephanie McCurry, *Masters of Small Worlds: Yeoman Households, Gender Relations, and the Political Culture of the Antebellum South Carolina Lowcountry* (New York, 1995).

36. James D. Richardson, *A Compilation of the Messages and Papers of the Presidents* (Washington, D.C., 1897), V: 452.

37. Jeremy Atack and Fred Bateman, *To Their Own Soil: Agriculture in the Antebellum North* (Ames, Iowa, 1987).

38. Alan L. Olmstead and Paul W. Rhode, "Beyond the Threshold: An Analysis of the Characteristics and Behavior of Early Reaper Adopters," *Journal of Economic History* 55 (1995): 27–57; J. H. Williams to James Williams, Homer, Iowa, December 12, 1858, in John K. Folmar, ed., *This State of Wonders: The Letters of an Iowa Frontier Family, 1858–1861* (Iowa City, 1986), pp. 17–18.

39. Marshall, *Land Fever*, pp. 50–80; David W. Galenson and Clayne L. Pope, "Economic and Geographical Mobility on the Farming Frontier: Evidence from Apanoose County, Iowa, 1850–1870," *Journal of Economic History* 49 (1989): 635–655, notes the advantages often gained by early settlers. Gregson, "Wealth Accumulation and Distribution," notes that early settlers' knowledge of soil conditions and markets also gave them income advantages over later settlers in a region.

40. On the general point, see Gray, *The Yankee West*, pp. 159–168.

41. Basler, ed., *The Collected Works of Abraham Lincoln*, III: 459, 468; V: 36, 52–53.

42. Ibid., III: 481.

43. Carey, *The North and the South*; see also Sarah T. Phillips, "Antebellum Agricultural Reform, Republican Ideology, and Sectional Tension," *Agricultural History* 74 (2000): 799–822.

44. Amos Lawrence to Robert Barnwell Rhett, Boston, December 12, 1849, in Lawrence, ed., *Extracts from the Diary and Correspondence of the Late Amos Lawrence,* pp. 274–276.

45. Hammond, *Secret and Sacred,* entry for November 7, 1861.

46. Francis Parkman, "Aristocrats and Democrats," *Boston Daily Advertiser,* June 14, 1863, in Jacobs, ed., *Letters of Francis Parkman,* I: 163.

Chapter 7. The Civil War: Two Kinds of Revolution

1. James M. McPherson, *Abraham Lincoln and the Second American Revolution* (New York, 1991), argues that the Civil War brought dramatic change. On the absence of marked changes in Northern society during the war, see J. Matthew Gallman, *Mastering Wartime: A Social History of Philadelphia During the Civil War* (Cambridge, England, 1991), and J. Matthew Gallman, *The North Fights the Civil War* (Chicago, 1996).

2. On the later influence of a "Southern" interpretation of the Civil War, see David W. Blight, *Race and Reunion: The Civil War in American Memory* (Cambridge, Mass., 2001).

3. Leonard L. Richards, *The Slave Power: The Free North and Southern Domination, 1780–1860* (Baton Rouge, 2000).

4. "Charleston, March 27, 1865," *New-York Daily Tribune,* Tuesday, April 4, 1865, at History Matters: http://historymatters.gmu.edu/d/6381 (consulted May 5, 2005).

5. De Gasparin, *The Uprising of a Great People,* pp. 147–149.

6. E. W. Winkler, *Journal of the Secession Convention of Texas* (Austin, Tex., 1912), pp. 120–123.

7. Edward L. Ayers, *In the Presence of Mine Enemies: War in the Heart of America, 1859–1863* (New York, 2003), quotes Stuart on p. 99 and Baldwin on p. 125.

8. Gallman, *The North Fights the Civil War,* p. 14, on Maryland, and p. 83, discusses family splits.

9. De Gasparin, *The Uprising of a Great People,* p. 149.

10. For recruitment data, see Larry M. Logue, *To Appomattox and Beyond: The Civil War Soldier in War and Peace* (Chicago, 1996), pp. 12, 27; Gallman, *The North Fights the Civil War,* p. 16 (holiday), and pp. 67–68. On Stowell, see Peter R. Knights, *Yankee Destinies,* p. 41.

11. The story of Daniel Edwards's mower is in Sally McMurry, *Families and Farmhouses in Nineteenth-Century America: Vernacular Design and Social Change* (New York, 1988), p. 89.

12. Doyle, *The Social Order of a Frontier Community,* pp. 234–235.

13. Lee A. Craig and Thomas Weiss, "Agricultural Productivity Growth During the Decade of the Civil War," *Journal of Economic History* 53 (1993): 527–548.

14. Lori D. Ginzberg, *Women and the Work of Benevolence: Morality, Politics, and Class in the Nineteenth Century United States* (New Haven, 1990); Elizabeth D. Leonard, *Yankee Women: Gender Battles in the Civil War* (New York, 1994).

15. Palladino, *Another Civil War*, pp. 90–159; Daniel W. Wells and Reuben F. Wells, *A History of Hatfield, Massachusetts* (Springfield, Mass., 1910), p. 231.

16. Katherine A. Giuffre, "First in Flight: Desertion as Politics in the North Carolina Confederate Army," *Social Science History* 21 (1997): 245–263; Ira Berlin, et al., *Freedom: A Documentary History of Emancipation, 1861–1867*, Series I, vol. 1, *The Destruction of Slavery* (Cambridge, England, 1985).

17. Doyle, *The Social Order of a Frontier Community*, pp. 238–240.

18. On casualties and death rates, see Gallman, *The North Fights the Civil War*, pp. 74–75.

19. James H. Hudson, quoted in C. Peter Ripley, ed., *Witness for Freedom: African American Voices on Race, Slavery, and Emancipation* (Chapel Hill, 1993), p. 222.

20. Berlin, et al., *Freedom*, Series II, *The Black Military Experience* (Cambridge, England, 1982).

21. Barbara Jeanne Fields, *Slavery and Freedom on the Middle Ground: Maryland During the Nineteenth Century* (New Haven, 1985), chapter 5; Ayers, *In the Presence of Mine Enemies*, p. 168; Berlin, et al., *Freedom*, Series I, I: 2–3; on Iwen, see ibid., p. 177. For accounts of "contrabands" (possibly including Iwen) from the viewpoint of a member of the Tenth Massachusetts regiment, see David W. Blight, ed., *When This Cruel War Is Over: The Civil War Letters of Charles Harvey Brewster* (Amherst, Mass., 1992), pp. 57, 61–62, 78.

22. On "refugeeing," see Robert Edgar Conrad, *In the Hands of Strangers: Readings on Foreign and Domestic Slave Trading* (University Park, Pa., 2001), part 3.

23. Berlin, et al., *Freedom*, Series I, I: 217.

24. Ibid., p. 323; and Document 36.

25. De Gasparin, *The Uprising of a Great People*, pp. 195–196, discusses Tocqueville's and his own predictions.

26. On Conwell, see Blight, *Race and Reunion*, p. 154.

27. On Mary Jones, see Blight, *Race and Reunion*, pp. 41–42; Gerald D. Jaynes, *Branches Without Roots: Genesis of the Black Working Class in the American South, 1862–1882* (New York, 1986), p. 41; William T. Palfrey to John Gorham Palfrey, June 29, 1865, and August 8, 1867, in Frank Otto Gatell, ed., "The Slaveholder and the Abolitionist: Binding Up a Family's Wounds," *Journal of Southern History* 27 (1961): 376, 390. On Southern output and per capita income, see Engerman, "Slavery and Its Consequences."

28. In the Emancipation Proclamation, Lincoln wrote, "I recommend to them that in all cases when allowed, they labor faithfully for reasonable wages"; see Basler, ed., *The Collected Works of Abraham Lincoln*, VI: 30.

29. Jaynes, *Branches Without Roots*, pp. 107–109; see also pp. 169, 189–190.

30. Herbert G. Gutman, *The Black Family in Slavery and Freedom, 1750–1925* (New York, 1976), esp. chapter 9.

31. Jaynes, *Branches Without Roots*, p. 5.

32. Moore and Tobey quoted in Jaynes, *Branches Without Roots*, at p. 295 and p. 8 respectively.

33. Robert Tomson to William Preston, August 16, 1870, Wickliffe-Preston Family Papers, University of Kentucky Special Collections and Archives, Lexington,

Ky., http://www.uky.edu/LCC/HIS/scraps/jail.html (consulted November 29, 2004).

34. Jaynes, *Branches Without Roots*, pp. 39–44, 300–316.

35. Henry Grady, Speech to the Bay State Club of Boston, 1889, reprinted in Paul D. Escott and David R. Goldfield, ed., *Major Problems in the History of the American South, vol. II: The New South* (Lexington, Mass., 1990), pp. 71–73.

36. Steven Hahn, *The Roots of Southern Populism: Yeoman Farmers and the Transformation of the Georgia Upcountry, 1850–1890* (New York, 1983); David L. Carlton, "The Revolution from Above: The National Market and the Beginnings of Industrialization in North Carolina," *Journal of American History* 77, no. 2 (September 1990): 445–475.

37. James Guild, *Old Times in Tennessee* (Nashville, 1878), p. 13.

38. Jaynes, *Branches Without Roots*, pp. 256, 263.

39. Martha Hodes, *White Women, Black Men: Illicit Sex in the Nineteenth Century South* (New Haven, 1997).

40. On agricultural productivity, see Craig and Weiss, "Agricultural Productivity Growth," pp. 527–548; on commercialization and diversified output, see Mary Eschelbach Gregson, "Rural Response to Increased Demand: Crop Choice in the Midwest, 1860–1880," *Journal of Economic History* 53 (1993): 332–345.

41. R. Budd, "Factor Shares, 1850–1910," in Conference on Income and Wealth, *Trends in the American Economy in the Nineteenth Century*, Studies in Income and Wealth, no. 24 (Princeton, 1960), p. 392, table A-1. Johan Bauer is quoted in Kamphoefner, et al., ed., *News from the Land of Freedom*, p. 163. On the resurgence of family farming, see Harriet Friedmann, "World Market, State, and Family Farm: Social Bases of Household Production in the Era of Wage Labour," *Comparative Studies in Society and History* 20 (1978): 545–586.

42. Remington quoted in McFarland, *A Scattered People*, p. 168.

43. Joseph Hatton, *To-day in America: Studies for the Old World and the New* (London, 1881).

44. Interregional income comparisons in 1880 are from Paul M. Romer, "The Origins of Endogenous Growth," *Journal of Economic Perspectives* 8 (1994): 9.

45. Rutherford B. Hayes to William McKinley, Cincinnati, November 6, 1866, reproduced at Ohio Historical Society, Online Documents Collection, http://www.ohiohistory.org/onlinedoc/hayes/appendixa.html (consulted June 22, 2003).

46. Gilkeson, *Middle-Class Providence*, p. 95. On employees as a proportion of the workforce, see David Montgomery, *Beyond Equality: Labor and the Radical Republicans, 1862–1872* (New York, 1967), p. 449, and Daniel T. Rodgers, *The Work Ethic in Industrial America, 1850–1920* (Chicago, 1978), p. 37.

47. Kamphoefner, et al., ed., *News from the Land of Freedom*, p. 174.

48. "The Autobiography of Omar H. Morse," in Marshall, *Land Fever*, pp. 5, 77–80.

49. Patricia Nelson Limerick, *The Legacy of Conquest: The Unbroken Past of the American West* (New York, 1987).

50. David Montgomery, *Workers' Control in America: Studies in the History of Work, Technology, and Labor Struggles* (Cambridge, England, 1979).

51. Richard Franklin Bensel, *The Political Economy of American Industrialization, 1877–1900* (Cambridge, England, 2000), chapter 2, stresses the "uneven economic development" of the late-nineteenth-century United States.

52. On the limitations, for example, of married women's property laws, see Norma Basch, *In the Eyes of the Law: Women, Marriage, and Property in Nineteenth-Century New York* (Ithaca, 1982). My conclusion here is slightly more pessimistic than that of Shammas, *A History of Household Government*, which emphasizes the degree to which formal hierarchy and coercion had diminished in the regulation of households by the 1880s.

A Note on Sources and Further Reading

Preface. Households, Labor, and Society

A GENERAL reference work for themes raised in this book is Mary Kupiec Cayton, Elliott J. Gorn, and Peter W. Williams, ed., *Encylopedia of American Social History*, 3 vols. (New York, 1993). A useful general account is Robert H. Wiebe, *The Opening of American Society: From the Adoption of the Constitution to the Eve of Disunion* (New York, 1984).

David J. Weber, *The Spanish Frontier in North America* (New Haven, 1992); Edward Countryman, *Americans: A Collision of Histories* (New York, 1996); and Daniel K. Richter, *Facing East from Indian Country: A Native History of Early America* (Cambridge, Mass., 2001), revise the conventional East Coast orientation of early American histories. Of works placing the early United States in wider historical and geographical contexts, Felipe Fernández-Armesto, *The Americas: A Hemispheric History* (New York, 2003), is an accessible introduction. D. W. Meinig's classic *The Shaping of America: A Geographical Perspective on 500 Years of History*, 4 vols. (New Haven, 1986-2004), is an incomparable treatment of some themes covered in this book. The issue of regions in American history is discussed in Edward L. Ayers, et al., *All Over the Map: Rethinking American Regions* (Baltimore, 1996), while three works that explore the consequences of regional differences are W. T. Easterbrook, *North American Patterns of Growth and Development: The Continental Context* (Toronto, 1990); Marc Egnal, *Divergent Paths: How Culture and Institutions Have Shaped North American Growth* (New York, 1996); and Edward Grabb and James Curtis, *Regions Apart: The Four Societies of Canada and the United States* (New York, 2004).

Important accounts of wealth and wealth distribution at different periods include Alice Hanson Jones, *Wealth of a Nation to Be: The American Colonies on the*

A Note on Sources and Further Reading

Eve of the Revolution (New York, 1980); Lee Soltow, *Distribution of Wealth and Income in the United States in 1798* (Pittsburgh, 1989); Carole Shammas, "A New Look at Long-Term Trends in Wealth Inequality in the United States," *American Historical Review* 98 (1993): 412–431; and James L. Huston, *Securing the Fruits of Labor: The American Concept of Wealth Distribution, 1765–1900* (Baton Rouge, 1998).

Chapter 1. Households and Regions at the End of the Colonial Period

CAROLE SHAMMAS, *A History of Household Government in America* (Charlottesville, 2002), provides the best introduction to dependency in the household economies of early America and the changes that occurred up to the 1880s. Cornelia Dayton, *Women Before the Bar: Gender, Law, and Society in Connecticut, 1639–1789* (Chapel Hill, 1995), deals with the colonial period in the context of a study of women's appearances in court and court records. Michael Grossberg, *Governing the Hearth: Law and the Family in Nineteenth-Century America* (Chapel Hill, 1985), covers the early national period. Jeanne Boydston, *Home and Work: Housework, Wages and the Ideology of Labor in the Early Republic* (New York, 1990), discusses women's and men's economic relationships in households and early capitalism. An invaluable discussion of status, marriage, and economic relationships is Amy Dru Stanley, *From Bondage to Contract: Wage Labor, Marriage, and the Market in the Age of Slave Emancipation* (Cambridge, England, 1998).

Alan Taylor, *American Colonies* (New York, 2001), offers a continent-wide perspective. The essays in Jack Greene and J. R. Pole, ed., *Colonial British America* (Baltimore, 1984), and John J. McCusker and Russell R. Menard, ed., *The Economy of British America, 1607–1789* (Chapel Hill, 1985), provide essential background on colonial societies. Jackson Turner Main, *The Social Structure of Revolutionary America* (Princeton, 1965), remains a classic account.

Significant works on the eighteenth-century Middle Colonies include James T. Lemon, *The Best Poor Man's Country: A Geographical Study of Early Southeastern Pennsylvania* (Baltimore, 1972); Carville Earle and Ronald Hoffman, "The Foundation of the Modern Economy: Agriculture and the Costs of Labor in the United States and England, 1800–1860," *American Historical Review* 85 (1980): 1055–1094; Mary M. Schweitzer, *Custom and Contract: Household Government and the Economy in Colonial Pennsylvania* (New York, 1987); Sharon V. Salinger, *'To Serve Well and Faithfully': Labor and Indentured Servants in Pennsylvania, 1682–1800* (Cambridge, England, 1987); Barry Levy, *Quakers and the American Family: British Settlement in the Delaware Valley* (New York, 1988); and Brendan McConville, *These Daring Disturbers of the Public Peace: The Struggle for Property and Power in Early New Jersey* (Ithaca, 1999). On textile production, see Adrienne D. Hood, *The Weaver's Craft: Cloth, Commerce, and Industry in Early Penn-sylvania* (Philadelphia, 2003). Important studies of merchants are Thomas M. Doerflinger, *A Vigorous Spirit of Enterprise: Merchants and Economic Development in Revolutionary Philadelphia* (Chapel Hill, 1986), and Cathy Matson, *Merchants and Empire: Trading in Colonial New York* (Baltimore, 1998).

Ira Berlin, *Many Thousands Gone: The First Two Centuries of Slavery in North America* (Cambridge, Mass., 1998), introduces colonial slavery. Other works on slave societies include Edmund S. Morgan, *American Slavery, American Freedom: The Ordeal of Colonial Virginia* (New York, 1975); Allan Kulikoff, *Tobacco and Slaves: The Development of Southern Cultures in the Chesapeake, 1680–1800* (Chapel Hill, 1986); Ira Berlin and Philip D. Morgan, ed., *Cultivation and Culture: Labor and the Shaping of Slave Life in the Americas* (Charlottesville, 1993); and Philip D. Morgan, *Slave Counterpoint: Black Culture in the Eighteenth Century Chesapeake and Lowcountry* (Chapel Hill, 1998). Kathleen M. Brown, *Good Wives, Nasty Wenches, and Anxious Patriarchs: Gender, Race, and Power in Colonial Virginia* (Chapel Hill, 1996), takes a broader view of social relationships in the colonial South. On the gentry, see Rhys Isaac, *The Transformation of Virginia, 1740–1790* (Chapel Hill, 1982), and T. H. Breen, *Tobacco Culture: The Mentality of the Great Tidewater Planters on the Eve of Revolution* (Princeton, 1985); on yeoman farm societies, see Richard R. Beeman, *The Evolution of the Southern Backcountry: A Case Study of Lunenburg County, Virginia, 1746–1832* (Philadelphia, 1984).

Works on New England include William Cronon, *Changes in the Land: Indians, Colonists and the Ecology of New England* (New York, 1983); John L. Brooke, *The Heart of the Commonwealth: Society and Political Culture in Worcester County, Massachusetts, 1713–1861* (New York, 1989); Gloria L. Main, *Peoples of a Spacious Land: Families and Cultures in Colonial New England* (Cambridge, Mass., 2001); and Margaret E. Newell, *From Dependency to Independence: Economic Revolution in Colonial New England* (Ithaca, 1998). On the dual character of the New England economy, see Daniel Vickers, *Farmers and Fishermen: Two Centuries of Work in Essex County, Massachusetts, 1630–1830* (Chapel Hill, 1994). William D. Piersen, *Black Yankees: The Development of an Afro-American Subculture in Eighteenth-Century New England* (Amherst, Mass., 1988), discusses slavery and free black communities. On households and household production, see Laurel Thatcher Ulrich, *A Midwife's Tale: The Life of Martha Ballard, Based on Her Diary, 1785–1812* (New York, 1990); Laurel Thatcher Ulrich, *The Age of Homespun: Objects and Stories in the Creation of an American Myth* (New York, 2001); and Marla R. Miller, "Gender, Artisanry, and Craft Tradition in Early New England: The View Through the Eye of the Needle," *William and Mary Quarterly* 60 (2003): 743–776. Christine Leigh Heyrmann, *Commerce and Culture: The Maritime Communities of Colonial Massachusetts*

(New York, 1984), and Phyllis Whitman Hunter, *Purchasing Identity in the Atlantic World: Massachusetts Merchants, 1670–1780* (Ithaca, 2001), discuss commerce. On maritime society, see Daniel Vickers, *Young Men and the Sea: Yankee Seafarers in the Age of Sail* (New Haven, 2005), and Elaine Forman Crane, *Ebb Tide in New England: Women, Seaports, and Social Change, 1630–1800* (Boston, 1998).

On eighteenth-century immigration, see Bernard Bailyn, *The Peopling of British North America: An Introduction* (New York, 1986); Bernard Bailyn, *Voyagers to the West: A Passage in the Peopling of North America on the Eve of the Revolution* (New York, 1986); Marianne S. Wokeck, *Trade in Strangers: The Beginnings of Mass Migration to North America* (University Park, Pa., 1999); and Kerby A. Miller, et al., ed., *Irish Immigrants in the Land of Canaan: Letters and Memoirs from Colonial and Revolutionary America, 1675–1815* (New York, 2003). On German migrants, see Aaron Spencer Fogleman, *Hopeful Journeys: German Immigration, Settlement, and Political Culture in Colonial America, 1717–1775* (Philadelphia, 1996); Hartmut Lehmann, et al., ed., *In Search of Peace and Prosperity: New German Settlements in Eighteenth-Century Europe and America* (University Park, Pa., 2000), and A. G. Roeber, *Palatines, Liberty, and Property: German Lutherans in Colonial British America* (Baltimore, 1993).

T. H. Breen, *The Marketplace of Revolution: How Consumer Politics Shaped American Independence* (New York, 2004), adds to a growing literature on late-colonial consumption and culture; see also Cary Carson, "The Consumer Revolution in Colonial British America: Why Demand?" in Cary Carson, Peter Albert, and Ronald Hoffman, ed., *Of Consuming Interests: The Style of Life in the Eighteenth Century* (Charlottesville, 1994); Richard L. Bushman, *The Refinement of America: Persons, Houses, Cities* (New York, 1992); Carole Shammas, *The Preindustrial Consumer in England and America* (Oxford, 1990); and John E. Crowley, *The Invention of Comfort: Sensibilities and Design in Early Modern Britain and Early America* (Baltimore, 2001).

Studies of poverty are becoming equally prominent, including Billy G. Smith, *The "Lower Sort": Philadelphia's Laboring People, 1750–1800* (Ithaca, 1990); Richard Oestreicher, "The Counted and the Uncounted: The Occupational Structure of Early American Cities," *Journal of Social History* 28 (1994): 351–361; Ruth Wallis Herndon, *Unwelcome Americans: Living on the Margin in Early New England* (Philadelphia, 2001); and an important collection of essays, Billy G. Smith, ed., *Down and Out in Early America* (University Park, Pa., 2004).

Recent arguments emphasizing the cohesiveness of the pre-Revolutionary colonies include Jon Butler, *Becoming America: The Revolution Before 1776* (Cambridge, Mass., 2000), and David Hancock, *Citizens of the World: London Merchants and the Integration of the British Atlantic Community, 1735–1785* (New York, 1995); Jack P. Greene, *Pursuits of Happiness: The Social Development of Early*

Modern British Colonies and the Formation of American Culture (Chapel Hill, 1988), takes a different tack. In addition to the works on planters cited earlier, several studies have addressed the roles of colonial elites, including Marc Egnal, *A Mighty Empire: The Origins of the American Revolution* (Ithaca, 1988); Trevor Burnard, *Creole Gentlemen: The Maryland Elite, 1691–1776* (New York, 2002); Ronald Hoffman with Sally D. Mason, *Princes of Ireland, Planters of Maryland: A Carroll Saga, 1500–1782* (Chapel Hill, 2000); and Jeffrey Robert Young, *Domesticating Slavery: The Master Class in Georgia and South Carolina, 1670–1837* (Chapel Hill, 1999).

Chapter 2. Change and Continuity in the American Revolution

CONTRASTING INTERPRETATIONS of the social implications of the American Revolution are Gordon S. Wood, *The Radicalism of the American Revolution* (New York, 1992), and Edward Countryman, "Indians, the Colonial Order, and the Social Significance of the American Revolution," *William and Mary Quarterly* 53 (1996): 341–362, each of which was the subject of a critical symposium in that journal.

On the social origins of the Revolution and the rise of popular politics, see Gary B. Nash, *The Urban Crucible: Social Change, Political Consciousness, and the Origins of the American Revolution* (Cambridge, Mass., 1979); Dirk Hoerder, *Crowd Action in Revolutionary Massachusetts, 1765–1780* (New York, 1977); Alfred F. Young, *The Shoemaker and the Tea Party: Memory and the American Revolution* (Boston, 1999); and Gary B. Nash, *The Unknown American Revolution: The Unruly Birth of Democracy and the Struggle to Create America* (New York, 2005). Works on the background to revolution and on mobilization in particular towns and regions are cited in the endnotes.

Implications of revolution in rural societies are discussed in Allan Kulikoff, *From British Peasants to American Colonial Farmers* (Chapel Hill, 2000), and Peter C. Mancall, *Valley of Opportunity: Economic Culture Along the Upper Susquehanna, 1700–1800* (Ithaca, 1991). Recent local studies include John B. Frantz, ed., *Beyond Philadelphia: The American Revolution in the Pennsylvania Hinterland* (University Park, Pa., 1998), and Francis S. Fox, *Sweet Land of Liberty: The Ordeal of the American Revolution in Northampton County, Pennsylvania* (University Park, Pa., 2000). Recruitment, mobilization, and the difficulties of war-fighting are discussed in Paul A. C. Koistinen, *Beating Ploughshares into Swords: The Political Economy of American Warfare, 1606–1865* (Lawrence, Kans., 1996); Wayne E. Lee, *Crowds and Soldiers in Revolutionary North Carolina: The Culture of Violence in Riot and War* (Gainesville, Fla., 2001); E. Wayne Carp, *To Starve the Army at Pleasure: Continental Army Administration and American Political Culture, 1775–1783*

A Note on Sources and Further Reading

(Chapel Hill, 1984); Richard Buel, *In Irons: Britain's Naval Supremacy and the American Revolutionary Economy* (New Haven, 1998); Richard Buel, *Dear Liberty: Connecticut's Mobilization for the Revolutionary War* (Middletown, Conn., 1980); and Alfred F. Young, *Masquerade: The Life and Times of Deborah Sampson, Continental Soldier* (New York, 2004). John Resch, *Suffering Soldiers: Revolutionary War Veterans, Moral Sentiment, and Political Culture in the Early Republic* (Amherst, Mass., 1999), is the best study of soldiers' post-Revolutionary fortunes, drawing on nineteenth-century pension records.

On slavery, slaves, and the war, see Sylvia R. Frey, *Water from the Rock: Black Resistance in a Revolutionary Age* (Princeton, 1991); Woody Holton, *Forced Founders: Indians, Debtors, Slaves, and the Making of the American Revolution in Virginia* (Chapel Hill, 1999); Rhys Isaac, *Landon Carter's Uneasy Kingdom: Revolution and Rebellion on a Virginia Plantation* (New York, 2004); and David Waldstreicher, *Runaway Americans: Benjamin Franklin, Slavery and the American Revolution* (New York, 2004). On the consequences of revolution for black Americans, see Gary B. Nash, *Forging Freedom: The Formation of Philadelphia's Black Community, 1720–1840* (Cambridge, Mass., 1988); Shane White, *Somewhat More Independent: The End of Slavery in New York City, 1770–1810* (Athens, Ga., 1991); Joanne Pope Melish, *Disowning Slavery: Gradual Emancipation and "Race" in New England, 1780–1860* (Ithaca, 1998); Jon F. Sensbach, *A Separate Canaan: The Making of an Afro-Moravian World in North Carolina, 1763–1840* (Chapel Hill, 1998); and Mechal Sobel, *Teach Me Dreams: The Search for Self in the Revolutionary Era* (Princeton, 2000).

The implications of the Revolution for Native Americans are discussed in Gregory E. Dowd, *A Spirited Resistance: The North American Struggle for Unity, 1745–1815* (Baltimore, 1992); Colin G. Calloway, *The American Revolution in Indian Country: Crisis and Diversity in Native American Communities* (Cambridge, England, 1995); and Frederick E. Hoxie, Ronald Hoffman, and Peter J. Albert, ed., *Native Americans and the Early Republic* (Charlottesville, 1999). Richard White, *The Middle Ground: Indians, Empires and Republics in the Great Lakes Region, 1650–1815* (Cambridge, England, 1991), is particularly important. On the renewed pressure of Western settlement, see Gregory H. Nobles, *American Frontiers: Cultural Encounters and Continental Conquest* (New York, 1997); R. Douglas Hurt, *The Ohio Frontier: Crucible of the Old Northwest, 1720–1830* (Bloomington, Ind., 1996); and Elizabeth A. Perkins, *Border Life: Experience and Memory in the Revolutionary Ohio Valley* (Chapel Hill, 1998).

Studies of the Revolution's social and ideological consequences include Allan Kulikoff, "Was the American Revolution a Bourgeois Revolution?" in Ronald Hoffman and Peter Albert, ed., *The Transforming Hand of Revolution* (Charlottesville, 1996), pp. 58–89; the essays in Alfred F. Young, ed., *Beyond the*

A Note on Sources and Further Reading

American Revolution: Explorations in the History of American Radicalism (De Kalb, Ill., 1993); and David Waldstreicher, *In the Midst of Perpetual Fetes: The Making of American Nationalism, 1776–1820* (Chapel Hill, 1997). On agrarian protests, see David P. Szatmary, *Shays' Rebellion: The Making of an Agrarian Insurrection* (Amherst, Mass., 1980); Robert A. Gross, ed., *In Debt to Shays: The Bicentennial of an Agrarian Insurrection* (Charlottesville, 1993); Leonard L. Richards, *Shays's Rebellion: The American Revolution's Final Battle* (Philadelphia, 2003); Thomas P. Slaughter, *The Whiskey Rebellion: Frontier Epilogue to the American Revolution* (New York, 1986); Paul D. Newman, *Fries's Rebellion: The Enduring Struggle for the American Revolution* (Philadelphia, 2004); and Alan Taylor, *Liberty Men and Great Proprietors: The Revolutionary Settlement on the Maine Frontier, 1760–1820* (Chapel Hill, 1990).

Chapter 3. Social Change in the Early Republic

JOYCE APPLEBY, *Inheriting the Revolution: The First Generation of Americans* (Cambridge, Mass., 2000), and Joyce Appleby, ed., *Recollections of the Early Republic: Selected Autobiographies* (Boston, 1997), provide important overviews of social and political developments in the early republic. Charles Sellers, *The Market Revolution: Jacksonian America, 1815–1846* (New York, 1991), is one of the most widely debated syntheses of social change in the period; Melvyn Stokes and Stephen Conway, ed., *The Market Revolution in America: Social, Political, and Religious Expressions, 1800–1880* (Charlottesville, 1996), publishes papers from a symposium on Sellers's work held in London in 1994, to which Sellers contributes a response; Scott C. Martin, ed., *Cultural Change and the Market Revolution in America, 1789–1860* (Lanham, Md., 2004), collects recent essays on a range of topics.

On territorial expansion, see David J. Weber, *The Spanish Frontier in North America* (New Haven, 1992), chapters 10–12; William Earl Weeks, *Building the Continental Empire: American Expansion from the Revolution to the Civil War* (Chicago, 1996); and Gregory H. Nobles, *American Frontiers: Cultural Encounters and Continental Conquest* (New York, 1997). On the consequences of the Louisiana Purchase, see Roger G. Kennedy, *Mr. Jefferson's Lost Cause: Land, Farmers, Slavery, and the Louisiana Purchase* (New York, 2003), and Peter J. Kastor, *The Nation's Crucible: The Louisiana Purchase and the Creation of America* (New Haven, 2004). Among many works that discuss the impact of expansion on Native American societies, see Stuart Banner, *How the Indians Lost Their Land: Law and Power on the Frontier* (Cambridge, Mass., 2005), and Theda Perdue, *Cherokee Women: Gender and Culture Change, 1700–1835* (Lincoln, Nebr., 1998). Migration and land settlement are discussed in Malcolm J. Rohrbough,

A Note on Sources and Further Reading

The Trans-Appalachian Frontier: Peoples, Societies, and Institutions, 1775–1850 (New York, 1978), and Gerald W. McFarland, *A Scattered People: An American Family Moves West* (New York, 1985). John Lauritz Larson, *Internal Improvement: National Public Works and the Promise of Popular Government in the Early United States* (Chapel Hill, 2001), discusses the importance of government in the expansion of settlements. Important regional studies are Alan Taylor, *William Cooper's Town: Power and Persuasion on the Frontier of the Early American Republic* (New York, 1995), on central New York State; William Wycoff, *The Developer's Frontier: The Making of the Western New York Landscape* (New Haven, 1988); Charles E. Brooks, *Frontier Settlement and Market Revolution: The Holland Land Purchase* (Ithaca, 1996); Stephen Aron, *How the West Was Lost: The Transformation of Kentucky from Daniel Boone to Henry Clay* (Baltimore, 1996); Andrew R. L. Cayton, *The Frontier Republic: Ideology and Politics in the Ohio Country, 1780–1825* (Kent, Ohio, 1986); and Kim M. Gruenwald, *River of Enterprise: The Commercial Origins of Regional Identity in the Ohio Valley, 1790–1850* (Bloomington, Ind., 2002). See also Jeremy Atack, Fred Bateman, and William N. Parker, "Northern Agriculture and the Westward Movement," in Stanley Engerman and Robert E. Gallman, ed., *The Cambridge Economic History of the United States*, vol. II, *The Long Nineteenth Century* (Cambridge, England, 2000), pp. 285–328. Annette Kolodny, *The Land Before Her: Fantasy and Experience of the American Frontiers, 1630–1860* (Chapel Hill, 1984), comments on women's experience. Rachel N. Klein, *Unification of a Slave State: The Rise of the Planter Class in the South Carolina Backcountry, 1760–1808* (Chapel Hill, 1990), traces the beginnings of Southern territorial expansion, while Jean V. Cashin, *A Family Venture: Men and Women on the Southern Frontier* (Baltimore, 1991), offers an insightful interpretation of the family dynamics of migration among slaveholders.

Daniel Vickers, *Young Men and the Sea: Yankee Seafarers in the Age of Sail* (New Haven, 2005); W. Jeffrey Bolster, *Black Jacks: African American Seamen in the Age of Sail* (Cambridge, Mass., 1997); and Margaret S. Creighton, *Rites and Passages: The Experience of American Whaling, 1830–1870* (Cambridge, England, 1995), provide excellent studies of mariners' lives and their social contexts, while Lisa Norling, *Captain Ahab Had a Wife: New England Women and the Whalefishery, 1720–1870* (Chapel Hill, 2000), vividly discusses the women, families, and households overshadowed by seafarers' careers.

On rural life, see Steven Hahn and Jonathan Prude, ed., *The Countryside in the Age of Capitalist Transformation: Essays in the Social History of Rural America* (Chapel Hill, 1985); Joan M. Jensen, *Loosening the Bonds: Mid-Atlantic Farm Women, 1750–1850* (New Haven, 1986); Daniel Vickers, *Farmers and Fishermen: Two Centuries of Work in Essex County, Massachusetts, 1630–1830* (Chapel Hill, 1994); Allan Kulikoff, *The Agrarian Origins of American Capitalism* (Charlottesville, 1992); Christopher Clark, *The Roots of Rural Capitalism: Western Massachusetts, 1780–1860* (Ithaca, 1990); and Winifred B. Rothenberg, *From Market-Places to a Market Economy: The Transformation of Rural Massachusetts, 1750–1850* (Chicago, 1992). See also Reeve Huston, *Land and Freedom: Rural Society, Popular Protest, and Party Politics in Antebellum New York* (New York, 2000). Studies of agricultural improvements include Joyce E. Chaplin, *An Anxious Pursuit: Agricultural Innovation and Modernity in the Lower South, 1730–1815* (Chapel Hill, 1993); Peter D. McClelland, *Sowing Modernity: America's First Agricultural Revolution* (Ithaca, 1997); and Steven Stoll, *Larding the Lean Earth: Soil and Society in Nineteenth-Century America* (New York, 2002).

On early industry, see Gary Kornblith, "Artisan Federalism: New England Mechanics and the Political Economy of the 1790s," in Hoffman and Albert, *Launching the "Extended Republic": The Federalist Era* (Charlottesville, 1996), p. 249–272; Christopher Clark, "Social Structure and Manufacturing Before the Factory: Rural New England, 1750–1830," in *The Workplace Before the Factory: Artisans and Proletarians, 1500–1800*, ed. Thomas Max Safley and Leonard N. Rosenband (Ithaca, 1993), chapter 1; Clark, *The Roots of Rural Capitalism*, chapters 3 and 7; and the important synthesis in David R. Meyer, *The Roots of American Industrialization* (Baltimore, 2003). Thomas Dublin, *Transforming Women's Work: New England Lives in the Industrial Revolution* (Ithaca, 1994), focuses on household-based outwork. Gary Kulik, et al., ed., *The New England Mill Village, 1790–1860: A Documentary History* (Cambridge, Mass., 1982), and Donald R. Hoke, *Ingenious Yankees: The Rise of the American System of Manufactures in the Private Sector* (New York, 1990), are also important. On the cultural experience of early manufacturing economies, see Paul E. Johnson, *Sam Patch, the Famous Jumper* (New York, 2003).

Daniel Walker Howe, *Making the American Self: Jonathan Edwards to Abraham Lincoln* (Cambridge, Mass., 1997); Jon Butler, *Awash in a Sea of Faith: Christianizing the American People* (Cambridge, Mass., 1990); and Nathan O. Hatch, *The Democratization of American Christianity* (New Haven, 1989), discuss aspects of the emergence of self-reliance in the context of the Second Great Awakening.

Chapter 4. Two Directions for Labor

James Oakes, *Slavery and Freedom: An Interpretation of the Old South* (New York, 1990), and Peter Kolchin, *American Slavery, 1619–1865* (New York, 1993), provide overarching accounts of American slavery. Of a large literature on slave culture and family life, Ann Paton Malone, *Sweet Chariot: Slave Family and Household Structure in Nineteenth-Century Louisiana* (Chapel Hill, 1992), is a good example. Modern debates have been profoundly influenced by Eugene D. Genovese, especially his *Roll, Jordan, Roll: The World the Slaves Made* (New York, 1974); James Oakes, *The Ruling Race: A History of American Slaveholders* (New York, 1982), was one early critic. A summary of recent work on slavery is Stanley L. Engerman, "Slavery and Its Consequences for the South," in Engerman and Robert E. Gallman, ed., *The Cambridge Economic History of the United States, vol. II: The Long Nineteenth Century* (Cambridge, England, 2000). Among historians seeking to steer a new course in the debate, see Jeffrey R. Young, *Domesticating Slavery: The Master Class in Georgia and South Carolina, 1670–1837* (Chapel Hill, 1999); Mark M. Smith, *Mastered by the Clock: Time, Slavery, and Freedom in the American South* (Chapel Hill, 1997); Mark M. Smith, *Debating Slavery: Economy and Society in the Antebellum American South* (Cambridge, England, 1998); Larry Hudson, Jr., *To Have and to Hold: Slave Work and Family Life in Antebellum South Carolina* (Athens, Ga., 1997); and Christopher Morris, *Becoming Southern: The Evolution of a Way of Life: Warren County and Vicksburg, Mississippi, 1770–1860* (New York, 1995). See also Christopher Morris, "The Articulation of Two Worlds: The Master-Slave Relationship Reconsidered," *Journal of American History* 85, no. 3 (December 1998): 982–1007; Norrece T. Jones, Jr., *Born a Child of Freedom, Yet a Slave: Mechanisms of Control and Strategies of Resistance in Antebellum South Carolina* (Hanover, N.H., 1990); William Dusinberre, *Them Dark Days: Slavery in the American Rice Swamps* (New York, 1996); Winthrop D. Jordan, ed., *Slavery and the American South* (Jackson, Miss., 2003); and Joseph P. Reidy, *From Slavery to Agrarian Capitalism in the Cotton Plantation South: Central Georgia, 1800–1880* (Chapel Hill, 1992). John Ashworth, *Slavery, Capitalism, and Politics in the Antebellum Republic: vol. I: Commerce and Compromise, 1820–1850* (Cambridge, England, 1996), is an important study of the ideology and politics of slavery. John Hope Franklin and Loren Schweninger, *Runaway Slaves: Rebels on the Plantation* (New York, 1999), and Sally E. Hadden, *Slave Patrols: Law and Violence in Virginia and the Carolinas* (Cambridge, Mass., 2001), discuss slave escapes and white societies' measures to counter them. Walter Johnson, *Soul by Soul: Life Inside the Antebellum Slave Market* (Cambridge, Mass., 1999), is a key account of the domestic slave trade, a subject that is now attracting increasing attention from historians; see also Michael Tadman, *Speculators and Slaves: Masters, Traders, and Slaves in the Old South* (Madison, Wisc., 1989), and Michael Tadman, "The Demographic Cost of Sugar: Debates on Slave Societies and Natural Increase in the Americas," *American Historical Review* 105, no. 5 (December 2000): 1534–1575.

Lacey K. Ford, Jr., *Origins of Southern Radicalism: The Southern Upcountry, 1800–1860* (New York, 1988), examines the yeoman South; Charles C. Bolton, *Poor Whites of the Antebellum South: Tenants and Laborers in Central North Car-*

olina and Northeast Mississippi (Durham, N.C., 1994), is a fine account of non-landholding whites; Wilma F. Dunaway, *The First American Frontier: Transition to Capitalism in Southern Appalachia, 1700–1860* (Chapel Hill, 1996), presents important material on poverty, wealth, and power in the upland South.

Studies of African Americans outside the plantation South include Julie Winch, ed., *The Elite of Our People: Joseph Willson's Sketches of Black Upper-Class Life in Antebellum Philadelphia* (University Park, Pa., 2000); James Oliver Horton, *Free People of Color: Inside the African American Community* (Washington, D.C., 1993); James Oliver Horton and Lois E. Horton, *In Hope of Liberty: Culture, Community and Protest Among Northern Free Blacks, 1700–1860* (New York, 1997); Christopher Phillips, *Freedom's Port: The African American Community of Baltimore, 1790–1860* (Urbana, Ill., 1997); and Graham Russell Hodges, *Slavery and Freedom in the Rural North: African Americans in Monmouth County, New Jersey, 1665–1865* (Madison, Wisc., 1997), an important study of the countryside.

On the connections between Western expansion, urbanization, and commercial development, see Carol Sheriff, *The Artificial River: The Erie Canal and the Paradox of Progress, 1817–1862* (New York, 1996). Other aspects of the evolution of Midwestern societies are addressed in Jeremy Atack, Fred Bateman, and William N. Parker, "Northern Agriculture and the Westward Movement," in Stanley Engerman and Robert E. Gallman, ed., *The Cambridge Economic History of the United States, vol. II: The Long Nineteenth Century* (Cambridge, England, 2000); Andrew R. L. Cayton and Stuart D. Hobbs, ed., *The Center of a Great Empire: The Ohio Country in the Early Republic* (Athens, Ohio, 2005); Kenneth J. Winkle, *The Politics of Community: Migration and Politics in Antebellum Ohio* (Cambridge, England, 1988); John Mack Faragher, *Sugar Creek: Life on the Illinois Prairie* (New Haven, 1986); Don Harrison Doyle, *Social Order in a Frontier Community: Jacksonville, Illinois, 1820–70* (Urbana, Ill., 1978); Susan E. Gray, *The Yankee West: Community Life on the Michigan Frontier* (Chapel Hill, 1996); and Douglas K. Meyer, *Making the Heartland Quilt: A Geographical History of Settlement and Migration in Early-Nineteenth-Century Illinois* (Carbondale, Ill., 2000).

Urban developments and social experience are discussed in Carole Shammas, "The Space Problem in Early U.S. Cities," *William and Mary Quarterly* 57 (July 2000): 505–542; Edwin G. Burrows and Mike Wallace, *Gotham: A History of New York City to 1898* (New York, 1999); William H. Pease and Jane H. Pease, *The Web of Progress: Private Values and Public Styles in Boston and Charleston, 1828–1843* (New York, 1985); Stephan Thernstrom, *Poverty and Progress: Social Mobility in a Nineteenth-Century City* (Cambridge, Mass., 1964); Mona Domosh, *Invented Cities: The Creation of Landscape in Nineteenth-Century New York and Boston* (New Haven, 1996); Sean Wilentz, *Chants Democratic: New York City and*

A Note on Sources and Further Reading

the *Rise of the American Working Class, 1788–1850* (New York, 1984); Christine Stansell, *City of Women: Sex and Class in New York, 1789–1860* (New York, 1986); Timothy J. Gilfoyle, *City of Eros: New York City, Prostitution, and the Commercialization of Sex, 1790–1820* (New York, 1992); Patricia Cline Cohen, *The Murder of Helen Jewett: The Life and Death of a Prostitute in Nineteenth-Century New York* (New York, 1998); and Roy Rosenzweig and Elizabeth Blackmar, *The Park and the People: A History of Central Park* (Ithaca, 1992). Elizabeth Blackmar, *Manhattan for Rent, 1785–1850* (Ithaca, 1989), traces urban tenancy and class relationships, while Elizabeth Collins Cromley, *Alone Together: A History of New York's Early Apartments* (Ithaca, 1990), chapter 1, discusses responses to overcrowding. On early suburbs, see John R. Stilgoe, *Borderland: Origins of the American Suburb, 1820–1939* (New Haven, 1988); Henry C. Binford, *The First Suburbs: Residential Communities on the Boston Periphery, 1816–1860* (Chicago, 1985); and Tamara Plakins Thornton, *Cultivating Gentlemen: The Meaning of Country Life Among the Boston Elite, 1785–1860* (New Haven, 1989).

Farley Grubb, "The End of European Immigrant Servitude in the United States: An Economic Analysis of Market Collapse, 1772–1835," *Journal of Economic History* 54 (1994): 794–824, discusses one facet of the decline of unfree labor. Martin J. Burke, *The Conundrum of Class: Public Discourse on the Social Order in America* (Chicago, 1995), is an essential account of contemporary discussions of class. The emergence of free labor and its ideologies are discussed in Robert J. Steinfeld, *The Invention of Free Labor: The Employment Relation in English and American Law and Culture, 1350–1870* (Chapel Hill, 1991); Christopher Tomlins, *Law, Labor, and Ideology in the Early American Republic* (Cambridge, England, 1993); and David Montgomery, *Citizen Worker: The Experience of Workers in the United States with Democracy and the Free Market During the Nineteenth Century* (Cambridge, England, 1993). Robert J. Steinfeld, *Coercion, Contract, and Free Labor in the Nineteenth Century* (Cambridge, England, 2001), analyzes the elements of compulsion in wage labor.

Bruce Laurie, *Artisans into Workers: Labor in Nineteenth-Century America* (New York, 1989), provides an overview of changes in the social relations of industrial work. Peter Way, *Common Labour: Workers and the Digging of North American Canals, 1780–1860* (Cambridge, England, 1993), discusses "unskilled" manual labor. Studies that trace developments in specific industries or localities include, for New England: Robert F. Dalzell, Jr., *Enterprising Elite: The Boston Associates and the World They Made* (Cambridge, Mass., 1987); Thomas L. Dublin, *Women at Work: The Transformation of Work and Society in Lowell, Massachusetts, 1826–1860* (New York, 1979); Jonathan Prude, *The Coming of Industrial Order: Town and Factory Life in Rural Massachusetts, 1813–1860* (Cambridge, England, 1983); Alan Dawley, *Class and Community: The Industrial Revolution in Lynn* (Cambridge, Mass., 1976); and Mary H. Blewett, *Men, Women and Work: Class, Gender and Protest in the New England Shoe Industry, 1790–1910* (Urbana, Ill., 1988). Important works on Philadelphia and its environs are Diane Lindstrom, *Economic Development in the Philadelphia Region, 1810–1850* (New York, 1978); Anthony F. C. Wallace, *Rockdale: The Growth of an American Village in the Early Industrial Revolution* (New York, 1978); Bruce Laurie, *Working People of Philadelphia, 1800–1850* (Philadelphia, 1980); Philip Scranton, *Proprietary Capitalism: The Textile Manufacture at Philadelphia* (Cambridge, England, 1984); and Cynthia J. Shelton, *The Mills of Manayunk: Industrialization and Social Conflict in the Philadelphia Region, 1737–1837* (Baltimore, 1986). See also Anthony F. C. Wallace, *St. Clair: A Nineteenth-Century Coal Town's Experience with a Disaster-Prone Industry* (New York, 1987). Rosalind Remer, *Printers and Men of Capital: Philadelphia Book Publishers in the New Republic* (Philadelphia, 1996), and Donna J. Rilling, *Making Houses, Crafting Capitalism: Builders in Philadelphia, 1790–1850* (Philadelphia, 2001), trace the development of trades in which there was a constantly shifting line between wage-earning status and proprietorship.

Chapter 5. Crisis and Expansion

ON PRODUCERISM and its implications for politics and religion, see Tony Freyer, *Producers Versus Capitalists: Constitutional Conflict in Antebellum America* (Charlottesville, 1994); Ronald Schultz, "God and Workingmen: Popular Religion and the Formation of Philadelphia's Working Class, 1790–1830," in Ronald Hoffman and Peter J. Albert, ed., *Religion in a Revolutionary Age* (Charlottesville, 1994), pp. 125–155; Jama Lazerow, *Religion and the Working Class in Antebellum America* (Washington, D.C., 1995); and William R. Sutton, *Journeymen for Jesus: Evangelical Artisans Confront Capitalism in Jacksonian Baltimore* (University Park, Pa., 1998).

On immigration and the labor market, see Joseph P. Ferrie, "The Entry into the U.S. Labor Market of Antebellum European Migrants, 1840–1860," *Explorations in Economic History* 34 (1997): 295–330. Dirk Hoerder, ed., *Labor Migration in the Atlantic Economies: The European and North American Working Classes During the Period of Industrialization* (Westport, Conn., 1985), is among several important essay collections produced by Hoerder and colleagues; see also Christiane Harzig, ed., *Peasant Maids—City Women: From the European Countryside to Urban America* (Ithaca, 1997). Irish immigrants are discussed in Howard Harris, "'The Eagle to Watch and the Harp to Tune the Nation': Irish Immigrants, Politics, and Early Industrialization in Paterson, New Jersey, 1824–1836," *Journal of Social History* 23 (1990): 575–597; Hasia R. Diner, *Erin's Daughters in America: Irish Immigrant Women in the Nineteenth Century* (Baltimore, 1983); Kerby Miller,

A Note on Sources and Further Reading

Immigrants and Exiles: Ireland and the Irish Exodus to North America (New York, 1985); and J. Matthew Gallman, *Receiving Erin's Children: Philadelphia, Liverpool, and the Irish Famine Migration, 1845–1855* (Chapel Hill, 2000). The classic work by Oscar Handlin, *Boston's Immigrants, 1790–1865: A Study in Acculturation* (Cambridge, Mass., 1941), remains valuable. On English migrants, see Charlotte Erickson, *Invisible Immigrants: The Adaptation of English and Scottish Immigrants in Nineteenth-Century America* (Coral Gables, Fla., 1972), which contains interpretive essays and a collection of emigrants' letters, and Charlotte Erickson, *Leaving England: Essays on British Emigration in the Nineteenth Century* (Ithaca, 1994). Jon Gjerde, *From Peasants to Farmers: The Migration from Balestrand, Norway, to the Upper Middle West* (Cambridge, England, 1985), is a good study of early Norwegian migration.

Much recent work has been done on the influence of race on class, politics, and identity in white societies, pioneered by Alexander Saxton, *The Rise and Fall of the White Republic: Class Politics and Mass Culture in Nineteenth-Century America* (London, 1990). David Roediger, *The Wages of Whiteness: Race and the Making of the American Working Class* (London, 1991); Noel Ignatiev, *How the Irish Became White* (New York, 1995); Eric Lott, *Love and Theft: Blackface Minstrelsy and the American Working Class* (New York, 1993); and Matthew Frye Jacobson, *Whiteness of a Different Color: European Immigrants and the Alchemy of Race* (Cambridge, Mass., 1998), are also important.

Edward J. Balleisen, *Navigating Failure: Bankruptcy and Commercial Society in Antebellum America* (Chapel Hill, 2001), and Scott A. Sandage, *Born Losers: A History of Failure in America* (Cambridge, Mass., 2005), explore the consequences of economic depression, and Balleisen in particular connects this with middle-class development. On the new middle class, see Stuart M. Blumin, *The Emergence of the Middle Class: Social Experience in the American City, 1760–1900* (Cambridge, England, 1989); Karen Halttunen, *Confidence Men and Painted Women: A Study of Middle Class Culture in America, 1830–1870* (New Haven, 1982); the essays in Burton J. Bledstein and Robert D. Johnston, ed., *The Middling Sorts: Explorations in the History of the American Middle Class* (New York, 2001); and Catherine E. Kelly, *In the New England Fashion: Reshaping Women's Lives in the Nineteenth Century* (Ithaca, 1999). Nancy Isenberg, *Sex and Citizenship in Antebellum America* (Chapel Hill, 1998), traces the legal and political position of women. Other aspects of middle-class life are addressed in Mary P. Ryan, *Cradle of the Middle Class: The Family in Oneida County, New York, 1790–1865* (Cambridge, England, 1981); Nathan O. Hatch, "The Second Great Awakening and the Market Revolution," in David Thomas Konig, ed., *Devising Liberty: Preserving and Creating Freedom in the Early American Republic* (Stanford, 1995), pp. 243–264; Lori Merish, "Sentimental Consumption: Harriet Beecher

Stowe and the Aesthetics of Middle-Class Ownership," *American Literary History* 8 (1996): 1–33; and Lori Merish, *Sentimental Materialism: Gender, Commodity Culture, and Nineteenth-Century American Literature* (Durham, N.C., 2000). The experience of young men in cities and commercial employment is discussed in Thomas Augst, *The Clerk's Tale: Young Men and Moral Life in Nineteenth-Century America* (Chicago, 2003). Alfred D. Chandler, *The Visible Hand: The Managerial Revolution in American Business* (Cambridge, Mass., 1977), is a fundamental and much-discussed account of the early growth of large organizations in mid-nineteenth-century business. See also John Lauritz Larson, *Bonds of Enterprise: John Murray Forbes and Western Development in America's Railway Age* (Cambridge, Mass., 1994).

Studies of Northern elites include Peter Dobkin Hall, *The Organization of American Culture, 1700–1900: Private Institutions, Elites, and the Origins of American Nationality* (New York, 1982); Betty G. Farrell, *Elite Families: Class and Power in Nineteenth Century Boston* (Albany, N.Y., 1993); Joseph F. Rishel, *Founding Families of Pittsburgh: The Evolution of a Regional Elite, 1760–1910* (Pittsburgh, 1990); and Sven Beckert, *The Monied Metropolis: New York City and the Consolidation of the American Bourgeoisie, 1850–1896* (Cambridge, England, 2001).

Chapter 6. From Regional Differences to Sectional Divide

AMONG MANY studies of North-South differences, see the essays by Bertram Wyatt-Brown, *Yankee Saints and Southern Sinners* (Baton Rouge, 1985), and, in economic terms, John D. Majewski, *A House Dividing: Economic Development in Pennsylvania and Virginia Before the Civil War* (Cambridge, England, 2000). See also Roger L. Ransom, *Conflict and Compromise: The Political Economy of Slavery, Emancipation, and the American Civil War* (Cambridge, England, 1989). Discussions of slavery and Southern manufacturing are in Charles B. Dew, *Bond of Iron: Master and Slave at Buffalo Forge* (New York, 1994); Midori Takagi, *"Rearing Wolves to Our Own Destruction": Slavery in Richmond, Virginia, 1782–1865* (Charlottesville, 1999); and Tom Downey, "Riparian Rights and Manufacturing in Antebellum South Carolina: William Gregg and the Origins of the 'Industrial Mind'," *Journal of Southern History* 65 (1999): 77–108.

Important studies of Missouri include David Thelen, *Paths of Resistance: Tradition and Dignity in Industrializing Missouri* (New York, 1986), and Jeffrey S. Adler, *Yankee Merchants and the Making of the Urban West: The Rise and Fall of Antebellum St. Louis* (Cambridge, England, 1991). On Texas, see Randolph B. Campbell, *Gone to Texas: A History of the Lone Star State* (New York, 2003); Gary Clayton Anderson, *The Conquest of Texas: Ethnic Cleansing in the Promised Land, 1820–1875* (Norman, Okla., 2005); and, on the development of slavery there,

A Note on Sources and Further Reading

Randolph B. Campbell, *An Empire for Slavery: The Peculiar Institution in Texas, 1821–1865* (Baton Rouge, 1989). The sesquicentennials of the California Gold Rush and California statehood inspired a flurry of good new books, including Malcolm J. Rohrbough, *Days of Gold: The California Gold Rush and the American Nation* (Berkeley, 1997); Stephen Schwartz, *From West to East: California and the Making of the American Mind* (New York, 1998); and Brian Roberts, *American Alchemy: The California Gold Rush and Middle-Class Culture* (Chapel Hill, 2000). Susan Lee Johnson, *Roaring Camp: The Social World of the California Gold Rush* (New York, 2000), concentrates on the "southern mines" region. Essay collections, including Kenneth N. Owens, ed., *Riches for All: The California Gold Rush and the World* (Lincoln, Nebr., 2002), and Kevin Starr and Richard J. Orsi, ed., *Rooted in Barbarous Soil: People, Culture, and Community in Gold Rush California* (Berkeley, 2000); and volumes accompanying exhibits, such as Peter J. Blodgett, *Land of Golden Dreams: California in the Gold Rush Decade, 1848–1858* (San Marino, Calif., 1999), and J. S. Holliday, *Rush for Riches: Gold Fever and the Making of California* (Berkeley, 1999), offer an abundance of information.

On the wealth of slaveholders and the comparative value of property in slaves in 1860, see James L. Huston, *Calculating the Value of the Union: Slavery, Property Rights, and the Economic Origins of the Civil War* (Chapel Hill, 2003). On the struggle to assist runaways along the borders of free and slave states, see Thomas P. Slaughter, *Bloody Dawn: The Christiana Riot and Racial Violence in the Antebellum North* (New York, 1991). On the political power of planter elites, see J. Mills Thornton, *Politics and Power in a Slave Society: Alabama, 1800–1860* (Baton Rouge, 1978); Shearer Davis Bowman, *Masters and Lords: Mid-Nineteenth Century U.S. Planters and Prussian Junkers* (New York, 1993); and Stephanie McCurry, *Masters of Small Worlds: Yeoman Households, Gender Relations, and the Political Culture of the Antebellum South Carolina Low Country* (New York, 1995). State-based accounts of the connections between slaveholding and the political movements that eventually led to secession include Manisha Sinha, *The Counterrevolution of Slavery: Politics and Ideology in Antebellum South Carolina* (Chapel Hill, 2000), and William A. Link, *Roots of Secession: Slavery and Politics in Antebellum Virginia* (Chapel Hill, 2003). William Dusinberre, *Slavemaster President: The Double Career of James Polk* (New York, 2003), offers both a chilling account of Polk's activities as a slaveholder in Tennessee and Mississippi and an interpretation of the origins of secession that challenges conventional emphases on South Carolina. But political allegiances were not fixed by class or by sectional identity, as William K. Scarborough, *Masters of the Big House: Elite Slaveholders of the Mid-Nineteenth-Century South* (Baton Rouge, 2003), and particularly Margaret M. Storey, *Loyalty and Loss: Alabama's Unionists in the Civil War and Reconstruction* (Baton Rouge, 2004), remind us.

A Note on Sources and Further Reading

Eric Foner, *Free Soil, Free Labor, Free Men: The Ideology of the Republican Party Before the Civil War* (New York, 1970), is the classic account of the free-soil movement and its emergence in national politics in the 1850s. John Ashworth, *Slavery, Capitalism, and Politics in the Antebellum Republic. Vol. I. Commerce and Compromise, 1820–1850* (Cambridge, England, 1995), and Michael A. Morrison, *Slavery and the American West: The Eclipse of Manifest Destiny and the Coming of the Civil War* (Chapel Hill, 1997), contribute notably to an understanding of slavery's increasing centrality to national debates. Essays in William W. Freehling, *The Reintegration of American History: Slavery and the Civil War* (New York, 1994), and studies by Leonard L. Richards, *The Slave Power: The Free North and Southern Domination, 1780–1860* (Baton Rouge, 2000), and Susan-Mary Grant, *North over South: Northern Nationalism and American Identity in the Antebellum Era* (Lawrence, Kans., 2000), reflect on aspects of the emergence of sectional identities and antagonisms.

Chapter 7. The Civil War: Two Kinds of Revolution

JAMES M. MCPHERSON, *Battle Cry of Freedom: The American Civil War* (New York, 1988), remains one of the best standard accounts of the war. Gabor S. Borritt, ed., *Why the Civil War Came* (New York, 1996), is an important collection of essays. Charles B. Dew, *Apostles of Disunion: Southern Secession Commissioners and the Causes of the Civil War* (Charlottesville, 2001), is a recent study of efforts for secession. Edward L. Ayers, *In the Presence of Mine Enemies: War in the Heart of America, 1859–1863* (New York, 2003), is a significant account of the early phases of the war in the Middle Atlantic states, where sectional opinion was perhaps least polarized. Barbara Jeanne Fields, *Slavery and Freedom on the Middle Ground: Maryland During the Nineteenth Century* (New Haven, 1985), demonstrates the wartime role of slaves in ending slavery in this key border state.

Recent works on soldiering and the military experience include Larry M. Logue, *To Appomattox and Beyond: The Civil War Soldier in War and Peace* (Chicago, 1996); James McPherson, *For Cause and Comrades: Why Men Fought in the Civil War* (New York, 1997); Reid Mitchell, *The Vacant Chair: The Northern Soldier Leaves Home* (New York, 1993); J. Tracy Power, *Lee's Miserables: Life in the Army of Northern Virginia from the Wilderness to Appomattox* (Chapel Hill, 1998); and the large collection of documents on African-American soldiers in Ira Berlin, et al., *Freedom: A Documentary History of Emancipation, 1861–1867*, Series II, *The Black Military Experience* (Cambridge, England, 1982).

In addition to the works by Lori D. Ginzberg and Elizabeth Leonard cited in the endnotes, recent books on women in the Civil War include Drew Gilpin Faust, *Mothers of Invention: Women of the Slaveholding South in the American Civil*

War (Chapel Hill, 1996), and Jeanie Atie, *Patriotic Toil: Northern Women and the American Civil War* (Ithaca, 1998). Philip Shaw Paludan, *"A People's Contest": The Union and Civil War, 1861–1865* (New York, 1988), helped pioneer attention to the Civil War "home front," a theme followed up by J. Matthew Gallman, *Mastering Wartime: A Social History of Philadelphia During the Civil War* (Cambridge, England, 1991), and J. Matthew Gallman, *The North Fights the Civil War* (Chicago, 1996); Joan E. Cashin, ed., *The War Was You and Me: Civilians in the American Civil War* (Princeton, 2002), and Paul A. Cimbala and Randall M. Miller, ed., *An Uncommon Time: The Civil War and the Northern Home Front* (New York, 2002), gather more recent work on this topic. Studies addressing social and political conflict during the war include Grace Palladino, *Another Civil War: Labor, Capital, and the State in the Anthracite Regions of Pennsylvania, 1840–1868* (Urbana, Ill., 1990), and Iver Bernstein, *The New York City Draft Riots: Their Significance for American Society and Politics in the Age of the Civil War* (New York, 1990). Heather Cox Richardson, *The Greatest Nation of the Earth: Republican Economic Policies During the Civil War* (Cambridge, Mass., 1997), traces afresh the impact of secession on the North's ability to shape national policy.

For community studies of the wartime South, see David Williams, *Rich Man's War: Class, Caste, and Confederate Defeat in the Lower Chattahoochee Valley* (Athens, Ga., 1998), and Martin Crawford, *Ashe County's Civil War: Community and Society in the Appalachian South* (Charlottesville, 2001), together with the essays in David Williams, Teresa Crisp Williams, and David Carlson, ed., *Plain Folk in a Rich Man's War: Class and Dissent in Confederate Georgia* (Gainesville, Fla., 2002), and Kenneth W. Noe and Shannon H. Wilson, ed., *The Civil War in Appalachia: Collected Essays* (Knoxville, Tenn., 1997).

Michael Vorenberg, *Final Freedom: The Civil War, the Abolition of Slavery, and the Thirteenth Amendment* (Cambridge, England, 2001), discusses the legal and constitutional implications of ending slavery. Amy Dru Stanley, *From Bondage to Contract: Wage Labor, Marriage, and the Market in the Age of Slave Emancipation* (Cambridge, England, 1998), and David W. Blight, *Race and Reunion: The Civil War in American Memory* (Cambridge, Mass., 2001), follow its implications into other important aspects of social experience, politics, and memory. A significant social history of the end of slavery is Leon F. Litwack, *Been in the Storm So Long: The Aftermath of Slavery* (New York, 1979). Recent works particularly emphasize the influence of freedpeople in shaping their own economic circumstances, under constraints, after Emancipation: see Julie Savile, *The Work of Reconstruction: From Slave to Wage Laborer in South Carolina, 1860–1870* (Cambridge, England, 1994); Leslie A. Schwalm, *A Hard Fight for We: Women's Transition from Slavery to Freedom in South Carolina* (Urbana, Ill., 1997); and Sharon Ann Holt,

A Note on Sources and Further Reading

Making Freedom Pay: North Carolina Freedpeople Working for Themselves, 1865–1900 (Athens, Ga., 2000). Steven Hahn, *A Nation Under Our Feet: Black Political Struggles in the Rural South from Slavery to the Great Migration* (Cambridge, Mass., 2003), provides a new, authoritative account of African-American politics in the aftermath of Emancipation.

The best single account of Reconstruction remains Eric Foner, *Reconstruction: America's Unfinished Revolution, 1863–1877* (New York, 1988). See also Eric Foner, *Politics and Ideology in the Civil War Era* (New York, 1980). Gavin Wright, *Old South, New South: Revolutions in the Southern Economy Since the Civil War* (New York, 1986), and Edward L. Ayers, *The Promise of the New South: Life After Reconstruction* (New York, 1992), discuss the complexities of Southern development after the Civil War period; see also Harold D. Woodman, "Class, Race, Politics, and the Modernization of the Postbellum South," *Journal of Southern History* 63 (1997): 3–22.

The consolidating tendencies of postwar Northern development are picked up in Richard Franklin Bensel, *Yankee Leviathan: The Origins of Central State Authority in America, 1859–1877* (Cambridge, England, 1990), and in Alan Trachtenberg, *The Incorporation of America: Culture and Society in the Gilded Age* (New York, 1983). Ron Chernow, *Titan: The Life of John D. Rockefeller, Sr.* (New York, 1998), and Jean Strouse, *Morgan: American Financier* (New York, 1999), are lively biographies of individuals emblematic of Gilded Age power and success, though Naomi R. Lamoreaux, Daniel M. G. Raff, and Peter Temin, "Beyond Markets and Hierarchies: Toward a New Synthesis of American Business History," *American Historical Review* 108, no. 2 (April 2003), argue for a renewed emphasis on the importance of small as well as large businesses.

William Cronon, *Nature's Metropolis: Chicago and the Great West* (New York, 1991), traces the social, institutional, and environmental implications of the growth of national commodity markets. David Blanke, *Sowing the American Dream: How Consumer Culture Took Root in the Rural Midwest* (Athens, Ohio, 2000), examines the beneficiaries of this development, while Robert C. McMath, Jr., *American Populism: A Social History, 1877–1898* (New York, 1993), provides a succinct introduction to its harsher outcomes.

Walter Licht, *Getting Work: Philadelphia, 1840–1950* (Cambridge, Mass., 1992), discusses the experience of obtaining wage work in the later nineteenth century; Alexander Keyssar, *Out of Work: The First Century of Unemployment in Massachusetts* (Cambridge, England, 1986), considers the difficulties of holding on to it. David Montgomery, *Beyond Equality: Labor and the Radical Republicans, 1862–1872* (New York, 1967), remains an important study of the labor movement; Kim Voss, *The Making of American Exceptionalism: The Knights of Labor and Class Formation in the Nineteenth Century* (Ithaca, 1993), suggests that business power effectively defeated it. Heather Cox Richardson, in *The Death of Recon-struction: Race, Labor, and Politics in the Post-Civil War North, 1865–1901* (Cambridge, Mass., 2001), applies a similar insight: that a mutual concern to assure control over labor encouraged elites and proprietors North and South to compromise the antagonisms between them that the war had aggravated.

Index

Index

Index

Index

A NOTE ON THE AUTHOR

Christopher Clark was born in Kingston-upon-Thames in England and studied history at the University of Warwick and at Harvard University, where he received a Ph.D. He has also written *The Roots of Rural Capitalism* (which won the Frederick Jackson Turner Award of the Organization of American Historians) and *The Communitarian Moment*, and edited, with Kerry W. Buckley, *Letters from an American Utopia*. He is now professor of history at the University of Connecticut and lives in Storrs, Connecticut.